Neal Fain has penned a treasure trove of information concerning Bible prophecy and what prophecy means for today's Christian. Brother Fain's patient and diligent research has resulted in some amazing insights into how Bible prophecy works. It has been my privilege to personally know Brother Fain for several years and I count him, not only as a friend, but also as a serious student and Bible scholar. This book promises to add valuable perspective and research material for Bible teachers, church leaders and anyone else who is seeking to know God more fully. The solid Biblical principles taught in this manuscript will serve as an anchor for anyone seeking to have a more clear understanding and appreciation of Bible prophecy. I give Prophecy Principles my highest recommendation.

Dennis Jones, President
HERITAGE CHRISTIAN UNIVERSITY

In this age of almost fanatical fascination with end times prophecies—the interpretations of which seem to constantly shift like windblown sand dunes depending on this week's current world events—Neal Fain's Prophecy Principles offers a welcome corrective. Relying on sound principles of interpretation rather than fanciful geo-political speculations, Fain presents an approach to biblical prophecy that takes in all of biblical history, not just the immediate future. While he does move us ultimately toward the return of Christ—and emphasizes how important it is to be prepared—he is more concerned with demonstrating how prophecy strengthens our faith even now as we engage in battle with the forces of evil and unbelief. Unlike today's "experts on end time prophecies," Fain's work encourages faithful trust, not fear.

Dennis Connor
Raleigh, North Carolina

This is about
the fulfillment
of John 16:13

Prophecy Principles

The Background We Need for Bible Prophecy, and How it Works.

Second Edition

Neal Fain

AngleofEntry .com
Learning for the Journey

ISBN 978-0-9786866-8-0
(based on *Prophecy Sketches*, first published 2011)

AngleofEntry.com
P. O. Box 384
Lawrenceburg, TN 38464

Library of Congress Control Number 2017913860

Introduction

This is a book to read more than once. There is a lot that is being addressed here. Hopefully, this is not a book about me or my ideas. Nor is it a survey of available literature, nor a compendium of all the exotic theories which have been advanced about prophecy and its applications. The goal has been to make this about what God says, dealing with but not concentrating on what man says, and perhaps helping us to see more clearly the Word of God. This is a Bible study with many quotes from Scripture. A main objective has been to demonstrate the unity of God's Prophetic Word from the very beginning to the very end. This is only an overview but it has been written with the idea to make it useful for many years, even over many changes in culture and perspective which must inevitably come.

There are many problems in learning to deal with Biblical prophecy. Most have little to effectively guide them, and many just do not believe there can be such a thing. On one hand, most "scholarship" for the last four hundred years has not just disbelieved but has in addition taken a presumption against God and anything He would say, especially prophetically. Many modern Christians have taken on these attitudes, and even many Christians who consider themselves "conservative Bible believers" often approach prophecy with an attitude of rationalistic unbelief. None of this is conducive to understanding such a specialized body of literature. On the other hand, many of the popular teachers on prophecy have been little more than con artists in the employ of this group or that. A crowd of political cliques would like to have their schemes endorsed as planned by God. Often the public learns to distrust them, without really knowing why. So often people thrash around without ever really coming to see how prophecy works.

More attention needs to be paid to ancient Rome than is given here, but not as much as liberal scholarship has given her. She is there, but she is a figure of greater things.

Nothing here is being dealt with exhaustively. The concentration is on the Bible texts as they apply and illuminate our present world, not primarily about past centuries, although one must all along look at the past for perspective. This is intended to be a "tie things together" book, a book designed to give one perspective and insight in dealing with the issues of prophecy **to make it useful in ordering your life**. Indeed, that is what prophecy is about: perspective. Whole books have and will be written on what is here only chapters, but hopefully this will show some of the limitations of many of the major "systems" of understanding Bible prophecy.

This is a topical and a systematic treatment. Sorry, but this does not look either first or mainly at the book of Revelation, but rather it is a look at Scripture as a whole. The presentation uses a general chronological order, but no one can absolutely do this. For instance: Moses says in Deuteronomy 18 that the

Lord will send a prophet like himself (the Christ) whom everyone must listen to. So in one breath there is a jump from the fifteenth century BC to the first century AD. Wow. One can seldom go from beginning to end in any single passage or book of Scripture, while never going forward or never coming back again. That is part of the limitations of this sort of study, and any commentator or student must deal with these things. So this is nothing like a rigid numbers game. There are neither section nor chapter numbers. Is it logical? Hopefully yes. Is it rigidly topical or chronological? No, and really it cannot be. It is hoped that these admitted limitations are outweighed by the benefit in perspective. The plan is to speak of early events and then practice on fulfilled prophecies and only then of principles. Lastly comes the time to make application to these principles to those events which must yet come to pass. Some seventeen charts are also used which are listed under "Charts" in the Index.

There is much quoting of the Word of God and citing of the references to Scripture, because after all, that is the central matter, not what one might think or say. So the key issue for the reader is whether Scripture is used properly, and whether the conclusions reached are supported by the Word of God. The rest is immaterial.

I have tried as best I know how to let the LORD speak for Himself, and if this plan has succeeded, then at the end, prophecy will be an open book to you. To those who stay awake, all will become clearer as the end comes closer.

If this plan is successful, this should be a readable excursion into prophecy dealing with the main issues for men. Has your author been presumptuous? Please forgive him. Don't count those things against the LORD! The mistakes are all mine. On the other hand, if there is any benefit here it is probably because a dull pupil feebly listened as the LORD demonstrated the continuity of the story.

Preface to the First Edition

Prophecy Principles: The Background We Need for Bible Prophecy, and How it Works.

Previously issued as *Prophecy Sketches*, it was felt both by myself and others that the title did not properly do justice to the intent and scope of the work. Further there were many small corrections which needed to be made, none of which really affected the sense of the passages, or the final conclusions. The closest thing to a "change" is to insert to Bible words "pattern," or "shadow," as another alternate for the Bible terminology of "type" (symbol).

Nothing of substance has been changed. ... Even where because of further studies, my understanding of many issues has increased from what you see reflected here, the basic statements of the original ideas has remained unchanged, and any new insights are left for future works.

We need to be able to see how prophecy is thoroughly grounded in reality.

Nor is it apart from the very commands of God. It is very much a part of the whole counsel of God. For instance, Jesus tells us,

> "He who has believed and has been baptized shall be saved; but he who has disbelieved shall be condemned." Mark 15:16 NASB

This statement is a prophecy, a "shall be." It is of the future. It has not happened yet in any visible form, but it is a "shall be." If you believe what Jesus said, then you will conform yourself to what He said "shall be." If you despise His words, do not believe His vision of the future, you may very well say, "Well I am not sure I really believe that." That is the real issue.

Key people in helping me correct this volume to its present state, are my daughter Alicia Hickman, and my dear friend from my Alaska days, Allen Houtz. But any mistakes which remain are all mine, no matter their nature.

My God bless you the reader in seeking the counsel of the Lord.

Neal Fain
July, 2016

Preface to The Second Edition

This is a translation independent and condensed edition of *Prophecy Principles*. This work was originally composed using the New American Standard Bible, 1995 edition NASB, but is not dependent on any single translation. This edition has for the most part used the readings of the King James Version KJV. Many of the useages, word forms, and spellings in the KJV, though obsolete, present no problem to the modern reader. 'Sinneth,' 'calleth,' 'covereth,' etc., are antiquated useages, but still very clear. At other times, old useages may be puzzling to many readers. Where it might not be completely clear to the modern reader, I have mainly used the New King James Version NKJV, or New American Standard Bible, 1995 edition, NASB. In all cases I have tried to give preference to those translations which appear to be closest to the Hebrew and Greek originals, or (if no special issue is at stake) at least give reasonable renderings. In preparing this edition I was amazed at how closely both the NKJV and the NASB follow the KJV. I have given preference the NKJV here, as possibly the closest of the modern translations to the KJV. In every case I can think of, if an important point cannot be proved from a particular verse in your favorite translation, then it can be proved from other verses in that same translation. Occasional special notes have been added, for instance on the KJV's translation of the Greek word *aion* on page 103, but such added notes are few. This is truly a translation independent subject.

Also this is a carefully condensed edition of the original *Prophecy Principles*. So what has been left out? **First**, there are fewer long quotations of Scripture. Scriptures are more often cited than quoted in full. An example: in the first edition 12 long verses were quoted from Jeremiah chapter 46. In the present edition, only 5. Adaptations in wording have been made to fit with different translations. In all though, everything is essentially the same. **Second**, the discussions of a Biblical Philosophy of History have been shortened. This is a closely related topic, but it is not the primary subject of this book. Having wrong views of God or His Word, or how He works in history, *often* keep us from seeing what the Scriptures have to say to us. Even so, many of these discussions, though necessary, were shortened. **Third**, the abundant teaching summaries have in this edition been either shortened or, on occasion, deleted as unnecessary repetition. Much of it is still there, but perhaps not too much. **Fourth**, the discussion of some associated issues have been eliminated. Related subjects were carefully evaluated as to whether they were really necessary for complete coverage of "prophecy principles." On closer reading, much of the section "Satan and the Evil Empire," was found to overlap one or more of these categories, was shortened from over 12 pages in the first edition, to 3 pages in the present text. Only one section of the original book has been completely eliminated as unnecessary to the main subject: "God Often Uses the Lowliest of Men." It is an important topic, but not the primary subject, and is otherwise dealt with in this volume.

The principles and background that are really necessary for an understanding prophecy all remain intact. Minor corrections have been made in places. Most of the original illustrations survive into this edition, and all of the charts. Most of the charts have been redone for this edition.

And What is the Object of These Changes?

Plainly, a shorter and more focused book, and the use of translations more familiar to many dedicated Bible believers, for a wider readership. And yes, perhaps even an improved edition of *Prophecy Principles*, and indeed I think it is.

These are subjects that both the general public, and the Bible believing public, deserve to know about!

May you the reader be blessed as you seek the truth of God's Word!

Neal Fain

September, 2017

Acknowledgements

My daughter Christi has always been a stern critic and helpful advisor. I have very much appreciated her input, and her attempting (not always successfully) to set me straight. The reading by her and her husband Phillip was especially helpful.

Grammatical correction fell to Alice Stofel. I owe much to her for plowing through this forest of words while still teaching school and tending to her family. If there is an awkward phrase or a misplaced comma here, it is probably because I foolishly ignored her advice.

I hope you enjoy the old illustrations that have been used and that they aid in thinking about the issues of Scripture. Many of the engravers are unknown to us today, but the majority of these are from the most excellent nineteenth century work of Gustave Doré. Portions of Doré prints are seen on pages, 2, 11, 13, 14, 31, 37, 72, 104, 105, 153, 195, 249, 285, and 323. There has been some editing here and there, and all I can do is offer apologies to Gustave. There does not seem to be a definitive edition of Doré prints from either the nineteenth or the twentieth centuries. I do not always agree with his theology, but much admire his skill and his artistic sense. The full page engraving on page 137 is by A. B. Walter, and the one on page 343 is by H. Melville (and also I admit to doctoring Mr. Melville's print quite a bit to make it more reproducible). Both of these are from "The Complete Works of John Bunyan," Bradley, Garretson & Co., Philadelphia, 1873.

If some old engraver was slighted who deserved special recognition, only apologies can be offered.

The variety of spellings in historical and scholarly sources, especially of foreign names, is dismaying. For consistency, where these touch on Scripture I have followed the New American Standard.

Corrections have been made following the first printings, mainly small things, including bad spacing, line breaks, punctuation and minor rewording in places. My thanks go especially to my daughter Alicia, and my dear friend Allen Houtz and their very sharp eyes in these matters.

Abbreviations and Emphasis.

I view the New American Standard Version, 1995 edition, as overall the most accurate, but not necessarily always the most readable, of the current mainline translations. In the main translations used here, including the New American Standard Bible, the translators used italics "to indicate words not found in the original Hebrew and Greek but implied by it." I have tried to retain those italics in my quotes of Scripture. (Also note that the New King James Version also uses italics for New Testament quotes of Old Testament passages.) On those occasions where it was felt emphasis was needed to make a point, I have used **bold face type**, or, very infrequently, <u>underline</u> and have inserted words at the end of the quote like "(*emphasis added*)."

Often there are references to the Greek or Hebrew words used in the Greek or Hebrew texts of the Bible. The Greek or Hebrew word is given first in an English transliteration, followed by the actual word in Greek or Hebrew letters. For instance, "angel *angelos* ἄγγελος," on page 2. Regretfully there is more than one system of transliteration around, and at times I have used my own system. If there is any defect here, it is clearly my own fault.

I have adopted the New American Standard's convention of capitalizing all references to God. Some seem to be ruffled at such treatment, but to me it seems appropriate, and I cannot help but notice the sounds of silence when leading worldly writers give similar treatment to pagan "gods"! I have chosen to use the abbreviations BC and AD, instead of "B. C." and "A. D.", or BCE and CE. Your author obviously believes that Jesus is now Lord and King of ALL in heaven and earth.

Where there is a reference to a chapter in Scripture as a whole, the name of the book is spelled out in full, as in "Genesis 12". If there is a reference to particular verses in a chapter (such as Gen 12:1-3), then the abbreviations used for the book names are as follow:

Abbreviations of Bible Books

1 Chron	1 Chronicles	Heb	Hebrews
1 Cor	1 Corinthians	Hos	Hosea
1 Jn	1 John	Isa	Isaiah
1 Kgs	1 Kings	Jas	James
1 Pe	1 Peter	Jer	Jeremiah
1 Sam	1 Samuel	Jn	John
1 Thes	1 Thessalonians	Job	Job
1 Tim	1 Timothy	Joel	Joel
2 Chron	2 Chronicles	Jonah	Jonah
2 Cor	2 Corinthians	Jos	Joshua
2 Jn	2 John	Jude	Jude
2 Kgs	2 Kings	Judg	Judges
2 Pe	2 Peter	Lam	Lamentations
2 Sam	2 Samuel	Lev	Leviticus
2 Thes	2 Thessalonians	Lk	Luke
2 Tim	2 Timothy	Mal	Malachi
3 Jn	3 John	Mic	Micah
Acts	Acts	Mk	Mark
Amos	Amos	Mtt	Matthew
Col	Colossians	Nah	Nahum
Dan	Daniel	Neh	Nehemiah
Deut	Deuteronomy	Num	Numbers
Eccl	Ecclesiastes	Obad	Obadiah
Eph	Ephesians	Phil	Philippians
Esth	Esther	Philem	Philemon
Ex	Exodus	Prov	Proverbs
Ezek	Ezekiel	Psa	Psalms
Ezra	Ezra	Rev	Revelation
Gal	Galatians	Rom	Romans
Gen	Genesis	Ruth	Ruth
Hab	Habakkuk	Song Sol	Song of Solomon
Hag	Haggai	Titus	Titus
		Zech	Zechariah
		Zep	Zephaniah

Translation Abbreviations

ESV	English Standard Version
KJV	King James Version
NASB	New American Standard Versions, 95 ed.
NIV	New International Version
NKJV	New King James Version
NET	New English Translation
RSV	Revised Standard Version

Other Works Cited

Generally, the references to other works are put with the quotes in as tolerable a form as possible. First and Second Maccabees are listed as "1 Mac" and "2 Mac."

Of Edward Gibbon's *Decline and Fall of the Roman Empire*, there are so many editions that I despaired of giving page numbers that will be useful to the reader, and have instead just referenced his chapter and "Part" numbers. I would think that the quotes I have given could be searched on the Internet.

I have on occasion modernized Whiston's translation of Josephus' works, strictly to improve readability, hopefully with no damage to Whiston's intentions. The citations are abbreviated as "*Wars*" for Josephus' *The Wars of the Jews*, and *Ant* for his *Antiquities of the Jews*. Then are given the volume number and then the paragraph number (like "Wars II, 364"). Once again, there are too many diverse editions to make page numbers useful.

Other references are handled in a more traditional fashion.

Table of Contents

We Sit

We wake up one day
in the middle of a war!

And choose the wrong side!

As It Was All Beginning

Originally, there was a Rule and an Order in Creation. It was glorious in those days of old when first the worlds were formed, and grace and life was given to matter. Some very high orders of beings were created first, but none were created without Jesus Christ. He was there in the beginning. He was "with" God, and He

> [1] ... was God. [2] He was in the beginning with God. [3] All things were made through Him, and apart from Him nothing was made that was made. Jn 1:1-3 NKJV

These higher beings were called by many names. They are commonly called "angels," which is a translation of the Hebrew word *malak* מַלְאָךְ which means a messenger. It is also used in the sense of an ambassador or an envoy, but *malak* is mainly used for someone sent with a message, or alternately that special order of higher beings that often called "angels." The English word for "angel" comes from the Greek word for messenger or angel *angelos* ἄγγελος. The Greeks also had other words for an envoy or an ambassador, and some of those words are also used in Scripture, but *angelos* in the New Testament is once again used for someone you send with a message, or that higher order of beings who are God's "messengers." Messengers? Yes, they are "greater in might and power" than men, 2 Pe 2:11. They are moral creatures, but

> ... God did not spare angels when they sinned, but cast them into hell and committed them to chains of gloomy darkness, to be kept until the judgment; 2 Pe 2:4 ESV

They are rather like men in the sense that they are capable of wrong doing. So of these servants of God, it says that God, "put no trust in his servants; and his angels he charged with folly:" Job 4:18 KJV.

Now these are powerful beings but not "creator" beings. They are powerful, but not life-giving beings. Angels are *not* gods. You can forget the Gnostic pictures of "creator" angels, or of life and worlds as made by some funny little elf-like creatures, as have been portrayed in some movies. Some men have corrupted themselves insisting on worshipping these subordinate lower beings, "taking delight in *false* humility and worship of the angels," Col 2:18 NKJV. Many of the angels have indeed been an alien spiritual reality in this world, and so we are warned,

> [20] No, but the sacrifices of pagans are offered to demons, not to God ... 1 Cor. 10:20 NIV

When we have been taken captive and served these lower beings (as we all have in the course of our lives) then it says of us that "you were slaves to those which by nature are no gods," Gal 4:8 NASB. But as Creator there was none but the LORD God, for

Thus says the LORD, your Redeemer,
And He who formed you from the womb,
"I am the LORD, who makes all things,
Who stretches out the heavens all alone
Who spreads abroad the earth by Myself," Isa 44:24 NKJV

Or again from Isaiah the prophet,

¹² "Listen to Me, O Jacob, even Israel whom I called;
I am He, I am the first, I am also the last.
¹³ Surely My hand founded the earth,
And My right hand spread out the heavens;
When I call to them, they stand together." Isa 48:12-13 NASB

But of the angels, what is there to say? They are called "sons of God" more than once in Scripture, and they appear before the LORD, as in Job 1:6. They are called "stars" in the occult and in astrology, and also in Job chapter 38, where it says of creation,

⁴ "Where were you when I laid the foundations of the earth?
Tell *Me*, if you have understanding ...
⁷ When **the morning stars sang together**
And all **the sons of God** shouted for joy?" Job 38:4,7 NKJV *(emphasis added)*

It was a glorious day when these morning stars sang together at creation, but the Lord created and some of the angels (also created beings), were watching the completion of this work. But names and titles used of angels indicate great power for these mere "messengers," and "sons of God" is only a start. Even if you discount the occult terms for these angels, words like "demiurges," "spheres," or "aeons," there are plenty of powerful terms used to describe these beings in Scripture. The KJV translates "rulers or authorities" as "principalities, or powers," Col 1:16. That is a translation you will often see in literature about these beings. Some of these beings rule over others, and over other things, so some are called archangels, from *archangelos* ἀρχάγγελος, or literally speaking "ruling angels." Once again these terms are an indication of rule and authority, as do the other the names given these powerful beings in passages like Col 1:16 and Eph 6:12.

Another of the names for a type of angel is that of a cherub *keruv* כְּרוּב or the plural would cherubim *kiruvim* כְּרֻבִים. It is customary in the West to think of cherubim as naked little baby boys with wings, but the Biblical picture is a far cry from this. One theory of cherubim is that the name indicates a being that was created for the praise and glory of God. Such creatures appear in Ezekiel chapters 1, and 10, and other places, as surrounding and protecting the throne of God. Glorious creatures they are, having all the attributes of the humanity and the intelligence of a man, the sight of an eagle, the ferocity and power of a lion, and the power of an ox. Such cherubim may be what is pictured as a "living creatures, each one of them with six wings, are full of eyes around and within; and day and night they do not cease to say, "Holy, holy, holy is the Lord God, the Almighty, who was and who is and who is to come,"" Rev 4:8 ESV. Read Ezekiel's accounts of these creatures surrounding the throne of God to see really awesome descriptions. A special cherub is described in Ezekiel 28, a "covering cherub."

> "Thou art the anointed cherub that covereth; and I have set thee so: thou wast upon the holy mountain of God; thou hast walked up and down in the midst of the stones of fire." Ezek 28:14 KJV

One artist's concept of the mercy seat on ark of the covenant.

Notice that this is a covering cherub, perhaps like those spoken of in Revelation, or perhaps like those angels who are pictured as covering the mercy seat of God in the ark of covenant. A dazzling creature is this one in Ezekiel 28, who is beautiful and powerful and important and stunningly clothed, but who is also someone who has a lot trouble with pride and selfish ambition.

> " ... Every precious stone was your covering:
> The sardius, topaz, and diamond,
> Beryl, onyx, and jasper,
> Sapphire, turquoise, and emerald with gold.
> The workmanship of your timbrels and pipes
> Was prepared for you **on the day you were created**.
> Ezek 28:13 *(emphasis added)* NKJV

This cherub had a day he was created, but he was in heaven itself, on the mountain of God. It was noted above that he was a "covering" being, and that he walked in heaven "in the midst of the stones of fire." Ezek 28:14. It says, in addition, that "God saw all that He had made, and behold, it was very good," in Gen 1:31 KJV, so also it says of this cherub, that,

> Thou wast perfect in thy ways from the day that thou wast created, till iniquity was found in thee. Ezek 28:15 KJV

But this cherub, this angel, although a very high level creature, was a moral creature, a fallible creature, and he corrupted himself.

> [16] "By the abundance of your trade

You were internally filled with violence,
And you sinned;
Therefore I have cast you as profane
From the mountain of God.
And I have destroyed you, O covering cherub,
From the midst of the stones of fire.
[17] Your heart was lifted up because of your beauty;
You corrupted your wisdom by reason of your splendor.
I cast you to the ground; ..." Ezek 28:16-17 NASB

This creature of wonder and majesty and ruin, we are told, was not only in heaven, but also in the garden of Eden, for it also says, "Thou hast been in Eden, the garden of God," Ezek 28:13 KJV. This creature is the one known as Satan, the adversary. It has been an Ancient Enmity. Man was intended to be the ruler of God's creation. Man was placed in Paradise, and that is what it was, paradise, because God planted a garden. The Hebrew word for garden is *gan* גן and it means a garden, especially an enclosed garden. The Greek word for garden, the word that was used in New Testament times, was the word *paradeisos* παράδεισος, literally Paradise! A paradise is literally a garden. So from the start, man had a job, even in paradise, and that job, the duty of man, was to rule God's creation, including:

> ... the fish of the sea, and over the fowl of the air, and over the cattle, and over all the earth, and over every creeping thing that creepeth upon the earth. Gen 1:26 KJV

God also told man to do some things, for instance to multiply, Gen 1:28. It is a responsibility of men to multiply; that is what he is *supposed* to do. Man is supposed to "fill" the earth. That is an order. Now many *object to* men filling the earth. They think the earth should be empty of men and free for other critters to fill; in other words men should be few. So when men move away from the Lord, they stop multiplying, stop filling; *but that is what God said for men to do!* And man is supposed to "subdue" the earth according to Gen 1:28. Man is *supposed* to dominate the earth, put it under his control. That is his job. Now the "environmental" religions (and that is what they really are, religions) have a different view. They do promote a religious view of man, a non-Christian religious view of man. A view that man is no more important than any other creature, and that he shouldn't crowd any other creature out, or subdue anything else. *But that is a different **spiritual** view of man, really a different **religious** assessment of man, and what he is intended to be, and how he should hold back from his natural ability to dominate.* However in the record the LORD our God had written, man **should** subdue and rule, and that indicates many things *may be out of order,* **needing** to be set in order, **needing** to be ruled *so that earth will serve its purposes, and that this is the desired result of what has been made.* God gave man everything he needs.

[29] And God said, Behold, I have given you every herb bearing seed, which *is* upon the face of all the earth, and every tree, in the which *is* the fruit of a tree yielding seed; to you it shall be for meat. [30] And to every beast of the earth, and to every fowl of the air, and to every thing that creepeth upon the earth, wherein *there is* life, *I have given* every green herb for meat: and it was so. Gen 1:29-30 KJV

Now some who had been given the power to make choices were already making other choices, as has been shown, but when God saw everything He had made, it was good. Let me repeat what the Scripture says exactly, that "it was very good," Gen 1:31.

What then of these other, more powerful, more intelligent creatures and in a real sense even more wonderful creatures? They are to be ruled by man? They are not to judge man, but they are to be judged *by man*, for as the prophet Paul says, "Do you not know that we will judge angels?" 1 Cor 6:3. It is hard to disagree with the prophet David when he speaks in Psalm 8.

[4] What is man that You are mindful of him,
    And the son of man that You visit him?
[5] For You have made him a little lower than the angels,
    And You have crowned him with glory and honor.
[6] You have made him to have dominion over the works of Your hands;
... Psa 8:4-6 NKJV

And the ultimate role of angels?

Are they not all ministering spirits, sent forth to minister for them who shall be heirs of salvation? Heb 1:14 KJV

Staggering, but true. A truth of both the Old Testament and the New Testament. The purpose of angels is to "serve those who will inherit salvation," those who will live forever and rule with the Lord.

Not to deny these truths, but for some of the angels of glory, this must have had part of what some of them thought was an intolerable situation. I mean the very idea, that they "the powerful" should serve this miserable little critter made of dirt? So there was a revolt. It was not all the angels, but indeed among a significant number of the angels. The special covering cherub mentioned in Ezekiel 28 had decided on revolt. So the Lord says of this revolting angel,

[13] "But you said in your heart,
'I will ascend to heaven;
I will raise my throne above the stars of God,
And I will sit on the mount of assembly
In the recesses of the north.
[14] I will ascend above the heights of the clouds;
I will make myself like the Most High.'" Isa 14:13-14 NASB

And now the Lord says,

> "How you have fallen from heaven,
> O star of the morning, son of the dawn!
> You have been cut down to the earth,
> You who have weakened the nations!" Isa 14:12 NASB

This cherub is no longer the beautiful and wonderful creature it once was. Like a handsome man or beautiful woman that has been ruined by their adulteries and their drugs, so Satan was once a beautiful cherub but has morphed into nothing more than a disgusting and vicious reptile, a beast, a monster, a dragon.

> And there appeared another wonder in heaven; and behold a great red dragon, having seven heads and ten horns, and seven crowns upon his heads. Rev 12:3 KJV

It describes then in Revelation a

> [7] ... war broke out in heaven: Michael and his angels fought with the dragon; and the dragon and his angels fought, [8] but they did not prevail, nor was a place found for them in heaven any longer. Rev 12:7-8 NKJV

Also angels are again called "stars," for it says of the dragon,

> And his tail drew the third part of the stars of heaven, and did cast them to the earth. ... Rev 12:4 KJV

So this "dragon," this powerful and once beautiful being, manages to sweep a third of the angels of heaven into this revolt, and they make war on the woman who gives birth to a male child.

> And the great dragon was cast out, that old serpent, called the Devil, and Satan, which deceiveth the whole world: he was cast out into the earth, and his angels were cast out with him. Rev 12:9 KJV

In this way an implacable enmity against man was set, and the stage for the story which prophecy tells.

A Seed War and Dominions

Serpents have always had an evil connotation. People were told to detest them in Lev 11:42, but clearly there is often no need to tell us to detest them. Perhaps this antipathy had its origins in the fall of our race. Now the serpent was the devil, or Satan, so it is told in more than one passage, as in Rev 20:2. He is the one who deceived Eve, and he deceives the whole world, Rev 12:9. Now the serpent, as he is called in Genesis, was a subtle creature, a crafty creature, Gen 3:1. The word is *arum* עָרוּם which means to be shrewd, crafty, prudent, cunning. This serpent ends up being cursed above all creatures, Gen 3:14. It is from this point on the serpent will crawl on its belly on the ground and eat dirt. Surely this is no good way to get around! Satan had taken on the form of some creature, or perhaps he got inside this creature. This creature (at the beginning it seems) had legs, but which after the curse no longer had legs and will forever go on its belly. It was damaged, physically changed. It was changed because of sin. Now all of creation is cursed because of men's sin, but the serpent is cursed more, again in Gen 3:14.

> "Because you have done this,
> Cursed are you more than all cattle,
> And more than every beast of the field; ..." NASB

There is opposition now. Opposition between the man and "the serpent," between the "principalities and powers" and "the woman." Enmity! So God says to the "serpent,"

> "And I will put enmity
> Between you and the woman," Gen 3:15 NKJV

This is a battle, a warfare, that began near the beginning, and it involves not only the man and the woman and Satan, but also all their "seed," their offspring, their descendants. Thus from the first it spoke of the seed (singular) of the woman and the seed (singular) of serpent, Gen 3:15. The seed of the woman is a thread that goes throughout Scripture. The promise runs through Abraham, as can be seen in Gen 12:3, and other passages. Later in history it also runs through David. It is called "a root of David."

> and one of the elders said to me, "Stop weeping; behold, the Lion that is from the tribe of Judah, the Root of David, has overcome so as to open the book and its seven seals," Rev 5:5 NASB

It is again in Rev 22:16, where it says,

> I Jesus have sent mine angel to testify unto you these things in the churches. I am the root and the offspring of David, and the bright and morning star. KJV

This was something spoken of old about David, before the house of David had fallen, because Isaiah had spoken of a time when an offspring will come from "the root of David." "Then a shoot will spring from the stem of Jesse, And a branch from his roots will bear fruit," Isa 11:1 NASB. The word root is *shoresh* שֹׁרֶשׁ. "From the stump of Jesse" it says in the NIV and some other translations. Of this seed, this root, Paul comments in Galatians, where it says,

> Now to Abraham and his Seed were the promises made. He does not say, "And to seeds," as of many, but as of one, *"And to your Seed,"* who is Christ. that is, Christ. Gal 3:16 NKJV

So the "seed" was singular and was a long line leading to one man, "that is, Christ." So from the beginning the seed was of woman, not of the man. Christ was born of a woman, *not* of man but rather of God Himself by His Holy Spirit. So by the woman came the deception leading to the fall, and by the woman came God's only begotten Son to redeem us from the fall.

But there are two seeds spoken of in Gen 3:15.

> "And I will put enmity
> Between you and the woman, and between your seed and her seed;
> He shall bruise you on the head,
> And you shall bruise him on the heel." NASB

So there is also **a seed of the serpent**, a seed of Satan, an evil one born of Satan, and also, eerily, singular. He too is spoken of in many places in Scripture, many times in terms of types or symbolic rulers. He is pictured as plotting against the LORD God.

Out of the serpent's root a viper will come out Isaiah says in Isa 14:29, "For from the serpent's root a viper will come out, And its fruit will be a flying serpent," NASB. And it is the same word for root, *shoresh* שֹׁרֶשׁ. There is a root of David, and there is a root of the serpent. A discussion of the details of Isaiah 14 will come later. Clearly there will be a day for punishing the serpent, Gen 3:15. Only the heel of the seed of woman is harmed, clearly not a fatal blow, but the head of the serpent is harmed. That could indicate that either the head of evil is punished (that is Satan) and/or that evil will receive a fatal blow. Clearly both things are within reach of the passage. Satan suffers eternal death in Rev 20:10 and many other passages. On that day the serpent will be punished.

> In that day the LORD will punish Leviathan the fleeing serpent,
> With His fierce and great and mighty sword,
> Even Leviathan the twisted serpent;
> And He will kill the dragon who lives in the sea. Isa 27:1 NASB

So Isaiah speaks of a special day, called "that day," when the serpent will be punished. Notice the associations here. The serpent is associated with a dragon, and that is the same association seen in the book of Revelation. There he is called "the great dragon, the serpent of old" Rev 12:9. And the dragon, Satan, is of course to be punished. Then there is another association, because the dragon is called two other things in Isaiah 27. He is called "the twisted serpent." The NIV calls him "the coiling serpent," and the KJV calls him "the crooked serpent." How should we take all this? As literal? As metaphorical? Maybe it should be taken as both. It is not beyond belief that Satan's spiritual body was twisted. At one time he was beautiful and good, Ezek 28:12-13. Sin does change creatures, even physically. The immediate physical change in Adam and Eve was that they started to die physically. When you look at people who have been deeply enmeshed in sin, the dragging, aging, marring, twisting effects of sin are visible. In the main, those who stay pure and sweet looking, are those who overall live the best. My middle daughter was doing some work among those at a local homeless shelter. She told me of a lady there who was soon to die of cancer. I asked her how old this lady was, and she replied that she couldn't tell, because "You know how people are in such shelters. They have lived such hard lives, and have often aged so rapidly, that it is hard to tell how old they really are." There are exceptions, but these are still "the rules" that are clearly seen among men. Sin changes us even physically, and as is seen in how the serpent was changed.

Satan can still "appear," **take on the form**, of an angel of light, 2 Cor 11:14-15. Is that like his "appearing" as a serpent? In Revelation the serpent is described as a dragon, a monster, not something beautiful. So it is not beyond consideration that the cherub who became the devil and Satan came to be "twisted" in body. Distorted!

Also the serpent is seen as living in the sea in Isa 27:1. Now the serpent was cast out of heaven, down to earth, in a battle at some point during history as seen in Rev 12:7-13. Here in Isaiah 27 he is pictured as living in the sea. And when the dragon at the end of time gives his special powers and authority to the one he selects, listen to how it describes him.

> And I stood upon the **sand of the sea**, and saw a beast rise up out of **the sea**, ... Rev 13:1 KJV (*emphasis added*)

The other association is that the serpent, the sea creature, is called "Leviathan." This sea monster, who is spoken of in other passages in Scripture, and who was it would seem, a literal creature which is in our own times extinct, has wide associations. Even the occult in their movies and books and plans use "Leviathan" as a name for Satan himself.

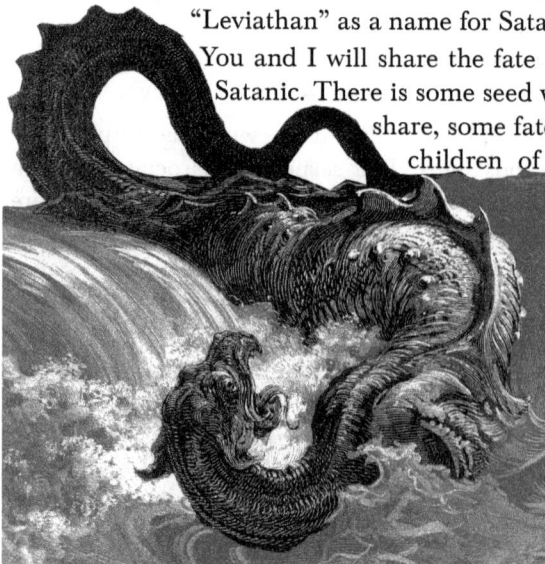

You and I will share the fate of one seed or another, godly or Satanic. There is some seed we are born of, some ancestry we share, some fate to which we go. You and I were children of wrath before we came to the Lord, Eph 2:1-3. We needed to "*escape* from the snare of the devil, having taken captive by him *to do* his will," 2 Tim 2:26 NKJV. Still, God loved us and was willing to give us a rebirth in Christ, Eph 2:4-5. We will share the fate of some master. Who is your master? Satan or Jesus? *And how does this "seed" idea work out on the Satanic side?*

For starters, look at the

mighty men of old: giants and the issues in Gen 6:1-4. These are harder things to think about in our age for Satan is restrained until just before the end, Rev 20:1-3; and many of his angels are still imprisoned, Jude 6.

Over 1,500 years have passed as one comes to the time of Noah, and this number is arrived at by adding the years given in Genesis 5. Noah has been around for 500 of those 1,500 years, and it mentions him as the father of three particular sons, Gen 5:32. People were really multiplying on the earth, Gen 6:1. And notice what is said next, for it says that the "sons of God" thought that the daughters of men were beautiful, Gen 6:2.

Many discuss what is meant by the phrase "the sons of God." If you look closely at Scripture you can see that the term "son of God" is used in more than one way, especially in the New Testament. When Scripture says we are "sons of God" it means it in two senses. First of all, we are born again of God, and secondly we are becoming more and more like God. We become more and more "like" the LORD of Hosts. We are His sons. So the term "son of God" is used of Christians, those righteous by faith. Again of us it says in Rom 8:14, "For as many as are led by the Spirit of God, they are the sons of God." KJV Also in Rom. 8:19, "For the earnest expectation of the creation eagerly waits for the revealing of the sons of God." NKJV

But the term "sons of God" is used another way, especially in the Old Testament. Look at Job 1:6 where it says "Now there was a day when the sons of God came to present themselves before the LORD, and Satan came also among them," KJV. And it is clearly speaking of the angels of heaven presenting themselves before the Lord, as most acknowledge, and perhaps it is acknowledging that they came from God and are "like" God in some way, although Satan is contrasted with the faithful sons of God. The same thing is in Job 38:7 when it says, "When the morning stars sang together and all the sons of God shouted for joy?" KJV. It is clearly talking about the angels singing for joy at God's creation of the world, and seems to imply that the spiritual powers, the angels, were created before the material world was formed.

Now angels are very different creatures as seen in Scripture. They are spirit beings, greater in power than men (2 Pe 2:11), and are described as having incredible traits and powers in passages like Ezekiel chapter 1 and in Revelation chapter 4, as already discussed. **But the first time an angel is seen in Scripture he is assuming the *bodily* form of a serpent in Genesis 3.** Also, they can assume a human form to appear to men, and **three angels appear to Abraham as "three men," Gen 18:2.** Abraham then prepares bread and butchers a young calf to feed them, and then stood "by them as they ate," Gen 18:8, which was not exactly what you would expect. But there is nothing in Genesis 18 and 19 that indicates that the "angels" looked like anything more or less than "men," Gen 18:2. Abraham fed them, and the men of Sodom a little later wanted to rape them. Later in Hebrews we are all counseled to,

Be not forgetful to entertain strangers: for thereby some have entertained angels unawares. Heb 13:2 KJV

So yes, someone might think of angels as almost aliens from another dimension but still able to "take on" a physical form and talk and eat with us, as any other man might. It is then obviously easy to make some very naive assumptions about these powerful creatures, beings that the faithful will judge one day, 1Cor 6:3.

Gen 6:2 says that the sons of God were marrying the daughters of men. So who is it talking about? Some people think it is speaking of the sons of Seth or Enoch or someone "righteous" marrying the daughters of Cain. God says He is not going to fight with man forever, Gen 6:3. Among other things, God seems to be talking about how long it will be before He destroys the earth with water, but notice what it says next. The Nephilim were on the earth in this time, Gen 6:4 NASB. The Nephilim were one of the races of giants who were on the earth, Num 13:33. Now it says there that the Nephilim were the sons of Anak, (called the Anakim), and it describes them as very tall in Deut 9:1-2. They were related to some other races of giants such as the Rephaim, Deut 2:10-11. Hebrew words are far fewer than the number of words in Greek or English, and Hebrew words often have a wider range of meaning than their Greek or English cousins. The Hebrew word Rephaim seems to refer to someone who is strong, or who is "sunk" or abandoned, and it also may be used to refer to spirits or ghosts. One of these Rephaim in Deut 3:11, had a bed thirteen feet long and six feet wide. Of course, most are familiar with the nine foot tall giant Goliath. Scripture does not argue these things, merely mentions them as facts.

Look carefully at the story of angels in Jude. Here it talks about the angels who "left their own abode," NKJV Jude 6-7. The KJV says the angels "left their

The three angels who visited Abraham appeared to be nothing more nor less than mere men.

own habitation," and their own habitation was of course in heaven, and these angels, who were punished, had left their home in heaven. It doesn't seem to indicate that these angels just made a trip out of heaven, but rather that they "abandoned" their home in heaven to make a home somewhere else. Then it says that "Sodom and Gomorrah and the cities around them in a similar manner to these, having given themselves over to sexual immorality and gone after strange flesh," NKJV. So Sodom and Gomorrah engaged in fornication "in the same" way as the angels did who had abandoned their habitation. How did Sodom and Gomorrah "in the same way" commit gross immorality? They went after "strange flesh," Jude 7. They engaged in *unnatural* intercourse. The angels who did this are in prison awaiting the judgment day. They are being "reserved in everlasting chains under darkness unto the judgment of the great day," Jude 6 KJV. Likewise Sodom and Gomorrah who also committed great unnatural sin, are "set forth for an example, suffering the vengeance of eternal fire," Jude 7 KJV. Listen carefully to Peter about where these angels are, because,

> For if God spared not the angels that sinned, but cast them down to hell, and delivered them into chains of darkness, to be reserved unto judgment;
>
> 2 Pet. 2:4 KJV

The word translated "hell" here, is not the regular word for hell, but it is from the Greek word for Tartarus or *Tartaro-ō* ταρταρόω, which is described as "chains of darkness, to be reserved unto judgment." Also there are angels fallen from heaven. Jesus said "I beheld Satan as lightning fall from heaven," Lk 10:18 KJV; and the rest of the evil angels are cast out heaven in Rev 12:7-9. Lastly notice that a special man called "the lawless one" will come by "the activity of Satan," 2 Thes 2:3, 9 NASB; this same body of evil angels.

So what is the name for these giants in Genesis 6? It is the Hebrew word *Nephilim* נְפִילִים, and the name Nephilim comes from the Hebrew word *nephal* נָפַל "to fall," so Nephilim literally means "the fallen ones." The giants, the men of renown of old, are literally "the fallen ones." Other cultures also have traditions of giants in ancient times. For instance, the Greeks have more than one tradition of giants on the earth. Some they called the Titans (although some quibble about them as "giants"). The Greeks called their lower gods "demons," just like in Acts 17:18 where the Greeks said of Paul, "He seems to be a proclaimer of strange deities," (literally "foreign" "demons"/"gods," *xenōn diamoiōn* ξένων δαιμονίων). The Titans were supposedly the children of Uranus (heaven), and Gia (earth)! Supposedly they rebelled against the higher gods and were thrown into Tartarus! (And it is the same Greek word which Peter uses.) But back to the text, when "the sons of God came in to the daughters of men," Gen 6:4; it says it produced the Nephilim who were mighty men of old, Gen 6:4. Now some people think this is talking about some good boys (who were descendants of Seth or Enoch or whomever) who were marrying those good looking (but very bad) girls who were descendants of Cain. First, notice that it is contrasting "sons of God" with "men," then some questions must be asked:

1. Are you sure there were some "good boys" around? At this time "the earth was corrupt before God," Gen 6:11 KJV. None found favor except Noah and his family, and the wickedness described seems to be more than just a poor choice of a wife, serious though that can be!

2. Since when does good boys marrying bad girls (good looking no doubt) produce giant children? Maybe deformed children because of sin or disease, but giant children? That *also* doesn't match what is known about genetics. And,

3. This happened again after the flood, because it says of the Nephilim that they were "in the earth in those days; and also after that," Gen 6:4a KJV.

Maybe this is just stumbling at Scripture. Maybe angels going after "strange flesh" is the answer after all. Angels leaving their home in heaven to marry human women! Unnatural fornication! And these beings who can assume human bodies, and eat food, were it would seem, also capable of producing offspring with women, offspring who were giants.

So the issues of "seed" and "offspring" and "descent" works more than one way. There is also more than one unusual seed which can be produced. **We speak of angels in human form.**

Then looking ahead in Scripture, there is a turn from the seed of the serpent to the seed of woman, and the seed of the woman means God is with us in Isaiah 7. The time given in Isa 7:1 is in the days of Ahaz king of Judah, and Rezin king of Aram, and Pekah king of Israel, somewhere around 735-734 BC.

At this time, Rezin and Pekah got together to wage war on Judah. The people of Judah heard about this great alliance, and that the Arameans were already camping in Ephraim. The hearts of the leaders and the people "shook as the leaves of the forest shake with the wind," Isa 7:2 NASB. Ephraim is in fact the northern ten tribes of Israel. It was perhaps two or three times as large as Judah. What the NASB and the NIV call Aram (as in the Hebrew text), most would call Syria today (as in the KJV and NKJV), and it was a large and very powerful nation, a very warlike nation, with its capital in Damascus. The two nations ganging up on little Judah would be like Japan finding out that America and Russia were about to gang up on her. It's on the news every day now. That's all the television is talking about, and now God gives the prophet instructions. He tells him to go with his son Shear-jashub to meet the President, the king, King Ahaz (whom you can read about in 2 Kings 16), and give him a message. And here is what you are to tell him:

Be careful, be calm, Isaiah says to Ahaz! Isa 7:4-9. Don't be afraid, he says, because these two kings are just smoldering sticks who will soon perish. Their anger is not to be feared. This will not happen, the prophet says. Aram and the Northern Ten Tribes will not invade Judah, Isa 7:7. For the head of Aram is Damascus, Isa 7:8. And Damascus will be crushed, and in 65 years the Northern Ten Tribes, called "Ephraim" in this passage, will cease to be a people according to Isa 7:8. It is unclear to me why Isaiah mentions 65 years. Perhaps that includes the time it will take for Ephraim/Israel to be completely dismantled. Syria was in fact conquered by the Assyrians under Tiglath Pileser in 732 BC. Then a mere ten years later Israel fell in the year 722 B.C. to King Shalmaneser of Assyria, and almost the entire nation was deported to Assyria to live. So don't worry about the northern ten tribes, called Israel or 'Ephraim'. Isaiah also warns Ahaz, a political leader in a war situation, that if he does not stand by faith, he won't stand at all! Isa 7:9.

So ask for a sign, Ahaz is told by Isaiah in Isa 7:10-11. It can be any kind of sign, in heaven above or earth beneath or all the way down to Sheol. In this case, Ahaz is instructed to ask for a sign. No, more than that, he is commanded. It is not something men are to even ask for normally. Do not put the Lord to the test, Deut 6:16. Jesus took note that the wicked often demand a sign, Mtt 12:38-40, but He said in essence that the men of His day were not going to get any sign except for Jesus' death burial and resurrection. But even so, Isaiah wants to convince Ahaz that it makes sense to follow the Lord and trust in Him, not in treaties or combinations, or powerful backers from other nations, and Ahaz is actually encouraged to ask for any sign he wants, to convince him that he should really trust in God, not in some Assyrian "deliverer."

By this time Isaiah is angry with King Ahaz. You are trying my patience, he says. So if you are not going to *ask* for a sign, then Isaiah says he is going to *give* him a sign. Here is that sign, a sign which the Lord Himself will give. "Behold, a virgin shall conceive, and bear a son," Isa 7:14 KJV. The Hebrew word that is used here can either mean a virgin or it can mean just an unmarried young woman, a maiden, or what is in German called a Fräulein, a young

"Miss." So he is saying that a young woman will have a child (a son) and further that the virgin will call this young son "Immanuel."

Around this same time, some of Isaiah's children are presented as signs of the moral disintegration and international turmoil which was occurring. Indeed, in Isa 8:1 it is the same general international situation that the Lord is speaking of, and the Lord told Isaiah to take a large tablet and to write "*Maher-shalal-hash-baz,*" which means "Swift is the booty, speedy is the prey," or as in the NIV notes, "quick to the plunder, swift to the prey." So Isaiah had a child by his wife, and the Lord told him to name the child "Maher-shalal-hash-baz." Can you imagine calling this son in for a meal, or to do his studies? Isa 8:3-4 is very similar to what is seen in Isaiah 7. The Lord says that before the child, the child of the "virgin," is able to call out "Mama" or "Daddy," that all Aram with its capitol in Damascus, and all of Israel with its capitol in Samaria, will be carried away as booty (as loot) for the taking to the land of Assyria.

Likewise the boy that was with Isaiah when he met Ahaz at the upper pool, Shear-jashub, whose name means '"a remnant will return," is the theme of Isaiah's prophecy in Isaiah 10. There Isaiah says that only a small portion of Israel or Judah will survive in that day, though one day Israel will be like the sands of the sea.

> 21 The remnant will return, the remnant of Jacob, To the Mighty God.
> 22 For though your people, O Israel, be as the sand of the sea,
> 　　A remnant of them will return;
> 　　The destruction decreed shall overflow with righteousness.
> 23 For the Lord GOD of hosts
> Will make a determined end
> In the midst of all the land. Isa 10:21-23 NKJV

Similarly it appears that some young woman in Isaiah 7 would have a child, a son named "Immanuel." That is not a name that would be unthinkable to a devout Jew in those days. It means "God is with us." As this child starts to grow up, he will eat curds and honey when he is old enough to take what is good and reject what is bad. But way before the child is able to eat any "baby food" as it was in that day, while he is still a nursing infant, the land of the Arameans, and the land of the Northern Tribes of Israel will be ruined in battle, ruined by the invasion of the Assyrians. Further though, this nation Assyria will also "shave" Judah, the land King Ahaz rules. The Lord will bring something that Ahaz would not believe, Isaiah says in Isa 7:15-20. The Lord's razor will come. You are afraid of the wrong things he says. You are afraid of Ephraim and Aram. They do not even matter in this situation. They will never be a threat, and here you are afraid of them. But I tell what God will do. He will bring Assyria, and they will scrape this land clean as if it had been shaved with a razor, Isa 7:18-25. The Lord will bring on Judah not the northern ten tribes of Israel whom they fear so much, nor the feared Syrians. Rather someone else that

Ahaz doesn't even think of fearing: the Assyrians, Isa 7:17. Isaiah describes Assyria as a razor that is hired from beyond the river Euphrates, and that will shave the land clean, not only shave the head and legs, but the pride of men, their beards. The Assyrians will shave the land so clean that if a man is careful he may be able to keep a cow alive and couple of sheep, and so keep himself from starvation. But the fields and pastures will be desolate, not farmed, uncultivated, because of invasions, Isa 7:17-23.

So evidently some "young woman," had this child named Immanuel. Still part of this doesn't really seem to fit the context. The word for 'virgin' or 'maiden' is the Hebrew word *almah* עַלְמָה, which normally means a young and tender unmarried woman, and in the strictest sense, and ideally, really would be a virgin, and that seems to have been the normal use of this word—someone young and fresh and pure. A sexually ripe but unspoiled young woman. The Jewish translators of approximately the second century BC took the word this way, for in the Greek Septuagint translation of the Old Testament they translated *almah* in Isa 7:14 as *parthenos* παρθένος, literally and specifically a virgin.

Now this young woman in Isaiah's day might have been a sweet young thing! She might have looked very youthful. I do not know. Perhaps she is the original one who has this baby as a sign. But can you really say that she is a 'Miss', a 'M-I-S-S', a Fräulein, a virgin? Some have suggested that it is Isaiah's wife of which he speaks as bearing a baby as a sign to Ahaz. Maybe this is so or maybe not. Maybe Isaiah himself had another child as a type, as a symbol, and named him Immanuel for Ahaz's benefit, or perhaps it was another young lady who had this child by her husband. If it is indeed Isaiah's wife, she has already had at least one child previously, and that boy is old enough to walk with his daddy to meet Ahaz at the water pool. You can just hear the neighbors talking: Now *how* can you call Mrs. Isaiah a Fräulein, a 'virgin'? I don't mean anything against her, she's a nice lady, and that's a sweet little baby, but your going to call her 'Miss' Isaiah? Huh? I just can't see it, I just can't see it. What in the world is going on? Indeed, there was more going on. She was probably not a real "virgin," not a *real almah,* having a child back in the eight century BC. So at the very least there were some loose ends, at least as far as someone like Ahaz was concerned. But of course Jesus says that not even "the smallest letter or stroke shall pass ... until all is accomplished," Mtt 5:18 Therefore, the complete fulfillment of the prophecy had to come later.

So what is seen in Isaiah 7 is evidently symbolic. The Bible sometimes calls these things a "type." The child born in the eight century BC was thus a type or symbol of the Messiah, the Christ, who is the Ultimate One who is "God with us," because He was with God and He was God, Jn 1:1. The promises of a virgin birth were made to Mary, for she was told that, *"The* Holy Spirit will come upon you, and the power of the Highest will overshadow you; therefore, also, that Holy One who is to be born will be called the Son of God," Lk 1:35

NKJV. Then at the proper time the virgin was with child.

> [18] Now the birth of Jesus Christ was as follows: when His mother Mary had been betrothed to Joseph, before they came together she was found to be with child by the Holy Spirit. ... [22] Now all this took place to fulfill what was spoken by the Lord through the prophet: [23] "BE-HOLD, THE VIRGIN SHALL BE WITH CHILD AND SHALL BEAR A SON, AND THEY SHALL CALL HIS NAME IMMANUEL," which translated means, "GOD WITH US." Mtt 1:18, 22-23 NASB

Jesus is this Ultimate One who is God with Us, the Ultimate One who is a sign of God's deliverance, that we might be saved from the tragedy of a world gone awry. The Messiah was to come as a child, Isa 9.6-7. He was the Mighty God. He was literally, God with us, Jn 1:1, 14. The child is a sign then of two things: of God being with us and He was worshipped as God during His time here on earth (as when He stilled the waters of a raging sea in Mtt 14:28-33). That's why the Jews tried to kill Him, because He verified that He was Himself God.

> Therefore the Jews sought the more to kill him, because he not only had broken the sabbath, but said also that God was his Father, making himself equal with God. Jn 5:18 KJV

Additionally, this child is a sign for those rejecting the Lord's ways, of God's coming judgment, for those like Ahaz who think themselves too clever to trust in God. And He is coming again.

> [9] You shall make them as a fiery oven in the time of Your anger;
>   The LORD shall swallow them up in His wrath,
>   And the fire shall devour them.
> [10] Their offspring You shall destroy from the earth,
>   And their descendants from among the sons of men.
> Psa 21:9-10 NKJV

Are you afraid of your boss, teacher, husband or wife? Your bills, grades, education or job? Oh no, no, no! Fear God and keep his commandments, for this is the whole duty of man, Ecc 12:13! For though the foreign enemy is about to engulf us, those in the Lord are able to say to their adversaries, "Take counsel together, and it shall come to nought; speak the word, and it shall not stand: for God is with us." Isa 8:10 KJV. "Do not fear," Mtt 10:28.

There is a seed war, and there is a seed of the woman (singular), and there is a seed of the serpent (*also singular*); and God will come and He will come to "comfort My people," as it says in Isaiah 40. In the book of Isaiah, the prophet has been talking by the Word of God, over and over again, about punishment, about annihilation, and about death for sins in the earlier chapters of the book of Isaiah. However, in Isaiah 40 the tone and the emphasis changes.

"Comfort, yes, comfort My people," God says in Isa 40:1-2 NKJV. Speak kindly to Jerusalem, the capital of God's people, both spiritually and physically, and tell her that difficult times are over, and that her sins have been removed, and that everything is to go well from this point. These are powerful words for 7th century BC Judah, which was full of much immorality and trouble of every sort. Who was not in those times surrounded by enemies and perhaps very close to being overcome by invaders. And not only they might ask, but we also might ask, When is this? When are the troubles of God's people to be complete, and all of this to be fulfilled? Then it describes a voice is calling in the wilderness, Isa 40:3. It is a voice in the wilderness, meaning unpopulated places, to clear the way for God, to clear the way for *Yahweh/ Yehovah* יהוה, that is the name of God. Following ancient Jewish custom, often *Yahweh* is translated "LORD" with a capital "L" and small caps for "ORD." Look carefully at your Bible. The name of God comes from the Hebrew word "to be" and it is seen in Ex 3:14, where "God said to Moses, "I AM WHO I AM"; and He said, "Thus you shall say to the sons of Israel, 'I AM has sent me to you.'" NASB So Isaiah 40 is saying that God Himself is going to come, and that He is going to come in the wilderness! It says to straighten out the road for Him, Isa 40:4. It refers to the practice of sending out road crews to straighten out the road and fill in the potholes *if the king was coming that way!* And the King of all the Universe is to be coming that way! It says that the people will see *God Himself,* because

> "The glory of the LORD shall be revealed,
>   And all flesh shall see it together;
>   For the mouth of the LORD has spoken." Isa 40:5 NKJV

It may even be speaking of more than one event, for it says "all flesh shall see it **together,**" *emphasis added.* That would mean that the first event will be a type, a symbol, for the second event. I will let you just think about that one for a while, and type and anti-type will be discussed in more detail later. At this they ask: "What shall I call out?" Isa 40:6a. The answer is all flesh is grass! It is a truth of our being! Job said similar things. "He comes forth like a flower and fades away; He flees like a shadow and does not continue," Job 14:2 NKJV.

In the same way Isaiah says "... Surely the people are grass. The grass withers, the flower fades, But the word of our God stands forever." Isa 40:7-8 NKJV Peter quotes these verses in 1 Peter chapter 1, and James in James chapter 1.

In Isa 40:9 it is talking about good news coming. You can see from the end of verse 9 that it is good news *because* **God** is coming, and they will say it in Judah, so it identifies where God will come, and they will say **in Judah** *Here is your God!* All I can say is "Wow!" Judah, of course, did see our Lord, did see God in an earlier day. Jesus Himself said to His disciple Philip, "Have I been so long with you, and yet you have not known Me ... ? He who has seen Me has seen the Father ..." Jn 14:9 NKJV. In Isaiah 40 it says the Lord God will come with might, and will have His reward with Him, Isa 40:10, and God will come ready to pay back all around. And He will tend His flock like a shepherd, Isa 40:11, and "In

His arm He will gather the lambs And carry *them* in His bosom; He will gently lead the nursing *ewes*." NASB

Clearly it is speaking of "God" in Isaiah 40, not just "A" "god" or a "A" divine person, but God Himself. This is clearly seen in the next few verses when it asks in those next few verses about who is really like God, Isa 40:12-18. Who has taken in His hands and measured the oceans, or measured the mountains on scales? The nations are literally just a drop in the bucket to Him. They are like dust on some scales. They are less than nothing. They are meaningless. And then it asks, "To whom then will ye liken God?" So the passage is not vaguely about "divinity." It is about the True and Living God.

Of course this is all speaking of Jesus, and Judah did see Him! Jesus is this true shepherd, and He calls His own sheep by name, as the One who created them and knows them, and His own sheep recognize His voice and follow Him. They will never follow a stranger, Jn 10:3-5. This good shepherd says of Himself, "I am the good shepherd. The good shepherd gives His life for the sheep," Jn 10:11 NKJV.

He is *really* God. He was with God in the beginning, and He was God, and nothing was made without Him, Jn 1:1-5. When He came to His own, those who should have had salvation, those who should have known Him and followed Him, they didn't receive Him. But to those who did receive Him, He gave the right to become children of God. And the apostle John says that

> And the Word was made flesh, and dwelt among us, (and we beheld his glory, the glory as of the only begotten of the Father,) full of grace and truth, Jn 1:14 KJV

The voice that Isaiah speaks of crying out in the wilderness, preparing the way for Jesus, is John the Baptist. He was out in the wilderness, eating wild food, and he came telling people to repent for the kingdom of heaven was at hand, and everyone was in that day coming to him to listen and be baptized. The apostle Matthew says in Mtt 3:1-6 that John was the fulfillment of Isa 40:3.

The fact that God Himself was coming to deliver His people is the good news, and that is really what the word "gospel" means: good news. Jesus and John were proclaiming it and showing the power of healing redemption that was in Him, Mtt 4:23.

God Himself came down to accept a place among men, and to fully be a man; and to taste of death, so that by our participating in His death, we might escape the bondage and death that has come through our sins. Later on the Jews were offended at Jesus because He was saying He was God. Again you can see it in Jn 10:31-33.

> [31] Then the Jews took up stones again to stone Him. [32] Jesus answered them, "Many good works I have shown you from My Father. For which of those works do you stone Me?" [33] The Jews answered Him, saying,

"For a good work we do not stone You, but for blasphemy, and because You, being a Man, make Yourself God." NKJV

They were offended that a man would claim to be *God Himself.* But notice carefully, that Isaiah 40, written centuries earlier, *clearly says that* **God Himself** would come to Judah itself. That is the point of the passage, the clear meaning that God Himself would come, and would send a man, John the Baptist, to prepare the way for His coming, and that this would lead to God's people having their sins removed and their warfare ended, and that He would in fact come in the wilderness! ***What excuse did these Pharisees have for their unbelief?*** They had none, absolutely none.

Also this God who would come is The Mighty God. He is the one who made the earth, Isa 40:12. Who can give God advice? Who can tell Him what to do? Who does He need to talk to, Isa 40:13-14? All of the nations of the earth, even together, amount to nothing, Isa 40:15, 17. There is no idol that is like the Lord our God, Isa 40:18-20. The earth is nothing before Him, Isa 40:21-22. Notice that it speaks of the earth as a globe, as circle; and men as like grasshoppers, and our earthly rulers are next to nothing, Isa 40:22-24.

Psalm 2 says that Jesus Himself personally rules these kings. It is talking about the gospel period. It is speaking of that period after Jesus is on the throne of His kingdom. It says that the kings of the earth should be smart about this. If they don't bow before Jesus and worship and serve Him, He (the Son) may destroy them in a minute, Psa 2:10-12.

Who is like this God who will come to Judah, who will appear in the desert? Lift up your eyes and see the One who created the stars, who brought them out by number and who calls all of them by name. Why should Israel think for a minute that they are hidden or forgotten by this God, or that He won't call us to account?

> [29] He gives strength to the weary,
> And to *him* who lacks might He increases power.
> [30] Though youths grow weary and tired,
> And vigorous young men stumble badly,
> [31] Yet those who wait for the LORD
> Will gain new strength;
> They will mount up with wings like eagles,
> They will run and not get tired,
> They will walk and not become weary. Isa 40:29-31 NASB

It is talking about heaven. Why shouldn't you and I be a part of this? We have to make Jesus our Master and work for Him. The shepherd will take care of us, but we must commit ourselves to His care. We must follow Him.

Jesus, as you may know, is the Greek form of the name Joshua, *yehoshua* יְהוֹשֻׁעַ in Hebrew, which means "The Lord is Salvation." Also the high priest

Joshua in the time of Zechariah was evidently a symbol of Jesus, thus telling before hand the Savior's name, for as it says,

> 'Now listen, Joshua the high priest, you and your friends who are sitting in front of you — indeed **they are men who are a symbol**, for behold, I am going to bring in My servant the Branch.'
> Zech 3:8 NASB *(emphasis added)*

There is an old joke, many would say a bad one, about "What is a cross between an owl and a billy goat?" The answer is a hoot-nanny. But really, what is the son of deer, but a deer? Or what is the son of a lion, but a lion? Jesus is from the seed of woman, but he is also not from man. He is the "Son of God," Lk 1:35. And so as the "son of God," He is therefore "God."

> ^{6} who, being in the form of God, did not consider it robbery to be equal with God, ^{7} but made Himself of no reputation, taking the form of a bondservant, *and* coming in the likeness of men. Phil 2:6-7 NKJV

In these verses and those following in Philippians chapter two, more than one word for the idea of "form" is used. One is the Greek word *morphē* μορφή, which is the word for the inner "form" of something, the inner nature of something, what it is like "inside." From this root comes the word "metamorphosis," which means to change the inner nature of something. Another Greek word for "form" that is used in this passage, is the word *schēma* σχῆμα, which is a word for the outward form of things, the outward appearance or "scheme" of things. In addition there is another word used here, and that is the Greek word for "likeness" or *homoiōma* ὁμοίωμα, which is a word that describes what something looks like.

Phil 2:6 tells us that Jesus was in the form (*morphē* μορφη) of God. That is to say He had the inner nature of God. But Jesus took the "form" of a bondservant/slave, and once again it is the word *morphē* μορφη, the word for having the inner nature of something. So Jesus had the inner nature of God Himself, and took on the inner nature of man also. Jesus was really God, and also really became a man! "And being found in appearance as a man," there is a different word that is used here. He had the appearance, the *homoiōma* ὁμοίωμα of a man. He was both truly God, and truly man, but he looked like, had the likeness, the appearance of, a man, Phil 2:6.

This Christ will unify both heaven and earth at the last day. Jesus created all things, whether in heaven or on earth, and whether visible or invisible, Col 1:16. It was God's good pleasure for all the fullness of God to dwell in Jesus, and through this One who is both fully God, and became also fully man; to reconcile "all things to Himself." KJV Is it just men that Jesus is to reconcile to Himself? No! In fact Jesus is to reconcile everything to Himself, "whether *they be* things in earth or things in heaven." Has there been sin even in heaven? How is this God/man to reconcile all things to Himself? It is "through the blood of

His cross," Col 1:19-23. So whether we are creatures in heaven, or creatures on earth; whether we are visible or invisible; we will all be reconciled to God by Jesus' blood, *if we are to be reconciled!*

As Jesus approaches thirty years of age, John the Baptist comes preaching, Mtt 3:1- 2. John the Baptist, the voice in the wilderness of Isaiah 40, had truly come in the wilderness, the outlying, unpopulated, parts of Judea. Luke dates this in Luke 3 as being the fifteenth year of Tiberius Caesar, when Pontus Pilate was governor of Judea; all of which means that this is about AD 25-26.

The way had to be prepared for the Lord, both to satisfy the objectives of His ministry, and to fulfill the requirements of prophecy. John had to build up every place that might be too low and to remove every obstacle out of the way of Israel, so that they might receive the good news of the Messiah, Isa 57:14. This would mean that when Jesus came all would be ready, and everything that could be done, had been done, so they might believe. But in the end, who would receive Him? With whom might the Lord dwell? He tells us that,

"... I dwell in the high and holy *place*,
With him *who* has a contrite and humble spirit,
To revive the spirit of the humble,
And to revive the heart of the contrite ones," Isa 57:15 NKJV

Matthew tells us that this John was the voice in the wilderness in Isa 40:3, thus John would be the one to say "Here is your God" as in Isa 40:9, to fulfill this preparation. There is a very interesting passage, reflecting the interpretation of prophecy, when the Pharisees approach John the Baptist in John chapter one. They asked him, "Who are you?" John immediately told them, "I am not the Christ." Then they asked, "Then who are you? Are you Elijah?"

At this point one can get into a couple of involved questions dealing with some Old Testament prophecy. You see, quite a mystique had arisen around the Old Testament prophet Elijah. He had been the persistent foe of the un-faithful King Ahab of Israel and his pagan wife Jezebel, from Sidon (starting in 1 Kings 16 and going through 2 Kings 2). Elijah had preached the word faith-fully and had opposed wickedness even in high places, as if not even counting the risk to himself. To turn his nation around and to get his people to repent of their sins, Elijah had even asked God that it might not rain on the land of Israel. His prayers were answered and he was even able to tell Ahab that there would not be any dew or rain for years, *except at his word.* James gives him as an exam-ple of a man *just like us*, who was able to do powerful things through believing prayer (see James 5).

He had to flee his own country for a while and seek safety in pagan Sidon. But he was able to raise the dead, make food last almost endlessly, face all the false prophets on Mount Carmel, put them first to shame, and then to death. In the end, the Lord had Ahab put to death, but Elijah was basically still on the run from persecution.

But the final glorification of Elijah by his Lord was the way in which he left this earth. First he passed on his ministry and prophetic office to Elisha. Then while walking along with Elisha, a chariot of fire and horses of fire separated them, and Elijah was swept up to heaven in a whirlwind, 2 Kings 2. So Elijah is one of only two known men who did not leave this world by death. The other was Enoch. Scripture says that after Enoch had his son Methuselah, Enoch walked with God for 300 years, and "he was not, for God took him," Gen 5:22.

This fiery exit of Elijah from this life left many questions unanswered. A group of the sons of the prophets searched for his body after his leaving, without success. Then several hundred years later the prophet Malachi spoke of the

Elijah being taken to heaven in a firey chariot 2 Kings 2.

Messiah and of Elijah.

> Behold, I will send my messenger, and he shall prepare the way before me: and the Lord, whom ye seek, shall suddenly come to his temple, even the messenger of the covenant, whom ye delight in: behold, he shall come, saith the LORD of hosts. Mal 3:1 KJV

So Malachi seems to speak of two messengers. One is the messenger of the covenant who is going to come to "his temple." And the other is "my messenger" who will clear the way before Me, and that was discussed in two passages from Isaiah of the special preparations to clear the way for the Messiah. Then Malachi speaks of these things again, and he says,

⁵ Behold, I will send you Elijah the prophet before the coming of the great and dreadful day of the LORD: ⁶ And he shall turn the heart of the fathers to the children, and the heart of the children to their fathers, lest I come and smite the earth with a curse. Mal 4:5-6 KJV

The language is not vague, nor is it necessary (on the face of it) to take the passage as symbolic. The Lord says He will send Elijah. The language itself does not say "like Elijah," rather it says "I am going to send you Elijah." In addition, since Elijah did not die like ordinary men, many could not help but wonder if he would come back as he left, to complete his mission. One may be reminded here of the two prophets in Revelation 11.

³ "And I will give *power* unto my two witnesses, and they shall prophesy a thousand two hundred *and* threescore days, clothed in sackcloth ⁴ These are the two olive trees, and the two candlesticks standing before the God of the earth. ⁵ And if any man will hurt them, fire proceedeth out of their mouth, and devoureth their enemies: and if any man will hurt them, he must in this manner be killed. ⁶ These have power to shut heaven, that it rain not in the days of their prophecy: and have power over waters to turn them to blood, and to smite the earth with all plagues, as often as they will."
Rev 11:3-6 KJV

Say what you like, these two prophets in Revelation 11 sound very Elijah-like, with a little bit of Moses kicked in. They call down fire from heaven to devour their foes. They are able to shut the sky so that it does not rain. They do all of this for twelve hundred and sixty days, or forty-two months, the same amount of time that Elijah cut off rain from Israel, 1 Kgs 18:1, Jas 5:17. Also this is the length of the time the beast of Revelation reigns! It is almost as if it is Elijah and Elisha finishing their mission, and witnessing to Jerusalem in that final day. All of this is indeed, "before the great and dreadful day of the LORD ," Mal 4:5, if you are talking about the final day of the Lord, the second coming. The "beast" then makes war on them and kills them, before one final time they rise to heaven in front of their foes! But although there is "likeness," "similarity," there are no names given there, nothing but similarities. Remember this text later when the discussion of type and anti-type comes up.

But listen to what the angel tells John the Baptist's father, Zacharias, when announcing the birth of John in Luke 1. The baby is announced as one who would be a *de facto* Nazirite, or at least that is what it sounds like when it speaks of no wine or strong drink. He is to be filled with the Holy Spirit of God from the womb, and he will turn the sons of Israel back to their God, much like "he shall turn the heart of the fathers to the children, and the heart of the children to their fathers," in Mal 4:6 KJV. But notice the additional words of the angel Gabriel,

"It is he who will go as a *forerunner* before Him **in the spirit and power of Elijah,** TO TURN THE HEARTS OF THE FATHERS BACK TO THE CHILDREN, and the disobedient to the attitude of the righteous, so as to make ready a people prepared for the Lord."
Lk 1:17 NASB *(bold emphasis added)*

The angel quotes Mal 4:6 and says John the Baptist is the man. He is the fulfillment of the prophecy of Malachi. Then listen to what Jesus says at the death of John the Baptist in prison. He says that John was the messenger sent ahead of Him, and He quotes Mal 3:1 about the two messengers previously discussed. Then our Lord goes on to say that, if you will accept it, John himself is Elijah who was to come, Mtt 11:9-15. In other words, the announcement "I am going to send you Elijah," meant sending someone in the spirit and power of Elijah. Elijah was a type of John the Baptist, a model, a prototype. There you have laid before you the evidence. It is evidence to be understood if you want to understand, or to trip over, if you want to stumble. The angel prophesied that the boy would called a prophet of God and that he would go before the LORD to prepare His ways, to give the people knowledge of salvation, Lk 1:76-79.

The Pharisees had asked John if he was the Christ, and he had said plainly, "I am not the Christ," Jn 1:20. But the Lord had said, "I am going to send you Elijah the prophet," so the Pharisees had then asked, "What then? Are you Elijah?" Are you literally Elijah? And John answered no, I am not literally Elijah. And then they asked, are you **the** prophet, **the** special prophet of Deut 18:15? That prophecy will be covered in detail later, but the Pharisee do not seem to realize that "the Prophet" *is the Christ*, and they have *already* asked John if he was the Christ, and he had said no, so now once again John says no. Then they said, Well then tell us who you are so that we can give an answer to the people who sent us? Jn 1:22.

How does John answer them? As a prophet, his answer was from the Holy Spirit of God. One should not be surprised if the answer was just like the normal answers one often gets from prophecy. It tells us the truth but leaves us room to avoid the truth, *if that is what we want to do.* Does he answer their question directly? He leaves them in their muddle but tells them the truth. He tells them in Jn 1:23 that he is the voice of the one crying in the wilderness in Isaiah 40, "Make straight the way of the Lord."

The Pharisee's next question is staggering because they ask, "Why then are you baptizing, if you are not the Christ, nor Elijah, nor the Prophet?" Jn 1:25 NASB. The Pharisees though muddled and confused, misunderstanding a lot, distracted by their desires and ambitions and greed; never the less understand that the Christ, and "the Elijah to come," and "the Prophet" are **all** to come baptizing. *Take note that the Pharisees were able to understand from prophecy that Elijah, and the Christ, and the Prophet **all** were to come baptizing, and if we are not able to see this from prophecy,* **then we are not even as good of students of prophecy as the**

Pharisees! It is nothing short of incredible what they did and did not understand.

There are only a few references to washing with water in the Old Testament, but there are some references. In Ezek 36:25 God says that He will sprinkle you with clean water and you will be clean. Isaiah commands the Jews, "Wash you, make you clean; put away the evil of your doings from before mine eyes; cease to do evil; Learn to do well ..." Isa 1:16-17 KJV. Is that perhaps a reference to baptism? In Isaiah 4 the prophet speaks of a future day called "that day," when the Lord will have washed away the filth and bloodshed from Jerusalem, Isa 4:4. Could that be a look ahead at baptism? Also the Lord says that He will pour out waters on a thirsty land in Isa 44:3-5. Lastly note that submerging in water was associated with cleansing in Elijah and Elisha's time, and that is how Naaman was told to be cleansed in 2 Kings 5. No, this is not talking about "water salvation" as some say; but salvation is associated with water, in both the Old Testament and the New Testament. Jesus says that unless we are born of **water** and the Spirit, we **cannot** enter the Kingdom of God, Jn 3:5. The apostle John says that John the Baptist came as a witness.

> [6] There was a man sent from God, whose name *was* John. [7] The same came for a witness, to bear witness of the Light, that all *men* through him might believe. [8] He was not that Light, but *was sent* to bear witness of that Light. Jn 1:6-8 KJV

John's baptism was from God, and it was only replaced by baptism into Christ. In Acts 19:1-5, Paul runs into some disciples who have only been baptized into John's by then obsolete baptism, and who are then baptized into Jesus Christ. So someone can have a baptism of repentance, even sincere repentance, and it not be good enough to be a saved believer in Jesus Christ. You can have a baptism, even a Scriptural baptism, that is not good enough to really be a Christian; that is, not good enough for salvation. You must be baptized into Jesus Christ for the forgiveness of your sins, Acts 2:38.

At one point in Matthew 3 John saw many of the Sadducees and Pharisees coming to be baptized along with the rest of the people, and he told them, You bunch of snakes, who warned you to run from the wrath to come? John told them to bear the type of fruit they should bear if they are really repentant. He went on to tell them not to assume that just because they were descendants of Abraham that they would be all right, because the LORD could make descendants of Abraham out of the rocks on the road!

There is an old gospel song called "The World's Bible." This song says that "Christ has no hands but our hands To do His work today, He has no feet but our feet To lead men in His way; He has no tongue but our tongues To tell men how He died, He has no help but our help To bring them to His side." The sentiments seem well intended. They are trying to say that God wants us to do our job in spreading His gospel. But the sentiments express a rationalistic point of view, that *God **only*** works through men, and that indeed God is helpless without us! The prophet John the Baptist *says that these sentiments are wrong.* God can work His will without us.

God does not depend on us. God does not depend on our strength, and God says that in fact that His power is made perfect in weakness, 2 Cor 12:9. God does not depend on our wisdom. Instead God has chosen the foolish things of the world to shame the wise, and the weak things to shame the strong, and the despised things to bring to nothing the "things" which think they are something, 1 Cor 1:27-29. The key word is "chosen," for God actively chooses and acts in history. No, God doesn't "need" us, doesn't "depend" on us to carry out His desires, no matter what some beloved song says. Instead it is God who gives us success, not *us* giving Him success.

The axe is already being laid at the root. John the Baptist pictures the Pharisees of his time as a weak and sickly tree that is not bearing fruit but is just taking up the ground of God's garden of men, Mtt 3:10-12. So the farmer has placed his axe at the root of the tree and he is ready to start chopping to bring it down and carry it off for burning to make room for those who bear fruit for the kingdom. The Lord will separate the good from the bad, put the good seed in his barns, and will burn the trash and all that is not worth keeping.

So this is what is seen from the first. **With the prospect of both a singular seed of God and also of a (singular) demonic seed, a Satanic seed.**

We Stand

How does God operate?

How does He talk,
and what might He say?

So we learn a prophetic syntax,
another class, another genre,
of literature.

We Measure the Words

One of the most curious of questions that often come to men is of the ways in which God instructs men or of the ways in which men may "allow" the Lord to speak to us. In a way it is a bizarre, even ridiculous, the idea that the creature, might decided how the LORD of Glory may or may not act, may or may not speak, what manners or modes of speech He may use, and what manner of language he can or cannot use. However, that is how some men talk! Scripture is not a science textbook, but some expect it to be so, and expect it to use the terminology only recently invented. (For instance, the word "dinosaur.") Science, true science, is a bottle weighed and measured. It is about "facts," never really coming close to "truth," for there are far too many "facts" yet to find. The Bible is a book of truth and life, and it is really the truth that determines how we look at the facts. Still some would want God to conform to the understanding of the facts *that we have* **today**, and then to change it again to what we may "learn" tomorrow. Incredible!

This sort of foolishness has all sorts of ridiculous results. Men who readily accept hyperbole or highly symbolic imagery in secular literature, may want to say that God can not talk that way, would never communicate with us that way. Men who would readily accept insight or foresight in secular writers, maintain that no insight or foresight can be allowed in our understanding of any prophet of God, that we must a priori rule out foresight in Scripture.

Now the LORD God spoke to men many ways in the past, Heb 1:1. God used dreams at times, as with Joseph in Genesis 37, but it was all true. God was revealing to men what He was going to do in such a way that when it happened, it would be plain that He was doing it. Sometimes God even gave these dreams to pagans, like King Abimelech in Gen 20:3-6. In the book of Job it talks of God sending dreams to ordinary men in order to, if you will pardon the expression, "scare the hell out of them." That is not just a figure of speech; but it is literally to scare them out of their sins.

> 14 "Indeed God speaks once,
> Or twice, yet no one notices it.
> 15 In a dream, a vision of the night,
> When sound sleep falls on men,
> While they slumber in their beds,
> 16 Then He opens the ears of men,
> And seals their instruction,
> 17 That He may turn man aside from his conduct,
> And keep man from pride;
> 18 He keeps back his soul from the pit,
> And his life from passing over into Sheol." Job 33:14-18 NASB

So the Lord says He often acts even toward sinful men to turn them back from their iniquity. If you say, "Don't you know that the age of miracles is past?" I would then say, who is talking about "miracles"? Rather this is about men having dreams that scare them out of their wits! If you protest that God would never do anything to scare someone, then I would say, Oh? Where do you get that, in either the Old Testament or the New Testament? Are you not ignoring a great bulk of Scripture in both the Old Testament and the New Testament? You sure wouldn't get that from Rom 1:18 where it says that, "the wrath of God **is** revealed **from heaven** against all ungodliness and unrighteousness of men who suppress the truth in unrighteousness" (*emphasis added*). The words "is revealed" is the Greek form *apokaluptetai* 'αποκαλύπτεται, present middle indicative, meaning literally that "it is being revealed" *presently* and *continuously*. And the rest of Romans chapter 1 is about God **acting** against sin, both in revealing to men His divine nature and in **acting** against the sins of men, to bring punishment for sins! You wouldn't get anything different from Revelations chapters 7 through 9 which pictures God as sending a series of disasters on the earth which are intended to turn men to repentance from their sins, Rev 9:20-21.

If you then protest that God has not guaranteed to transmit truth to us through dreams, and there is no assurance that any specific dream is from God; I would immediately agree that is true. There is no Scripture that says or even insinuates this. But that does not mean that God might not use it at times for His purposes, much as Job tells us (I am being facetious). I would argue that God has not specifically agreed that He *will* send a man to *you* to turn you from your sins, but God does send men with such a purpose and has instructed His followers to approach you in Mk 16:15-16, and many other passages.

In the past God sometimes gave the dream to one person, and the interpretation to another person. This was true of Pharaoh's dreams in Genesis, which Joseph interpreted; and Nebuchadnezzar's dreams in the book of Daniel, which Daniel interpreted. God also used visions at times and had angels explain them as in Dan 8:15-23. For all that, a vision is not necessarily the same as a dream. When God spoke to the apostle John in Revelation 1, John seems to be awake, and he says only that he was in the Spirit on the Lord's day in Rev 1:9-11. Then God presented many "visions" to Him, as in Rev 9:17.

God has often used comparisons, parables, and allegories to teach men. Some of the most extreme are in the prophets, and it was noted earlier of some of the names of Isaiah's children. It seems that when God's people become the most sinful, and their hearts the hardest, the imagery becomes the most intense, the examples the most graphic, and the models for instruction often the crudest; perhaps because that is what is necessary to communicate with those who have gone so far into sin and have suffered the worse for their wrongs but who still will not change. There is no more astonishing example of these things than the prophet Ezekiel, although such things are not restricted to Ezekiel. Ezekiel starts his ministry in Ezekiel chapter 4, where he is told to get a brick and etch into its surface a map of the city of Jerusalem and lay siege to the city. He makes a ramp up to it walls and places model battering rams against the walls. He is told to lie first on one side of his body and then the other, with a sheet of iron between his face and the city—390 days for Israel on his left side and 40 days on his right side for Judah. This was for the sins of his people while he lays siege to the model city. For this siege Ezekiel is told to make himself bread of various grains and beans and lentils, and to eat the bread by weight, as if rationed, and his water by measure, as in a siege. It would seem that Ezekiel is acting all of this out in his house; or perhaps just outside of his house, so that all of his neighbors and the captives in Babylon will hear of what he is doing and know from the Lord that Jerusalem will fall and will be completely destroyed.

God went even further in His instructions in Ezek 4:12 and tells Ezekiel to bake his special bread over human dung. Ezekiel protests this and says he has never eaten anything unclean, so as an exception to the first instructions, the Lord allows him to bake his bread over cow dung instead. At least he would be allowed to bake his bread over the dung of a clean animal: a cow. And God then tells Ezekiel explicitly the purpose of his pantomime.

> Moreover he said unto me, Son of man, behold, I will break the staff of bread in Jerusalem: and they shall eat bread by weight, and with care; and they shall drink water by measure, and with astonishment:
> Ezek 4:16 KJV

Then Ezekiel is told in chapter 5 that he is to shave his head with a barbers razor, and then take some scales and weigh the hair that he gets. A third of the hair he is to burn in a fire on the brick diagram of the city Jerusalem. Then he is to take a third of the hair and scatter it around the brick diagram of the city and strike it with a sword all around the city. Then a third of hair he is throw up into the wind, and let it blow away; but to chase it with a sword, where ever it blows. This is perhaps an indication that Ezekiel is performing this ritual outside of his house. Indeed, has not Israel been chased by the sword for their sins even to this day? But more about these things will come later. Lastly Ezekiel is to take a few of the hairs of his head which are still at hand, which have not blown away while being chased by the sword, or burned in the city ... a few, a remnant; and put them in the edges of where his robe tied around his body. Then he takes some of these out of his robes, and throws them into the fire.

God adjusts His imagery to fit the morals and values and the situation of the people. Ezekiel was among the first of the people of Judah to go into captivity, while Jerusalem had yet to be destroyed for her rebellion against the Lord their God, and the king of Babylon. Ezekiel was among the people taken to Babylon as "security" for the good behavior of the people left in their place. Even so, Ezekiel lets the people know that the city will not last, and they will never be able to return home in their time. The people of Judah have refused to be faithful to their God. They have worshipped all of the gods of the pagans, especially the "nature" gods of Baal, and his companion Asherah (mother nature?), who is called "the queen of heaven" in Jer 44:15-19. As part of their worship of "nature" they have committed sexual immorality with the priests and priestess of the "nature gods" and offered the products of their fornication in fiery sacrifices.

> [37] They even sacrificed their sons And their daughters to the demons,
> [38] And shed innocent blood,
> The blood of their sons and daughters,
> Whom they sacrificed to the idols of Canaan;
> And the land was polluted with blood.
> [39] Thus they were defiled by their own works,
> > And played the harlot by their own deeds. Psa 106:37-39 NKJV

Paul says of the spiritual creatures they served, and which we have served,

> However at that time, when you did not know God, you were slaves to those which by nature are no gods. Gal 4:8 NASB

Jeremiah also warns about these so-called "gods" who will perish.

> Thus you shall say to them: "The gods that have not made the heavens and the earth shall perish from the earth and from under these heavens." Jer 10:11 NKJV

The ancient attitudes toward life and death were much different from ours. An example is seen in a well-known letter from Roman times found in Egypt. It is the letter from an Egyptian laborer named Hilarion to his wife Alis (both are Greek names, and the letter is written in Greek). It was written in Alexandria, Egypt, June 17, 1 BC, where Hilarion was laboring at a job away from home.

> Hilarion to Alis his sister, many greetings.
> Also to Berus my lady and Apollonarin.
> Know that we are still even now in Alexandrea. Be not distressed if at the general coming in I remain at Alexandrea. I ask and beg of you, take care of the little child. And as soon as we receive wages I will send to you. If you have delivered, if it was a boy, let it (live); if it was a girl, throw it out.
> You said to Aphrodisias, "Don't forget me." How can I forget you? I ask you to not be in agony.
> In the year 29 of the Caesar, Pauni 23 (from Deismann, *Light From the Ancient East*, 1927, George H. Doran Co., NY, pg 168)

He plainly intends to say he cares for his wife and cannot forget her, and he will send some money when he gets some. But the child? It is not a big thing if the child is left out somewhere to die, or to be taken up by others if they want a girl. Such were common ancient values, and such values as these and even worse were among the Israelites of Ezekiel's time.

God spares no effort to deliver those destined to burn forever with the

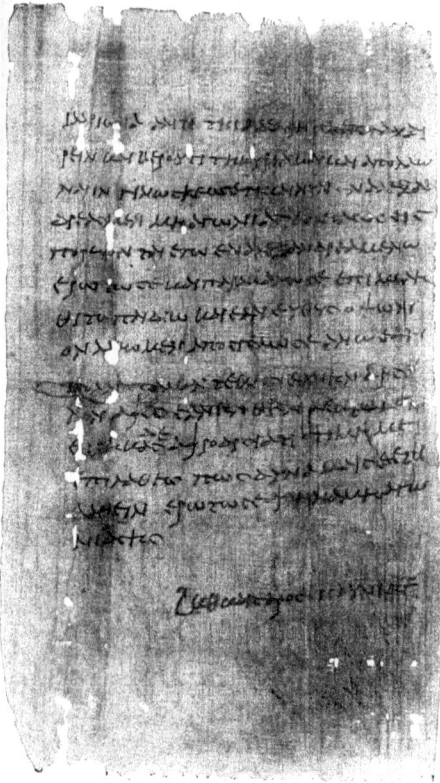

Hilarion's letter to his wife Alis.

trash of the universe, to communicate with them, to turn them from their great wickedness, that they might be fit for redemption; that they might live forever and not remain under permanent punishment for their sins. As striking an example as you will find in the Word of God is in Ezekiel chapter 16. God says that He is dealing with an Israel, which is really of gentile parentage! Wow! What a start for a sermon to some Jews! He tells them, "your father was an Amorite and your mother a Hittite," Ezek 16:3 NASB. In other words, He says the Jews are of the same parentage as the present Palestinians! The Lord says to Israel, they were a cast off baby girl, left to die in an open field.

4 "As for your birth, on the day you were born your navel cord was not cut, nor were you washed with water for cleansing; you were not rubbed with salt or even wrapped in cloths. 5 No eye looked with pity on you to do any of these things for you, to have compassion on you. Rather you were thrown out into the open field, for you were abhorred on the day you were born." Ezek 16:4-5 NASB

All of which is just like what Hilarion would have his wife to do with any baby girl that they might have. I know that there was much hardening of hearts in those days even as in our day. Still I'm sure many women felt much anguish at these things, surely worse than a woman losing a baby in our own times. And I'm sure that some of those fathers, though feeling it was an economic necessity, will remember on the day of judgment the beautiful and innocent child crying for help and will recall with anguish their sin. Even though we become hardened, we still often really know our sins.

Then a man came by looking for a girl. The Lord came by and saw this naked little baby girl, squirming and crying in her blood, with no one to care.

> "And when I passed by you and saw you struggling in your own blood, I said to you in your blood, "Live!' Yes, I said to you in your blood, 'Live!'" Ezek 16:6 NKJV

So the little girl was raised in the man's house. She is a slave, she is a servant, she is whatever the Master of the house desires. Finally the time came when her breasts grew and new hair grew, but she was naked before the One who took her in, Ezek 16:7. Then one day the One who took her in as a baby, He passed by her, and saw it was the time of love for her, and He spread His skirt over her, which seems to be an expression they used for marriage, and made a covenant with her, which definitely speaks of marriage. So the One who saw this abandoned and naked baby girl, and took her in, and at the proper time loves her and marries her, and provides all the very best for her, is the LORD of Hosts. This abandoned baby girl, squirming and crying in her blood, then becomes like a royal princess, beautiful and adored by all.

> 9 "Then I washed you in water; yes, I thoroughly washed off your blood, and I anointed you with oil. 10 I clothed you in embroidered cloth and gave you sandals of badger skin; I clothed you with fine linen and covered you with silk. ... 13 Thus you were adorned with gold and silver, and your clothing was of fine linen, silk, and embroidered cloth. You ate pastry of fine flour, honey, and oil. You were exceedingly beautiful, and succeeded to royalty." Ezek 16:9-10, 13 NKJV

The imagery is so vivid and plain and bare, that we are stunned at the picture which it paints. For we, the people of God, are the naked baby girl, flailing and floundering in the blood of our birth, abandoned and without hope in a world that would destroy us and think nothing of it. A picture of such love and grace in a world without love or grace, is without parallel. But then the beautiful little girl, who is now adored by all, comes to trust in her beauty and plays the role of a harlot, and the second half of this story is as stunning as the first part. This little girl is God's people. In context she is Judah, and her sisters are Sodom and Samaria (the ancient Sodom, and the Northern ten tribes of Israel), Ezek 16:55. In Ezekiel 16 it is pointed out that both Sodom and Samaria have been destroyed for their sins, but Judah has not learned from their fate.

> 32 "*You are* an adulterous wife, *who* takes strangers instead of her husband. 33 Men make payment to all harlots, but you made your payments to all your lovers, and hired them to come to you from all around for your harlotry." Ezek 16:32-33 NKJV

What would happen to a young girl in those times, who had been so graciously delivered from death to be the wife of the Master of the house, and who then acted so disgustingly? Ezekiel 16 also describes that, plainly and in detail. The imagery is vivid, stunning, suitable to the audiences He intends to enlighten, with no holds barred in language or treatment, if such stands a chance of securing repentance. Then as now, some will listen, and some never will.

One time God used the mouth of an ass, Num 22:26-31. Some with a laugh say that God has used the mouth of an ass more than once to communicate with sinful men. On another occasion God spoke to Elijah in a still small voice, 1 Kgs 19:11-13. In Daniel 5 the Lord communicated His decisions by having a hand appear that wrote on the wall during a drunken feast, Dan 5:1, 4-6. At this they called for Daniel to interpret the words, Dan 5:25-30. The Greek historian Herodotus tells the story of how the city of Babylon fell that night, by hidden entry to the city when they were all in the middle of drunken celebration. On the other hand, God spoke to Moses face to face, Num 12:6-9. So God has spoken a lot of different ways in the past.

It finally came about that in our time God has spoken through Jesus, Heb 1:2. God has appointed Him to inherit all things, Heb 1:2, even the very ends of the earth according to Psa 2:8. Now Jesus, as always, has used many means to speak to us. He told His apostles He had some things to tell them *after* His death, by the Holy Spirit, Jn 16:12-13.

This Jesus is the One who speaks to us in our day and has often used men to transmit His commands to us. He has told His servants to preach the gospel to every creature, teaching them to observe ***everything*** which He has command-ed, Mtt 28:19-20. According to prophecy, Jesus is supposed to "Rule in the midst of" His enemies, Psa 110:1-2; and Jesus is of course doing this in our pre-sent time. He will rule until he puts down all His enemies, 1 Cor 15:25-26, and then Jesus will hand over the kingdom to His Father.

If you and I want to be saved, we have to listen to Jesus. There is salvation no where else, Acts 4:12, for "there is none other name under heaven given among men, whereby we must be saved." KJV

So in the very basics of the issues, it is absurd to assume that the Lord God of Heaven and Earth must always be simpler that the simplest of men, not as sophisticated as the most learned of men, never employing the subtlest forms of language and instruction.

How long, ye simple ones, will ye love simplicity? Prov 1:22 KJV.

At this point comes a key issue for many: What use is prophecy to us? Bear with us as we walk through some of these issues. And there is also the problem of Rationalism! Man often wants to accept as real only what his mind can un-derstand and clearly explain. Yet in many of the simplest and most necessary things of life we often have no real explanations.

Philosopher Francis Bacon was one of the first to clearly say that for us to use sound reason we must be ruling out God; that is, if we cannot experimen-tally determine it, then it "isn't so." Now this may help us to concentrate on what we may sometimes call "natural causes," but is it really "natural" to rule out God? In John 1 when it speaks of Jesus as both creator and God, it says

> [3] All things were made by him; and without him was not any thing made that was made. [4] In Him was life, and the life was the light of men," Jn 1:3-4 KJV

So Jesus is the source of *everything*, literally *everything*! Leave Jesus out of the start of anything? Impossible. But also Jesus as God, as Creator, is more than just a maker who forgets. He is indeed "the image of the invisible God." In

Him indeed "were all things created, that are in heaven, and that are in earth, visible and invisible," Col 1:15-16 KJV. Beyond all of that, "in Him all things hold together," Col 1:17 NASB. So in answer to the question "What makes the world go around?", the answer is Jesus from the beginning to now and to the end. It says that in Jesus "all things hold together." The Greek word used in Col 1:17 is *sunistāmi* συνίστημι, which means literally "together-to-stand," to establish something, to make it stand. Jesus is the glue that transcends of all our experiments. God is always involved, you might say "naturally."

This can be seen in both the Old Testament and the New Testament. Take for instance Psalm 104. It starts off speaking of the majesty of God and His creative powers. Then it starts talking about God working in His creation, and tending to it; and here is where it speaks of God using His angels to accomplish His works, and says that "He makes the winds His messengers, Flaming fire His ministers," Psa 104:4 NASB. There is more than a little double meaning here. In both Hebrew and Greek the word for "wind" and the word for spirit are the same. The Hebrew word is *ruach* רוּחַ. The Greek word is *pneuma* πνεῦμα (from which we also get the word "pneumatic"). Remember this! Also in both Hebrew and Greek the word for messenger and angel are the same. (The Hebrew word is *malak* מַלְאָךְ and the Greek word is *angelos* ἄγγελος.) You might ask, looking at the context in Psalm 104 whether it means winds or spirits, and whether it means "messengers" or angels; and in context the answer would be an emphatic yes! It is talking about things we would call "natural" and it also includes what we would call "spirit." The King James Version translates the verse, "Who maketh his angels spirits; his ministers a flaming fire," and that is emphatically correct, and that is the way the verse is taken in Heb 1:7, where it says in the KJV "Who maketh his angels spirits, and his ministers a flame of fire." Then in Psalm 104 the author moves *immediately* to God working in the "natural environment" to provide good "natural" things for His creatures, as He may desire.

> 10 He sends the springs into the valleys;
>   They flow among the hills.
> 11 They give drink to every beast of the field;
>   The wild donkeys quench their thirst.
> 12 By them the birds of the heavens have their home;
>   They sing among the branches.
> 13 He waters the hills from His upper chambers;
>   The earth is satisfied with the fruit of Your works
> 14 He causes the grass to grow for the cattle,
>   And vegetation for the service of man,
>   That he may bring forth food from the earth,
> 15 And wine *that* makes glad the heart of man,
>   Oil to make *his* face shine,

And bread which strengthens man's heart. Psa 104:10-15 NKJV

But none of this is a process which is outside of God's majesty and control. It is not just a mechanical toy, which will "work" with out its maker. God is the glue, which keeps the substance of His creation "working." He decides and it happens, or He decides "No," and it doesn't, according to His will and wisdom.

> [27] They all wait for You
>> That You may give *them* their food in due season.
> [28] *What* You give them they gather in;
>> You open Your hand, they are filled with good.
> [29] You hide Your face, they are troubled;
>> You take away their breath, they die and return to their dust.
> [30] You send forth Your Spirit, they are created;
>> And You renew the face of the earth. Psa 104:27-30 NKJV

You O man, whoever you are, will meet this One and Only God, and will bend you knee in worship to Him, Rom 14:11; because it is appointed to man to die once, and after that comes judgment, Heb 9:27. He is a God who deals with His creation "naturally," and can do *whatever* He wants to do. Nor is it only about what men would call "natural" events. The range of verses and topics covered as being under God's care and guidance is both wide and varied.

> The plans of the heart belong to man,
> But the answer of the tongue is from the LORD. Prov. 16:1 NASB

> The LORD has made everything for its own purpose,
> Even the wicked for the day of evil. Prov 16:4 NASB

> The mind of man plans his way,
> But the LORD directs his steps. Prov 16:9 NASB

> The lot is cast into the lap,
> But its every decision is from the LORD. Prov 16:33 NASB

And last, but in human terms by no means least,

> The horse is prepared for the day of battle,
> But victory belongs to the LORD. Prov 21:31 NASB

This is a unified view in Scripture. So Jesus says,

> [29] "Are not two sparrows sold for a copper coin? And not one of them falls to the ground apart from your Father's will. [30] But the very hairs of your head are all numbered. [31] Do not fear therefore; you are of more value than many sparrows." Mtt 10:29-31 NKJV

It is not that things are really unnatural. Rather it is natural that the bird which you saw this afternoon *cannot* die or be killed, apart from the Lord's will. It was discussed from Proverbs earlier that the Lord also works in and by man's will, even in the most sinful of men, from the beginning and *all the way to the end.* So it will be, toward the end of time, that the Lord is angry with "the great city, which <u>rules over</u> the <u>kings</u> of the earth." (*emphasis added*). And ten kings come to power and give their "power and authority to the beast." Then "These will wage war against the Lamb ..." Rev 17:18, 12-14 NASB. But also God uses these kings to destroy "the harlot," "the great city."

> **"For God has put it into their hearts** to fulfill His purpose, to be of one mind, and to give their kingdom to the beast, until the words of God are fulfilled." Rev 17:17 NKJV (*bold emphasis added*)

It does not mean of course that a microscope or oscilloscope or imaging radar can prove God's presence, or verify His working, or weigh His working, although they will often be able to "see" the results.

> "Indeed God speaks once,
> Or twice, yet no one notices it," Job 33:14 NASB

Men often sense it but cannot place it on scales or run it through a volt meter.

> [11] Lo, he goeth by me, and I see him not: he passeth on also, but I perceive him not. [12] Behold, he taketh away, who can hinder him? who will say unto him, What doest thou? Job 9:11-12 KJV

Can we detect and prevent Him? He has stealth and ability to prevent which we cannot imagine.

> "All the inhabitants of the earth are accounted as nothing,
> But He does according to His will in the host of heaven
> And *among* the inhabitants of earth;
> And no one can ward off His hand
> Or say to Him, 'What have You done?' " Dan 4:35 NASB

See how this reverses all of our primitive concepts of when God works, and when He doesn't. So let's talk about "miracles." There are two regular New Testament words that are often translated miracle. One is the word *dunamis* δύναμις, and the word dynamite comes from this Greek word. It literally means power or strength or might or force. Jesus did perform a lot of powerful works, which indicated He was God, and often times these powerful works (*dunamis*) are translated miracle in our English Bibles. In Acts 2:22 it speaks of Jesus as a man who was proven by God with many miracles. Jesus said in Mark 9:39 there is no one who does a "miracle" in His name, who will soon be able to talk badly of Him. In both of these cases the word is *dunamis*, and it indicates powerful actions.

Another word that is sometimes translated as miracle is the Greek word sign, *sāmeion* σημεῖον. In the King James Version it is translated as miracle in Jn 2:11 when it is speaking of Jesus turning water into wine. Several translations say miracle in Acts 4:16 when it is talking about a powerful work which the apostles had done, but the Greek word is *sāmeion* or sign.

Let's take the easy one first, "signs." Signs communicate information, but not all signs are what one would call miracles. The sun and the moon are given as signs to tell time, Gen 1:14. When the Israelites were commanded in Ex 12:13 to put blood over the door of their houses for the Passover. It was to be a sign that they belonged to God and that they would not be subject to the plague of the death of the firstborn which would come on the Egyptians. It was just men putting blood over the entrances to their homes. Similarly, circumcision is called a sign in Gen 17:11. It is a physical action, minor surgery, but it acts as a sign that a man belongs to God. I once saw a sign on a church which said, "If you are looking for a sign from the Lord, this may be it!" There are also stop signs, and slow down signs, and street signs. A sign from God may be powerful, but not all signs are miracles, even from God.

Not all "signs," even from God, are "miraculous."

There are many different types of "power" from God. As noted earlier, a normal word for miracle as it is used in most of our English translations is the Greek word *dunamis* δύναμις, and it is a word that means power or ability. It is used for all sorts of power. For instance, it is used for the normal powers of the heavens, like the sun and the moon and the stars moving around, but one day these powers will be shaken, Mtt 24:29. In Rev 1:16 the word *dunamis* is used of the natural power or strength of the sun.

The first letter to the Corinthians speaks of what many would call the natural powers of people because Paul says he will come to find out the real strength or power of some of the Christians, 1 Cor 4:19. It is a word that is also used of men's natural ability to make and give their money as they have been prospered. So it says the Macedonians gave money beyond their ability (*dunamis*, power) to give, in 2 Cor 8:3. It is a word used of men's natural strength, and so Paul says that they were tested beyond their strength (*dunamis*, power) in 2 Cor 1:8. Jesus says some men were given money according to their ability (*dunamis*, power) to make money in Mtt 25:15. It is used of the power (ability) to have babies in Heb 11:11. The Hebrew prophet James, the half brother of Jesus, says of course that every good and perfect gift, *everything good we have or we are*, is from the Father of lights, Jas 1:17!

The views of the reprobates of the pagan Renaissance of past centuries have so distorted our view that we cannot even begin to comprehend the simplicity of the Biblical view on these matters. The emphasis of our humanists has made such a point of asserting the autonomy of man that the views of even Bible believing Christians have been extremely distorted on these issues. The truth of these things often escapes all of us, even when we see it.

The cross is also the power (*dunamis*) of God, 1 Cor 1:18. Obviously it is not speaking of what most would call miracles. It is rather speaking of the preaching of God's Word. Peter says "his divine power (*dunamis*) hath given unto us all things that pertain unto life" through the knowledge of Jesus, 2 Pe 1:3 KJV. It is not talking about "miracles," but just the working of Scripture.

Consider carefully: When a certain power comes from God, the Bible doesn't distinguish whether that power breaks the laws of nature or not. We often do that. Americans do that, the ancient Romans did that, and Catholics do that. **The Bible does *NOT* do that.** *If* it is from God, ***then it is from God***, whether it so called "breaks" the laws of nature or not. Not a bird can fall apart from the Father's will Mtt 10:29, but it is not talking about miracles, rather God's day-to-day management of this earth. We have a hands-on God.

Also power is used of angelic beings. Jesus has been exalted far above every rule and authority and **power** (*dunamis*) and dominion, Eph 1:21. Peter says in 1 Pe 3:22 Jesus has gone into heaven, after angels and authorities and **powers** (*dunamis*) had been subjected to Him. The job of these angels/dominions/powers is to serve the Christians of our present age, Heb 1:14. Paul says "Jesus shall be revealed from heaven with his **mighty** angels, In flaming fire" 2 Thes 1:7-8 KJV, and the word "mighty" there is our old word *dunamis*. In the last days the man of lawlessness will come by Satan's help "with all **power** (*dunamis*) and signs and lying wonders," 2 Thes 2:9 KJV. God will use His power to meet our needs. Don't be anxious about anything Paul says in Phil 4:6-7. "For God has not given us a spirit of timidity, but of power (*dunamis*) and of love and discipline," 2Tim 1:7 NASB. In 2 Cor 12:9 God says that "My grace is sufficient for you, for **power** (*dunams*) is perfected in weakness." NASB Paul says he is not ashamed of the gospel because it is God's power (*dunamis*) for salvation to all who believe. Rom 1:16. Again, "if the Spirit of Him ... dwells in you, He ... will also give life to your mortal bodies." Rom 8:11 NKJV. So the Spirit of God living in the bodies of Christians gives life to our mortal bodies so that it will make them live forever! What more power can you ask for?

Do we have the power of great works? ***Yes!*** Prayer is powerful enough to change the weather according to Jas 5:16-18. Eph 3:20 tells us that God can do things beyond *anything* we can even *think* about, "according to the **power** (*dunamis*) that works in us," NKJV. 1 Pe 1:5 says Christians "are protected by the **power** (*dunamis*) of God through faith for a salvation," NASB. It is not necessarily speaking of breaking *what we know* about the laws of the universe, but it does speak of the Living God working in us. We have the power to overcome the world, 1 Jn 5:4, but again it is speaking of our faith that gives us this power to overcome. Do we have great power? Yes, Eph 3:20, unless we don't believe!

On the other hand, do we have the powers of the apostles? For Paul **God** was performing "extraordinary" **powerful** works it says in Acts 19:11-12. Miracles it calls them in the NASB. Notice that it calls them "extraordinary" in the

NASB and the NIV. It calls them "special" in the KJV, and "unusual" in the NKJV. It is speaking of something that is not normal. **These were *out of the ordinary powers*** which were happening through the apostle Paul in Acts 19:11.

We don't have signs of being the Messiah, do we? Why? Because we are not the Messiah, the Christ. Nor do we have the signs and wonders and the **powers** of an apostle as in 2 Cor 12:12. Why? We are not apostles; we have not seen the resurrected Lord here on earth, 1 Cor 9:1. In Hebrews it describes these powers to confirm the word, as having already passed away. God **was** "testifying **with them**, both by signs and wonders," (*bold emphasis added*) in Heb 2:3-4!

The debate over miracles has a wrong footing. It assumes that *what we understand* about nature *must be broken for it to be the power of God.* **This is not true,** but any way you turn it there is a difference in quality and strength between what the apostles and prophets were able to do, and what we can do. However, we will not, in the effort to deny the false signs of false teachers, teach a form of godliness but deny its **power** (*dunamis*), 2 Tim 3:5. Still, God is able to do beyond anything we can even think or imagine, according to the power (*dunamis*) that works in us, Eph 3:20.

Prophecy is a Lamp in a Dark Place

In dealing with these questions, a bigger issue is often America and the church are often in conflict with faith. Society is rejecting faith, and the church struggles against it. Are we missing something?

Faith means you believe in God. Heb 11:6. You can not be an atheist. But more than this, faith means you believe God. You believe what He says. The example of Abraham is instructive. He believed God (not just *in* God), Genesis 15, Romans 4, Hebrews 11. What did Abraham believe? He believed a *prophecy*, a prophecy that he would have a son, and that God would make him a great nation. Paul emphasizes in Rom 4:19-22 that Abraham did not stagger at the promise. He did not think about the fact that his body was ninety-nine years old and as good as dead, and that his wife was in her late eighties, but he believed with a growing confidence in God's announcements and did not stagger at the promises. He felt that if God had promised any thing, He could fulfill the promise. For this reason God counted Abraham's *belief* as if it were righteousness! He had plenty of reason in human terms to not believe. He was seventy-five when he was first called, and told God would make him a great nation," Gen 12:2. But twenty-four years later, at age ninety-nine, he was still without a son.

Now you might say, it didn't matter what Abraham thought. God would do what He would do, and it didn't matter *as long as Abraham obeyed!* But God thought it mattered whether or not Abraham believed Him. He was pleased that Abraham believed, and He counted it for righteousness, Gen 15:6.

God tells us things, and we should trust Him, believe Him. That is faith! Without faith it is impossible to please Him, Heb 11:6. Noah believed *a prophecy* of how the world would be destroyed and acted and saved his life. Some hear God tell us that the music He desires is "singing and making melody in your heart" Eph 5:19 KJV, and some believe it. But also many more "can't really see it," and don't really believe what He says.

Unbelief says:

- I don't understand that. It can't be so.
- This contradicts what I think I know. It must not be so.
- I haven't heard this before: it must not be so.
- This contradicts what I know of the world. This must not be so. Nicodemus stumbled at the new birth. It seemed to contradict how he thought things work in John 3. So he stumbled in unbelief, but perhaps not to death.
- I like something different. I don't like that. I like this. (And here are the sources of our great sins of worship.)

If you hear the promises, and say in your heart, "it is not so," then you are not the children of Abraham. Unbelief is a curse that destroys people and families and churches and nations. "... if you will not believe, surely you shall not be established." Isa 7:9 KJV.

Why did the Pharisees stumble? They did not believe PROPHECY. They did not believe *the prophets*, as many don't even today. They read, and understood some of it, but did not believe the *nature* of the prophecies of the Messiah. They should have been the mature teachers of Scripture, but instead they transmitted their own unbelief. Now many people, *common people*, believed Jesus was The One, before His death. But the Pharisees didn't believe *the prophecies* and so they **failed in salvation**. *Prophecy and our believing it, and salvation are linked.* Jesus says they did not really believe Moses!

> [46] For had ye believed Moses, ye would have believed me: for he wrote of me. [47] But if ye believe not his writings, how shall ye believe my words? Jn 5:46-47 KJV

They were blind guides. They refused to see. So what was that generation like? Jesus says it was faithless and perverse, Mtt 17:17. My friends, beware of the leaven of the Pharisees.

> [11] How is it that ye do not understand that I spake *it* not to you concerning bread, that ye should beware of the leaven of the Pharisees and of the Sadducees? [12] Then understood they how that he bade *them* not beware of the leaven of bread, but of the doctrine of the Pharisees and of the Sadducees. Mtt 16:11-12 KJV

Beware. Unbelief can become permanent. Most of the ancient Pharisees ended up staying in theirs, so they were broken off, Rom 11:20. Six hundred thousand men died because they did not believe prophecy! When the Lord had led the children of Israel out of Egypt, He first led them to Mount Sinai and formed a covenant with His people, and then He led them close to the land of Canaan—the land promised to their forefathers, the land where Abraham, Isaac and Jacob lived during their time here on earth. Then upon coming close to the land, the Lord commanded Moses to send some spies into the land at the beginning of Numbers 13, a man from each of the tribes.

It was near harvest time when the spies went into Canaan. The land was so productive that when they cut *a single cluster of grapes* from the valley of Eshcol, they had to carry it on a pole between two men. At the end of forty days they returned and gave their report. The land certainly was certainly a land of milk and honey, as the Lord had promised. It was very different from Palestine today which has been ruined by the sins of many nations. They had seen the descendants of the races of giants there, the descendants of Anak; and they said they seemed like grasshoppers to them, and they seemed that to themselves.

So ten of the twelve spies gave what is called "a bad report." They didn't think that Israel could take the land. They felt the Canaanites were too strong for them to conquer. Joshua and Caleb tried to persuade them to trust the Lord in this matter, but people listened to the ten spies who had brought a "negative," unbelieving, report. They had prophecies that they would receive the land. To Abraham it was promised, "To your descendants I will give this land," Gen 12:7. Also God had promised them victory in battle against the Canaanites.

> "For My angel will go before you and bring you in to the land of the Amorites, the Hittites, the Perizzites, the Canaanites, the Hivites and the Jebusites; and I will completely destroy them," Ex 23:23 NASB

The greatness of the conquest they would have had been stated in Ex 23:31.

"And I will set your bounds from the Red Sea to the sea, Philistia, and from the desert to the River. For I will deliver the inhabitants of the land into your hand, and you shall drive them out before you."

The spies returned with abundant evidence of the goodness of the land in that day, but without confidence in God's promises.

All the details have not pointed out, but it is clear

that there was little ambiguity in God's promises of victory. They were told to enter the land. They had a prophecy that they would win, but *they didn't see **how** it would be*, or see **why** *they should be able to do it*, or **where** *they would get the strength*. They didn't understand *the **means*** of their victory, or *feel* that they could win, **and so they perished.** The whole nation became infected by the bad report of the ten spies. They griped at Moses and Aaron and asked why they had been brought out Egypt just to perish by the sword in the desert. They talked of selecting a leader to bring them back to the "security" of slavery in Egypt, Num 14:4. Moses, Aaron, Joshua and Caleb tried to convince them, four men against 600,000; but they wouldn't listen ... even despite the prophecies.

They had plenty of reason to trust God, after their deliverance from Egypt and wonders God performed there. Moses at this point interceded for the people, and said to the Lord that the heathen would think God had killed them because He could not bring them into the land, because He wasn't powerful enough. Moses asked God to pardon the sin of His people. So the Lord answered,

> [20] Then the LORD said: "I have pardoned, according to your word; [21] but truly, ... [22] ... all these men who have seen My glory and the signs which I did in Egypt and in the wilderness, and have put Me to the test now these ten times, and have not heeded My voice, [23] they certainly shall not see the land of which I swore to their fathers, nor shall any of those who rejected Me see it." Num 14:20-23 NKJV

However the Lord said that the faithful spies had a different spirit, and He would spare them. Then the ten spies who had given an unbelieving report died of a plague from the Lord, Num 14:37-38; but Joshua and Caleb remained alive. Slowly the people began to realize what a mistake they had made.

You cannot play games with God and win. You cannot in effect say to His face, "It is not so," and have His support and His blessings in the things of this life. " Do not be deceived, God is not mocked; for whatever a man sows, that he will also reap," Gal 6:7 NKJV. There comes a time in the affairs of men when they have drunk His goodness, seen His glory, heard His Words; when we know these things and still will not follow Him, and the LORD Himself says, "Enough!"

We are warned of these things in Heb 3:12. You see, unbelief is a plague. It is disease that spreads like the flu. It spread *quickly* from *ten spies to 600,000 men ... in a few days.* True belief **always** causes **action**, and unbelief **always** causes **action**. One is action to life, and the other is action to death. Unbelief causes you to concentrate on your life here. This is why liberalism grows in the church. It causes you to focus on your tent in the wilderness because you don't think you will really get a house in Canaan. It causes you to focus on what *might happen* in following, rather than focus on the reward promised for following. Unbelief means you sit rather than march at your Lord's command. They had *decided* to not believe, and God held them to it.

[18] And to whom did He swear that they would not enter His rest, but to

those who did not obey? [19] So we see that they could not enter in because of unbelief. Heb 3:18-19 NKJV

Did they realize this ahead of time? I do not think so. At least they did not remember it when they confronted a challenge. **So the key is believing God or not believing God.** Why was Abraham justified? He believed God, and it was credited to him as righteousness, Rom 4:9. Why did Moses *not* enter the land of Canaan? It is seen the clearest in the NIV. He didn't believe *enough* to treat God as holy according to Num 20:12. If you don't really believe, you won't act. **Belief in *what* is said, gives you the strength and courage to act.** Belief says:

- I don't understand it, but I will do it. I can't figure it all out, but I will follow. Faith says it is close to you, Rom 10:6-8, and grabs hold of things not present.
- Faith says: I will think about your Word, I will search your Word. Those of faith are more noble than those at Thessalonica.
- Faith says: "Speak Lord, your servant is listening," and does whatever is said.

Prophecy is about far more than "theory" about what "may" happen. It is God's ***instructions*** about the things His people will face, ***so that they may be prepared.*** And if you believe, you take these thing seriously. By the promises we become partakers, Peter says.

For by these He has granted to us His precious and magnificent **promises, so that by them** you may become partakers of *the* divine nature, having escaped the corruption that is in the world by lust.
2 Peter 1:4 NASB (*bold emphasis added*)

Now this is not just talking about commands. It is talking about *prophecies*, the **promises**. It is by *the promises* that you become more than a mere man. Without them there is no escape from the human dilemma. So are the promises unimportant? Are they to be despised and ignored? Not hardly. This presents the promises, the prophecies, **as something to act on**, something we should act on, **not** an *optional extra*. The taint of Rationalism which has infected us, and led us to ignore the promises, the prophecy, could hardly have served us worse!

You do well to pay attention to the prophetic Word, Peter says in 2 Peter 1:19. He says this Word has been made more sure in the Christian age, since there is such a record of its accuracy and power. Notice carefully. It is the ***prophetic*** Word that gives us light in a dark place! It is not obsolete. It is **not** an *optional* part of strength and maturity. It is *not* something *irrelevant*, or of no concern to the modern church. Observe carefully that it is the Word spoken (*past tense*), of old by "men moved by the Holy Spirit," 2 Pe 1:20-21 NKJV, which gives us this lamp, so that one can see in this *present* darkness.

In addition, the prophetic Word does not mean just anything you or I want it to mean. It is of no "private interpretation," 2 Pe 1:20-21 KJV. It does not mean just any thing you may think it means, or just anything you may *want it* to mean. It has an objective sense. It means some things in particular. It has the meaning intended by its author, the Lord God of Hosts! It does not promise just *anything*; it promises *some thing*.

Believing and watching, has a moral quality to it. "And what I say to you I say to all, Watch.'" Mk 13:37 KJV. However, unbelief so often grabs hold.

- We often have not read the promises.
- We have often not *believed* the promises! The Word! And so ...
- We don't *act* on the promises, rather we act on sin. It is a faith and works thing. *Believing causes action.* The church doesn't have vision, and so as Scripture says, "Where *there* is no vision, the people perish:" Prov 29:18 KJV. Who then has been guilty of this sin? At times, almost all of us.

How do one correct the situation? Read the Word. Read all of it. Use the Word to interpret the Word, and believe it. Don't falter at the Word. Don't stumble, don't trip. It seems some are constantly looking for something to stumble over. *Assume that it is true. All of it.* And cling to it. "And Jesus said to his disciples, "O fools, and slow of heart to believe all that the prophets have spoken." Luke 24:25 KJV.

Realize that it is not necessary to *figure everything out* or be able to explain everything for it to be true. Might true faith included some misunderstanding? Yes, but faith is able to work with that. Abraham figured wrong when he was commanded to sacrifice Isaac. God was testing Abraham to see if he would obey even if he thought it would cost him his true heir and son Isaac. You see, Abraham thought that God was able to raise up Isaac from the dead to fulfill His promises through Isaac.

> [17] By faith Abraham, when he was tested, offered up Isaac, and he who had received the promises was offering up his only begotten *son;* [18] *it was he* to whom it was said, "in Isaac your descendants shall be called." [19] He considered that God is able to raise *people* even from the dead, from which he also received him back as a type. Heb 11:17-19 NASB

You see *it seemed* that the prophecy was contrary to the command God had made. Even so Abraham *assumed* God was right, and he gave God *the benefit of the doubt* and did not stumble at either the prophecy or the command.

We don't have to let our sins have the victory over us. Believe, resolve, plan, act, win ... by faith in Jesus. If we are losing, it is unnecessary. But without faith it is impossible to please Him, Heb 11:6. God wants to be believed. He wants to be trusted. The Lord's recruiting a few good men for life in another world, men like those of old looking for a city, a heavenly city.

> But now they desire a better country, that is, an heavenly: wherefore God is not ashamed to be called their God: for he hath prepared for them a city. Heb 11:16 KJV

If all of this is true, then how should we be approaching prophecy?

First, we need to just admit that some passages are difficult, and we may not be able to understand all of it, and surely won't understand all of it at first. In a real way this is no different from the rest of Scripture, or the rest of life. Seek help from God in prayer. Read other passages that bear on the subject.

Before you study prophecy in depth, make sure that you understand the basics of the gospel, the new covenant, and the New Testament church. If you are mixed up on these things, then you will surely get mixed up trying to interpret obscure prophecies. By learning these things you will be entering the school of the prophets and will learn first principles of prophecy, much as the coverage in these opening sections.

Make sure that you have read all of the Bible first. They are all parts of the whole, and the different parts—from Genesis to Revelation—all fit together. To concentrate on an obscure passage before reading all of the Bible is like trying to put together a large picture puzzle without first looking at all of the pieces. This doesn't mean that you shouldn't read or think about these passages, but you may not be able to put these things together before you get a broader knowledge of the Scripture.

Make sure to use clear passages to regulate the interpretation of obscure passages, not obscure passages to regulate the clear. It should not be necessary to say this, but even highly trained theologians will sometimes take an obscure passage and try to change even the clearest passages in the Bible to conform to their interpretation of what is otherwise obscure.

Make sure to approach it cautiously. Do not be dogmatic unless you are absolutely positive. For instance, this book will not try to explain to you what *all* of Daniel 11 means, mainly because I don't know *every-thing* it means. But we can understand some things, a bit at a time, can expand our understanding. Remember you do not have to understand *everything* to learn *some* worthwhile *things*. Lessons of faith, fortitude in suffering, and God's acting in history are easy to learn even in the most obscure passage. As you progress, more and more things will start to fit together.

A good way to start off in studying prophecy (after you have read the entire Bible more than once) is to practice reading fulfilled prophecies, especially the ones that are quoted in the New Testament. This in itself can be a challenging exercise. See if, without referring to the New Testament, you can understand the Old Testament prophecies. If we can't, that means either the New Testament authors were mixed up, *or you and I are mixed up!* (Probably us! Eh?) Often we need to back up, figure out what we are doing wrong, and not be dogmatic.

Most of the important points in Scripture are repeated in more than one way. A good example is the parables of the kingdom in the gospels. He describes the kingdom from several points of view, perhaps so that if we don't understand one parable, we may understand another. It is the same way with prophecy. For instance the visions of Daniel (much like the parables of the kingdom) overlap each other. So the kingdom of Babylon is in Daniel chapters 2, 7, and 8, the Medo-Persian and the Greek empires in chapters 2, 7, 8, and 11, and the Roman empire is in Daniel 2, and is also mentioned in chapters 9 and 11. These overlapping visions. Thus you have more than one opportunity to understand these truths.

There is a need to understand the nature of the covenants involved, in order to get a good feel for the Scriptures. Promises were made to man early in the Scripture. Man had lost his place in Paradise because of the temptation of the devil and man's own fall into sin. A warfare is promised between the "seed of woman" and the "seed" of the serpent. It is promised that man will bruise the head of Satan, and Satan will bruise his heel, Gen 3:15.

Then more promises of a seed came. The word for "seed" and the word for "descendant" are basically the same. The Hebrew word *zera* זֶרַע is the word for "seed" (and it is often singular, just as in English we speak of a bag of "seed.") This is additionally the regular word for a "descendant," and it is often translated this way in many translations. Your descendants in Hebrew are your "seed," and if you keep that in mind it will help you to more clearly follow the seed promises, regardless of your main translation. The promise of a special seed is passed on to Abraham, and it says that in his seed *all* the nations of the earth will be blessed, Gen 22:18, and Gen 12:3, etc.

They were promised moreover that a prophet like Moses was to come, a prophet that all must obey, Deut 18:15. The profile of Moses is a dynamic one that begins early with the attempt of the ruler of the land to have Moses and all the male infants killed at birth. Even at this point the likeness of the special prophet to Moses is clear because the rulers of this world tried also to kill Jesus at His birth. It continues with Moses being raised as royalty and attempting to release his people from bondage. Moses had supposed that Israel understood that God had sent him to deliver them from bondage, but instead they rejected him, so he went to a far country to live, in Moses case for forty years.

Later the Lord God sent him to effect the deliverance of His people, to lead them from the Egypt of this world to the promised land of Canaan.

Jesus also was rejected by those who should have been His, as was prophesied. He came to His own, and His own didn't recognize Him or accept Him, Jn 1:10-11. Likewise Jesus went away to a far country to receive a kingdom and then return, Lk 19:12. The Jews would have thought of someone like Herod the Great going off to Rome to receive the kingdom of Judea and then returning to rule. However, the far country Jesus went to was heaven and He went to receive the kingship of ALL and He went there to prepare a place for us, Jn 14:2. He now rules from there in the midst of His enemies, Psa 110:1-2. Like Moses, He will return from that far country and call to account all of those who did not want this man to rule over them, Lk 19:27. He will call His elect and have them gathered by the angels from one end of heaven to another, Mtt 24:31; and He will lead them to the ultimate promised land, the new heavens and new earth where righteousness lives, Rev 21:1-7.

This is but a bare outline of how Jesus is "a Prophet like me from your midst, from your brethren." Deut 18:15 NKJV. There is much more to the story. For instance, Moses was a giver of a new law and a new covenant: The Mosaic Law. Everyone had to listen to Moses and the laws he laid down or he was stoned, Heb 10:28. Similarly of this prophet like Moses who would come from the Jews, God says He will require ALL to obey Him.

> [18] I will raise up for them a Prophet like you from among their brethren, and will put My words in His mouth, and He shall speak to them all that I command Him. [19] And it shall be that whoever will not hear My words, which He speaks in My name, I will require it of him. Deut 18:18-19 NKJV

A primary question is: what is the Old Testament? Jesus referring to it, calls it "the law or the prophets" in Mtt 5:17. Thus, the first reference to the Old Testament that is in the New Testament says there is more to it than "the law of Moses," but the very next verse seems to use the word law to refer to all of what most call "the Old Testament." Jesus also spoke of a three part Old Testament in Lk 24:44, composed of 1.) the Law, 2.) the Prophets and 3.) the Psalms. So the basic divisions of the Old Testament speak of more than "the Law of Moses" in what is called the "Old Testament." The prophets may later quote the law, but they do not add to it. They may point out its deeper meaning, but they cannot change it, Deut 12:32.

It must be carefully pointed out that Moses' Law did not affect the promises to Abraham. The Law came 430 years after the promises to Abraham and his seed, Gal 3:16-17, and did not alter that covenant already ratified by God. All *Christians* are part of that seed, and heirs according to the promises to Abraham, according to Paul in Gal 3:26-29. So also, the promises to Noah, his descendants, and the animals were also not changed by either the Law of Moses or the New Covenant. What you learned in Sunday school and what you taught in Sunday school about the promise of the rainbow is true! And if the promises are still true, so are the requirements.

Realizing this and knowing the divisions of the Old Testament that Jesus pointed out, puts us in a little better position to understand some of the radical conservative rabbis who claim that Joshua through Malachi is not part of the Law of Moses. Not part of the Law of Moses? Right! Inspired and authoritative? Definitely! Even though parts are often lumped together with the Law in common language by the Jews, the New Testament writers, and us.

But it was really only Moses' Law that was removed with the coming of the Messiah. So when did it end? Some gospel passages seem to indicate that the period of the Old Testament (as it is often called) was proclaimed until the time of John the Baptist, Lk 16:16. Paul speaks in more specific terms in Col 2:14 where he says Christ nailed it to the cross. He abolished the law in His flesh, so that He might make an international and permanent reign of peace by destroying the division between Jew and gentile (the Law) and give one law of peace.

> [14] For He Himself is our peace, who made both *groups into* one and broke down the barrier of the dividing wall, [15] by abolishing in His flesh the enmity, *which is* the Law of commandments *contained* in ordinances, so that in Himself He might make the two into one new man, ... [16] and might reconcile them both in one body to God through the cross, by it having put to death the enmity. Eph 2:14-16 NASB

Paul then quotes Isaiah as to the reason the Messiah (the Christ) would come. The Messiah was to bring peace to *ALL*, not just those who were close to Him in the Old Testament period but also those who were far away from Him.

> I create the fruit of the lips; Peace, peace to him that is far off, and to him that is near, saith the LORD; and I will heal him. Isa 57:19 KJV

It should also be understood that the Old Law was completely given before Moses died. Scripture plainly says, "the Law was given by Moses," Jn 1:17 KJV. Now Moses died somewhere about 1406 BC, by a Biblical chronology. Yet most of the Old Testament, almost all of it, was written after Moses died. Still it was the law which was given through Moses. The same can be seen in Heb 9:19, where it says Moses spoke "every commandment" to them NASB. So what did Moses read to the people? All the commands of the Law, that is to say, what is in the books of Exodus through Deuteronomy. Of Joshua it later says, "There was not a word of all that Moses commanded, which Joshua read not before all the congregation," Jos 8:35 KJV, although most the Old Testament was likewise written *after* Joshua's time. So everything after the book of Deuteronomy is **not** part of Moses' law! Some of it talks about Moses Law, and some of this or that event of olden times, and some of it speaks of the Christian age! But the Law was all read by Moses before he died in about 1406 BC, and shortly after by Joshua!

So what does all of this mean? This is really very simple, and this message is well understood in many sermons and lessons that many have heard from the Old Testament. All of what is called the Old Testament, *whatever* was written in the past times, was written to instruct *US*, Rom 15:4. The regulations of our covenant are not here, but it is still for our learning, for doctrine, for teaching (which is what the word "doctrine" really means). The Greek word for what is sometimes translated as "doctrine," is *didaskalia* διδασκαλία, that is to say, teaching, 2 Tim 3:16. The Bible is not a dead letter, New Testament or Old Testament. It is *all* intended for our teaching. Even the old rules about pigs and cows and cloth and washings were written for us, the Christians of the New Covenant. In Deut 25:4 it says "You shall not muzzle the ox while he is threshing." NASB Now Paul says that Deut 25:4 was written for us and then tells us *why*.

> [9] ... God is not concerned about oxen, is He? [10] Or is He speaking altogether for our sake? **Yes, for our sake it was written**, because the plowman ought to plow in hope, and the thresher to thresh in hope of sharing the crops. 1 Cor 9:9-10 NASB (*bold emphasis added*)

In other words, we should learn that whoever works on a project should be able to partake of the products or profits of that work. Is this a law for us not to muzzle oxen? No! Are we supposed to use it for teaching, use it for learning? Absolutely. Of the events that happened long ago, it implies that God had them happen as examples for us.

> [6] Now these things happened as examples for us, so that we would not crave evil things as they also craved. 1 Cor 10:6 NASB

> [9] nor let us tempt Christ, as some of them also tempted, and were destroyed by serpents; [10] nor complain, as some of them also complained, and were destroyed by the destroyer. [11] Now all these things happened to them as examples, and they were written for our admonition, upon whom the ends of the ages have come.
> 1 Cor 10:9-11 NKJV

So of the very first things written in the Scriptures—written of people under different cultures and different laws from us—even those stories are written for our benefit. The author of Hebrews says that Prov 3:11-12 was written, not just to Jews, but to you, Heb 12:5-6!

> [5] and **you** have forgotten the exhortation which is addressed to **you as sons**,
> "MY SON, DO NOT REGARD LIGHTLY THE DISCIPLINE OF THE LORD,
> NOR FAINT WHEN YOU ARE REPROVED BY HIM;

[6] FOR THOSE WHOM THE LORD LOVES HE DISCIPLINES, AND HE SCOURGES EVERY SON WHOM HE RECEIVES." NASB (*bold emphasis added*)

Not only does the author of Hebrews say it was written to you but even written to you "as sons." Solomon says by the Holy Spirit that whipping a child gives him wisdom, Prov 29:15. That is a statement of truth that did not become false because Jesus died on the cross. It is not part of the Law of Moses because Moses had completely stated the Law about 400 years earlier. Is this proverb taken out of the way? By no means! Should you learn from it? By all means!

There are many age lasting issues that are only dealt with in detail, or only used with examples, in the Old Testament. For instance, many of the issues concerning civil government and war, images and idolatry, details of the nature of God, examples of faith under pressure are seen in the lists in Hebrews 11, and are *only* discussed in the Old Testament. Again, Isaiah says that all wars will cease, Isa 2:4. This not a veiled prophecy. But wars are still going on, both physical and spiritual. Paul says to fight the good fight, 1 Tim 6:12. He says to put on the full armor of God so that you can fight well, Eph 6:11-12. All of that not withstanding, will the prophecy of Jesus ending all wars one day come to pass? Yes it will! Mtt 5:18. So has Isaiah 2:4 been taken out of the way? Nailed to the cross? By no means. It was spoken over 600 years *after* the law of Moses was given, and it has nothing to do with the Law of Moses being taken out of the way. Has this happened yet? Not in any way!

All this is said in 2 Tim 3:15-17. *All* of Scripture is inspired by God, and *all* of it is profitable for doctrine, for reproof, for instruction in righteousness. If we are not using *all* of the Bible, there is no promise that you have *everything* you need or that you will be *thoroughly* furnished. Still, many both inside and outside of the Lord's church only use a subset of Scripture and not the whole.

Many foolishly will not believe God's Word that was written before the time of Christ, unless they can verify it by the New Testament. But the noble Bereans, instead, *successfully used the Old Testament to verify the New, Acts 17:11!*

Should we study the prophets now? For sure! Peter says we now have the prophetic Word made more sure, 2 Pe 1:19! It has been truly said of the Scriptures, properly handled that: "The Old Testament is the New Testament concealed, and the New Testament is the Old Testament revealed."

The Foundations of Order and Another Kingdom

The flood is over as the reader comes into Genesis 9. Noah and his family and the animals have come out of the ark. Noah has offered a sacrifice of thanks to the Lord, and the Lord has promised that He will never again destroy all the earth with a flood, as long as summer and winter last, Gen 8:21-22. At this point, the Lord prepares a covenant with the survivors. By implication the covenant really begins in the end of Genesis 8. The chapters divisions are an invention of men, and in this case one might argue that this is a clumsy place to divide the material. All of that aside, God has made a promise and binds together a series of promises and commands into a covenant.

A covenant is a contract of sorts, but one in which someone who is the superior party dictates the terms, and binds both himself and the other parties to certain terms. The technical term for what is seen here and in other passages of Scripture is a suzerainty treaty or covenant.

Who is under this covenant, and how long does it last? It is with Noah and his

descendants, Gen 9:9. That includes *every* human being who has lived since the flood. Moreover this covenant also includes all the animals and "every living creature" on the earth, Gen 9:10. Yes, you heard right. The deer and the dogs and the possum and the snakes are all under this covenant.

How long does it last? It basically lasts *until the end* of this present world, and ***it was not taken away by the cross of Christ!*** It is Moses' law that was taken away at the cross. With Noah it is approximately four to five hundred years until the covenant with Abraham is to be given, and nearly a thousand years until the law of Moses is to be given, but Paul says that the Law of Moses *does not abolish a covenant previously confirmed by God,* Gal 3:17. So Paul argues that the covenant with Abraham is still valid, and you and I as Christians, are heirs of that covenant with Abraham, Gal 3:29. In fact, the covenant with Abraham goes on into eternity, with blessings for all of the saved. But if Abraham's covenant is still intact then so also is the covenant with Noah and his descendants and the living creatures of the earth. It is not affected by the coming or going of the Law of Moses. This Noahic covenant will not meet its end, "While the earth remains ... day and night Shall not cease," Gen 8:22 NKJV.

So what are some of the terms of covenant for us? God has already begun by making a promise of no more world wide floods. We are to fill the earth. Also, to protect us during this age, God put the fear of man on all creatures, Gen 9:2. This is part of man's advantage, and it is a gift from God. This gives us a terrific advantage over the other creatures. It does have some limitations, just as someone being afraid of you does not automatically mean they will not fight. It does not give us automatic full domination, but it does give us a terrific advantage. Often we can bluff our way through a confrontation with an animal, when otherwise we would be very vulnerable. It is a gift from God.

Man is also *given* "everything moving that lives" for food, Gen 9:3 NKJV. *Everything* that moves, it says, is *given* to man for food. (Yes Ma'am, this means your boy being a "Snake Eater" is alright!) This is the same answer that is given in 1 Timothy. False teachers in the Christian age sometimes say we should not eat or drink certain things, 1 Tim 4:3. However everything created by God is good, 1 Tim 4:4. Thus the New Covenant follows the Noahic Covenant. This is the same answer given in Gen 1:31. It was all *very* good!

But there are two other requirements given. We are not to eat flesh with the blood in it, Gen 9:4-5. This is repeated in Acts 15:19-20 where Peter said,

> [19] Therefore I judge that we should not trouble those from among the Gentiles who are turning to God, [20] but that we write to them to abstain from things polluted by idols, *from* sexual immorality, *from* things strangled, and *from* blood. NKJV

In other words, the only ritual requirement of Moses' law to be continued into our covenant is the one first stated in the Noahic covenant: we are not to eat the blood of either man or beast, and so once again the New Covenant follows a key command of the Noahic Covenant.

Then one more requirement is given: the death penalty for murder. You might call this the ultimate requirement of the Noahic covenant, and with this God established the foundation for all civil government during remaining history: a community duty (a duty of all the people) to put to death whoever murders a man.

> 5 "Surely I will require your lifeblood; from every beast I will require it. And from *every* man, from every man's brother I will require the life of man.

> 6 "Whoever sheds man's blood,
> By man his blood shall be shed,
> For in the image of God
> He made man," Gen 9:5-6 NASB

With this commandment, God put the sword in men's hands to punish the wicked, and made it a requirement to punish those who shed blood. By implication, if the thugs are organized, then the retribution may be organized. So wars are thus authorized, if necessary for bringing the wicked to accountability. The particulars of organization and finance are not dictated. The rest is history, but in this way God has clearly indicated His intention to use the swords of men to punish much of men's wickedness *within history*. So the governing authorities are to impose limits on men's wickedness for the good of all, and they are,

> ... the minister of God to thee for good. But if thou do that which is evil, be afraid; for he beareth not the sword in vain: for he is the minister of God, a revenger to execute wrath upon him that doeth evil. Rom 13:4 KJV

Thus the New Covenant follow the Noahic Covenant. Thus, men have responsibilities, but **proper government derives its authority from God**, Rom 13:1, **not from the consent of men**. So this covenant establishes a rule of law under God in which God also uses men to bring His retribution for sin. This is surely one of the most telling assignments of authority to sinful man in all of history. An assignment which will soon after Noah's time be divided and expanded.

Still perhaps there is a need to emphasize in passing, but still firmly, that this is a care taking role. People need shepherds. They are often like sheep without a shepherd. So Jesus saw the people.

> But when he saw the multitudes, he was moved with compassion on them, because they fainted, and were scattered abroad, as sheep having no shepherd. Mtt 9:36 KJV

Rulers are meant by the Lord to rule, be caretakers of the peoples under them. God, for instance, appointed Saul as king to be a shepherd to his people, and then when Saul proved unfaithful, God replaced Saul with David to that post of shepherd of His people.

> "... and the LORD said to you, 'You shall shepherd My people Israel, and will be a ruler over Israel.' " 2 Sam 5:2b NKJV

When evil king Ahab was about to go to his death because he had not been a faithful shepherd, prophecy speaks as if for a while the people will be like sheep without a shepherd, 1 Kgs 22:17. And when God speaks of Cyrus king of Persia, He calls him "my shepherd" in Isa 44:28. Of course the true and final Shepherd is Jesus Christ. He will take care of His own, Jn 10:1-5, 8-11.

Then comes Babel and the making of nations in Genesis 11. In the early days the whole earth had one language, and few words, Gen 11:1. So the people came out of the ark, still living a comparatively long time (that is compared to how long we live now), and they settled on the plains of Shinar, Gen 11:2. (The plains of what was later the land of Ur, or the land of Babylon.) This same area is what is today southern Iraq. This was a very prosperous and fertile area in ancient times, nothing like it is today. Then they said, let's make a name for ourselves, and build for ourselves a big city, centered around one big tower, that reaches all the way to heaven, Gen 11:4. It is easy to see that they wanted to be one people, and they wanted to be famous, and not be scattered over all the earth. So they said, we'll build the city and tower out of fired brick, Gen 11:3.

Then the Lord came down to see the city, Gen 11:5. God looks down from heaven to see what men are doing, how they are acting, and tests them, Psa 11:3-5. God made some observations about what is going on. He says that indeed the men of the earth are all one language and people, Gen 11:6a. They are united and of one mind and one spirit, and they will be able to do anything that they want to do and nothing will be impossible to them, Gen 11:6b. So far these assessments coincide.

Have you listened to any of the United Nations propaganda? The UN propaganda in essence says that if we would just all abandon our independence, and give our obedience to a one-world government, and follow one-world customs, then (they say) nothing would be impossible to us! That is the gist of much of the One World propaganda. In Genesis 11 God says, That is true! But there is another part of God's response: God didn't think that men's plans were for the good!

First, God had wanted men "To be fruitful and multiply and replenish the earth." Gen 9:1 KJV. Which means they would scatter out and fill things up. But scattering out over the earth is not part of the new plan among men. They want to build a tower "lest we be scattered abroad upon the face of the whole earth," Gen 11:4 KJV. (And that is still the plan: to keep men close together for control.)

You see, mankind has been ruined. Yes, they were created upright, but they have sought out many inventions, Ecc 7:29. God does not seem to think that it is a good idea for sinful mankind to be united, not a good idea for them to be able to do *anything* they want. For *many* of the things they might want to

do are *evil*! So God brought confusion to sinful men's plans.

Then it was that God scattered mankind all over the earth, Gen 11:8. So GOD created the nations and tribes, languages and tongues, of the earth! In the confusion of languages men were alienated from each other, by tribe and family, and they were scattered all over the earth. Babel got its name from each man's speech becoming babbling to his neighbor, Gen 11:9. So God *Himself* did not think it would be good for **sinful** man to be united!

Even so this lost unity has for ages been the goal of sinful men. Especially, this has been the objective of those who thought they would be the ones who would be able to rule any one-world-kingdom. A successful one-world wide empire which will come is known in Scripture as "Mystery Babylon" in Rev 17:5, or "Babylon the Great" in Rev 14:8. Also it will be completely destroyed *within history*, never to rise again.

It is interesting to see in the current European Union that the Council of Europe has incredibly created a European Union poster (see the next page) picturing the tower of Babel, and the motto "Europe: Many Tongues, One Voice," and has the Tower capped with Satanic stars! It is hard to not notice the block-like/robot-like character of these "builders" of Babylon in the poster.

Not that the European Union is necessarily the ultimate Mystery Babylon, although some may attempt to use her in such a way. Many nations have been proposed as fulfilling this "Mystery Babylon" of Scripture, including ancient Rome, Venice, the Holy Roman Empire, the Catholic church, the British Empire, the United States of America, and others. Many of the occult powers, when

In the occult, an upright star (as to the left) stands for man, and a canted star (to the right) represents Satan.

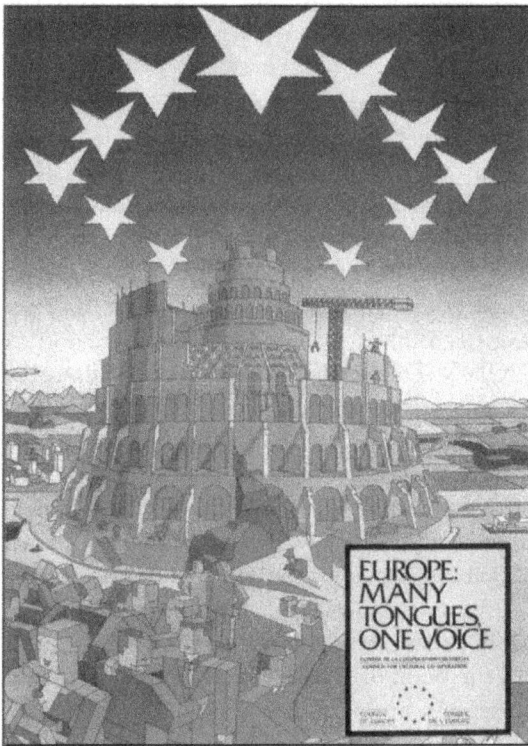

EUROPE:
MANY
TONGUES,
ONE VOICE

they have been in the drivers seat of various nations throughout history, have *tried* to fulfill this. But all of these, though indeed powerful in their own way, have *all* fallen short of the breadth of power seen in Revelation chapters 14 through 18, or the other criteria, such as is seen in Revelation 18. (More details will be discussed later.) Still, it is striking that some in the Council of Europe would choose such symbolism. **So the point is that:**

The spiritual and political issues of Genesis 11 are ALIVE EVEN TODAY.

But God Himself divided the nations for His purposes. So the effect is an ethnic division of the authority to punish sin, which was established with the Noahic covenant. God Himself established the divisions and now uses men's divisions to limit the effect and the spread of our sins. It was God Himself who had placed the sword in men's hands, to punish the evil doer, as was noted earlier in Gen 9:4-7. Also God ensured that the authority to punish sin would never be a monopoly. If in one ethnic group this power has been subverted and rather become an instrument of evil, then other such powers have likewise been established to oppose them. Since these times God has pitted good men against bad men, and bad men against bad men, so as to limit and punish sin, and to leave room for men with "honest and good hearts" (Lk 8:15) to seek God. These purposes were discussed by Paul in Athens, when he said of the Lord that

> "26 ... He made from one *man* every nation of mankind to live on all the face of the earth, having determined *their* appointed times and the boundaries of their habitation, 27 that they would seek God, if perhaps they might grope for Him and find Him, though He is not far from each one of us;" Acts 17:26-27 NASB

So God's purposes through the raising and lowering of nations are to encourage men to seek Him. Indeed, I think the greatest glories of the church in history are yet to come. In the end, all will serve God's purposes in history. For "The LORD hath made all *things* for himself: yea, even the wicked for the day of evil." Prov. 16:4 NKJV.

Then comes the issues of other kingdoms and what God will do. To begin looking at these subjects let us turn to Daniel the second chapter. Daniel the second chapter actually starts in the year 604 B.C. This is roughly five years after King Josiah of Judah died. Nebuchadnezzar has for the first time taken Jerusalem from King Jehoiakim of Judah, Josiah's son, about a year before.

Egypt is no longer the power she was. She can no longer project her power over all of the Mideast, so she stays at home while all of this happens. Batches of "Prisoners Of War" (POW's) have been taken to Babylon for control and as security. In these early batches of POW's is the young man Daniel and some of his friends, all very religious young men, who are first seen in Daniel chapter one. At some point in Daniel 2, Nebuchadnezzar has had some wierd dreams. He calls for his magicians and conjurers and sorcerers to interpret his weird dream. He tells them he has had a dream, and he is impatient to know its meaning. In ancient times the courts of almost all nations were surrounded by groups of occult seers of various types, anxious to provide their ruler with advice and guidance from beyond the bounds of human experience. Most of the time these were politically canny groups, anxious to please their sovereign, as can be seen with the group surrounding Ahab in the book of 1 Kings (that will be discussed later). Their value ran from being wise but ambiguous counselors, all the way to out and out charlatans, and even to the demonic, as indeed can be seen with Ahab. As often demonic counsellors, they often had all of that "value" implicit in their "advice." In Scripture, any real power in these occult arts are associated with the demonic. Compare the story of the demon possessed girl in Philippi in Acts 16:16-21.

The king's occult advisors gave their "long live the king," and ask him to tell them his dream so they can interpret it! The history of the manipulation of rulers in these things is legendary. God even used such a group to influence Ahab so that he would go to his death at Ramoth-gilead. Many others have used such groups for this or that purpose. The stories are sprinkled throughout history, even into our own times. It is well known that Abraham Lincoln and his wife dabbled in the occult and sought such advice from the beyond. Adolph Hitler, as well, was a fanatic about the occult and sought such advice, insight, and talismans. Fictional exaggerations of these things are well-known in some of the Lucas-Spielberg Indiana Jones movies, but the truth is fantastic enough. For instance during, World War II, Hitler was following a "famous" Hungarian astrologer Louis de Wohl. He was getting world-wide publicity for his accuracy, and he was (who would guess) a captain in British Intelligence. British Intelligence was giving him bits and pieces of real information to bolster his credibility, and he was being used to try to manipulate Hitler. The story is told in William Stevenson's *A Man Called Intrepid*. There are many such dazzling stories down through history. Closer to our own time, Ronald and Nancy Reagan consulted astrologers.

But king Nebuchadnezzar seems to have had some experience with such false seers and is in no mood to be played with. They claim to be able to really "see" into the spirit world which controls the material world (and here the occult and Scripture are the same basic side of the issue), but *IF* they can see into the spirit world ... then ... the "seers" and magicians of the court will not need the king to tell them his dream, so Nebuchadnezzar decided.

> [5] The king answered and said to the Chaldeans, "My decision is firm: if you do not make known the dream to me, and its interpretation, you shall be cut in pieces, and your houses shall be made an ash heap. [6] However, if you tell the dream and its interpretation, you shall receive from me gifts, rewards, and great honor. Therefore tell me the dream and its interpretation." Dan 2:5-6 NKJV

The sorcerers and medium pleaded for the dream, and they said *then* you will get the interpretation. Nebuchadnezzar must have had some bad experience with such men. He is adamant. He thinks they are playing for time so they can deceive him with lying words. The sorcerers say that no man can do what the king is asking, and they are right. They say no one has ever asked for something like this. No one except "gods" could do this! The execution of these men is at hand, and Daniel and his friends were among these spiritual advisors who are about to be killed. Daniel found out what was going on and asked the king for time to bring him the dream and the interpretation. They prayed to the Lord, asking for "compassion from the God of heaven concerning this mystery," Dan 2:18, so that they might not die. Then the "mystery" was revealed to Daniel in a dream.

Then Daniel approached the king to tell him the dream and the interpretation. Daniel does not claim any special power for himself, but he says, "But there is a God in heaven that revealeth secrets, and maketh known to the king Nebuchadnezzar what shall be in the latter days," Dan 2:28 KJV. Isn't it incredible who God decides to tell his message?

"Thou, O king, sawest, and behold a great image," Dan 2:31. And it was a splendid and awesome looking statute. The head was made of gold, its chest and arms were made of silver, its belly and thighs were made of bronze, its legs were made of iron, and its feet of part iron and part clay. As Nebuchadnezzar looked on there was a rock cut out of a mountain without hands, and it struck the statue on its feet of iron mixed with clay and crushed the gold and silver and bronze and iron and clay, and the wind carried them away so that nothing remained of their presence. This was the dream.

This then is the interpretation Daniel gave. Nebuchadnezzar is the "king of kings" to whom the Lord has given power and glory and whom the LORD has given to rule on the earth. Nebuchadnezzar is the head of gold. After Babylon will come another kingdom, inferior to Nebuchadnezzar's. This was the Medo-Persian which followed, which was not quite as rich or powerful as the Babylonian empire, although it did last longer. The Medes and Persians are the chest and arms of silver, with the Medes being dominant in the early empire and the Persians being dominant in the late empire; and perhaps the two arms representing the two "arms" of the empire. Then will come a third kingdom of bronze which would rule the earth. The Greeks were never quite as rich as the Babylonians or the Persians (they did not seem to be able to hold on to their money as well), but the Greeks were well known for their excellent bronze armor and so are pictured as the belly and thighs of bronze. They came to power through the victories of Alexander the Great and their military and cultural dominance continued until the Romans took over. After this kingdom of bronze will come the fourth kingdom which was as strong as iron, which was the Romans who followed the Greeks.

> [40] And the fourth kingdom shall be as strong as iron, inasmuch as iron breaks in pieces and shatters everything; and like iron that crushes, *that kingdom* will break in pieces and crush all the others. [41] Whereas you saw the feet and toes, partly of potter's clay and partly of iron, the kingdom shall be divided; yet the strength of the iron shall be in it, just as you saw the iron mixed with ceramic clay. [42] And *as* the toes of the feet *were* partly of iron and partly of clay, *so* the kingdom shall be partly strong and partly fragile. [43] As you saw iron mixed with ceramic clay, they will mingle with the seed of men; but they will not adhere to one another, just as iron does not mix with clay." Dan 2:40-43 NKJV

What is depicted here is an empire with the strength of iron which is able to smash all opponents—an empire that is a "divided kingdom," but which also has a weak foundation. It has the weakness of iron mixed with clay, which gives the origins of its own demise, even though with the strength of iron it will last longer than any of these other kingdoms. It would eventually crumble away, even if merely left to itself. Then comes the decisive end of the vision. Daniel says that,

And in the days of these kings the God of heaven will set up a kingdom which shall never be destroyed; and the kingdom shall not be left to other people; it shall break in pieces and consume all these kingdoms, and it shall stand forever. Dan 2:44 NKJV

Now look at some of the particulars of this kingdom which is announced. It will come "In the days of those kings .." That seems to say that it will come in the days of the kingdom of iron, the days of the Roman empire. It is a kingdom which "will never be destroyed." It will not be left for another people, as perhaps you might argue that the Persians took over the kingdom and dominated the empire first dominated by the Medes. There will be no such thing in this kingdom to be established in the days of the Roman empire. Lastly, notice that this kingdom which is to be established "in the days of those kings" will "consume all these kingdoms, **but it shall stand forever."** A kingdom which "will break in pieces and consume all these kingdoms."

This special kingdom will be specially set up by God, seemingly in contrast to the empires established by men (although it has already been discussed that in a real sense all the powers that exist are ordained of God). It describes this permanent kingdom in surreal terms in Dan 2:45. It will be a stone "cut out of the mountain without hands." Clearly this repudiates any human origin or building at all. Clearly God does the building in a superlative sense. Then this special kingdom crushes all the preceding empires, and Nebuchadnezzar is told that this "will take place in the future," verse 29. The Roman empire was to replace the Greeks over three hundred years into the future, and that was only the beginning of the empire which the English historian Sir Edward Gibbon traces until the 1500's AD.

Nebuchadnezzar asked to even be told the dream. At this point, he has been told the dream which he determinedly told no one else. Now he has the dream and the interpretation which he can hardly refute. Then Nebuchadnezzar did homage to Daniel and said, "Surely your God is a God of gods and a Lord of kings and a revealer of mysteries, since you have been able to reveal this mystery," Dan 2:47 NASB. He gave Daniel many gifts and a high position.

The "empires" of Daniel 2 fit history, up to the last kingdom. It requires no crystal ball from our perspective to identify Babylon and the next three empires which followed. Then at the last kingdom, secular empires fail us for even any passably sensible identification. Those ancient empires indeed passed away, you might say were crushed; but there has been no secular successor.

Even so, in the days of Rome another prophet, Jesus, came to Galilee preaching the gospel and declaring that "The time is fulfilled, and the kingdom of God is at hand; repent and believe in the gospel," Mk 1:15. The apostle Paul spoke of these things and their purpose.

4 But **when the fullness of the time was come**, God sent forth his Son, made of a woman, made under the law, 5 To redeem them that

were under the law, that we might receive the adoption of sons.
Gal 4:4-5 KJV (*bold emphasis added*)

In Lk 8:1 it describes Jesus' teaching as "proclaiming and preaching the kingdom of God," NASB. When Jesus is telling a man what he should do, He says, "as for you, go and proclaim everywhere the kingdom of God," Lk 9:60 NASB. The kingdom of Daniel 2 was to be a kingdom the God of heaven will set up according to Dan 2:44. and Jesus in His teaching repeatedly represents His teaching as bringing about "the kingdom of God" or as "the kingdom of heaven." See, for instance, Mtt 12:28 where He talks about the kingdom of God as having "come unto you" or the parables in Matthew 13 of "the kingdom of heaven." When Jesus was about to go into heaven in Acts 1, His disciples seem to think the time had been fulfilled and they asked Him, "Lord, is it at this time You are restoring the kingdom to Israel?" Acts 1:6 NASB. The details will be discussed later, but notice that Col 1:13 speaks in the past tense saying that "He rescued us from the domain of darkness, and transferred us to the kingdom of His beloved Son." *In other words it speaks of "The Kingdom" as already in existence.* Paul emphasizes that this is not a kingdom of this world, even though historians like Gibbon have credited Christianity with being a major factor in the fall of Rome. At this point though, there is a need to look at some other prophecies which bear on our subject. First, look at the subject of the Son of David who will be king according to Jeremiah 23, and the prophet Zechariah.

In Scripture rulers are often called "shepherds." When Moses is about to die, he asks the Lord to appoint a man to rule over them, so that they will "be not as sheep which have no shepherd," Num 27:17 KJV. The Lord said to David, "You shall shepherd My people Israel, and be ruler over Israel," 2 Sam 5:2 NKJV. So it is implicitly David's task to care for God's people as a shepherd. In earlier times the judges were to shepherd God's people. The kingdom became very corrupt in the time before the deportation to Babylon. It has been pointed out that when Ahab was to be killed in battle, Israel was to be "scattered upon the hills, as sheep that have not a shepherd," 1 Kgs 22:17 KJV. The same is true of the rulers of the gentiles (that is to say of the other nations of the world). The LORD in Isa 44:28 said of Cyrus king of Persia "*He is* My shepherd," NASB When Assyria is about to fall, Nahum tells the king of Assyria, "Your shepherds are sleeping, O king of Assyria; Your nobles are lying down," Nah 3:18 NASB.

But in the end times of the Davidic kingdom, Jeremiah preached repentance.

> [10] For the land is full of adulterers;
>> For **because of a curse the land mourns.**
>> **The pleasant places of the wilderness are dried up.**
>> Their course of life is evil,
>> And their might is not right.
> [11] "For both prophet and priest are profane;
>> Yes, in My house I have found their wickedness," says the

LORD. Jer 23:10-11 NKJV (*emphasis added*)

Here is a picture of a country being ruined, even "environmentally," by the sins of the people. The so-called prophets are prophesying false things, and Jeremiah says they are "speaking a vision of their own imagination," Jer 23:16 NASB. If these men of their age had really spoken to the LORD, they would have been able to turn God's people away from their wickedness, Jer 23:22. Of course, part of the fault for these things is with the rulers. When the shepherds, the rulers, fail to do their work, the Lord has some things to say about it.

> [1] "Woe to the shepherds who destroy and scatter the sheep of My pasture!" says the LORD. [2] Therefore thus says the LORD ... "You have scattered My flock, driven them away, and not attended to them. Behold, I will attend to you for the evil of your doings," says the LORD. Jer 23:1-2 NKJV

Judgment is coming on Israel and Judah for their sins, but Jeremiah promises in chapter 23 that a day is coming when the Lord will gather the remnant of His people, and put shepherds over them who will tend the sheep, and make sure that none of them are missing or afraid. The Lord says that He will raise up a ruler for them of the house of David, what they Lord calls "a Branch of righteousness" to be their king and to bring both "judgment and righteousness," Jer 23:5 NKJV.

> In His days Judah will be saved,
>> And Israel will dwell safely;
>> Now this is His name by which He will be called:
>> THE LORD OUR RIGHTEOUSNESS. Jer 23:6 NKJV

So it is to be a descendant of David, "a Branch of righteousness" of the house of David who will be the ultimate shepherd, and make things right and bring justice to God's people.

Later the prophet Zechariah speaks of those future times. Zechariah similarly speaks of the Branch of David. Some speak of the ultimate savior of God's people as a "people" or "group" or a special holy nation who will save all, but Zechariah clearly speaks of Him as a "man." "Behold, **the man** whose name *is* Branch," Zech 6:12 says, KJV. The parallels between the book of Zechariah and the book of Revelation are many, the interrelations between the books are such that I do not see how you can really understand one without the other, although many seem to try. In Revelation chapter six is what many call the "Four Horsemen of the Apocalypse." In Zechariah chapter six there is a more vague four chariots coming between bronze mountains. There is far less explanation or reason given in those first few verses of Zechariah 6. The first chariot had red horses, and the second black horses, and the third white horses and the fourth chariot most translations say have dappled horses. Zechariah asked the angels about these things, much as John does in the book of Revelation. Zechariah is told these are the four spirits of heaven patrolling the earth. Are these the same as the four horsemen or the four creatures which surround the throne of God in Revelation four? It is not told, but it is told that those spirits which are going to the north have pacified God's wrath in the land of the north (the place from which the Medes and the Persians are then ruling).

Then Zechariah is told to take an offering of the exiles from Babylon and make an expensive crown for the high priest, for Joshua son of Jehozadak. Now Joshua is a common name in Israel, especially since the time of Joshua, *Yehoshua* יְהוֹשֻׁעַ, son of Nun, the faithful spy who succeeded Moses in ruling over Israel. Of course the Greek form of Joshua's name is *Iēsous* Ἰησοῦς as in Acts 7:45, or more simply in English, the Greek form of Joshua's name is "Jesus."

This Joshua/Jesus the priest is seen earlier in the book of Zechariah. In the first few verses of Zechariah chapter three he is seen standing before the angel of God and Satan was appearing at His right hand to accuse Him. Then the LORD said to Satan, "The LORD rebuke thee," Zech 3:2. This Joshua was one who had been pulled out of the fire according to that same verse. (Of hell, one might truly ask, or does He refer to the fire of the burning of the first temple in Jerusalem? Both would truly fit, as shall be seen.) The Joshua in Zechariah 3 is dressed in the filthy clothes of a refugee. Then a clean turban and festive garments are given to Him while the angel was standing there, and Joshua is told,

> Thus saith the LORD of hosts; If thou wilt walk in my ways, and if thou wilt keep my charge, then thou shalt also judge my house, and shalt also keep my courts, and I will give thee places to walk among these that stand by. Zech 3:7 KJV

Joshua is told even more in verse 8. He and his friends are symbols as was pointed out earlier, for the Lord is going to bring in His servant "the Branch," and he says in verse 9 that the Lord "will remove the iniquity of that land in one day." Of this "man whose name is Branch," this Joshua/Jesus, it says that He will branch out and build the temple of the Lord, Zech 6:12, and moreover,

> Even he shall build the temple of the LORD, and he shall bear the glory, and shall sit and rule upon his throne; and he shall be a priest upon his throne: and the counsel of peace shall be between them both. Zech 6:13 KJV

Here then are a couple of key prophecies in a single verse because it speaks of "he who shall build the temple of the LORD." The issue of where and how to approach the Most High God has been the issue since the beginning of religion. It has been an issue since Cain first decided to offer whatever *he* desired in worship of God. It has *always* been an issue, a point of contention which often led to profane worship or even the worship of other gods.

In the book of Leviticus, Moses conveys to Israel God's instructions about sacrifices and the new tabernacle of the Lord, which was literally a "tent," a dwelling, a resting place. The Tabernacle was the "tent of meeting," a phrase which first seen in Ex 27:21 NASB. The tabernacle which the Israelites built in the wilderness was to be a dwelling place of God and a place of meeting God for worship and instruction. God laid it down that any ox, goat, or lamb which a man might sacrifice in any other place than the tent of meeting was to be counted as bloodshed worthy of death, Lev 17:3-4. The reason given is that those offerings previously made in the open fields might now be part of an offering to God, and that the blood of those offering might be sprinkled on the altar of the LORD and the fat be burned as a pleasing aroma to the Lord, and that,

> "They shall no longer sacrifice their sacrifices to the goat demons with which they play the harlot. This shall be a permanent statute to them throughout their generations." Lev 17:7 NASB

So worship in unstructured places often led to the worship of evil things, and here are seen some of the first associations in Scripture between Satan and goats, an association which is also seen among the pagans in the god Pan, and in modern and semi-modern representations of Satan. The word paraphrased as "goat demon" in the NASB, and as "goat idols" in the NIV, and as "devils" in the King James Version, and "demons" in the New King James version, is the word *sair* or *sayer* שָׂעִיר , a word for shaggy male goat, and from which we get the word satyr, which the *New Oxford American Dictionary* defines as "... Mythology one of a class of lustful, drunken woodland gods. In Greek art they were represented as a man with a horse's ears and tail, but in Roman representations as a man with a goat's ears, tail, legs, and horns."

In Lev 17:9 God commands that if anyone will not bring his offering to the tent of meeting, that person was to be "cut off" (literally removed, killed, or to use our phrase, "taken out") from Israel. The term "cut off" is seen as putting to death in passages such as Gen 9:11, and Ex 9:15.

Later it was appointed by the Lord that the place of worship should stay in one location (symbolic perhaps of a stable heaven) on mount Zion in Jerusalem, 2 Chron 6:4-6, Psa 11:4. Of course, this restriction of place ran head on into the "high places," hill tops/mountain tops where people often wanted to worship.

But the ongoing conflict between a sovereign God and rulers who in themselves wanted to be sovereign was an ongoing thing. Priests of any and every religion which claimed to speak for "God" or "gods" often found themselves in conflict with rulers who felt their proper authority was threatened. This can be seen in many national groups all across the world and through world history. King Saul of Israel was about to go into battle in 1 Samuel 13, but there seemed to be some hitches in approaching God through the normally accredited means, so Saul forced himself to violate the rules and directly offer sacrifice to God in the place where he was, and he was condemned for his violations. Solomon himself it seems was brought up sacrificing to the LORD on various high places which were unauthorized, 1 Kgs 3:2-3; and in his final days these lapses led to his undoing. Jeroboam I in 1 Kings chapter 12, was afraid that submitting to

God's regulations of worship would undermine his political authority, and so he invented his own priesthood, places of worship, and regulations of worship.

The conflict continued between the Caesars and the church of the living God in the early centuries of Christianity and continued with the papacy claiming sovereignty over the kings of the earth and coming to focus mainly on temporal power. It goes on into our own times in the conflict between church and state, with some bizarre twists and turns. Some, it would seem, would to like to divorce all government from any sense of right and wrong. (Maybe they really *do* want anarchy!) The government of the United States of American presents the bizarre spectacle of trying to separate all government and education from all religion, while on the other hand supporting

At the left is a representation of the ancient "god" Pan, as half man, half goat. At the right is an edited version of French occultist Eliphas Levi's hermaphrodite Satan. Many curiosities are here. He has the wings of an angel, the head and horns and feet of a goat, the body and hands of a man, and the pentagram is mostly upright, indicating a man. But then his lower torso seems to have scales like a fish (an issue which will later discussed is Satan and the sea), and a staff with serpents much as in medical symbolism. These associations, as seen from passages like Lev 17:7, go back to remote antiquity.

the Jewish religious state of Israel, and then working in the twenty-first century to make sure that the new governments of Iraq and Afghanistan are separated from religion! Babylon reigns! Confusion everywhere!

But look at what Zechariah says that the Messiah, the Christ, the Branch of David will do. He will build the temple of the Lord. The implication is that He will build the true temple of the Lord. He will also be the ruler. He "shall bear the glory and shall sit and rule on His throne," Zech 6:13. He further "shall be a priest on his throne, and the counsel of peace will be between them both," in other words, between king and priests. The Messiah will once and for all end the conflict between church and state, between priest and king, between throne and altar, between politics and religion. The Christ will be both High Priest and King. Jesus of Nazareth fulfills the prophecies of the Messiah.

The Lord Our God will Reign

The latter part of Isaiah chapter one is about the times of the Messiah. It is about Zion, capitol hill in Jerusalem, where both the temple and the palaces of the king stood. It speaks of a time when Zion, with all the repentant, would be ransomed. It is to be a time when all of the sinners who refuse repentance are crushed. Israel will in those times be ashamed of the oaks under which they have committed fornication, but they will themselves be like oaks which are used for a long lasting fire. The strong men will become the tinder for the fire, and they will burn a long time. Indeed, it could be added that they will burn forever, with nothing to stop the fire, Isa 1:27-31.

It has been prophesied by Moses that the Jews are to return to the Lord, when they are in a great distress in what the Scriptures call "the latter days," Deut 4:30, NASB, NKJV, et al. Isaiah 2 talks of these last days. In these last days, the mountain of the Lord's house is to be established, Isa 2:2. Jerusalem is then to be a city of peace. Melchizedek, king of Salem, was the first king of this place in Gen 14:18 (and 'salem' of 'Jeru'-'salem' means Peace). David then took this city from the Jebusites in 2 Sam 5:6-9. It is called Zion, the city of David, 1 Kgs 8:1. It is called the Holy Mountain, the Holy Hill, in Dan 9:16, 20. It is called the Throne of the Lord by Jeremiah in Jer 3:17. This last is a telling reference, because in actuality the throne of God is in heaven according to Psa 11:4, and many other passages. Zion, physical Zion here on earth, is just symbolic of the true throne in heaven. Physical Zion is just a model, a type, or what Scripture also calls a pattern or a shadow. The *true* temple is also in heaven. The earthly Mount Zion, where David acting by the Holy Spirit of God put the altar of the Lord, is but a shadow of the real.

Presently Zion is to be made the highest of the mountains, Isa 2:2. It says it will be the chief of the mountains in the NASB. The religions of old commonly made some mountaintop or hill their center. There is Mount Olympus, the mountain of Samaria and the mountains of Lebanon. There are the seven hills or mountains on which Babylon sits in Rev 17:9, "Here is the mind which has wisdom. The seven heads are seven mountains on which the woman sits," NASB. And the Greek word in Rev 17:9 is indeed "mountain," *oros* ὄρος, which is not really the word for "hill." Scripture says that all of these mountains will be envious of the Lord's mountain, the Lord's religion. I think that the NIV is faithful to the sense of Psa 68:15-16.

> [15] The mountains of Bashan are majestic mountains; rugged are the mountains of Bashan..
> [16] Why gaze in envy, O rugged mountains,
> at the mountain where God chooses to reign,
> where the Lord himself will dwell forever? Psa 68:15-16 NIV

The religion of Yahweh, the Lord our God is to be supreme. It is the Lord's temple which will reign supreme, above every other religion. The role of this temple is to draw all men, all nations will stream to it, flow to it, according to the end of Isa 2:2. "Many peoples shall come and say, "Come, let us go up to the mountain of the Lord,"" Isa 2:3 NKJV. They will not be held back. There will be no obstacle. They will come willingly. They will not be forced. The tribes of the Old Testament were required to go up to Jerusalem 3 times a year according to Deut 16:16. But the nations of the world in Isaiah 2 will say "Let us go up ..." Isa 2:3. Look at how different this is from the picture in Isaiah 1, which was a picture of sin and rebellion. The temple is the center here in Isaiah 2, the base of pilgrimage to God and instruction to all nations. *And it is from Zion's God that all men will learn.* "... He he shall bear the glory, and shall sit and rule upon his throne; and he shall be a priest upon his throne: and the counsel of peace shall be between them both." Zech 6:13 NKJV.

Man's need is uncompromising truth. The people in Isaiah 2 respond to "*the law ... of the LORD.*" The Hebrew word for law is *torah* תּוֹרָה, and also represents teaching, doctrine, instruction, as has been discussed.

So what is the fulfillment? What is the house of God? It is where God dwells, but God doesn't really live in houses of wood or stone, as Solomon says,

> But will God indeed dwell on the earth? behold, the heaven and heaven of heavens cannot contain thee; how much less this house that I have builded? 1 Kgs 8:27 KJV

Solomon is telling us that God cannot even dwell in the *entire* universe, for it is too small (although some media "science" programs try to use the immense size of the universe as an implicit argument against any single "God"). So the "house" of God which Solomon has built is way too small for God to really live in. It is only a model of the true temple in "heaven," a "type" if you will (as has been pointed out) and here you see once again that Scripture is consistent.

> For the law having a shadow of good things to come, and not the very image of the things, ... Heb 10:1 KJV

God's true dwelling place is the church which is the true "house" of God.

> But if I tarry long, that thou mayest know how thou oughtest to behave thyself in the house of God, which is the church of the living God, the pillar and ground of the truth. 1 Tim 3:15 KJV

Once more in Heb 10:21 it says "And *having* an great priest over the house of God," KJV. And this house is a structure of people.

> [4] And coming to Him as to a living stone which has been rejected by men, but is choice and precious in the sight of God, [5] you also, as living stones, are being built up as a spiritual house for a holy priesthood, to offer up spiritual sacrifices acceptable to God through Jesus Christ. 1 Pe 2:4-5 NASB

It is built into a household for God, a house or household made of people.

19 So then you are no longer strangers and aliens, but you are fellow cit-
izens with the saints, and are of God's household, 20 having been built
on the foundation of the apostles and prophets, Christ Jesus Himself
being the corner *stone*, Eph 2:19-20 NASB

This church-household of God grows into a temple, a dwelling of God, in
Eph 2:21-22.

21 in whom the whole building, being fitted together, is growing into a
holy temple in the Lord, 22 in whom you also are being built together
into a dwelling of God in the Spirit. NASB

It is **the** *true* temple of God, and in the final analysis it is the final temple of
God. To mess with it is to mess with God.

16 Do you not know that you are a temple of God and *that* the Spirit of
God dwells in you? 17 If any man destroys the temple of God, God will
destroy him, for the temple of God is holy, and that is what you are.
1 Cor 3:16-17 NASB

But is it really called Zion? Indeed it is for,

22   But **you have come to Mount Zion** and to the city of the living
God, the heavenly Jerusalem, to an innumerable company of angels, 23
to **the general assembly and church of the firstborn** who are
registered in heaven, to God the Judge of all, to the spirits of just men
made perfect, Heb 12:22-23 NKJV (*bold emphasis added*)

It is the mountain of the Lord's house, a city set on a hill that cannot be
hid, Matt 5:14. It is be established "in the last days," according to Isa 2:2, and
so it was. Peter is explaining the outpouring which has occurred in Acts chapter two, and this is what he says.

16 But this is that which was spoken by the prophet Joel; 17 And it shall
come to pass in the last days, ... Acts 2:16-17 KJV

Which is a quote from Joel 2:28. The word of the Lord shall come from
Jerusalem is what it says in Isa 2:3. "For out of Zion shall go forth the law, And
the word of the LORD from Jerusalem," NKJV. It is to come *from the Jews*, for as
Jesus says "for salvation is of the Jews," Jn 4:22 KJV. That is Jesus' words, dispute
them if you will. It is a word of "peace on earth among men with whom He is
pleased," according to Lk 2:14 NASB. Peace I leave you, Jesus says in Jn 14:27.
And it is *from Jerusalem*, for Jesus told His disciples before he left this earth,
"that repentance and remission of sins should be preached in his name among
all nations, beginning at Jerusalem," Lk 24:47 KJV. So as seen in Acts 1 and Acts
2 that it indeed *did go forth* from Jerusalem. Also, it was a message for all nations,
as said in Isa 2:2. So when Peter preached the first gospel sermon, he said in
Acts 2:39, "For the promise is unto you, and to your children, and to all that
are afar off ..." KJV. It is God who teaches, His Word that we receive, just as it

says in Isaiah 2. He alone is the key, for they shall all be taught of God.

> It is written in the prophets, And they shall be all taught of God. Every man therefore that hath heard, and hath learned of the Father, cometh unto me. Jn 6:45 KJV

This is talking about being taught things that men could not know on their own. This temple, this church, is *God's teaching agency*: not a Christian college or university, not a monastery, or an evangelical association, or a missionary alliance, or a Bible school. It is the very thing men look down on, the thing men will not work for, the thing men despise, the plain old church of our Lord.

> [11] And He gave some as apostles, and some as prophets, and some as evangelists, and some as pastors and teachers, [12] for the equipping of the saints for the work of service, to the building up of the **body** of Christ; Eph 4:11-12 NASB (*bold emphasis added*)

The body is, of course, the church, of which "... he is the head of the body, the church," Col 1:18. We are to carry this message into all the world, Mk 16:15-16.

Then comes the problem in Isaiah 2: the mighty God, the Lord Jesus Christ, will judge between the nations, and "... nation shall not lift up sword against nation, **neither shall they learn war any more**," Isa 2:4 KJV (*bold emphasis added*). "Never again"? It is possible that,

1. This means that the gospel and church would bring a reign of peace to all in this present earth. This is called "Post-Millennialism," the idea that Christ will come *after* a reign of peace is brought to the earth through Christianity. But at least in current cultural terms, this doesn't seem to be the answer. Again it seems that America about to enter another perhaps extensive war, and the *majority* of the people of the earth seem unlikely to draw near to God. However, there are other points to consider later which will bear on this answer.

2. This means there will be peace in the church, the household of God. But there are wolves among the sheep of God's pasture, and Paul warns "I know that after my departure savage wolves will come in among you, not sparing the flock;" Acts 20:29 NASB. That doesn't sound like "peace" does it?

Jesus says rather he came to divide men between good and bad.

> [34] Think not that I am come to send peace on earth: I came not to send peace, but a sword. [35] For I am come to set a man at variance against his father, and the daughter against her mother, and the daughter in law against her mother in law. [36] And a man's foes shall be they of his own household. Mtt 10:34-36 KJV

Once again, that does not sound like peace. This conflict here on earth between the world and the church is a fact of life. The church is to be ready for war against the evil spiritual powers that seek to destroy it.

> [11] Put on the full armor of God, so that you will be able to stand firm against the schemes of the devil. [12] For our struggle is not against flesh

and blood, but against the rulers, against the powers, against the world forces of this darkness, against the spiritual *forces* of wickedness in the heavenly *places*.

¹³ Therefore, take up the full armor of God, so that you will be able to resist in the evil day, and having done everything, to stand firm.

Eph 6:11-13 NASB

This is war. This is battle. This is the struggle of Christians throughout the Christian Age. This is surely not "peace" on this present "earth" is it?

3. Next it is possible that the way to peace is through religion and doing away with all armies and having a good, world-wide, civil government. Outside of United Nations headquarters in New York there is a partial quote of Isa 2:4. But the Bible does not indicate that human civil government of *any kind* is the answer to the problem. It indicates that this same Jesus and *His kingdom* is the answer, and salvation is not by any kingdom of this world, **not** any of this present **realm**, Jn 18:36.

4. Also it is possible, as some think, the answer is not the church/kingdom at all, *as indicated by the New Testament*, but a rather a kingdom of Jews will rule over all men and bring world wide peace *under a world wide implementation of the law of Moses*. But the law of Moses has been done away with by God, nailed to the cross Col 2:14. No to detract those good things of Moses law, but since when has Moses law brought peace to the Jews *in any of history*?

If this number 4 is the answer, *then the New Testament is **false***, the *apostles were **liars***, and the verses we read were not true, and ... the Pharisees would then have been right and not Jesus. Beyond that, *any* "this worldly" kingdom which puts a *permanent* end to war *precludes* an end-times revolt against righteousness, *which as will be seen is clearly forecast in Scripture!*

But if you look carefully at the prophecies of Isaiah, this is a peace that comes after the passing away of this present creation. And the last option is:

5. This peace is with the church, the blessed of the Lord, in the kingdom of God, *in the age to come!* A time when every knee will bow to Jesus. There is a time to come when He will make *all* wars cease,

He **maketh wars to cease unto the end of the earth**; he breaketh the bow, and cutteth the spear in sunder; he burneth the chariot in the fire. Psa 46:9 KJV

So one day the last battle in an age long war will be fought, and the last enemy that will be destroyed is death, 1 Cor 15:26.

But it is not during this age that final peace comes. "And ye shall hear of wars and rumours of wars: see that ye be not troubled: for all *these things* must come to pass, but the end is not yet," Mtt 24:6 KJV. So not all of Isaiah 2 has happened yet! The final peace and justice has not come yet. But it is coming very soon. The pride of man will be humbled on ***that day***, Isa 2:17 NASB.

Peter describes the future days of glory in the later part of Acts chapter 3.

Peter, James and John and the other first Christians have been worshipping in the temple courts and have been meeting from house to house. Peter has healed a man in the early verses of Acts 3, a lame man, a cripple, and the crowds are amazed, but Peter puts all of this in perspective. He tells the crowd they should not be astounded as if he had done this by his own righteousness. He says that it is the same Jesus, whom the Jews had murdered, who had healed this man. But he also emphasizes that the great body of Jews, *just like us of the nations ...* acted in ignorance, and Peter acknowledges that was the same for the rulers, they also had acted in ignorance, Acts 3:17. Jesus Himself recognized on the cross that it was in ignorance that they had in these ways fulfilled the Word of God. He said, Father forgive them, they don't really know what they are doing, Lk 23:34. But the things which God had previously announced by His prophets (that the Christ must be rejected as it says in Psalm 22, and be condemned by judicial proceeding as in Isa 53:7-9, and suffer and die as it says in these passages) these things "He has thus fulfilled," Acts 3:18.

In this way Peter speaks of the key Scriptures which Jesus has fulfilled. Jesus had a *wisdom* which none of the rulers of this age has understood; for if they had understood it they would not have crucified the Lord of glory; 1 Cor 2:8. Jesus said it well. "And these things will they do unto you, because they have not known the Father, nor me," Jn 16:3 KJV. But God was fulfilling His promises by the prophets.

So what God has done is what He said He would do, Acts 3:18. Old Testament prophecy has been fulfilled of Jesus' death, burial, and resurrection. What God had said would happen *in Jesus first coming* **has come to pass**. Jesus *had to* suffer, Acts 17:3. He did not cover His face from humiliation, and the only man who could fulfill these prophecies is one like Jesus, who

> .. gave my back to the smiters, and my cheeks to them that plucked off the hair: I hid not my face from shame and spitting. Isa 50:6 KJV

Any so-called Messiah who is not disowned as Jesus of Nazareth was, could not fulfill the scriptures of the deliverer of the world.

> [3] He is despised and rejected of men; a man of sorrows, and acquainted with grief: and we hid as it were *our* faces from him; he was despised, and we esteemed him not.
>
> [5] But he *was* wounded for our transgressions, *he was* bruised for our iniquities: the chastisement of our peace *was* upon him; and with his stripes we are healed. [6] All we like sheep have gone astray; we have turned every one to his own way; and the LORD hath laid on him the iniquity of us all. Isa 53:3, 5-6 KJV

As Jesus told His disciples after His resurrection, it was necessary, it *had to* happen, and they, the believers, had been fools to not see these things *had to* happen, Lk 24:26-27, 44. They were foolish (as we also often are) because they were so slow to believe all that had been spoken by the prophets, Lk 24:25. Jesus died in accordance with the Old Testament Scriptures which said that He had to both suffer and die and be raised again on the third day, 1 Cor 15:3-4.

Some maintain that part of Jesus' first coming failed because the Jews rejected Jesus and that these things will be fulfilled at His *second coming* when He establishes a Jewish kingdom on earth. Some think that present day Israel is the fulfillment of ancient prophecy. However Scripture does not speak of Jesus' failing, does not speak of prophecies falling through, does not speak of postponed governments or kingdoms. Scripture does speak of fulfillment and success, and of the rejection of the Jews as something foreseen by God. **To suggest that God could not pull off His plans, or *failed because of men* is in fact little short of blasphemy.** God is all powerful and can do **what** He wants, **when** He wants. The Scriptures previously discussed prove that those ideas are not true and that the things God announced He has thus fulfilled, Acts 3:18.

With these things being true, you and I need to be among those gently correcting others, 2 Tim 2:25-26. The true answer to men is that they need to turn to God, Acts 3:19a. Repent and be baptized for the forgiveness of sin, Peter had said when he first used the keys of the kingdom in Acts 2:38. We need to not only repent (and to repent means to change our mind) but also we need to turn from our evil ways, and submit to God's ways.

> 6 Seek the LORD while He may be found;
> Call upon Him while He is near. Isa 55:6 NKJV

The most sublime book of prophecy is Isaiah, in this author's opinion. Perhaps it is the most sublime book of all times, excepting perhaps the Gospel of John. Perhaps when the true Glorious Revolution comes, Isaiah will get the recognition in literature which he deserves. Greater things are still to come. We need to repent so that times of refreshing will come.

> 19 Repent ye therefore, and be converted, that your sins may be blotted out, when the times of refreshing shall come from the presence of the Lord; 20 And he shall send Jesus Christ, which before was preached unto you: Acts 3:19-20 KJV

The most accurate technical description of these times of refreshing is in Rom 8:18-25. That passage will be dealt with in detail when heaven is discussed near the end of this volume. The outline is that Christians are to rule "the world to come," the new heavens and new earth, Heb 2:5. You and I can have a foretaste of the world to come, Heb 6:4-5.

At the end time all men will see Jesus sitting on His throne, Mtt 25:31-33. Men will receive the rule of cities and of angels, Lk 19:12, 16-19, 1 Cor 6:2-3. The apostles will rule with the Lord himself, Mtt 19:28-30, and you and I will sit with Jesus on His throne, Rev 3:21. He will wipe away every tear, Rev 21:4. The entire universe will rejoice on that day, Psa 98:1-9. It will be a day of refreshing and wealth such as we have never seen, Isa 66:10-14. In the meantime

Jesus has to stay in heaven for a while.

> ²⁰ and that He may send Jesus, the Christ appointed for you, ²¹ whom heaven must receive **until *the period of restoration*** of all things about which God spoke <u>by the mouth of His holy prophets</u> from **ancient time.** Acts 3:20-21 NASB (*emphasis added*)

So Jesus must stay in heaven until the times of refreshing, the period of restoration, comes. Then men will see the sign of His coming, Mtt 24:30-31. All men will see it, even those who crucified Him, Rev 1:7. Jesus <u>is</u> that special prophet! Moses said that God would send a special prophet, Acts 3:22-24. *It is for <u>all</u> the earth that these blessing have come. Really* it was **from the first**, for **ALL** *the families of the nations*, but was always to come through the Jews, as it did.

> Ye are the children of the prophets, and of the covenant which God made with our fathers, saying unto Abraham, And in thy seed shall all the kindreds of the earth be blessed Acts 3:25 KJV

It is for the Jew first, Acts 3:26, but also for the Greek, that is to say, those of the other nations. The veil of the darkness of the Jews is only lifted in Jesus.

> But their minds were blinded. For until this day the same veil remains unlifted in the reading of the Old Testament, because the veil is taken away in Christ. 2 Cor 3:14 NKJV

We need to seek the water of life, the living waters!

Type and Anti-Type, Symbol and Fulfillment

Model and Fulfillment, **Symbol** and **Reality** is the subject. Sometimes one historical event, person, or thing is symbolic of another event, person, or thing. In Scripture this is often called a type (model/symbol), and anti-type (replacement/fulfillment). It is good for us to remind ourselves the real foundations of "morality" are in "reality". The philosophical names for these things are not that important to this discussion but the concepts are quite important, and the plan is to explore them and see how they work and what is their significance. However a key subject, and an important one, is to correctly apply the truth, recognizing symbolism in our texts, and to see that God generally uses history to produce His comparisons.

So what does the word "type" mean? The Greek word is *tupos* τύπος, meaning a model, a pattern, an example. It is used in passages like Rom 5:14, where Adam is described as a "type" (as it is in the NASB and in the Greek original), or a symbol of the Christ. Some of the "types" are simple, like the Passover lamb representing Jesus (1 Cor 5:7) or Noah's flood as representing baptism's waters (1 Pe 3:20-21).

On a more complex level, let's look in detail at 2 Sam 7:11-16. (See the chart on this page.) It is a prophecy about a son of David who would build a temple of God. Solomon was David's son, and he did build a temple of God. So Scripture says that *Solomon* fulfilled all of this, referring to 2 Samuel 7:

> [17] And it was in the heart of David my father to build an house for the name of the LORD God of Israel. [18] And the LORD said unto David my father, Whereas it was in thine heart to build an house unto my name, thou didst well that it was in thine heart. [19] Nevertheless thou shalt not build the house; but thy son that shall come forth out of thy loins, he shall build the house unto my name. [20] And the LORD hath performed his word that he spake, and I am risen up in the room of David my father, and sit on the throne of Israel, as the LORD promised, and have built an house for the name of the LORD God of Israel.
>
> 1 Kgs 8:17-20 KJV

But let's notice some things that do not seem right about the prophecy if the prophecy is left at this place! God said, "I will establish the throne of his

---

Solomon as a "type," a model, of the Christ, 2 Sam 7:12-15

Solomon fulfills this according to 1 Kgs 8:17-20, AND Jesus does according to Heb 1:5.

Both Solomon and Jesus are descendants of David and both build a "house" for God.

Solomon built a literal "house"/temple, 2 Chron 6:10.

Solomon's kingdom ended in 586 BC, 2 Kings 25.

God was **like** a father to Solomon (*figurative*).

Solomon did wrong and was punished, 1 Kgs 11:11.

God's love for Solomon could be lost, 1 Chron 28:9.

12 "When your days are complete and you lie down with your fathers, I will raise up your descendant after you, who will come forth from you, and I will establish his kingdom.
13 "He shall build a house for My name, and I will establish the throne of his kingdom forever.
14 "I will be a father to him and he will be a son to Me; when he commits iniquity, I will correct him with the rod of men and the strokes of the sons of men,
15 but My lovingkindness shall not depart from him, as I took it away from Saul, whom I removed from before you.
NASB95

Jesus built a spiritual "house"/temple of God, Mtt 16:17-18, 1 Cor 3:16-17, Heb 3:6.

Only Jesus throne is established forever, Lk 1:31-33.

God **was** Jesus Father, Heb 1:5.

Jesus was the Son who did no wrong, 2 Cor 5:21.

The sinless Son of God (and of David) will never lose God's love, Psa 91:11-16.

kingdom forever," 2 Sam 7:13. *However*, Solomon's kingdom did not last *forever*; in fact it only lasted about 400 years.

Also in 2 Sam 7:14 it says that God would be Solomon's father. That might be highly *symbolic* language, but it was not literally so. David was really Solomon's father. Again it says in 2 Sam 7:15, my love will never be taken away from him. But David clearly says that Solomon *could* lose God's favor.

> And thou, Solomon my son, know thou the God of thy father, and serve him with a perfect heart and with a willing mind: for the LORD searcheth all hearts, and understandeth all the imaginations of the thoughts: if thou seek him, he will be found of thee; but **if thou forsake him, he will cast thee off for ever**.
> 1 Chron 28:9 KJV *(emphasis added)*

So what is the story? Did some of this fail? I don't think so. For Heb 1:5 applies this same text, 2 Sam 7:14, to Jesus! Study the chart about Solomon and Jesus on the previous page. *Jesus* is the true son of God when it said God will establish the throne of his kingdom forever, and "I will be a father to him and he will be a son to Me" in 2 Sam 7:13-14 NASB. Solomon serves as a 'pattern,' a "shadow" of the Christ, a "type" if you want to use one of the Scriptural terms. Solomon was figuratively a son of God, and Jesus was literally the Son of God.

When you have language that **doesn't seem to fit**, or that **seems exaggerated**, it is often an indicator that **you are looking at is a 'pattern,' a 'type,' and NOT the completion of a prophecy!** The chart gives a detailed analysis of the passage and how it applies. Notice carefully that as given in the Old Testament, *if* Solomon *is not symbolic* of another greater son of David, ***then the prophecy has plainly failed!***

Now types and patterns provide models both for conduct, and for future events. A key point to remember is that imagery in prophecy is in fact little different in principle, from imagery in the parables. There is a lot to learn about models in Scripture, but there are often clues in the text itself. For instance, in 2 Samuel 7 David wishes to build a temple for the Lord. God denies David that right, but gives a prophecy about David's offspring.

So of this prophecy and fulfillment, ***notice three things:***

1. Both men are said by Scripture to fulfill this prophecy. Let's make the point more emphatic. *When both a "type" and an "anti-type" are considered in a prophecy, then **both are considered as valid "fulfillments" of the prophecy. Both or all** (or how ever many are involved) are considered as part of the prophecy. And if you lose sight of this you will quickly fall into confusion.*

2. When a passage has a type (such as Solomon as a model), and an anti-type (such as Jesus as the fulfillment), some parts may only fit the model, and some parts may only fit the fulfillment, and some parts may fit both the symbol and the fulfillment.

3. The text may go back and forth between the two subjects *with no single*

dividing line intended.

Oh how we often love simple, single, dividing lines which are often so very much contrary to reality.

Still desolate Babylon.

²² How long, ye simple ones, will ye love simplicity? and the scorners delight in their scorning, and fools hate knowledge? ²³ Turn you at my reproof: behold, I will pour out my spirit unto you, I will make known my words unto you. Prov. 1:22-23 KJV

Thus no later than 586 BC (the fall of Solomon's kingdom) a saint of old should have expected another son of David to come and build another temple. What may seem like "exaggeration," things that "don't seem to fit," often allow us to spot a "type."

Even so, "scripture cannot be broken." Jn 10:35 KJV. That is what Jesus said. Not even "the smallest letter or stroke" can fail, Mtt 5:18 NASB. So when the prophets of old said of Old Testament Babylon that she would be completely destroyed like Sodom and Gomorrah, Isa 13:19-22, then it *had to happen. Of Babylon it was said,* "It shall never be inhabited, neither shall it be dwelt in from generation to generation," Isa 13:20 KJV. Like Sodom and Gomorrah it fell in a single day. The historian Herodotus tells the story. And true to the Word of God, Babylon became totally desolate, and has literally never been rebuilt, it has totally ceased to exist as a city. Let's now look at a couple of easy examples of types in the Scriptures.

One is the king of Tyre in Ezekiel 28. Tyre was a city-state on the Mediterranean coast. Ezekiel 28 is talking about what "will" happen (future) to the king of Tyre. But look at the strange things it says about this king! Things which do not fit! It says he was in the garden of Eden, Ezek 28:13. It says that he was an "anointed cherub" (a form of angel) on God's holy mountain in heaven but was cast out because of sin. *Can it really be said that the king of ancient Tyre was an angel in heaven, or was in the garden of Eden?* Exactly who all was in the Garden of Eden? So before one has gone very far in Ezekiel 28, he should know that the king of Tyre is a type, a model of someone who thinks he is a god but it says that he is " a man not God," Ezek 28:2.

Of whom does this speak? You would have to study much further! **Clues:**

compare the destruction of Tyre as prophesied in Ezekiel 27, with the destruction of gospel age Babylon in Revelation 18. This will be touched again later on in Ezekiel 27 and 28.

Then there is the discussion of Babylon the Great in Revelation. When John the apostle describes a worldwide empire that persecutes the saints, he describes her as "Babylon the Great" in Rev 17:4. Thus at the beginning he lets us know that this gospel age empire is "like" literal Babylon of the Old Testament times which had already ceased to exist. That is to say Old Testament Babylon is a "type," a model of New Testament Babylon. Thus, we should not be expect to be able to unravel the prophecies of the gospel age "Babylon," without using the prophetic types in the Old Testament. Obliquely it may be telling us that many of the prophecies of Old Testament Babylon may be like the prophecy in 2 Samuel 7. Parts probably apply exclusively to New Testament "Babylon."

Even so, what is this "Babylon" that persecutes the Lord's holy church. Many "scholars" think it refers to ancient Rome. Rome did sit on seven "hills" (Rev 17:9, depending on your translation), and there are other similarities. But look at what it says about Babylon the Great in Rev 18:2, for she "will not be found any longer." Wow! Just like Old Testament Babylon. Further it says,

> [22] And the voice of harpers, and musicians, and of pipers, and trumpeters, shall be heard no more at all in thee; ... [23] And the light of a candle shall shine no more at all in thee; and the voice of the bridegroom and of the bride shall be heard no more at all in thee: ... Rev 18:22-23 KJV

But there are still weddings in Rome! There are still harpists, musicians, flute players. This is not that complicated. So ancient Rome may be a "type" or model of the gospel age Babylon that oppresses the church world-wide, but she is not the ultimate fulfillment! Rome may be one of the "types" of the New Testament Babylon, but in this matter she is not like Babylon of old; she still exists! She is not as a stone thrown into the sea, "and will not be found any longer." Rev 18:21. Is Rome no doubt included in the prophecy, just like Solomon was "included" in 2 Samuel 7? Yes. Is she the "anti-type," the ultimate fulfillment of Revelation 18? It does not appear so. She appears to be dropped off in a matter of speaking, much as one might say that Solomon is dropped off as being the ultimate "Son of David" who will build the true temple of the LORD.

So a couple of straight forward "models" in prophecy have been identified. Prophecy can get complicated, but seeing that a model is involved is often quite simple. More than that, if you miss these types in Scripture, you will miss a great deal of God's message for you.

John the Baptist and his disciples understood these principles, and they asked Jesus, "Are You the Coming One, or do we look for another?" Mtt 11:3 NKJV.

The next question is about how to follow these "types"/"models." How do you know when two prophecies are talking about the same thing?

A good example is following the prophecies of the Savior. How would you see the promises when they came about? How would you know when you saw the fulfillment? How would you gladly become a part of these things, instead like so many, stumbling at the prophecies.

This is about finding patterns, types, or themes in Scripture. Now type or *tupos* τύπος means a pattern, example, a model. *It is a 'type' of* something, or (to use the modern term) it is a "prototype" of something. In the NASB *tupos* is translated "example" (3 times), examples (twice), form (twice), images (once), imprint (once), model (once), pattern (3 times), and type (once). You may see other sets of variations in other translations.

A more modern word that fits the sense of *tupos* is the word "prototype." The dictionary defines it as "a first or preliminary model of something, ... from which other forms are developed or copied ... a typical example of something ... the archetypical example of a class" of things. We use "prototype" in the technical sense, and this is really the way I think we should consider the Old Testament and New Testament types—as sort of a prototype of the fulfillment.

God *often* uses symbolism, and this bears on how to properly treat the "truth" of something. Some want to ignore all symbolic language, however, just

The tabernacle (tent) of worship of Moses' Law was a "copy and shadow of the heavenly things," Heb 8:5 NKJV. We study "types" to learn of future things.

because a Scripture is symbolic does not indicate that it is meaningless. Jesus is pictured in the Old Testament as a shepherd and as a Passover lamb. Although this is not literal, it is definitely not meaningless. The parable of the sower in

Luke 8 is symbolic but not meaningless. As noted, it is good to practice reading prophecies that are already fulfilled. Moses tells us in Deuteronomy 18 (noted earlier) that the future special prophet of God (Jesus) will be like Moses. Think through these Scriptures, and then read about Moses in the Old Testament to learn how prophecy works. Scripture frequently uses one man or king in Scripture as a pattern or type for some future man or king. Or Scripture will use one event or happening as a pattern or type for some future event. These symbolic prophecies often form recurring themes which the alert reader should sense.

Sometimes there are indicators of a pattern or symbol. We are clearly told that Jesus is to be a pattern for our conduct.

5 Let this mind be in you, which was also in Christ Jesus: 6 Who, being in the form of God, thought it not robbery to be equal with God: 7 But made himself of no reputation, and took upon him the form of a servant, and was made in the likeness of men: Phil 2:5-6 KJV

So sometimes a pattern for our learning is not vague or subtle at all but is very straight forward. So the clear message is that you should use Jesus' attitudes as a pattern or model for our attitudes.

On the other hand, sometimes a symbol is very subtle. It says in Rom 5:14 that Adam was a type, a model, a pattern, of the Christ (NKJV, NASB, ESV, etc.

The KJV translates *tupos* 'type', as 'figure'). Then it explains about Adam as a type in Rom 5:16-19, and in 1 Corinthians 15. *It is more than fair after all, Paul says in Romans 5.* He talks about life and death in this text. You know, sin is a universal problem. The Bible did not invent sin, so to speak. If you threw away the Bible, you would still have the problem, but you would not know how or why it happened, nor have even a clue as to how this mess could be "cured.".

There are many types and symbols in Scripture. The tabernacle of the early ages of Israel is spoken of in Heb 8:5 as a copy and a shadow of God's throne in heaven. Adam was just one man, but his actions affected all who followed him. Christ was just one man, but his actions affected all who followed Him. There is a first Adam and a last Adam. It should be emphasized this is not speaking of myths. Rather it is LORD God having history happen in symbolic ways.

And so it is written, *"The first man Adam became a living being."*

The last Adam became a life-giving spirit. 1Cor 15:45 NKJV

But there are differences between the type and the fulfillment. Adam does symbolize Christ, but Paul emphasizes in Rom 5:15 that the free gift is not like the transgression. The Greek word for transgression or trespass or offense is the word *pa-ráp-tō-ma* παράπτωμα. It means a false step, a slip, fall, stumbling. So Paul says if many died through the offense, there was much more good effect which came from God's grace in Jesus Christ, abounding to many. It is not really

like the effect of sin, Paul says in Rom 5:16. Adam with one sin brought judgment and condemnation to our whole race. But Jesus coming after many sins, resulted in the free gift of God's Son, thus giving us forgiveness and justification.

By one man's sin, death came to reign over all men, Rom 5:17. Death was sovereign; death ruled. But now by one man, the Christ, life rules, life reigns, over those who will receive the free gift. Adam's one sin, Rom 5:12, led to condemnation to all, Rom 5:18a. But Christ's one act of righteousness on the cross of Calvary results in justification to all, Rom 5:18b. Adam's disobedience made many men sinners, Rom 5:19a. But now Christ's obedience, will make *many* righteous, Rom 5:19b.

The old head of the race of fleshly men was Adam, and his offspring are all like him in sin and death. The new head of the new race of spiritual men is Jesus Christ. Those who really belong to Him, those who are born of Him (as also men were formerly born of Adam) become like Him in righteousness and life.

> [21] For since by man *came* death, by man *came* also the resurrection of the dead. [22] For as in Adam all die, even so in Christ shall all be made alive. 1Cor 15:21-22 KJV

The symbolism in this case has most of all to do with the breadth and depth of their effects. Each had in their own way very profound effects on all who followed them, on all who were born of them; although the effect of each was actually the exact opposite of the other. The parallel is that each was the head and the fountain of a new race of men, with all of their posterity playing out their particular moral qualities. But each in his own order will be made right.

> [23] But every man in his own order: Christ the firstfruits; afterward they that are Christ's at his coming. [24] Then *cometh* the end, when he shall have delivered up the kingdom to God, even the Father; when he shall have put down all rule and all authority and power. [25] For he must reign, till he hath put all enemies under his feet. [26] The last enemy *that* shall be destroyed *is* death. 1Cor 15:23-26 KJV

Christ is the first fruits and the rest is about those who are Christ's at His second coming.

> [45] And so it is written, The first man Adam *was made* a living soul; the last Adam was made a quickening spirit. [46] Howbeit that *was* not first which is spiritual, but that which is natural; and afterward that which is spiritual. [47] The first man *is* of the earth, earthy: the second man *is* the Lord from heaven. [48] As *is* the earthy, such *are* they also that are earthy: and as *is* the heavenly, such *are* they also that are heavenly. [49] And as we have borne the image of the earthy, we shall also bear the image of the heavenly. 1Cor 15:45-49 KJV

The full change will be later. We who are flesh and blood cannot inherit the kingdom of God, but at the last trumpet of God we who are Christ's will be changed, and death will be swallowed up in victory, 1 Cor 15:50-55.

Notice the balance in *things!* The effects of Jesus Christ are as wide as the effects of Adam. *By one man's sin,* death came to all men. We did not deserve it. But also *by one man's obedience* righteousness came to all men. We did not deserve that either. In fact, we really deserve death *for our own sins.* By one sin we became liable to death! *We did not deserve it.* But by one man's obedience we became liable to be justified. *We did not deserve that either.* By one man's sin we received a tendency to sin. *We did not really deserve it, but that is how sin works.* But we really did not have to sin.

> The soul that sinneth, it shall die. The son shall not bear the iniquity of the father, neither shall the father bear the iniquity of the son: the righteousness of the righteous shall be upon him, and the wickedness of the wicked shall be upon him. Ezek 18:20 KJV

So Jesus was like Adam, not that He was a sinner, but that
1. He was the beginning of new race of men, created in the image of God for good things and for ruler-ship.
2. His actions affected all of His descendants after Him. Adam's actions condemned all men to sin and death, and Jesus' actions gave life and peace and righteousness to all those who are born of Him, who are born of water and the Spirit Jn 3:5.

If we perish, it will be for our own sins, not those of others. But God has made a way out for those who will receive it. Count the cost, Lk 14:28, and determine to give yourselves to Jesus. But if you refuse?

What will you do, when the angels come for you?
What will you say,
when God asks you to pay?

So notice that the links between many themes and types are often very loose, and the points of similarity are often related to a few key ideas, not to everything concerning the model. A "seed" of woman theme starts in Gen 3:15.

> And I will put enmity between thee and the woman, and between thy seed and her seed; it shall bruise thy head, and thou shalt bruise his heel. KJV

But there is precious little direct reference to these "seed" who will strive with each other. Later there are the promises made to Abraham, Gen 12:2-3, and there is the promise to what is in Hebrew called the "seed" of Abraham, Gen 12:7. Again it speaks of Abraham's "seed" in places like, Gen 22:18, and it speaks of "O ye **seed** of Israel his servant, ye children of Jacob, his chosen ones." 1Chron 16:13 KJV.

"Seed" (as used of the promise) is normally, and strangely, singular. The promise is "Thy seed will I establish for ever, and build up thy throne to all generations." Psa 89:4. And Zech 8:12 says "*there will be* peace for the seed," it will be prosperous, NASB. It is all in all quite a collection of promises made to "the seed."

There is a special prophet promised—a prophet like Moses who has to be listened to Deut 18:15, 18-19.

There is also a special king. A king who is the "seed" in Hebrew, the seed/descendant of David, 2 Sam 7:12-13. So now the seed idea of the woman and the seed of Abraham, begins to overlap with a special descendant of Abraham, David, and his "seed." That special king was evidently not Solomon, even though Solomon was a type of this king, as in Scriptures like 2 Chron 6:10, along with those Scriptures looked at earlier. But also in Hebrews it quotes these verses as speaking of Jesus Christ, Heb 1:5.

Then hundreds of years after Solomon died Isaiah speaks of this king as still to come. It clearly speaks of a king because it says He will be on the throne of David's kingdom. It says this king will come as a child, Isa 9:6-7. So no later than the time of Isaiah there is an additional line of evidence that Solomon was not that special one, even though he was a king and a lawgiver and prophet whose words we read in Scripture even today. *No! Solomon was just a "parable," so to speak, of Jesus. He was a foretaste, a prototype to use the modern term, but not the ultimate fulfillment of the special seed of David!* There are wonderful things the king will do, establishing justice and truth and delivering the poor.

> ⁴ But with righteousness He will judge the poor,
> And decide with fairness for the afflicted of the earth;
> And He will strike the earth with the rod of His mouth,
> And with the breath of His lips He will slay the wicked.
> ⁵ Also righteousness will be the belt about His loins,
> And faithfulness the belt about His waist.
> ⁶ And the wolf will dwell with the lamb,
> And the leopard will lie down with the young goat,
> And the calf and the young lion and the fatling together;
> And a little boy will lead them. Isa 11:4-6 NASB

Obviously not *all* of this has come to pass *yet*. The desire for compassion and peace in all of the world of nature is at the root of the appeal of many of our modern cartoons and animated stories for children. They reflect something missing in our hearts and in our lives, that will only be fulfilled in Jesus Christ.

Also see there is a "Branch," Isa 4:2. It will be a **"man"** called Branch, Zech 6:12, who builds the temple. So the Branch is clearly identified as a man. And Jeremiah says the Branch is of David.

> In those days, and at that time, will I cause the Branch of righteousness to grow up unto David; and he shall execute judgment and righteousness in the land. Jer 33:15 KJV

Now the prophecies of Branch link to the "seed" of David. Much later we see ourselves as becoming part of the Branch so to speak, for

I am the vine, ye are the branches: He that abideth in me, and I in him, the same bringeth forth much fruit: for without me ye can do nothing. Jn 15:5 KJV

Most of the links between these topics are "loose"! But they are true links; one might call them "soft" links, but they are links all the same. Seldom are there any direct statements that all these things are equal.

So you have to look for:
Recurring Words and Ideas.
Sometimes you are looking for synonyms
or other words that have the same general idea in more than one way.

You are looking also **for overlapping thoughts/concepts**. The idea of
the great prophet being like Moses, a ruler and a leader and a lawgiver
of God's people is *related to the concept* to being a king over
God's people. A king's job is to make laws and
lead God's people, and rule them.

Don't ignore facts that "don't seem to fit!" These are often the signal that you are dealing with a model, not a fulfillment. The models are often very figurative (like Isaac in Heb 11:18-19), while the fulfillment is often very literal (like Jesus resurrection).

Notice as a side point that *the most important commands of the* Old *Testament are NOT in the Ten Commandments*! They are in Deut 6:5,

You shall love the LORD your God with all your heart, with all your soul, and with all your strength. NKJV

and in Lev 19:18.

You shall not take vengeance, nor bear any grudge against the children of your people, but you shall love your neighbor as yourself: I *am* the LORD NKJV

The Ten Commandments only *reflect* these central ideas! They were placed so that men had to study to figure it out! Would we have noticed that these were the central commands of the Old Testament on our own? Some did.

25 And behold, a certain lawyer stood up and tested Him, saying, "Teacher, what shall I do to inherit eternal life?" 26 He said to him, "What is written in the law? What is your reading *of it*?" 27 So he answered and said, ""*You shall love the LORD* your God with all your heart, with all your soul, with all your strength, and with all your mind,' and '*your neighbor as yourself.*'" 28 And He said to him, "You have answered rightly; do this and you will live." Lk 10:25-28 NKJV

Would we have noticed these things? Or do we need to change the way we study? Notice how easy it would be to miss ALL of these themes! So there is a need for care in reading noted in passages like, "(let the reader understand)"

Mark 13:14. It is often left to the intelligent reader to figure it out, and see the links! There is a need *to think through **the ideas** and **not just the words***. In this way the minor differences between translations may not be significant, and may sometimes even help you link topics to together, if they "click" with you. **If we think through the ideas we will see that these things are related, and start talking about them together and it will be natural to see there is a link!**

One last thing should be noted about types and their fulfillments, the anti-types. **The types often come close after the prophecy, but the anti-type is often at considerable distance from the type, maybe thousands of years.** So it was that Moses (the type) lived in the fifteenth century BC, but Jesus (the anti-type) came over fourteen hundred years later. Solomon (the type) came soon after the prophecy in 2 Samuel 7, but Jesus (the anti-type) came nearly a thousand years later. *This is not an ironclad rule, but it is a very common pattern in prophecy.*

What then is God's strategy in giving us these various *examples*?
1.) Things are arranged so that *we won't "get it"* **unless** *we are **really** looking and studying.* God rewards those who "diligently seek him," Heb 11:6 KJV. **2.)** If we are really looking for it and cannot understand what is about to happen one way, we may understand it another way. So we have more than one opportunity to "get it." This is similar to the parables of the kingdom. First Jesus tells us the kingdom is like this, and then tells us it like that or the other thing ... so that if we do not understand this way, we may understand it that way. But if you are not thinking and comparing, you will not get any of it. **To get what you need, you have to be dedicated to the Word of God.**

Faith is such a theme. Faith or belief in what God said is implied in the story of Abel in Gen 4:4, but not specifically mentioned. But later it specifically talks of Abel's faith in Heb 11:4. One more time, look for the *same* or *similar* words, but also look for the same *concepts* in action. Faith is mentioned in the story of Abraham as the very basis for God counting him as righteous in Gen 15:6. Now faith overlaps with the subject of being trustworthy, so there is a need to consider the idea of trust in studying about faith, as Jeremiah says,

> [7] Blessed is the man that trusteth in the LORD, and whose hope the LORD is. [8] For he shall be as a tree planted by the waters, and that spreadeth out her roots by the river, and shall not see when heat cometh, but her leaf shall be green; and shall not be careful in the year of drought, neither shall cease from yielding fruit. Jer 17:7-8 KJV

The real issue is not really believing Scripture, Lk 24:25. The Pharisees had trouble with this. The rich man and his brothers had trouble with this in Luke 16. If we really believe, it will change how we live. The 600,000 men of Israel had trouble with this as can be seen in Hebrews 3. We need to make sure we don't have trouble with this.

> [12] Take heed, brethren, lest there be in any of you an evil heart of unbelief, in departing from the living God. [13] But exhort one another

daily, while it is called Today; lest any of you be hardened through the deceitfulness of sin. Heb 3:12-13 KJV

We need to be born of the seed of Jesus Christ by the living and abiding Word, 1 Pe 1:23. The idea of a descendant crosses with the idea of the Word, and with you and me. Jesus plants the seed, and He said, "He who sows the good seed is the Son of Man," Matt 13:37 NKJV. And you get into Jesus only one way, by baptism, Gal 3:27.

> **A lot of ground has been covered here. These ideas will**
> **come back again and again. Mark this section,**
> **so you can easily review type and anti-type.**

Time and Image in Prophecy

Now is the time for a genuine Prophecy Laboratory. Now this Christ who is to have such tremendous effects is spoken of in many passages and in many ways. Some of this is written in the first person by someone else, like for instance David in Psalm 22, who at first seems to speak of himself until you look deeper. This is a test of these ideas about prophecy, looking to see how or why we understand prophecy, *or how or why* we *misunderstand* it, and to learn by practice how to listen to the Words of the Spirit. Read along in Psalm 22 in your Bibles, and follow the study this psalm.

Someone is in trouble in Psa 22:1-2. This is written by David (as it says in the title), but it is also written about Jesus, for He also says *"My God, My God, why have you forsaken Me?"* Mtt 27:46 NKJV.

But He still trusts God, Psa 22:3-4.

"I'm a worm and no man," He says in Psa 22:6-11 KJV. I have been the "worm" on a job before, and perhaps you have too. This idea of the Messiah as someone who is despised is, of course, the same spoken of in other prophecies.

> ² For he shall grow up before him as a tender plant, and as a root out of a dry ground: he hath no form nor comeliness; and when we shall see him, there is no beauty that we should desire him. ³ He is despised and rejected of men; a man of sorrows, and acquainted with grief: and we hid as it were our faces from him; he was despised, and we esteemed him not. Isa 53:2-3 KJV

Then bulls of Bashan surround Him, Psa 22:12-13. It is males that surround Him. They are strong well fed bulls, and Bashan is on the eastern shore of the Sea of Galilee, famous for its fertile pastures, and it includes the Golan heights of fame in the Mid-Eastern wars of the past generation. It seems to be saying it is Jews who surround Him.

It describes the crucifixion in Psa 22:14.

Of course, the truth is that Jesus died of a broken heart. Literally! Out poured water *and* blood, a ruptured heart is what is seen in Jn 19:31b-34, an aneurysm. Notice that the time element as described here is almost colloquial. Jesus is already dead in Psa 22:15. Next, it describes a method of execution, exactly what happened in gospels.

> 16 For dogs have surrounded me;
> A band of evildoers has encompassed me;
> They pierced my hands and my feet.
> 17 I can count all my bones.
> They look, they stare at me;
> 18 They divide my garments among them,
> And for my clothing they cast lots Psa 22:16-18 NASB

Jesus was crucified by the Romans. *No one* seriously doubts the authenticity of this psalm. This psalm was written by David about 1000 BC, but Rome itself was not even established until about 756 BC, or about 250 years *after* the prophecy was written! It's nearly a 1,000 years later that Rome gained control over Palestine and used their horrible method of execution—death by crucifixion.

When the chief priests want to taunt the dying Messiah, they use words from Psalm 22:8, as can be seen in Mtt 27:41-43. They think it is a joke that He claims to be the Messiah of Psalm 22. They recognized that Psalm 22 was Messianic but didn't recognize that they were fulfilling it!

But it really seems contradictory here!

He says His strength is dried up in Psa 22:15. Well I guess so, because His heart had ruptured in verse 14! And His tongue cleaves to his jaws? Hadn't he already died, and He was laid in the dust of death? At any rate, He is definitely dead *and* buried by verse 15.

However notice what happens next, a band of evil doers surround Him, "dogs" it says. But didn't that happen *before* He died? Anyway, they did surround Him. But look at what is next! They pierce His hands and His feet, Psa 22:16. What? They kill Him, His heart ruptures, and *then* they make holes in His hands and His feet? His heart ruptures, they bury Him, and *then* they mutilate the corpse? That is not impossible, but it doesn't sound normal. This doesn't seem in order does it? As has been pointed out, the very first verse says, "My God, My God, why have you forsaken me," which is really in the middle of the story. What's going on? This is an advanced concept in prophecy:

The principle of "Kitchen Table Time."

It just like talking around the kitchen table describing our trip to town: "Oh, we went to town. We went to the bookstore, and to the mall, and we had to get some groceries. Oh yeah, we saw Tommy and Melissa eating at the restaurant. Did you know that Melissa is pregnant? And we found some good deals on shirts at the mall. Late in the afternoon we were so tired we had to eat, and we had to get some auto parts. We didn't have enough money so we had gone to the bank first. And after we had gotten the groceries we were so tired we just had to go home and plop down and rest!"

Did you notice this story was not told in order? The book store was mentioned first but we actually went to the bank first. We mentioned Tommy and Melissa early, but actually that was near the end of the day. And you cannot tell (from what we told you) exactly *when* we went to the mall. You just know we *did* in fact go to mall! Of course, this is the normal way we talk to each other.

And this is the normal way God talks to us!

Do you always speak in strict chronological order? No way! Neither does God! When God is telling His saints what the future holds, He speaks to us the same way we speak to each other, as a friend. He uses "kitchen table time" with us. How do you tell what happens first or second? You have to listen to the conversation. You have to think!

I can count all my bones, Psa 22:17.

Now that didn't happen *after* they laid Him in the dust of death, did it? Or after His heart ruptured did it? Not a chance! They gambled for His clothes in Psa 22:18. That is recorded of course in Mtt 27:35. But did this happen *after* they laid Him in the dust of death? Positively not! Pay attention to the conversation. It is kitchen table time. It is a colloquial time element in prophecy.

But then there is a prayer for deliverance, Psa 22:19-21. Notice that the "sword" in verse 20 is "symbolic" of violent death. He wasn't literally killed by a "sword," but a literal spear did pierce His side *after* His death. But you have to ask, what do you mean save Him? He's dead! **How can you say, God help Him**, God has already forsaken Him? He is dead. His heart ruptures in verse 14, He is buried in verse 15. His body is pierced? **How can you say**, "O Lord, be not far off"? **GOD WAS FAR OFF! WHERE WAS GOD?** But I speak as a man and God did hear Him, and deliver Him. But then ...

He breaks into praise in Psa 22:21!

It seems to be talking about the subject of this psalm praising God in the assembly, in the church, in the synagogue. It seems to be speaking of the one in trouble, the dying one, the dead one. But stand in awe of God the psalmist says.

> [22] I will declare thy name unto my brethren: in the midst of the congregation will I praise thee. [23] Ye that fear the LORD, praise him; all ye the seed of Jacob, glorify him; and fear him, all ye the seed of Israel. [24] For he hath not despised nor abhorred the affliction of the afflicted; neither hath he hid his face from him; but when he cried unto him, he heard. Psa 22:22-24 KJV

But how can you say He has not abhorred nor despised the affliction of the afflicted? Didn't He die? And all of this by the Word of the Holy Spirit of God? **This passage is of course, in these subtle ways, speaking of the resurrection of Jesus Christ, a thousand years before hand.**

Then it describes the preaching of the gospel. "From you *comes* praise in the assembly ... All the ends of the earth will ... turn to the LORD," Psa 22:25-28 NASB. The afflicted shall eat because of Him, just as it says in Isa 53:5-6. This is being fulfilled now! America IS the end of the earth from Jerusalem, and this gospel of salvation is being declared in assemblies in America and all over the world. All the ends of the earth will hear, for at the last day some will be saved from every nation, tongue and tribe, Rev 7:9. Look, all the proud, the prosperous, will bow down before Him.

> All the prosperous of the earth will eat and worship,
> All those who go down to the dust will bow before Him,
> Even he who cannot keep his soul alive. Psa 22:29 NASB

So let's dare to make a dogmatic statement here:
This part of Psalm 22 is not yet fulfilled.

There are many proud outside our services today. Today they refuse to bow their knee before the Lord and God of heaven and earth. But one day they will have to. This is the same prophecy given in Phil 2:9-11, and also in Rom 14:11, which there is not enough time to cover now. *This has not happened yet.* It will be fulfilled, will happen, but it has not happened yet.

Notice the time element in this psalm.

Time in this psalm is like that of a movie. There are flash-backs. There are visions of the future. In a modern movie, there are no signs saying, "meanwhile back at the ranch." Instead, you have to pay attention to the movie. Prophecy is in this way like an ancient play or a modern movie. *Notice that:*

- Verse 1 is in the middle of the crucifixion.
- Verses 2-18 cover the conflict with the Jews *and* the crucifixion.
- Verses 22-24 cover the resurrection itself.
- Verses 25-28 cover the <u>whole Christian age</u>, the preaching of the gospel up to and beyond our own time in human history.
- Verse 29 goes <u>beyond the end of time</u>, when all men will bow their knee to Jesus.
- Verses 30-31 drop back to speak again of the preaching of the gospel during our age.

See how easy it is to make foolish assumptions about time in prophecy?

And another dogmatic statement!

Not all Old Testament

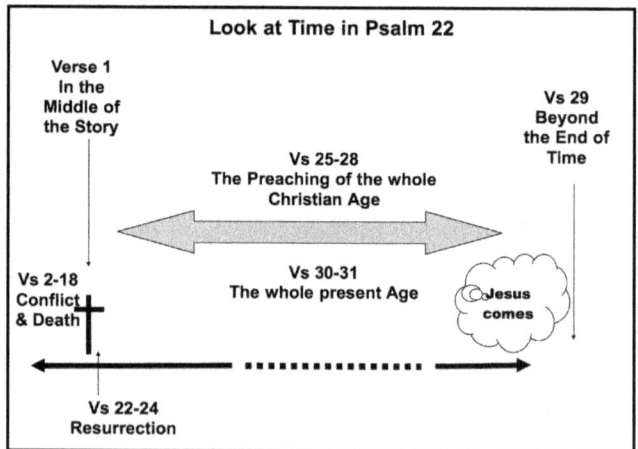

Look at Time in Psalm 22

Verse 1 In the Middle of the Story

Vs 29 Beyond the End of Time

Vs 25-28 The Preaching of the whole Christian Age

Vs 2-18 Conflict & Death

Vs 30-31 The whole present Age

Jesus comes

Vs 22-24 Resurrection

prophecy has been fulfilled. Now some in the church have misinterpreted Luke 24, and Acts 3, and claimed as much, but that is clearly not the case. Once you realize this, you can spot many prophecies that are not fulfilled. Take an easy one such as the ending of all wars.

> 8 Come, behold the works of the LORD,
> Who has wrought desolations in the earth.
> 9 He makes wars to cease to the end of the earth;
> He breaks the bow and cuts the spear in two;
> He burns the chariots with fire. Psa 46:8-9 NASB

This will happen one day, but it hasn't happened yet. There are still physical wars in our world, and there are still spiritual wars in our world, both inside and outside the church, and we are to put on the whole armor of God so we can wage a good warfare (Eph 6:12-13, 1 Tim 1:18).

So we have more homework to do!

We need to study in more detail Scriptures we have neglected. The gospel of Matthew makes an ideal prophecy laboratory for further study.

We are inviting you to become a good part of Psalm 22, that is to say part of Psa 22:30-31. He died for you, that you might not have to die forever. He lives for you, to deliver you at the proper time, and to protect you all the way. Will you accept Him now? Why wait until it is too late? Just like Paul, arise and be baptized and wash away your sins, calling on the name of the Lord, Acts 22:16.

Of the government of Christ and of the increase, there will be no end, Isa 9:6-7. Everyone will have to submit to this king. *Everyone*, Psa 22:28-29! Everyone has to bow to Him, Phil 2:9-11. *He is* Lord of lords, *He is* King of kings, *He is* the ultimate Master of all masters.

If we don't *worship and serve* this King ... we will be punished for our own sins forever, *as we deserve!* "And it shall come to pass, *that* every soul, which will not hear that prophet, shall be destroyed from among the people." Acts 3:23 KJV.

Look at some other patterns in prophecy. For instance, look at circumcision. Early in the Old Testament God made a covenant with Abraham, Gen 12:1-3. Then much later Paul says this promise means that Abraham's descendants would inherit the world, Rom 4:13. So a very valid question is how these promises apply. Circumcision was an important part of the covenant with Abraham.

> And the uncircumcised man child whose flesh of his foreskin is not circumcised, that soul shall be cut off from his people; he hath broken my covenant. Gen 17:14 KJV

In other words, it was to be the death penalty for those who are not circumcised. These principles came into operation later on, when Moses came under judgment because he had not kept this covenant with his sons. Perhaps because of pressure from his wife (but this is speculation), but the Lord sought to put Moses to death, and then Zipporah his wife circumcised their son.

[24] And it came to pass by the way in the inn, that the LORD met him, and sought to kill him. [25] Then Zipporah took a sharp stone, and cut off the foreskin of her son, and cast *it* at his feet, and said, Surely a bloody husband *art* thou to me. Ex 4:24-26 KJV

Circumcision was of course repeated in the Old Law, for instance in Leviticus 12. Even then it was recognized that the true circumcision was spiritual; it was of the heart. Deut. 10:16, "So circumcise your heart, and stiffen your neck no longer," NASB. And again in Deut. 30:6,

And the LORD thy God will circumcise thine heart, and the heart of thy seed, to love the LORD thy God with all thine heart, and with all thy soul, that thou mayest live. KJV

In other words, *even in the Old Testament* the true circumcision was to be of the heart. Along this line, Jeremiah told the men of Judah to circumcise their hearts, and not just their flesh, Jer 4:4.

It has already been pointed out, the covenant given through Abraham is still in effect. That is the whole point of Galatians 3. Moses' law "which came four hundred and thirty years later, does not invalidate a covenant previously ratified by God," Gal 3:17 NASB. Paul goes on to say that the old law was just a temporary schoolmaster to bring us to Christ, Gal 3:24. "But after that faith is come, we are no longer under a schoolmaster," Gal 3:25 KJV. Paul goes on to say "if ye *be* Christ's, then are *ye* Abraham's seed, and heirs according to the promise," Gal 3:29 KJV.

But many Pharisees began to teach physical circumcision as necessary to salvation, Acts 15:1. A debate occurred, and the end of it was that faith in Jesus was the center, and not the physical commands of the Old Testament.

[19] "Therefore I judge that we should not trouble those from among the Gentiles who are turning to God, [20] but that we write to them to abstain from things polluted by idols, *from* sexual immorality, *from* things strangled, and *from* blood. [21] For Moses has had throughout many generations those who preach him in every city, being read in the synagogues every Sabbath." Acts 15:19-21 NKJV

At this point comes the question: when does one leave the literal command behind, and concentrate on the "spiritual reality" behind the command? There are some clear statements in Scripture concerning circumcision. Christ abolished the law and commandments in His flesh, and the reasons are given for this abolition of the law, that the Jews and nations will be united. In Eph 2:13 it says that "you who once were far off have been brought near by the blood of Christ" NKJV, and Christ won the unity of Jews and the nations by breaking down the barriers. Eph 2:14, He has "abolished in His flesh the enmity, *that is*, the law of commandments *contained* in ordinances," Eph 2:15 NKJV. Christ abolished the law in His flesh. Abolished is the Greek word *katargeō* καταργέω, which means to "render ineffective, nullify, cancel; destroy, abolish, do away with (passive to pass away, cease); use up," "to cause to cease." Thayer says it means "to deprive of its strength, make barren (A.V. cumber), Luke 13:7; to cause a person or a thing to have no further efficiency; to deprive of force, influence, power (A.V. bring to naught, make of none effect)." So the **true** Jew is not physical, and the commands are not in the final sense physical, but spiritual.

> [28] For he is not a Jew, which is one outwardly; neither *is that* circumcision, which is outward in the flesh: [29] But he *is* a Jew, which is one inwardly; and circumcision *is that* of the heart, in the spirit, *and* not in the letter; whose praise is not of men, but of God. Rom 2:28-29 KJV

True circumcision is by the Spirit, and it is by the Spirit in true baptism.

> [11] In Him you were also circumcised with the circumcision made without hands, by putting off the body of the sins of the flesh, by the circumcision of Christ, [12] buried with Him in baptism, in which you also were raised with *Him* through faith in the working of God, who raised Him from the dead. Col 2:11-12 NKJV

Paul goes even further and says if any one wants to keep physical circumcision he is obligated to keep the whole law, and is fallen from grace, Gal 5:3-4.

There are many other examples where the type is spiritual and symbolic:

- Elijah is a 'pattern' of John the Baptist, Mal 4:5. And this was talked about by Jesus in Mtt 11:12-14.
- And Jesus was *like* Adam according to Romans 5, as was pointed out.
- And the Messiah had to be called out of Egypt, according to Mtt 2:15 and Hosea 11:1.

Now some things in prophecy are easier to grasp than others, and some are so casual, so subtle that they are very hard to recognize. In fact one wouldn't catch them unless they were reading and thinking and trying to catch shades of meanings in every line. Once again, most of the links between these topics are "loose"! By and large there are no direct statements that these things are equal. There is a need to think through *the ideas and not just the words*. If you think through the ideas you will see that these things are related and start talking about them together and it will be natural to see there is a link! But if you don't think through these things, you won't get any of it.

So there is a need to be put together what can be seen about patterns.

Let us look at how the author of the book of Hebrews detects a type. In Ex 33:14 God promised to go with the Israelites, and he said, "My presence shall go *with thee*, and I will give thee rest," KJV. Some did not receive it, but He gave rest to many, and God encourages those Israelites who have received an inheritance East of the Jordan to help their brethren in their conquest until they also receive their reward, Deut 3:20. But 400 years later David says "Today" they won't enter my rest, in Psa 95:7, 11. So the author of Hebrews says in Hebrews chapter 4 that Psalm 95 doesn't fit the physical rest in Canaan.

³ For we who have believed enter that rest, just as He has said,
  "As I swore in My wrath,
     they shall not enter My rest,"
although His works were finished from the foundation of the world. ⁴
For He has said somewhere concerning the seventh day: "And God
rested on the seventh day from all His works"; ⁵ and again in this
passage, "They shall not enter My rest." Heb 4:3-5 nasb

So what of the "rest" for God's people, Heb 4:1? Some had the gospel preached
to them, but it didn't do them any good, Heb 4:2. But those who have believed
will enter that rest, Heb 4:3. Now here in verse 3, the author of Hebrew quotes
from Psa 95:11 about many Jews not entering God's rest, and links this to
God's resting from the creation. Then he quotes Gen 2:2 in Hebrews 4. "For He
has said somewhere concerning the seventh day: "And God rested on the
seventh day from all His works"; and again in this passage, "They shall
not enter My rest,"" Heb 4:4-5 nasb. So God says in a future sense of the
Jews, "They **shall not** enter My rest," (future tense, emphasis added). At
this point the author of Hebrews reasons

⁶ Therefore, since it remains for some to enter it, and those who
formerly had good news preached to them failed to enter because of
disobedience, ⁷ He again fixes a certain day, "Today," saying through
David after so long a time just as has been said before, "Today if you
hear His voice, Do not harden your hearts." ⁸ For if Joshua had given
them rest, He would not have spoken of another day after that,"
Heb 4:6-8 nasb

So the land of Canaan was not the real rest for the children of God. Canaan
and the Sabbath days of old were symbolic of the eternal rest in heaven.

⁹ There remaineth therefore a rest to the people of God. ¹⁰ For he that
is entered into his rest, he also hath ceased from his own works, as God
did from his.
¹¹ Let us labour therefore to enter into that rest, lest any man fall after
the same example of unbelief. Heb 4:9-11 kjv

Those early covenants do not have the reality, but only "a copy and a shadow of the heavenly things," Heb 8:5 nasb. "... they *relate* only to food and drink
and various washings, regulations for the body imposed until a time of reformation," Heb 9:10 nasb. Christ did not enter a mere symbol or copy of the true
holy place of rest, but into heaven itself, Heb 9:24. The niv is giving the sense of
Col 2:17, when it says, "These are a shadow of the things that were to come; the
reality, however, is found in Christ." The Old Testament only contains "a
shadow of good things to come, and not the very image," Heb 10:1 kjv.

So there are **two rests!** And the land of Canaan is intended to be symbolic
of the final land of rest, what is commonly called "heaven." It is as sung in the

old hymn, "To Canaan's Land I'm On My Way."

It is not that we cannot or should not learn from the Old Sabbath. But Paul says to let no one judge you about food or drink or a sabbath day, because these things are mere shadows, Col 2:16-17. It is a lot like circumcision or giving. It is not that we cannot learn from physical circumcision (even physically and we should) but Old Testament physical circumcision was in the final sense *meant to be* symbolic, and not a permanent *law*. Also in the Old Testament they had giving, and they were commanded to give a tenth, a tithe, of what they had earned. Now all of Scripture is to learn from and to use for teaching, 2 Tim 3:16-17. Most certainly we should learn from the Old Testament on these things, and should be able to clearly see that to give a tenth is good example. But is it a command for the Christian? No! The command of the new law, the law of Christ, is to give as we have been prospered, 1 Cor 16:2. There is a different standard in "the law of Christ," Gal 6:2.

It is clear by example that men need to cease, to desist from all activity at times, to just *rest*, not play, but rest! If we do not know it by our bodies, we know clearly from Moses law that men need to stop a day each week, cease from work, to rest a day each week. Present day Americans have foolishly decided to throw away all true rest, and indeed most now need to "rest'" after their so-called "day off."

But the real sabbath—the real *shabat* שַׁבָּת, the real desisting, ceasing—is on that final and perfect day of rest in the paradise of God. There is a seventh day, a perfect day. There is a day when all work will cease, "that they may rest from their labours," Rev 14:13 KJV. What is the rest that is forever? My friend it is not of this world, but of the new heavens and new earth according to His promise, 2 Pe 3:10-13, Rev 21:1-2.

In addition, notice that not all patterns are even "announced." It did announce Moses as a type, but didn't with Elijah (it could have meant that he was literally coming back!), and it did not announce it with Adam. There should also be awareness that sometimes a pattern or 'type' refers to more than one thing! Just as we may use a paper pattern to make more than one dress or shirt or boat, and we may use Paul's example or pattern on more than one Sunday. So patterns in prophecy may be used more than once. If you will look, that has already been proved because in 2 Samuel 7 the prophecy talks about both Solomon and Jesus. Also this can seen in the seven heads in Rev 17:9-10.

> [9] "Here is the mind which has wisdom. The seven heads **are** <u>seven mountains </u>on which the woman sits, [10] **and** they are <u>seven kings</u>; five have fallen, one is, the other has not yet come; and when he comes, he must remain a little while." NASB (*bold and underline emphasis added*)

The seven heads in Revelation 17 represent *both* seven *mountains*, and seven *kings*! (The KJV says the same thing, but not as clearly.) So the assumption that a prophecy can only refer to one thing, is *incorrect!* Additionally, it can be seen that the completion of a prophecy is generally much greater than the type. Jesus is greater than Moses or Solomon or any Passover lamb. The final 'rest–the New Heavens and New Earth (2 Peter 3:13, Isa 65:17)–is much greater than the physical land of Canaan. Also it can be observed that a 'Pattern' in prophecy, often closely follows the prophecy, and the completion often comes *a long time* after the prophecy. So very soon after Nathan's prophecy in 2 Samuel 7, Solomon comes, but Jesus then does not come for another thousand years. The 'rest' of the land of Canaan happened soon after the first prophecies, but the 'rest' of heaven is yet to come. The Passover lamb was with the children of Israel every year, but Jesus didn't come for over 1400 years. To draw a further parallel that I think is valid, the 'patterns' for the final conflicts with Christianity occurred in centuries immediately following Jesus ascension to heaven, but the final conflicts are yet to come.

Last of all, plainly there are patterns for our conduct in the church. When God told Moses about building the physical temple, he told him build it *exactly* according to the patterns that were shown him, Ex 25:40. It tells us in Heb 8:5 that this was because these things (the tabernacle and its furniture and fixtures) were copies, shadows, or patterns of the great temple in heaven.

Clearly those in Christ are being made part of a great temple in which God does dwell. In 1 Cor 6:19 Paul says that your body is the temple of the Holy Spirit which is in you, which you have of God, and you are not your own. In 1 Peter 2:5 it says that we are living stones and are being built up into a spiritual house, a holy priesthood, to offer up spiritual sacrifices acceptable to God by Jesus Christ. For this temple, the church, the traditions of men are not authoritative. Jesus goes even farther than this, and says, "But in vain they do worship me, teaching *for* doctrines the commandments of men." Mtt 15:9 KJV.

So there are patterns for the New Testament church. Paul says in Phil 4:9 that those things which you have learned, and received and heard and seen in me (Paul), make sure that you do them. In other words, God has made Paul serve as a pattern for our conduct in the Lord. Again in 2 Thes 2:15, Paul says that we should hold to the traditions which we have been taught (the Greek word used here literally means "traditions"), whether by Paul's word, or by Paul's letters. So Paul represents himself as handing down to us, not the things of men, but rather the things of God. We have many of the letters of Paul, and read about Paul in the book of Acts. We are being told to use him as a pattern for our conduct in the church of our Lord.

It would not be hard to miss some of the themes and patterns that are in Scripture. Even so, once you spot a continuing subject, I am sure that from that point you will see it pop up over and over in your studies, just as it has in mine.

Should Christians, the true temple of God, use any less care in following God's patterns for the true spiritual temple than they did who built the physical temple years ago? Obviously not.

This also about using the Old Testament. Many of us have trouble using the Old Testament, some using it as a current law, when it is no longer intended to be used as current law. Others to avoid "abusing" the Old Testament, avoid it altogether. **Neither is the Christian position.** Scripture says that all Scripture is inspired of God and is profitable for teaching, 2 Tim 3:16.

Scripture says that everything that was written in the past was written to teach us, Rom 15:4. But having said that, how do you use it, how do you learn from it? Paul says Moses' Law was nailed to the cross, Col 2:14, and that it is **not** the agreement that we are under, so how *should* we use the Old Testament? In 1 Corinthians 10 there is some instruction and some examples of proper use. The first thing that Paul calls our attention to is that just as Christians are baptized into Jesus, so the Israelites were symbolically baptized into Moses.

> [1] Moreover, brethren, I would not that ye should be ignorant, how that all our fathers were under the cloud, and all passed through the sea; [2] And were all baptized unto Moses in the cloud and in the sea;
> 1 Cor 10:1-2 KJV

Also Paul says that the Israelites in Ex 14:19-22 were baptized in the cloud and the sea, and the Israelites of old drank of the same spiritual food and drink of which Christians drink.

> [3] And did all eat the same spiritual meat; [4] And did all drink the same spiritual drink: for they drank of that spiritual Rock that followed them: and that Rock was Christ. 1 Cor 10:3-4 KJV

Now some people think that the Old Testament was different *spiritually* from the New Testament. Some, most notably some of the occult, have even taught that the Old Testament was evil and the New Testament is good. But notice that even though the Old Testament has been nailed to the cross as previously noted, neither the Old Testament nor Moses Law is evil:

> What shall we say then? *Is* the law sin? God forbid. Nay, I had not known sin, but by the law: for I had not known lust, except the law had said, Thou shalt not covet Rom 7:7 KJV

> Wherefore the law is holy, and the commandment holy, and just, and good. Rom 7:12 KJV

So the Old Testament is not evil or to be avoided, as some false teachers say. Instead it is to be studied, and in 1 Cor 10:3-4 Paul even says they ate and they drank from the same *spiritual food and drink* as we eat and drink from! That is, they ate and drank from Jesus Christ.

Always keep this in mind: that the Old Testament is spiritually in "sync" with the New Testament. That is why we are told that *ALL* Scripture *is profitable* for doctrine, reproof, and correction in righteousness. It was in the Old Testament that it first said "But the righteous will live by his faith," in Hab 2:4 NASB. So if we have adopted a point of view that says that the Old Testament is evil, that means we are mixed up, and need to take another look at some things. But God was not pleased with many of them.

> [5] But with many of them God was not well pleased: for they were overthrown in the wilderness. [6] **Now these things were our examples**, to the intent we should not lust after evil things, as they also lusted. 1 Cor 10:5-6 KJV (*emphasis added*)

We may have become a Christian, we may have been baptized, we may have come out of bondage in Egypt, and we may have followed the light of Jesus Christ into the wilderness, and yet may still lose our soul by revolting against Jesus Christ and not following Him. We may not please God and we may, without always realizing it, decide not to stay in His salvation. Our bodies may be scattered over this earth, as their bodies were scattered over the desert ... in punishment of our sins.

We must not be idolaters, 1 Cor 10:7. It tells in Ex 32:4-6, 17-19 about how Israel made themselves some images of God when Moses stayed up on Mount Sinai. And many died of plagues from the Lord, Ex 32:27-28. Do not fall into using images my children, and so be destroyed.

We must not be sexually immoral, 1 Cor 10:8. The story is told in the book of Numbers. The girls from the church down the road invited the men to a wild party, and many of them went in Num 25:1-5. Read and learn my friends.

We must not test the Lord, 1 Cor 10:9. It also speaks of this testing in Psa 78:18-22. They asked the Lord and He gave them the food for which they asked in Num 11:31-32. But it was expensive meat.

> [13] They quickly forgot His works;
> They did not wait for His counsel,
> [14] But craved intensely in the wilderness,
> And tempted God in the desert.
> [15] So He gave them their request,
> But sent a wasting disease among them. Psa 106:13-15 NASB

This is an Old Testament message for us my New Testament friends ... don't test the Lord.

We must not grumble, 1 Cor 10:10. It is easy to see grumbling in a lot of places in the Old Testament and one of the places is Ex 16:2-3, and again in Ex 16:6-7. The lesson, among other lessons, is to accept whatever He gives you ... without complaining and with thanksgiving. Now these things happened as examples.

> Now these things happened to them as an example, and they were written for our instruction, upon whom the ends of the ages have come. 1 Cor 10:11 NASB

These things were written for **us**! The Old Testament was written for **us**! It was written *for* those who are in the end of ages! The *stories* were recorded for *us*! So learn from these things! Learn that you need to be careful because just when you think you are doing all right is when you need to be really careful that you do not destroy yourself. The types and patterns of Scripture and of prophecy are for our learning, so that we will inherit eternal life.

> Therefore let him who thinks he stands take heed that he does not fall. 1 Cor 10:12 NKJV

The key point here is that the Old Testament and the New Testament are in "sync" *spiritually*, and if we think other wise, we are not really understanding what we have received! We are playing with half a deck. Literally! We need to look again, and rethink the data we are using and how we are using it. God is willing to provide for us.

> No temptation has overtaken you except such as is common to man; but God *is* faithful, who will not allow you to be tempted beyond what you are able, but with the temptation will also make the way of escape, that you may be able to bear *it*. 1 Cor 10:13 NKJV

He will take care of us. He will make sure that we are never forced to sin, that there is *always* a way to escape. But we have to stay with Him, and have to learn from what He has had written for us. We have to stay with Him and plow with Him.

> [28] Come unto me, all *ye* that labour and are heavy laden, and I will give you rest. [29] Take my yoke upon you, and learn of me; for I am meek and lowly in heart: and ye shall find rest unto your souls. [30] For my yoke *is* easy, and my burden is light. Mtt 11:28-30 KJV

Now plowing must be kept straight, and the plowman must stay on the straight and narrow. We have to stay in harness. We have to stay in the harness so we will feel the pull of the Master, and pace of the Master, and the direction of the Master, as we walk along. We have to stay in the harness so we will feel the rubbing and pain of the harness when we try to go too fast or go too slow, or when we try to pull aside to the right or the left. If we don't stay in the harness (which means work, a yoke) and if we don't walk with the Master, then we won't stay on the straight and narrow, and we won't make it to the promised land.

This Age and the Age to Come

This world has been created by one God with more than one "person" involved, as is seen in Genesis 1. The Spirit of God was moving over the waters in verses 1 and 2, and in verse 26 God said, "Let Us make man ..." Of course we use the word "world," in more than one way. On one hand, we talk about the earth, the surface of the world where we all live. The devil showed Jesus all the kingdoms of the world from a very high mountain. The Greek word for "world" used in Mtt 4:8 is the Greek word *kosmos* κόσμος, which comes from a root that means something is orderly, systematic, even beautifully so. The parallel passage in Lk 4:5 the devil shows Him "all the kingdoms of the world," and it uses another word that means the whole "inhabited world" *oikoumenā* οἰκουμένη. So what the devil showed Him was the whole inhabited world, it appears from a dimension man cannot see. And Jesus tells us to go into all the world (*kosmos*) and preach the gospel to every creature in Mk 16:15-16.

We moderns use a form of the Greek word *kosmos* to describe not just this present earth, but also the whole universe. The Greek word *kosmos* also has some of these overtones, and is used to describe all that God has made under "heaven," as an ordered structure, as in Acts 17:24, where Paul says,

> God that made the world and all things therein, seeing that he is Lord of heaven and earth, dwelleth not in temples made with hands; KJV

Along this line notice that the NIV (which is very good at giving the "sense" of a passage), translates kosmos as "universe" in 1 Cor 4:9, and Phil 2:15, and translates the Greek word *pas* πᾶς or "all" as "universe" in Eph 4:10. It also translates the Greek word *aiōn* αἰών (which is often translated as "world" or "age,"and which will be discussed shortly) as "universe" in Heb 1:2 and Heb 11:3. The modern concept of universe is implicit in many passages of Scripture. Perhaps the Greek word *pas* πᾶς or "all," as in Eph 4:10, is the closest to our modern "uni-" (one) "-verse."

Next in line with such concepts, there is this present world—this present age. Jesus made this world, and He was in the world, even though the world (*kosmos*) did not know Him, Jn 1:9-10. The world (the *kosmos*, this present system) includes the people who are opposed to God whom Christians will judge at the last day, 1 Cor 6:2. Lastly, Satan is at least in some sense the ruler of the world (*kosmos*), for Jesus said "I will not speak much more with you, for the ruler of the world is coming, and he has nothing in Me ..." Jn 14:30, speaking of Satan coming to secure His death. Since Satan in some sense "rules" this world, listen to what James says again using the word *kosmos*,

> Ye adulterers and adulteresses, know ye not that the friendship of the world is enmity with God? whosoever therefore will be a friend of the world is the enemy of God. Jas 4:4 KJV

This, of course, is consistent with what Jesus said calling Satan "the ruler of this world." The world has turned against God, all the way from the evil spiritual powers who have ruled us, even to us. But God wants the world to repent, not to perish, so He says,

> [16] For God so loved the world, that he gave his only begotten Son, that whosoever believeth in him should not perish, but have everlasting life. [17] For God sent not his Son into the world to condemn the world;

but that the world through him might be saved. Jn 3:16-17 KJV

Jesus is the light of the world, as it also says in Jn 8:12; and yes, it is in both cases our old friend *kosmos*. He gives us enough light so that we will not stumble *if* we walk by the light. There is, of course, the other side. When Jesus died, He executed judgment on this world.

> [31] Now is the judgment of this world: now shall the prince of this world be cast out. [32] And I, if I be lifted up from the earth, will draw all *men* unto me. Jn 12:31-32 KJV

Even so, the Jews didn't understand this purpose, so when John the Baptist saw Jesus, he said to behold the Lamb of God sent to take away the sins of the world, Jn 1:29-34. This means that whoever is born of God overcomes the world, 1 Jn 5:4. Not that Christians convert all of it, but that they separate themselves from that part which will not repent, and overcome and reject that influence. Then they also become a light to this world, Mtt 5:14, and become part of the spectacle to this world, 1 Cor 4:9.

Also it speaks of this present age as this present "world" many times in our translations. Through Jesus, this age was made Heb 1:2 NASB. It is talking about the universe. **Jesus made this age, this aiōn αἰών.** *Aiōn* is a word that is used in a variety of ways, including to mean eternity or eternal, or as in Heb 1:2 to mean this present "age," this present "universe."

(Generally speaking the the Greek word for "world" is *kosmos* κόσμος, as in 1 Jn 2:15. The KJV for the most part translates *aiōn*, or literally "age," as another word for "world," or as "for ever" but does translate it as "ages" in for instance Eph 2:7 and Col 1:26.)

By faith the "ages" (the "worlds" as in the KJV and NASB) were prepared by God, Heb 11:3. The word age is used to mean eternal in passages like Rev 22:5, where the phrase "forever and ever" is literally "into the ages of the ages" (into the *aiōn* of the *aiōn*, εἰς τοὺς αἰῶνας τῶν αἰώνων). Jesus is the eternal king in 1 Tim 1:17 (literally 'the king of the ages'). Quite a title and totally true, right? The occult wishes to be the master of time, and fantasizes about having such mastery in their many movies and books, although they are not allowed such mastery. But Jesus is the master even of time. He is the Lord of the age**S**!

We are warned about trying to be wise in this age *aiōn*, 1 Cor 3:18, but then in 1 Corinthians 3 verses 19 and 22, it is once again our old word *kosmos*. This age, our present age, is the one which does not know God. The people of this age are those who do not know God. So the worldly master compliments the crooked steward who has stolen from him on his shrewdness because "the sons of this age are more shrewd in relation to their own kind than the sons of light," Lk 16:8 NASB. Also, the word age is used to mean "long ago," as He spoke by the mouth of His holy prophets "from of old" (*aiōn*), in Lk 1:70 (the KJV here paraphrases this as "since the world began.") At least in some sense, Satan is the ruler of **this** age. Certain things have been given to Satan; he has been allowed certain power. So he is given progressive authority to test Job in Job chapters 1 and 2. He has enough authority from God that he is called "the god of this age," and he can even cause intellectual blindness among us poor mortals according to 2 Cor 4:3-4 NASB, NKJV. The whole world is under the power of the evil one, 1 Jn 5:19, the whole *kosmos*. This present universe is. This age bothers us, blinds us, entangles us ... often to death. Sons of this age/world are wiser than the sons of light as you can see in Lk 16:8. The worries of this age aggravate us, "the worry of the world" (age), Mtt 13:22. And the form of this present *kosmos* is passing away.

> [29] But this I say, brethren, the time has been shortened, so that from now on those who have wives should be as though they had none; [30] and those who weep, as though they did not weep; and those who rejoice, as though they did not rejoice; and those who buy, as though they did not possess; [31] and those who use the world, as though they did not make full use of it; for **the form of this world** is passing away.
> 1 Cor 7:29-31 NASB (*emphasis added*)

The future is that there is another age coming. There is this age and the age to come, so Jesus says "Anyone who speaks a word against the Son of Man, it will be forgiven him; but whoever speaks against the Holy Spirit, it will not be forgiven him, either in this age or in the *age* to come," Mtt 12:32 NKJV. Again it speaks of this in Lk 18:29-30.

> [29] ... "Assuredly, I say to you, there is no one who has left house or parents or brothers or wife or children, for the sake of the kingdom of God, [30] who shall not receive many times more in this present time, **and in the age to come**, eternal life." NKJV (*emphasis added*)

As Christians we are teaching a wisdom **not of this age**, 1 Cor 2:6; **not of this dimension**, if you will pardon the expression. The ends of the ages have come on us 1 Cor 10:8-12; and according to Heb 6:5 we can even have a foretaste of the powers of the age to come. Jesus died at the consummation of the ages (the plural of *aiōn*), Heb 9:26 NASB NKJV; and Jesus has a name above every name, "not only in this age but also in the one to come," Eph 1:21 NASB NKJV. Men need to live for the age to come. You and I have in the past lived in accord with the course of this "world," this *kosmos*. We were dead in our sins, and walked according the principles of the prince of darkness, the spirit of wickedness, Eph 2:2. At that point Jesus came to "rescue us from this present evil age," Gal 1:4 NASB NKJV. So now we are to live a different way. The Lord doesn't want us to be conformed to this age, *aiōn*, Rom 12:2. The world should be crucified to me and me to the world, Gal 6:14. If you think you are wise in this age, 1 Cor 3:18, you should make yourself foolish before the world that you may become wise. In this present age *aiōn*, we are supposed to give up the "ungodly" desires of this age, Ti 2:12. A good Christian from Thessalonica lost his way in "having loved this present" age *aiōn*, 2 Tim 4:10. Lastly, Jesus will be with you to the end of the age, Mtt 28:20. The harvest is the end of the age *aiōn* Mtt 13:39, and so will it be at the end of the age,

> [49] "So it will be at the end of the age; the angels will come forth and take out the wicked from among the righteous, [50] and will throw them into the furnace of fire; in that place there will be weeping and gnashing of teeth." Mtt 13:49-50 NASB

These concepts are implicit in Scripture's viewpoints on reality and prophecy. *Misunderstand these things and you will also misunderstand and misapply prophecy!* Now prophecy, as has been pointed out, does not normally have a built-in time element. We are often assured that this or that will happen, given some hints about order or priority, but seldom told the time when these things will happen. There are exceptions. Abraham is told that Sarah will have a child "at this time next year," Gen 18:10 NASB; but such notices are rare. In a way it can be said that this is because Scriptures is written from a timeless perspective. It is enough to say it will happen, and all of this will soon be over anyway. However, there are some notices of "time" or "periods of time" given in some places in Scripture. Even so, when they are given, they often seem to be given in cryptic sorts of ways. The prophet Daniel talks about some of these transitions to "the age to come," as it is described in Heb 2:5.

The prophet Daniel had led an incredible and varied life, all the way from being a princely captive in Babylon, to time and training in the royal schools of Babylon, to climbing an incredible ladder of success in Babylon as part of the administration of a large and powerful multinational empire, to being favored by the Lord his God in his search for truth, and for understanding the things which were still yet to come. Daniel had visions of the near centuries, of the coming of the Christ and the establishment of God's Holy Kingdom. Some of these were typical of things right at the end, the end of *everything* it appears to mean. So at this point we come to the end of the book of Daniel. There are closing comments on the things Daniel has seen, on what will happen, on what has been said and what can be known.

At the time of the end Michael the great prince will come forward according to Dan 12:1. Michael is an angel, but not just any angel; he is a ruling angel, Jude 9. The Greek word is *archangelos* ἀρχάγγελος. An archangel means a ruling angel, or as some dictionaries put it, a chief of angels; that is to say that he directs the activities of others. Beyond all of that, Michael is not just *any* ruling angel, rather he is "the great prince who stands *guard* over the sons of your people," Dan 12:1.

Angels, as has been understood since ancient times, are emissaries—messengers—to transmit God's will and carry it out. They are not intended to be, or to be seen as, independent, but rather as servants. "He makes the winds His messengers," Psa 104:4 NASB, although "winds" could be translated "spirits" and it is so translated in many passages. That would make this verse read "He makes the spirits His messengers." And the last part is of course, "Flaming fire His ministers." This is quoted in Hebrews 1 where it is comparing the role of angels with the place of the Christ in the affairs of the universe. At the end of Hebrews 1, when it summarizes the role of angels, it says this of angels: "Are they not all ministering spirits, sent out to render service for the sake of those who will inherit salvation?" NASB. In other words, the proper function of angels is to serve, work for, and protect those who are going to inherit salvation. This is their *proper* function, not the subverting of the race into disobedience as the serpent in the garden of God was doing, and not to be worshipped as if they were gods (although many angels in defecting from faithfulness to the Lord have passed themselves off as "gods" to men), 1 Cor 10:20.

This particular angel Michael was seen earlier in Daniel 10 as coming to the aid of an angel who was being hindered in trying to get a message to Daniel. Michael also appears as leading the forces of righteousness in heaven in Revelation 12, and as being victorious in casting the devil and his angels out of heaven. Then at the very last, there will be stress and distress on the nations such as has never occurred since there have been nations. So when is this time of stress as described in Daniel 12? It is very specific. It is that same time when *everyone* whose name is written in the book will be rescued, Dan 12:1. There is only one time when *everyone* whose name is written in the book of Life will be delivered. That would only be at the very last day, at the trumpet of God, when the righteous dead and living rise to meet the Lord in the air, to be with Him forever, 1 Thessalonians 4. At that special time, when *everyone of God's people* are rescued who has been written in the book of life, is the time when stress will occur such as has never occurred since there has been a nation. All those other times of stress are at best just types, symbolic of that last great day. Of that special last day, when God's elect will be gathered by the holy angels from one end of the heavens to the other (Mtt 24:31), it says that men will be in awe about the roaring of the seas and the signs in the sun and moon, and men will be fainting at the thought of the things which will be happening as the heavens themselves are shaken, Lk 21:25-26. Of that day the psalmist writes,

> ³ A fire goes before Him,
>> And burns up His enemies round about.
> ⁴ His lightnings light the world;
>> The earth sees and trembles.
> ⁵ The mountains melt like wax at the presence of the LORD,
>> At the presence of the Lord of the whole earth.
> ⁶ The heavens declare His righteousness,
>> And all the peoples see His glory. Psa 97:3-6 NKJV

Definitely a day like no other in terms of stress for it will be terrifying to come face to face with the living God, Heb 10:31; who has come to avenge Himself on all those who know not God, and who will not obey the gospel which He has commanded, 2 Thes 1:7-9. In that special last day, the prophet Daniel tells us that many will arise from the dead to everlasting life, and others will arise "to shame *and everlasting* contempt" KJV, and some will shine like stars, especially those who lead many to righteousness, Dan 12:2-3.

At this juncture come other issues. What is to be known by men about these times, and what is sealed so that men cannot see all that will happen until the time is to occur? So in Dan 12:4 Daniel is told to seal the book, to hide the words he has been given "until the time of the end," the time being talked about in the text in Daniel 12. Indeed the passage in Daniel chapter 11 is among the most difficult in all prophecy.

Then Daniel looks to the angel messengers who have been speaking to him, and revealing things to him. One asked the other, How long will it be before all these wonders come to an end? At this the messenger swore by the Lord of Heaven and Earth: for a time, times and half *a time*, and as soon as "they" finish breaking the power of the holy people. Incredible! But it shouldn't be, should it? It is the same period of time which is given for the drought which fell on Israel at Elijah's prayer, Jas 5:17. It is the same length of time given for the rule of the beast in the last chapters of Revelation. The beast, who will be covered later, at the second coming of Jesus Christ will be thrown *alive* into hell. So the implication from the prophet Daniel and the apostle John is that their respective prophecies are related and intertwined.

Then Daniel asks in Dan 12:8 what will be the outcome of all these things. Now Daniel had been told of some things to come in Daniel 11, but what would be the outcome of all of this is something he is not specifically told in his prophecy. The answer he is given is that Daniel is to go on his way and not concern himself, "for these words *are* closed up and sealed until the end time," Dan 12:9 KJV. Daniel is told that many people will be purified and that many people will act sinfully, and that none of the "wicked" will understand but that "the wise will understand," Dan 12:10 KJV. The next part in Daniel 12 is probably the strangest part to the modern reader. It is not clear whether it applies to the "types" talked about especially in the book of Daniel, or the "anti-types." Daniel is told,

> [11] "From the time that the regular sacrifice is abolished and the abomination of desolation is set up, there *will be* 1,290 days. [12] How blessed is he who keeps waiting and attains to the 1,335 days! [13] But as for you, go *your way* to the end; then you will enter into rest and rise *again* for your allotted portion at the end of the age." Dan 12:11-13 NASB

Daniel 11 will be covered later, along with the principles to be used in understanding many of these sorts of prophecies. True and verified principles for approaching prophecy can be determined by analyzing fulfilled prophecies. However, I will not attempt in this work to make any sense of the dates and periods of time that are given here. Still it does give a couple of periods of time, and they seem to be related to the stories told in the book of Revelation.

However there is a bigger issue that should be covered at this time. That is-sue is that *there are things that are hidden from us, things which are "sealed," things which will not be understood until* **right at the end,** "until the time of the end," Dan 12:9 KJV.

Now what is told and what can be understood should be sufficient at any given point of history. Also since prophecy speaks of forces which will be active and working against the Christian all through history, *most of prophecy is therefore pertinent to Christians of all ages, and can be read and generally understood all through history.*

> The secret *things belong* unto the LORD our God: but those *things which are* revealed *belong* unto us and to our children for ever, that *we* may do all the words of this law. Deut 29:29 KJV

This thing of prophecy is, in essence, an overview of time and history, and our part in it. We are told what we ***need*** for every stage of history, and every stage of the Christian Age. Some things will no doubt be more perfectly un-derstood at the time that they happen. You can see examples of this all through the Scriptures. Peter tells us that the prophets made carefully searches and asked questions trying to understand what the Holy Spirit speaking through them was telling us. Peter says that they were told that they were serving ***us***, *not* ***themselves***, in things in which the angels desire to know more about, 1 Pe 1:10-12. So there were many things which *the prophets* ***themselves*** *didn't understand, things which they have told us!* But on the other hand, it has already been pointed out that there were many things which even the unbelieving Jews understood about the coming of the Messiah.

Still there were many things which were not plain until they started to hap-pen, and even then not everything was understood by everyone. There are plen-ty of illustrations of this. In Psalm 69, David speaks of both himself and Christ, and says in verse 9 that zeal for God's house has consumed him. This is the trait that is described that surely might to some extent apply to David, al-though it might seem to be to be a little bit of hyperbole. But a thousand years later the Messiah is angry at the desecration of God's Holy Temple by unscru-pulous selling and trading in a place which shouldn't be a market at all. Then He makes a whip and drives the sellers and money changers out of the temple. Naturally this causes no small disturbance among the elders who are profiting from the sales, and then the Messiah's disciples remember what was written in the psalms, and it is no hyperbole at all, because indeed, *"Zeal for Your house has eaten Me up,"* Jn 2:17 NKJV.

But still ... there are things which are "sealed" until the time of the end.

What is sealed I cannot deliver. It is hidden from me and from you. It is written for the future, and will be understood by God's Elect at the proper time, as the Truth is now. What has been given to me, I give to you, with the prayer that you will diligently search out whether these things are so.

All that being taken into account, *if indeed we have at each stage what we need,* then why do men so often stumble at the message? Stumbling often means you will fall, possibly hurt yourself, and if you fall from a great height, maybe even destroy yourself. Who would want to do such a thing? Despite these things, the truth is that some *do* want to stumble *in a way,* and wallow in the mire, and at times that might even include you and me.

You see, some are appointed to life. God has decided that His faithful ones will live forever, and He appoints them to eternal life. You and I as faithful Christians have come to Jesus Christ, the living stone rejected by men, but yet a stone which is precious in God's sight. We are spiritual stones being built on Jesus Christ, 1 Pe 2:4-7.

Then comes to the next part about the building of this temple. Jesus is also the stone which was rejected by the builders of God's holy temple made up of God's people, speaking of the Jewish leaders. He is the stone which, although rejected, has become the very cornerstone of God's Holy Temple, the true house of the Living God, the church of God. Compare also 1 Cor 3:16-17, and 1 Tim 3:15, among others. In this way it came about also that this key stone, this cornerstone Jesus, has become a "a stone of stumbling, and a rock of offence," 1 Pe 2:8 KJV. Peter is a quoting from Isaiah. The original says

> [14] "He will be as a sanctuary,
>> But a stone of stumbling and a rock of offense
>> To both the houses of Israel,
>> As a trap and a snare to the inhabitants of Jerusalem.
> [15] And many among them shall stumble;
>> They shall fall and be broken,
>> Be snared and taken." Isa 8:14 -15 NKJV

Isaiah has gone on to say that the words of this prophecy should be sealed (it is for sure, and it is finished, ready to be sent, to be unchanged). He also says that this applies in particular to the Jews, "the house of Jacob" from whom the Lord is hiding His face. So Isaiah emphasizes that the Jews are to stumble at the Messiah when He comes. The Jewish prophet Isaiah himself said this.

But in the first letter of Peter, the application is broader. Peter in effect says that everyone who rejects the Lordship of Jesus Christ is stumbling over this stone, and he goes on to say some particular things about how and why they stumble. He *is* saying "they were appointed" to stumble, but look at *why* he says they were appointed to stumble." He says it is "**because** they are disobedient to the word," NKJV (*emphasis added*). In other words, they don't *want* to receive it, therefore they don't want to obey the word, and so they are appointed to stumble.

In Scripture, obedience is part of faithful following. Jesus is the source of eternal salvation "unto all them who obey him," Heb 5:9 KJV. And how do you purify your soul? Peter tells us it is by your "obedience to the truth," 1 Pe 1:22 NASB; and the references could be multiplied over and over.

Then what about those who do not want to hear the word? The truth is that a lot of people judge themselves as unworthy of the gospel. They are many like Felix in Acts 24. He knew he was doing things which were wrong, and was frankly scared about what Paul was saying, and didn't want to hear it. He dismissed Paul and said that maybe when he found the time they could talk about these things. He didn't really want to hear. He didn't really want to change. He didn't really want to know.

They did have some opportunity to hear, but they didn't want to hear anymore. Look at what it says: *they judged **themselves** unworthy of eternal life!* How foolish we people often are! In effect they decided that *they didn't really want to obey the gospel,* that they were unworthy of the gospel, and unworthy of eternal life. People, many people every day, make such decisions about themselves for many reasons and refuse to obey the Word of truth. Paul talks about how we should deal with such people. They are truly caught in Satan's snares, however

> 24 The Lord's bond-servant must not be quarrelsome, but be kind to all, able to teach, patient when wronged, 25 with gentleness correcting those who are in opposition, if perhaps God may grant them repentance leading to the knowledge of the truth, 26 and they may come to their senses *and* escape from the snare of the devil, having been held captive by him to do his will. 2 Tim 2:24-26 NASB

Some are appointed to life. God foresees, and chooses, 1 Pe 1:1-2. In this same Antioch of Pisidia, where the Jews have now turned blasphemous, many of the pagans listened and rejoiced, and so Luke speaking by the Holy Spirit says of the crowd.

> Now when the Gentiles heard this, they were glad and glorified the word of the Lord. And as many as had been appointed to eternal life believed. Acts 13:48 NKJV

Appointed to life? Yes, as they respond and obey. But of those who disobey, Peter says they are often "appointed" to stumble. If we want more of the truth, if we want to understand more of what will be, then we have to be willing to obey. **We must be willing to submit to what we learn in Scripture and in prophecy *as we go along!*** Or in the end, we cut ourselves off from further insight and put ourselves in line to stumble, because we disobey.

> "If anyone is willing to do His will, he will know of the teaching, whether it is of God or *whether* I speak from Myself." Jn 7:17 NASB

> Jesus answered and said unto him, If a man love me, he will keep my words: and my Father will love him, and we will come unto him, and make our abode with him. Jn 14:23 KJV

We Walk, a Holy People

Seeing What We Can

Learning From the Past

Daniel's Visions

Warning to the Reader: *There is some very close
reasoning in this passage. If it gets too deep for you,
skim through the text and notice the main points,
and the sections on "Which Dates Start
the Prophecy," and "Atonement."
Then perhaps come back
to it later.*

Now the young man Daniel first went to Babylon as a hostage and a prisoner of war, and was (as you can see in Daniel 1) chosen to be trained as an administrator and servant, if you will pardon the expression, of the evil empire. Indeed, ancient Babylon is symbolic of the ultimate evil empire of the Christian Age. As the chapters of Daniel go along, this young man remains faithful to God all the way to the core of his being but still being a success and prospering in his day to day work for the empire. He was there not by choice but by the choosing of the rulers of Babylon and also clearly by the choosing of God. By the end of chapter 2, he is governor of the province of Babylon in the empire, and when the empire ends and is replaced by the Medes and the Persians, Daniel again survives and is a part of a body of commissioners over the satraps of the new empire. Turn now to Daniel 9, to follow the study.

In Daniel 9 this powerful administrator can be seen focusing once again on his roots, on what has happened to his people and what will happen to his people. It tells us in Dan 9:1 that this was in the first year of the Medo-Persian Empire, so that would seem to make it 539 to 538 B.C. in our calendar. Things at this time, as at many times in history, do not seem to be going well for the Jews, and Daniel, through whom God has chosen to work, wants to know what all of this is about. One cannot help but think here of 1 Pe 1:10-12.

> [10] As to this salvation, the prophets who prophesied of the grace that *would come* to you made careful searches and inquiries, [11] seeking to know what person or time the Spirit of Christ within them was indicating ... [12] ... —things into which angels long to look. NASB

Ah, these are things revealed to us which angels yearn to look into! How foolish for us then to seek wisdom from angels rather than from God and His Word! Compare if you will Col 2:18.

Daniel seems to be looking at Jeremiah 25, where it says,

> [11] And this whole land shall be a desolation, and an astonishment; and these nations shall serve the king of Babylon seventy years. Jer 25:11 KJV

He goes on to say the Lord would punish Babylon for her sin and make her "an everlasting desolation." The Lord would bring many nations against Babylon and pay her back for her deeds. So here is another of those infrequent *time references*, and like the present study, one of the key issues is knowing how to figure the start of this seventy years. Daniel is at the time of this writing still in Babylon, and the nations have come against Babylon to punish her, but the "everlasting desolation" which Jeremiah predicted has not yet happened!

Daniel started giving close attention to the things of the Lord, praying and fasting. He gives us some incredible lessons on prayer here. Daniel of all people, was one of the few who had nothing to do with those terrible sins which brought on the desolation of Israel for seventy years. Even so Daniel prays not just for himself, but for his people as they are. He is pleading their guilt before the Lord, admitting their not listening to what God has told them through the prophets, and confessing their shame and rebellion. Daniel acknowledges that these things were written as long ago as Moses in the Law, yet the Jews as a body had not turned their face to seek the Lord and to obey Him and to be guided by Him, so the Lord had finally brought on them all the calamities which He said. So Daniel now pleads, Lord you have done as you said, now Lord have mercy on your children. Look at what has happened to Jerusalem, and show the mercy for which You are known. Forgive! Forgive!

> O Lord, hear; O Lord, forgive; O Lord, hearken and do; defer not, for thine own sake, O my God: for thy city and thy people are called by thy name. Dan 9:19 KJV

Then as Daniel is praying, the angel Gabriel is sent to give him insight in these matters, for as was noted:

> Surely the Lord GOD does nothing,
> Unless He reveals His secret counsel
> To His servants the prophets. Amos 3:7 NASB

The angel Gabriel first appeared to Daniel in chapter 8, in explaining the things concerning the kings of Greece who were yet to come, and yes, I think also about events having links to the time of the end of all time. The angel Gabriel "one having the appearance of a man" in Dan 8:15 NKJV, is called a "man" in Dan 9:21, and is clearly called an "angel" in Lk 1:11 and verses 13 and 19 when he appears to Zacharias the father of John the Baptist. Also he is called an angel in Lk 1:26 when he is sent to explain things to Mary the mother of Jesus. Gabriel himself says in Lk 1:19 that he is one of that select group who stands in the presence of God. Gabriel then both talked to Daniel and gave him instructions in the verses which follow in Daniel 9. The angel tells Daniel that when he began his prayers the order was given to send Gabriel because Daniel was regarded highly. And then Daniel is told to pay attention to what is said so that he will gain insight into future events.

Seventy "weeks" (?) have been decreed, the angels says. The NIV says "Seventy's sevens" in Dan 9:24, and it does have the sense of a "seven." But this is also the regular word that is used for a "week" in the Old Testament, although this subject will come back later. He says that various things have to happen in this "Seventy weeks." These seventy weeks have been decreed, and I am using

the translation of the NASB:
- for your people
- and your holy city
- to finish transgressions
- to make an end of sin
- to make atonement for iniquity
- to bring in everlasting righteousness
- to seal up vision and prophecy
- and to anoint the most holy *place*

Wow! What a list! If you take it only as it appears on the surface, it seems to be speaking of a pivotal time in history, a time to which all other times of history must look forward to, or look backward at in perspective. It says that this period is "for" the Jews and Jerusalem. The KJV says that seventy weeks are determined "upon" the Jews and Jerusalem. Incredibly, it seems to limit the "period," if you will pardon the expression, for the Jews and Jerusalem. This also will be looked at later. This period is for making an end to sin and transgression, to make atonement of sin, and bring in everlasting righteousness. My goodness, how do *you* propose that this would be done, and what is it to look like after it has been done? After announcing what seems to be a "period" for the Jews and the city of Jerusalem, it also says it is a period "to anoint the most holy *place*." At least in human terms the most holy place was to be at "Jerusalem." Still this is quite a list.

Then Gabriel speaks of "a decree to restore and rebuild Jerusalem." Of course, if there is to be a *time* for "your people and your holy city," then that means it will have to be rebuilt. The fall of Jerusalem occurred in 586 BC, and the city and the temple were thoroughly looted, down to taking the "brass sea" of the temple for its bronze. Then the Babylonians burned the city, leaving just the lowliest of the people to remain in the city. So for Gabriel's vision to start, the city must be rebuilt, and he speaks of there being a decree to rebuild the city. Then he makes a clear statement: "that from the issuing of a decree to restore and rebuild Jerusalem until Messiah the Prince there will be seven weeks and sixty-two weeks;" Dan 9:25. "Time" is what is being talked about, precise time from the decree until the Christ, the Messiah, if we know how to figure it.

Gabriel gives some details about Jerusalem and its being rebuilt. He says that it "will be built again, with plaza and moat, even in times of distress," NASB. And a "moat"? That doesn't seem to fit. The Hebrew word is *charuts* חָרוּץ, a word for a trench or moat, a word which comes from *charats* חָרַץ, a word meaning to cut, or sharpen, or to make a decision (as we talk about "making a cut"). Clearly the NIV's translation of Jerusalem being rebuilt with a "trench" makes more sense for this water-poor city. The rebuilding, which at least in one sense went on all the way into the first century AD, was certainly turbulent times in the extreme, all the way from the beginning of the period to the end. If you want to know more of the details of those turbulent times, read the Jewish historian Josephus for a chronicle of almost continual troubles trials and tragedies.

So the period from the decree to rebuild until the Messiah "*shall be* seven weeks, and threescore and two weeks" and then he says the "Messiah be cut off, but not for himself" KJV after sixty-two weeks. The Messiah will be cut off? Now the word "cut off" is the Hebrew word *karath* כָּרַת. (Notice the phonetic relationship of this word to the word for "trench or moat" which was looked at above.) It means literally to cut something off, or to cut it down. For instance to cut down a tree, cut off a stick from a tree, cut off a tumor from your body, or to cut off your head! So it has the idea of killing someone who refuses this! So God said in Genesis He would never again cut off the people (kill all people) by a flood, Gen 9:11. It is clearly talking about putting to death. In Exodus 9 God says He could have already cut off (killed) all the Egyptians with disease if He had wanted to, Ex 9:15. So notice that **Dan 9:26 *clearly talks about the Messiah, the Christ, the Anointed One, being put to death!* ** Again, Wow! This is stunning that the Jews as a whole and the learned rabbis could miss it! And this is in a passage which purports to give the time of these things. Then it says:

> ... and the people of the prince that shall come shall destroy the city and the sanctuary; and the end thereof *shall be* with a flood, and unto the end of the war desolations are determined. Dan 9:26 KJV

So it looks like there is a particular period of the Jews being restored to their city, which will be rebuilt during turbulent times, and THEN the Messiah will be cut off, and THEN "the people" of a certain prince will come and destroy Jerusalem and the sanctuary (which by implication has been restored) *again.* And so it seems, the end will come like a flood and there will be wars (plural) all the way to the end of this period of "Seventy Weeks."

Now if you want to read a bizarre conglomerate of asinine theories of authorship, there is no better target than the book of Daniel. The real hurdle that many people have is the idea that no book can be as historically prescient, so very far in advance, as the book of Daniel. So-o-o-o *they figure*, it must be a fraud, and they want to post-date it to the second century B.C. Their linguistic evidences have been ably refuted many times, and their time lines do not really fit the text and still don't eliminate true prediction in the book. The reader should notice that Jesus accepts Daniel as the author of this book in Mtt 24:15.

Just the fact of these things happening according to prophecy is *astounding*, even if you discount all the dates, and even if you were to falsely post-date the book of Daniel until the second century B.C. (What can you tell me my friend, *with confidence*, of *anything* which will be 200 years from now?) The old German commentators Keil and Delitzsch, in their discussion of Dan 9:24-27, give a good summary of principle points of view on this passage.

1. Most of the church fathers and the older orthodox interpreters find

prophesied here the appearance of Christ in the flesh, His death, and the destruction of Jerusalem by the Romans. 2. The majority of the modern interpreters, on the other hand, refer the whole passage to the time of Antiochus Epiphanes. 3. Finally, some of the church fathers and several modern theologians have interpreted the prophecy eschatologically, as an announcement of the development of the kingdom of God from the end of the Exile on to the perfecting of the kingdom by the second coming of Christ at the end of the days. Keil and Delitzsch, Vol IX, *Ezekiel, Daniel,* by C. F. Keil, (Two Volumes in One), Eerdmans, Grand Rapids, Michigan, 1988 pg 336.

The "modern interpreters" he speaks of are mainly the liberal commentators of the nineteenth century but truly continuing into the twentieth and twenty-first centuries. To give the liberals their due, it is more complicated than it looks, for in truth some of the visions which Daniel saw had "types," or "patterns," which overlap in history all the way to the end of time. Like Antiochus IV Epiphanes being a type of the beast of the last days, something again which will be talked about later in this volume. Indeed, mistaking a "type" for a conclusion, or for an "anti-type," a "fulfillment," can make wrong conclusions appear more reasonable. The key is that you have to sort out the other elements in the prophecies, ***so that you don't mistake a "symbol" for a "conclusion,"*** just as was shown with David in Psalm 22, and with Solomon in 2 Samuel 7.

So then comes the issue of the "weeks" as they are called in most translations. If you take the seventy "weeks" as literal, then you make the fulfillment as supposed to occur somewhere between 538 to 535 B.C., and you reduce the passage to absurdity. That is not enough time to rebuild anything like a "city." If you recognize that Daniel wrote this, you would then have him tearing up his copy about 534 B.C. On the other hand, who would invent something so improbable in language 200 or 400 years before Christ?

If you look closer at the language used, if the seventy weeks are instead taken as "seventy-sevens" as in the NIV, then the "weeks" become seventy "sevens" of something but it is clear on the surface, not "weeks" or "sevens" of days. So then comes the next part: sevens of what? If you talk about Seventy Sevens of months, then you have a little over forty years, which still not much time for rebuilding a city. The next most logical designation, unsaid in the vision itself, is that it is "sevens" of years!

There are in a sense some "sabbaths of years" or "sevens of years" in Scripture. You can see this in,

> And thou shalt number seven sabbaths of years unto thee, seven times seven years; and the space of the seven sabbaths of years shall be unto thee forty and nine years. Lev 25:8 KJV

This how the celebration of the Fiftieth year was figured, the year of "Jubilee," Lev 25:10. It was to be after "seven sabbaths of years," or so to speak, after seven weeks of years (forty-nine years). Here then are key facts of history to keep in mind in looking at Daniel 9.

- Daniel is writing this chapter about 538-539 BC
- Jesus the Messiah WAS cut off as best I can figure, in the year 30 AD, which is about **560 years** from this writing
- The holy city of Jerusalem, the sanctuary of the temple, and the power of the Jews were broken in a siege of Jerusalem which culminated in the year 70 AD, about **609 years** from this writing.

The general alignment to history at this point becomes too much to ignore. There is more than enough time here to allow for the rebuilding of a city, among other things. So you have to ask the question:

When is the time "from the issuing of a decree to
restore and rebuild Jerusalem"
Dan 9:25?

The liberals, buried in their naturalistic ideas that automatically rule out God, and rule out God dealing with us or speaking to us, and automatically rule out any true and accurate prediction of the future; would have us just bury all of this, but if you take a candid look, it is too much to ignore.

If you look at Scripture, then you find three options to consider for the "decree to restore and rebuild Jerusalem." The first option is the Persian edict found in Ezra 1.

538 BC   Persian Edict   (Ezra 1:1-2)

[1] Now in the first year of Cyrus king of Persia, that the word of the LORD by the mouth of Jeremiah might be fulfilled, the LORD stirred up the spirit of Cyrus king of Persia, that he made a proclamation throughout all his kingdom, and put it also in writing, saying, [2] "Thus saith Cyrus king of Persia, The LORD God of heaven hath given me all the kingdoms of the earth; and he hath charged me to build him an house at Jerusalem, which is in Judah. Ezra 1:1-2 KJV

This first option is really a decree to rebuild the temple. A second decree is mentioned in Ezra 7, and is being carried by Ezra himself.

458 BC   Ezra sent   (Ezra 7:6-9)

This Ezra went up from Babylon; and he *was* a ready scribe in the law of Moses, which the LORD God of Israel had given: and the king granted him all his request, according to the hand of the LORD his God upon him. Ezra 7:6 KJV

But really this passage looked at overall seems to concentrate on the temple issues. Then comes to the third option listed in Scripture.

445 BC   *when Nehemiah was sent in (Neh 2:1-9)*

The subject of the book of Nehemiah in truth seems to concentrate more on the actual rebuilding of the city of Jerusalem.

But then perhaps it should be asked: is there maybe another edict which we are missing, which the ancients had but which we are missing, which falls somewhere in the periods shown above? Such is not impossible, but then again, we may have all the options listed in Scripture above. So the question is: which date starts the prophecy? Of Literally "seventy sevens"

From: "shibim" שִׁבְעִים *meaning seventy*
and
"shabua" שָׁבוּעַ *meaning sevens*

Seven periods of seven years = 49 years

Sixty-two periods of seven years = 434 years

And if the Messiah is to be cut after Seven weeks and sixty two weeks, the Total then = 483 years, Dan 9:25. Then comes the last week for:

> "And he will make a firm covenant with the many for one week, but in the middle of the week he will put a stop to sacrifice and grain offering; and on the wing of abominations *will come* one who makes desolate, even until a complete destruction, one that is decreed, is poured out on the one who makes desolate." Dan 9:27 NASB

So in the middle of the last seven years, the "he" "will make a firm covenant with the many," a New Covenant one might say. Then "in the middle of the week he will put a stop to sacrifice and grain offering." So how would these options work out for seventy sevens or "Weeks" of years?

Options for the Seventy "Sevens"			
Start	Ezra 1:1	Ezra 7:6-9	Neh 2:1
70 x 7 _ 490	538 BC	458 BC	445 BC
7 x 7 years 49 years	**489 BC**	**409 BC**	**396 BC**
62 x 7 years 434 years	**55 BC**	**25 AD**	**38 AD**
Middle of the last 7 years	**51 BC**	**29 AD**	**42 AD**
End of the 70 sevens	**38 BC**	**32 AD**	**45 AD**

Which starting date should be used? None of these answers are without some issues on the fine points of interpretation, but generally the starting date of Ezra 7:6-9, when by Imperial edict Ezra starts for Jerusalem in 458 BC, seems the overall best fit. The end of the sixty-two sevens plus the seven-sevens (a total of 483 years) would fall in 25 AD, which would be very close to the start of Jesus of Nazareth's ministry here on earth. The middle of the last seven years would be around 29 AD, and my best guess right now is that Jesus was actually crucified in 30 AD, although there are some minor issues even here. This part is incredibly close. And in the middle of that week the daily sacrifices and grain offering would have been made pointless by the sacrifice of Jesus as atonement of all men's sins, from the start of the world until its end.

Then you have to deal with the issue of *when* Jerusalem is to be destroyed. It seems to link this destruction with the death of the Christ, and as will be shown later, indeed it was linked. But all the prophecy really says about the time of destruction is that it will happen, presumably, and actually, after the death of the Messiah. As you can see, it is no wonder that in the first century many were looking for the Messiah and the kingdom to come *at any time!* No wonder that when Jesus came He said, "The time is fulfilled, and the kingdom of God is at hand; repent and believe in the gospel." Mk 1:15. Clearly they were familiar with the general outlines of the prophecy and were doing their counting. The first option, Christ being "cut off" in 51 **BC,** is the only option which had clearly failed by the time John the Baptist and Jesus came preaching.

It is obvious which option should be accepted, unless you have some distorted view of prophecy! *Then comes the Main Points:*

1. Clearly Daniel prophesies the death of the Messiah around the first century AD.
2. Clearly Daniel prophesies the destruction of Jerusalem around the first century AD, after it had been first rebuilt.
3. When time indicators are given in Scripture, they are important so that you will be ready for the general time when the key events are about to happen.
4. The hardest part, when a definite length of time is given (as in the last few chapters of Revelation), is knowing how to calculate when the period of time starts. This is often a gray area.
5. Clearly Daniel prophesies an end to sacrifices, and the making of a "final" atonement for sin.

So all of this study is relevant to the study of the end things of this world, and cannot be avoided in Matthew 24. So then comes the last parts of the discussion of Daniel 9, that is the discussion of the Atonement, and what about the "abomination?"

An Atonement for Sin, and Everlasting Righteousness? You may have noticed that the first lines of the prophecy, or all of the last lines of the prophecy, have not been dealt with. Of all the first lines: it says as you will remember, that the Seventy seven's are "to finish the transgression, and to make an end of sins, and to make reconciliation for iniquity, and to bring in everlasting righteousness," Dan 9:24 KJV. Of course, all of this was accomplished at the cross, at the time when "shall Messiah will be cut off," Dan 9:26 KJV. The death of Jesus on the cross in the first century is truly the central event of history, and the final reason for stopping the "sacrifice and grain offering," Dan 9:27. **So take**

note that it is clearly forecast that "sacrifice and grain offering" would be stopped! Indeed it was stopped by force in the first century. The author of Hebrews gives the central issues of sacrifice.

> [4] For *it is* not possible that the blood of bulls and goats could take away sins. [5] Therefore, when He came into the world, He said:
>
> *"Sacrifice and offering You did not desire,*
> *But a body You have prepared for Me.*
> [6] *In burnt offerings and sacrifices for sin*
> *You had no pleasure.*
> [7] *Then I said, "Behold, I have come—*
> *In the volume of the book it is written of Me—*
> *To do Your will, O God.' "* Heb 10:4-8 NKJV

The victory is not "going to happen," rather it has happened. Jesus defeated Satan with His death on the cross for mankind.

> [14] Forasmuch then as the children are partakers of flesh and blood, he also himself likewise took part of the same; that through death he might destroy him that had the power of death, that is, the devil; [15] And deliver them who through fear of death were all their lifetime subject to bondage. Heb 2:14-15 KJV

Christ by His action on the cross has rendered Satan "powerless." All the rest is footnotes in history. In 2 Cor 2:14-16, Psa 68:18, and Eph 4:8, Christ is pictured as having the equivalent of a Roman Triumph (2 Cor 2:14) when He reentered heaven in Acts chapter one.

> Thou hast ascended on high, thou hast led captivity captive: thou hast received gifts for men; yea, *for* the rebellious also, that the LORD God might dwell *among them.* Psa 68:18 KJV

Psalm 68 thus pictures this event as in the future, but as a completed action. (There is no "typo" here, it was said correctly!) Eph 4:8 pictures it as in the past, "When He ascended up on high ..." KJV. So this is a picture of Jesus coming back to heaven, ascending to the Father. As the Roman conquerors of old had prize captives and prisoners of war on display in their victory parade, their "Triumph," so Jesus is pictured as leading in His victory parade the demonic powers as captives, soon to be put to death. Satan is "captive," defeated, from the cross onward. As Jesus was going to the cross He said, "I beheld Satan as lightning fall from heaven," Lk 10:18. Jesus says that He has bound Satan.

> [28] But if I cast out demons by the Spirit of God, surely the kingdom of God has come upon you. [29] Or how can one enter a strong man's house and plunder his goods, unless he first binds the strong man? And then he will plunder his house. Mtt 12:28-29 NKJV

So Jesus is saying that He had to bind Satan, tie him up, in order to be able to ravage his kingdom and carry off Satan's captives as His prize. Satan is thrown down to earth after the cross, Rev 12:9; and Satan is pictured as "bound" during the Christian age, Rev 20:2. You don't think Satan is "bound, " restrained during the Christian age? Wait until you see what happens when Satan is released in the last days, Rev 20:7. Then the demonic powers will be afflicting all men who do not have the seal of God's Holy Spirit, as in Revelation 9. This demonic release is being continually pictured on television and the movies as a great time when the evil spirits will do to men as they wish in order to command their obedience. Yes, at that future time it will be clear that Satan has been "tied up" for most of the Christian Age!

Christ has already "blessed us with all spiritual blessings in heavenly *places*," Eph 1:3. And of those whom He has chosen, He has (past tense),

> [6] ... raised us up together, and made us sit together in heavenly *places* in Christ Jesus: [7] That in the ages to come he might shew the exceeding riches of his grace in his kindness toward us through Christ Jesus.
> Eph 2:6-7 KJV

The defeat and atonement of sin, the reign of righteousness, is not seen as something possible in the future, but as something done in the past, and, "For he must reign, till he hath put all enemies under his feet," 1 Cor 15:25 KJV. It was all accomplished at the cross, when the Messiah, the Christ was cut off, killed, but later raised from the dead. Why bring up a postponement of this prophecy? Why propose a failure of God's clear plan in these verses? *UNLESS*:

1. You don't understand that the kingdom of God is "not of this world," "not of this realm," or else at Christ's first coming His servants would have been "fighting so that I would not be handed over to the Jews," Jn 18:36 NASB. Or

2. You don't believe in the victory at the cross, that sin has now been defeated and reign of righteousness has come, and that the rest is just a period of grace to give men a chance to turn and become a part of it; and *that the rest of history is the "mopping up operations" after victory at the Cross!*

Then what of the abomination which makes desolate? Notice that in Daniel 9 he seems to be associated with the Romans who destroy Jerusalem in 70 AD, in fulfillment of Dan 9:26-27. But there is more than one association here.

Let's draw a parallel. There is more than one "type" or symbol of the Messiah, the Christ. (These are interchangeable terms, Messiah being Hebrew and Christ being Greek for "Anointed One".) So for instance, Solomon is a type of the Messiah in 2 Samuel 7, and Moses is a type of the Christ in Deuteronomy 18, and there are also many other types of the Christ.

So also there is more than one type of the abomination which makes desolate. One is from the Romans in the first century, and the other is Antiochus IV Epiphanes who is talked about in Daniel 8 and Daniel 11; and it is the confusion of these types with each other and the final anti-type (fulfillment) that is in part responsible for the confusion of the liberals in the book of Daniel. **Indeed, it is**

misunderstanding of types and anti-types, symbols and fulfillment, that is responsible for much of the blindness of the modern church. The key information for these things in the section on Type and Anti-type on Solomon and Christ in 2 Samuel 7. Refer to that section if you need to, or if necessary review it again later as these principles are needed to understand prophecy. Also there will be a more detailed discussion of the abomination that makes desolate later.

Again, all you can say is, Wow! What an incredible prophecy, and what a pity it has been neglected because of the confusion *which has been sown.*

Now it is time to look at the kings of Daniel 11 and to get an overview of Daniel 11. Like it or not, consider it as positive or negative, but still it is a fact: prophecy does have to do with history, with what has gone on and will go on in the future. It does have to do also with particular rulers, particular kings, presidents, dictators in history. At this point many people start to snicker and laugh. After all, there have been so many wrong identifications with the prophecies of Scripture, *which means the prophecies can not be true! Right?*

Passage Fulfillment (rulers, years reigning, and parallels)

Dan 11:2 Three more kings Medo-Persian Empire

Cambyses 530-522 BC

Pseudo-Smerdis or Gautmata 522 BC

Darius I 522-486 BC   Chest and arms of silver, **Daniel 2**

The bear, **Dan 7:5**

The ram, **Dan 8:3, 20**

Dan 11:2 a fourth who sill invade Greece,   **Xerxes (Ahasuerus)** 486-465

Esther 1:1, Ezra 4:6

[not specifically mentioned in this prophecy:

Artaxerxes I 465-424 BC

Darius II 423-404 BC

Artaxerxes II 404-358 BC

Artaxerxes III 358-338 BC

Arese 338-336 BC]

Darius III 336-330 BC, **Ezra 4:7, Neh 2:1**(book of Malachi written)

Dan 11:3 a mighty king   **Alexander the Great** 336-323

The Greeks   Start of the belly and thighs of bronze, **Daniel 2**

The prominent horn on the goat, **Dan 8:5-8, 21**

Dan 11:4 four winds of heaven   Alexander's generals who divided up his kingdom four ways: they are the 4 wings and the 4 horns

Dan 7:6 and **Dan 8:8, 22**

1. **Antipater & Cassander** (joint rulers of Greece)

2. **Lysimachus** (Asia Minor)

3. **Seleucus I Nictor** (1st "king of the North, Syria)

4. **Ptolemy I Lagi Soter** (1st "king of the South, Egypt)

AFTER ALL: If thousands of smart people have gotten
wrong answers in doing algebra problems,
then algebra must not be reliable!
RIGHT?

I am being facetious. Biblical prophecy is reliable, but it must be used correctly. It does at times involve particular kings (like Jesus Christ for instance),
and so at times you must make correlations to history, to the real world. Some
preliminaries are in order, and I are going to use Daniel 11 for the text.

The first part of Daniel 11 (see the chart on the previous page) is relatively
easy. Dan 11:1-4 describes well known events in history. The succession of some
(but not all) of the kings of the Medo-Persian Empire in verses 1 and 2, and
then in verses 3 and 4 it describes the rise of Alexander the Great and his generals who succeeded him.

Dan 11:5-35 (see the chart on the next page) goes into detail about two lines
of these kings who succeeded Alexander the Great: the Seleucids kings of the
North; and the Ptolemies, kings of South. The portraits are from ancient coins.

For this kind of prophecy, you may have to read history and look for matches. These events are described in secular history by the Jewish historian Josephus,
the Greek historian Polybius, the Roman historian Livy, and others. For the
average reader, the easiest place to start might be Josephus *Antiquities of the
Jews*, especially Book XII, and 1 and 2 Maccabees (which are useful books of
history, but do not claim to be inspired. Copies are available at most Bible
bookstores). So it can be seen that most of Daniel 11 is fulfilled prophecy which
one can "practice on," to see how these prophecies work. Most of this was hard
to see ahead of time, but more understandable as it was happening.

I are not suggesting that you should dive into this history right now, or that
you necessarily have to at some point. This chapter is being used as an example of
how these things work, and identifying part of the fulfillment of Daniel 11.

Our Purpose: By seeing how these things have worked in the
past (and you may also need to look back at lessons like the
section on Type and Anti-type, 2 Samuel 7), then
*when you need to, you will be ready to start
looking for matches to prophecy!*

The real mystery is Dan 11:36-45. This passage doesn't fit what is known
about Antiochus IV Epiphanes, or any ancient ruler. In Bible prophecy such
things often means that the subject is a pattern or 'type' of someone in the future. For example the prophecy of Solomon building a temple for God, 2 Sam
7:12-16 as discussed in the lesson on Types, Solomon fulfilled (see 2 Chron
6:10). However his kingdom did not last forever (it ended in 586 BC), and he
was not really the son of God (2 Sam 7:14). So Solomon was just a pattern or
type of the Christ who completes this passage, Heb 1:5. Christ is, to use the
Greek phrase, the anti-type, the fulfillment.

Kings of the North	Kings of the South
(North of Palestine: Syria Asia Minor)	*(South* of Palestine: Egypt)
The Seleucids	The Ptolemies
Dan 11:5 Seleucus I Nictor 311-280 BC	**Ptolemy I Lagi Soter**
(At first a commander of Ptolemy I)	323-285 BC
Antiochus I Soter 280-261 BC	**Ptolemy II Philadelphus**
	285-246 BC. Commissioned a Greek translation of the Old Testament, the same translation used by the early church
Dan 11:6 Antiochus II Theos 261-246 BC	
----marries---------------------------	*Bernice, daughter of*
(after divorcing Laodice)	*Ptolemy II*
Dan 11:7 Seleucius II Callinicus	**Dan 11:7 Ptolemy III**
(246-226 BC)	**Eugeretes I** 246-221 BC
	Dan 11:11 Ptolemy IV
Dan 11:10 Seleucus III Ceraunus 226-223 BC	**Philopator** 221-203 BC
Dan 11:10,11,16-18 Antiochus III (The Great) 223-187 BC, takes Palestine away from the Ptolemies, 198 BC	
Dan 11:17, His daughter, Cleopatra *marries ------->*	**Dan 11:14 Ptolemy V Epiphanes** 203-181 BC
Dan 11:20 his son **Seleucus IV Philopater** 187-175 rules	
Dan 11:21,27,28-35 Antiochus IV Epiphanes, 175-164 BC	**Dan 11:25,27 Ptolemy VI Philometer** 181-146 BC
replaces his brother, invades Egypt, & is turned back by Rome, he	

1. Takes away the daily sacrifice, Dan 8:9-13

2. Is a stern faced, master of intrigue, destroys the holy people, Dan 8:23-26

3. Dan 11:31 Sets up an abomination that causes desolation

But 4. Dan 11:36-45 ???? This part doesn't fit what we know about Antiochus Epiphanes, or any ancient ruler.

For example, to understand more about Jesus, you may have to read more about Solomon. And to learn more about the abomination of desolation (Dan 11:31 and Mtt 24:15) and the final "king of the North," you may have to read secular histories about Antiochus IV Epiphanes!

Cautions: "The prophetic word" is to warn and strengthen us, and we "do well to pay attention as to a lamp shining in a dark place," 2 Pe 1:19 NASB.

1. We need to do our homework carefully so we do not "see" things which are not there. Many of us have had to deal with people who try to explain the meaning of the fourth freckle on the third horn of the fifth beast.

2. We should be patient with each other. We have all been caught off guard by the insights of others, and rejected them out of hand. We need to read, think, listen, and compare. We should work systematically, and carefully.

It was said before, but let's repeat it.

Don't ignore "facts" which "don't seem to fit!"
These are often the signal that you are dealing with a model,
not a fulfillment. The models are often very figurative
(compare Isaac in Heb 11:18-19 NASB), while the fulfillment is
often very literal (like Jesus resurrection).

There are many important stories in the Old Testament that are involved in sorting out the meaning of New Testament commands and prophecy. These stories are to be used as examples as Paul pointed out in 1 Cor 10:6. They are types and models. One of them is about Esau in Gen 25:27-34, and Esau is a type, a model. He is a model of those Christians who despise their inheritance in the heavenly land, and sell their right to heaven for a little bit of this world's goods, a bowl of beans in this case, Heb 12:14-17.

What Must Soon Take Place

The announcement of the purpose of the book is what is at the beginning of the prophecy of Revelation. It is about what must soon take place, Rev 1:1 NASB. It is a *foretelling* of what must happen. What does this mean "must soon take place"? It says at the end of verse 3 that "the time *is* at hand," KJV. What does that mean? How should that be understood and what should we expect from it? Let me suggest four things that give us a perspective through which to look at the book of Revelation, and the book of life:

1. These things are going to *start* happening *soon*. Soon in human terms. At hand in the ways of men. Soon in terms of local history and what happens to a people. *Not* centuries away, will this *start* to happen.

2. And once it starts it will run until the end ... the end of this present universe, and the beginning of a new universe. But there is something else to notice, to notice about man and history and time.

3. History, over all, is really very short. It seems like a long time now, but really, *even for us*, *at the end*, it will seem like *nothing*, it will seem very short. We are like children waiting to enter the first grade, and it seems

like it will be forever before it happens, but of course it is really not forever. As a young man I feared having children, and wondered whether I should have any because, you know, it takes *forever* to raise children. But as most of you know, it is really not forever. Now, over 40 years later I have raised two sets of children and am still here. Time is really not forever. Indeed it is very short. Today you are born. Tomorrow you are married. The third day you see your grandchildren. The fourth day you die. The fifth day the trumpet of Lord will sound, and you will arise to fame, glory and honor, or to continual destruction. If your life has been one of destructive behavior, you shall be subject to it forever.

4. And time is really, really, short to The One who sees all things.

> ^{8} But, beloved, be not ignorant of this one thing, that one day is with the Lord as a thousand years, and a thousand years as one day. ^{9} The Lord is not slack concerning his promise, as some men count slackness; but is longsuffering to us-ward, not willing that any should perish, but that all should come to repentance. 2 Pe 3:8-9 KJV

Do not seal up the words of this prophecy, is the message in Rev 22:10. The time is near. In other prophecies that have been examined, the prophet was told that those words were sealed, but John is told to not seal up this prophecy. I am coming soon He says in Rev 22:12, 20. The Judge is at the door, James the Lord's half brother tells us! Jas 5:8-9

It is not just a belief plea, not just a time plea. It is a moral plea. Time is short, even for the young. How old will you live to be? Your life and mine will be over before we know it.

> ^{29} But this I say, brethren, the time has been shortened, so that from now on those who have wives should be as though they had none; ^{30} and those who weep, as though they did not weep; and those who rejoice, as though they did not rejoice; and those who buy, as though they did not possess; ^{31} and those who use the world, as though they did not make full use of it; for the form of this world is passing away.
> 1 Cor 7:29-31 NASB

It is very soon and very short ... and you and I are like little children waiting for the birthday to come that never seems to come.

Revelation is a revealing of the truth, and God is the one making it known, because the book of Revelation is a Revelation of Jesus Christ which God gave Him to show to His slaves (and yes, the Greek word is the word for "slaves," doulos, δοῦλος Rev 1:1). This is not a hiding of the truth. "And he saith unto me, Seal not the sayings of the prophecy of this book: for the time is at hand," Rev 22:10 KJV. This is an open book to those who will listen and hear and obey. Obviously this is in contrast to at least part of the book of Daniel. It is a revealing of the plans of God. That is what the word "revelation," *apokalupis* ἀποκάλυψις, means: to disclose or tell; to reveal. The word is literally the opposite of covering up ... it means to uncover. It is the revealing the secrets of the ages. Here is the uncovering of the truth of the Christian age. As it says in the Book of Daniel: there is a God in heaven who reveals mysteries, Dan 2:28.

This word is used in the same way in other passages. It says in Romans 2:5 that at the last day we will have a "revelation" of God's wrath. It says the gospel came to Paul by "revelation," in Gal 1:12. And Jesus Christ will be "revealed" from heaven at that last day, 2 Thes 1:7, and all will see Him, every eye will see Him, even those who crucified Him, Rev 1:7. In all, the word 'revelation' is used 18 times in the New Testament; in cases like you see here, and the word is used only once in the book of Revelation, and that is in the verse you see right at the beginning of the book, that He makes it known to His servants, His slaves, Rev 1:1.

If you are not His servant (and the word used here is really the word "slave," as has been pointed out) then He is not revealing it to you. If you like to see, but do not like to "do" ... if you like to feel religious, but service with the people of God is a joke to you, this book is not for you. Typically it won't "pierce the void." If you like to feel good but don't want to be a "slave" to the religion of Jesus Christ, then this is not a revelation *to you*! It is a "secret" *revealed* to His *servants, His **slaves**!* When you stumble at the words and you start rejecting, not believing, it becomes a tremendous barrier to understanding. This is for Jesus' *slaves*. This is for absolute slaves of God ... which many sadly are not.

Many do not want to hear and are afraid of what this may cause them to do, what they may have to give up to follow this.

> [14] ..."*Hearing you will hear and shall not understand,*
> *And seeing you will see and not perceive;*
> [15] *For the hearts of this people have grown dull.*
> *Their ears are hard of hearing,*
> *And their eyes they have closed,*
> *Lest they should see with their eyes and hear with their ears,*
> *Lest they should understand with their hearts and turn,*
> *So that I should heal them.'* Mtt 13:14-15 NKJV

The wicked will never understand, Dan 12:10.

The great men of God all the way down through history have been called "slaves" of God. Sometimes that is translated "servant" in many of our Bibles, but the original word is 'slave'. The Apostle John is a slave to Jesus Christ in Rev 1:1. Paul the Apostle is a slave of God, Ti 1:1. The Apostle James is also a slave, Jas 1:1. Moses is called a slave of God in 2 Kgs 18:12 and other passages.

Surely the Lord does nothing without telling his people, His servants the prophets, Amos tells us in Amos 3:7. The word "servant" used in this verse in Hebrew is the word *ebed* עֶבֶד, which can mean servant, but it is also the regular word for slave in the Old Testament. Isn't it curious that ancient Hebrew distinguishes between slavery and working for wages, only by the context? Perhaps that is more realistic than a lot of our thinking. However in the Greek translation of the Old Testament, *ebed* is translated slave in Amos 3:7 and in many other passages.

And if you don't understand what this book is about, then what? Two distinct possibilities are that either you are not using your light to open the book, or you are not understanding because you are not walking in the light. Do you have your Bible with you? The keys are in your hand, with a heart that can see and feel and hear.

Repentance heals. Circumcision, true circumcision of the heart ... enables you to be sensitive and feeling and responding and really living. He sent his angel to show his servants in Rev 22:6-7, and again it is really the word "slave," *doulos* δοῦλος.

There is also a blessing with the Book of Revelation.

> Blessed *is* he that readeth, and they that hear the words of this prophecy, and keep those things which are written therein: for the time *is* at hand. Rev 1:3 KJV

The end of all things is near according to Peter in 1 Pe 4:7-8. To understand as you should, to grow as you should, to be first, you must be a slave first, Mtt 10:24-25. You need to circumcise your heart, Rom 2:29. That circumcision which is necessary is that made without hands, the circumcision of your heart by the Spirit, so that you can see and feel and know.

> [11] In whom also ye are circumcised with **the circumcision made without hands**, in putting off the body of the sins of the flesh by the circumcision of Christ; [12] **Buried with him in baptism**, wherein also ye are risen with *him* through the faith of the operation of God, who hath raised him from the dead. Col 2:11-12 KJV (*emphasis added*)

So that you too can become a slave of God.

Revelation is a difficult book for many. One that many often avoid because they just do not know what to do with it. I am maintaining that it is understandable and not as "mystical" as some would make it. It was written for you and me. We have had help misunderstanding. Still the prophet Amos says,

> Surely the Lord GOD does nothing
> Unless He reveals His secret counsel
> To His servants the prophets. Amos 3:7 NASB

It's use of symbolism has precedent. Jesus' main form of teaching was using symbols (the parables), and you can practice there (so you see, reading it is not near as "mystical" as some have made it out to be). Daniel's prophecies also use symbolism in fulfilled prophecy to describe empires that have past. You can practice on Daniel's book. Both Daniel and Revelation are what the scholars call "apocalyptic" literature, a term that means to "reveal things" (which it does) but the muddling of men has turned things upside down. *Most (but not all)* of Daniel has been fulfilled. Daniel chapters 2, 7 and 8, are series of parallel /overlapping visions that cover ancient Babylon, Medo-Persia, Greece and Rome. These empires are described as "beasts," and their rulers are "horns" on the beasts. Some of these are identified by name, as Greece is in Dan 8:21, and Alexander the Great is clearly spoken of in Dan 8:5 (the prominent horn).

So for more trying times God has given us much material to "practice" on. Satan would much rather have us trip over what we *cannot* understand than have us learn from what we *can* understand, so he consistently tries to shy us away from studying the books of Daniel and Revelation, indeed really anything prophetic.

God shows us what will happen! This is seen in the symbolism in the Old Testament, and it is

Showing John the holy city in Rev 21:10.

not separate from the Old Testament! When John calls the empires of the gospel age beasts and refers to their "horns," it is clearly reminiscent of Old Testament prophecy and you can get clues from fulfilled prophecy. When the power behind the scenes is called "Babylon" (which no longer exists in New Testament times), or the prophet uses language reminiscent of Babylon, Tyre, Elijah and Elisha, the plagues of Egypt, it clearly intends to show us that these things are "types," "models" of the events and people of the gospel age. When it speaks of things like "Gog and Magog" in Rev 20:8, it clearly intends for us to consult Ezekiel 39, and Gen 10:2, and so on.

Revelation is a series of parallel visions. If you look around in Scripture, that is the normal way God speaks to His people, whether Jews or Gentiles. Who would do something so foolish as to try to put Jesus' parables of the kingdom end to end? No one! They are clearly parallel, overlapping accounts. The idea seems to be that if you don't understand it from one parable you may understand from another. That is the way the book of Daniel is organized, but some foolishly try to put the visions of the book of Revelation end to end.

If you are reading along in Rev 6:15-17, or Rev 11:18, or of the harvest in Rev 14:18-20, and you think to yourself, "that sounds almost like the end of time," that's because *it is* speaking of the end of time. You may well be identifying the end of some of the visions.

So in Daniel and the visions seen there, one can clearly see overlap. Let's look at the overall picture. In Daniel chapter two King Nebuchadnezzar sees a vision of an image, an image of succeeding empires, an image in which Nebuchadnezzar is clearly told that "... Thou art this head of gold," Dan 2:38 KJV. Then he is told that another kingdom inferior to his will follow his kingdom and is the chest and arms of silver, the Medo-Persian Empire which would follow his. Following that is the Greek empire of Alexander the Great as the belly and thighs of bronze, and the Greeks were known for their bronze armor. Following that is the legs of iron and the feet of iron mixed with clay, which represents the Roman Empire. The general outline of these empires is plainly represented in the visions. In the succeeding chapters these empires are represented in various ways, some easily seen, some requiring more investigation.

In Daniel chapter 7 these four ancient empires are represented, with Babylon as a lion with wings, Medo-Persia as a bear devouring prey, and Greece as a leopard with the four wings of a bird. Greece is the easiest to see for the modern reader, for at Alexander the Great's death, his empire was divided between his generals into four major competing kingdoms, all Greek. Thus you can see the four wings of the leopard. Last of all in Daniel 7 is the Roman empire as a terrible "beast" with great iron teeth that tore and devoured and trampled all the other empires down, and one of its "horns" (rulers) had "the eyes of man and a mouth uttering great boasts," Dan 7:8. At the end however, all these kingdoms were brought into judgment. There is more to tell in both Daniel 2 and Daniel 7, but the purpose is to show how the rough outlines of history are symbolically pictured there.

More instructive to us is perhaps Daniel 8 in its use of imagery, which can be then applied to these studies. First Daniel sees a ram running over the fields, butting down its opponents in every direction, and no one could oppose the ram. The ram represents the Medo-Persian Empire, and the ram is pictured as having one horn larger than the other. So it was that the horns represented the Medes and the Persians, with the Medes being dominant in the early part of the empire, but the Persians being dominant in the later empire and becoming both larger and greater.

Alexander the Great pictured on an ancient coin with horns like a goat. Compare Dan 11:3, and Alexander as the goat with horns in Dan 8:5-8, 21

Finally (after hundreds of years) a goat challenges the ram, and shattered his two horns. This is, of course, the Greeks who came some two hundred years after Daniel's time. The goat had one outstanding horn between his eyes, unicorn-like you might say. That horn (a person) was Alexander the Great; that horn was broken off (Alexander died), and then four outstanding horns rise up in his place. These are the four generals of Alexander the Great who divided up his kingdom at his death. They are Antipater and Cassander who jointly ruled Greece, Lysimachus who ruled what we would now call Turkey, Seleucus I Nictor (the first "king of the North" of Daniel 11, that is north of Palestine) who ruled over what we would call Iran and Iraq and Syria, and lastly Ptolemy I Lagi Soter (the "Great Savior"), the first "king of the South" in Daniel 11, that is to say, south of Palestine. The kings of the north and of the south fought back and forth for control of Palestine, with great effects on the Jews and their development. The four generals of Alexander the Great's empire are variously represented as four wings, and four heads in Dan 7:6, and as four prominent horns in Dan 8:8, 22. This part of the interpretation is easy to see in Daniel 8, and if you have even skimmed the book of Revelation, then you can see the significance of a lot of the symbolism used in the book of Revelation. So a "beast" *can be* an empire. It is a brute, a monster in our terms. *Also,* it *can be* a particular king. A horn similarly can represent either a line of rulers or a particular ruler.

If you miss the instruction in the book of Daniel, you will surely miss the Revelation of what will shortly come to pass in the New Testament. This will be discussed again later.

Similarly the prophet Hosea has a series of visions. If you look at the book, it has a series of overlapping visions, variations on the same theme, different facets of the same gem of truth, and most would not think of dealing with the book otherwise. But when we come to the book of Revelation, the tendency is to lose all of our bearings, forget every precedent, refuse to consider Old Testament parallels, and then add the visions of the book of Revelation end to end from the first century AD to the end of time.

An Overview: The book of Revelation has some natural divisions. Chapters 1-3 deals with seven lamp stands. Chapters 4-7 deals with seven seals on a book. Chapter 8-11 speaks of seven special trumpets. These are natural divisions which really cannot be avoided. Chapters 12-14 deal with the "dragon" Satan fighting against the male child who is to rule all nations (Rev 12:5), and Satan gives his authority to a "beast." This beast has a resurrection of sorts (its fatal wound is healed! Rev 13:3), all the world worships him, and he wages war on the saints (Rev 13:5). Chapters 15-16 speak of the seven **last** plagues from God! You cannot get around it, that is the subject. Chapters 17-18 tell of the *age long power* and the *doom of Babylon,* although she is first mentioned in Rev 14, and from there it moves to describe the final battle against God in chapter 19. Chapters 20-22 seem to span all the way from the binding of Satan at the cross, to his end release and rampage at the end of time, through the judgment and to the new creation spoken of by Peter in 2 Pe 3:13, by Isaiah in Isa 66:22, and also by others. Each vision indeed seems to cover all of our age, with more emphasis on the end of the age as you progress through the visions.

The book is instruction for us! It views all of our age. It describes those things which are at work *all through* the Christian age. War, famine, plague, oppression, and persecution are all part of our age from Roman times even until now and all the way to the end. The book clearly has to do with the early Christians (Rev 1:3), and clearly has to do with the last Christians (Rev 20:7-10). So it seems best to think of much of the imagery as picturing the spiritual battles and punishments that go on all through the Christian age. There are a series of powers that oppose the true and living God, but they are defeated, one after another.

Indeed, all who desire to live godly in Christ Jesus will be persecuted, 2 Tim 3:12. Wars are not a part of the end, for "but the end is not yet," Mtt 24:6 KJV. Instead the end will come when they say peace and safety, 1 Thes 5:3. Still the plagues and environmental disasters pictured will be an ongoing part of our age. So without understanding *exactly* all the details, one can clearly see in Revelation that things get much worse before the end. Just as it says in 2 Tim 3:13: "Evil men and imposters will grow worse and worse, deceiving and being deceived." NKJV.

It seems that it is sort of an "Outsiders View" in Revelations chapters 1 through 11. These chapters seem to describe the Christian age as seen on the surface. There are wars and desolations and environmental disasters throughout our age. The true church is persecuted throughout our age. But God in heaven cares, and the disasters are in part the punishment for the sins and hard hearts of men.

Then it seems to be an "Insiders View" of our age in Revelation chapters 12 through 22. It seems to be a picture of the behind the scenes spiritual struggles in this world. A struggle between the Son and His church, who are opposed by the dragon, and the occult forces of our age. The forces of evil culminate in a true world empire, an empire that is destroyed near the very end of history but still before the second coming of Christ. There are a few time indications, but they are very few. For instance, Rev 19:20 coincides with 2 Thes 2:8, and says the beast will be personally destroyed by Jesus' second coming. So the beast does not appear in history until just before the end of time! Prophecy in both the Old Testament and the New Testament clearly speaks of a world wide "war," which the book of Revelation calls "Armageddon," in Rev 16:16, against the true and living God and His people, very near the end. The Son and His church are opposed by the dragon and the occult (the hidden) forces of our age. The forces of evil culminate in a true world empire, an empire that is destroyed within history near the very end in a conflict prompted by God, Rev 17:16-17.

Even though "the mystery of lawlessness was already at work" in the first century (2 Thes 2:7 NKJV), it will work until it is destroyed at Jesus' second coming, 2 Thes 2:8. No doubt many men of the last two thousand years have "woke up" to find themselves involved in Babylon and had to come out of her, Rev 18:4. If you take your clues from the Old Testament "types," her fullness of power will be brief, and clearly her fall will be complete before Jesus comes!

Also the kingdom of God has come! Jesus has gone into a far country to receive the kingship and will return to deliver and reward His servants (compare Lk 19:11-12). Now He rules in the midst of His enemies, Psa 110:1-2, and Jesus will continue to rule until the end, 1 Cor 15:25-26. *The kingdom is not future; it is present, even though we will not see its fullness until we get to heaven, for it is indeed a kingdom which is not of this world,* Jn 18:36, a kingdom literally of heaven.

Rulers of our age should take note and serve Him with fear, Psa 2:7, 10. The martyrs cry out "How long?" (Rev 6:10), and Jesus opens seals of judgment within history in Revelation chapters 6 and 7. Christ does rule. It *seems* that the church is overcome, but really God helps and protects those He calls. It *seems* that the enemy is winning, but really God uses the forces of wickedness against each other, and puts them all to destruction and delivers His people.

Satan's **final** release is going to be different. Satan is restrained for most of the Christian age, 2 Thes 2:6-7. At one time Satan was in heaven, as in Job chapters 1 and 2. But Jesus said, "I was watching Satan fall from heaven like lightning," in Lk 10:18. (Also compare Rev 12:7-12.) The restraining and binding of Satan started while Jesus was on earth, Mtt 12:28-29. But near the end of the time, he will be released from his prison, Rev 20:3, 7. We literally haven't seen anything yet!

It is often easy to mistake one of Satan's minor actors for one of Satan's special men like the beast of Revelation 13. All of Satan's men will bear some resemblance to their master, just like all of God's men bear some resemblance to their LORD. But the "types" and the "models" do not show the breadth of power that is in those final passages of Revelation.

None of this will make you an expert. I am not an expert! But if you will look, and think, you can see a great deal!

And there are some warnings:

> Blessed *is* he that readeth, and they that hear the words of this prophecy ... for the time *is* at hand. Rev 1:3 KJV

> ... if any man shall take away from the words of the book of this prophecy, God shall take away his part out of the book of life ...
> Rev 22:19 KJV

We can also see, as with Jesus' first coming, some of these things probably will not be well understood until the time they occur. Daniel speaks of words that "are closed up and sealed till the time of the end," Dan 12:9 KJV; and the end of time is clearly the time of the resurrection of the dead, Dan 12:2-3.

Many of the big "happenings" in the later chapters of Revelation will be toward the very end and will be impossible to miss. *You may misinterpret these things because of living in darkness ...* may worship *false christs* instead of Jesus the Christ, and may follow *false prophets* and their signs (Rev 16:13-14), but you will not miss these events when they happen! Their world-wide nature will make that impossible!

But **"Where there is no vision, the people perish,"** Prov 29:18 KJV. Not all Christians will witness Babylon's actual fall within historical time, but Babylon is evidently an age long force in history. If we are not alive in Jesus, we will be caught by surprise by these things, 1 Thes 5:4-6.

Then come the closing words of what we should do.

> He that is unjust, let him be unjust still: and he which is filthy, let him be filthy still: and he that is righteous, let him be righteous still: and he that is holy, let him be holy still. Rev 22:11 KJV

> And if any man shall take away from the words of the book of this prophecy, God shall take away his part out of the book of life. Rev 22:19 KJV

God Acts in History

The activity of God in history is something seen over and over in Bible history, and it is implied that this is something constant, only most of the time we do not have the behind the scenes details. This subject can be seen in more than one story in Scripture.

Ahab was one of the more notable kings of the Northern Kingdom of Israel. The Northern ten tribes of Israel had revolted against the oppressive taxation and conscripted labor of Solomon's late kingdom. In the late tenth century BC, Jeroboam I formed the breakaway kingdom of Israel and ruled it for 22 years, 1Kgs 14:20. Modern man seems ignorant of the fact, but it was well understood in ancient and medieval times **that a religious consensus is necessary to maintain a political consensus.** (Actually the enemies of Christianity also realize this but want to sabotage any attempt at a state based on the Messiah, Jesus of Nazareth.) So Jeroboam (Ahab's predecessor) early in his reign, sought to establish a stable state religion and one independent of neighboring and parent kingdom, Judah, 1 Kings 12:27-29

The issue of course was that the Lord God is the one who had put Jeroboam I on his throne and established his kingdom and promised to make his lineage a "sure house," if he would be faithful to the Lord (1 Kgs 11:38-39). Israel itself was still under covenant obligations to the Lord, which included worshipping only in Jerusalem, not using any images in worship, and only using the priesthood of the Levites, and on and on and on. But Jeroboam's savvy political sense would not allow him to trust God's promise of security for his kingdom if he was faithful to God. So Jeroboam choose to trust his political sensibilities rather than trust the Lord. So it came to be that "And this thing became a sin: for the people went *to worship* before the one, *even* unto Dan," 1 Kgs 12:30 KJV. These rotten foundations became those on which all succeeding generations in the northern kingdom of Israel were built.

There were a lot of ups and downs in the years to come. The Lord permitted the kingdom to continue, but all the kings of the north followed Jeroboam's lead in religion. Baasha reigned twenty-four years, but Elah only two, and Zimri only seven days. Ahab's dad Omri reigned twelve years, and then around 874 B.C. Ahab came to the throne, and Ahab was more wicked than all the kings of Israel who had gone before him.

> [32] He set up an altar for Baal in the temple of Baal that he built in Samaria. [33] Ahab also made an Asherah pole and did more to provoke the LORD, the God of Israel, to anger than did all the kings of Israel before him. 1 Kgs 16:32-33 NIV

Our historian in 1 Kings describes all of this in a very detached manner, and if you are not careful, you can miss the full impact of what is said here. It could be argued, and has been argued, that Jeroboam I had not rejected the worship of Yahweh/Jehovah as the God of all heaven and earth. I'm sure Jeroboam would have argued this. He would have said that he only gave them a different access to Yahweh and had given them a way to focus on their "god" through the images which he had made, the golden calves. Such are the arguments of idolaters all through history. Many would argue that only a simpleton would really confuse the "image" with the "god," but that they are only providing a way to focus on the true god.

But beyond all of this, Ahab is clearly going on to emphatically worship other "gods," which are not gods at all, but are "them which by nature are no gods," Gal 4:8 KJV. Baal and Asherah are the male and female companion "gods" of the Canaanites, the same ones that caused the fall of the early Palestinians (Gen 15:16), and they are the same ones warned of in Moses' Law and in the books of Joshua and Judges. Asherah herself was sort of a "mother earth" figure, and indeed our modern pagans consider her the same as Isis, Ishtar, Aphrodite, Venus, the love goddesses, and the fertility goddesses. The Asherah poles mentioned in Scripture were evidently obscene images of the naked goddess, and were placed in her temples and her "high places" (mountain top worship places) and gardens; and she was "worshipped" by various sacrifices and rituals, including ritual fornication to insure the bounty of their crops and fields and herds and wives. The later prophet Amos complained,

> [7] ... A man and his father go in to the *same* girl,
> To defile My holy name.

[8] They lie down by every altar on clothes taken in pledge,
> And drink the wine of the condemned *in* the house of their
> god. Amos 2:7-8 NKJV

This included the use of both male and female "ritual prostitutes," and the Lord said,

> I will not punish your daughters when they play the harlot
> Or your brides when they commit adultery,
> For *the men* themselves go apart with harlots
> And offer sacrifices with temple prostitutes;
> So the people without understanding are ruined.
> Hos. 4:14 NASB

I am not touching here on human sacrifices, which will become more prominent later, but it goes without saying that such evil worship was destructive of
both homes and society and clearly destructive of any blessings from God.

Then more to the point of this study, Ahab comes to be opposed by the
prophet Elijah. Now Elijah and his successor Elisha clearly seem to be types of
the two prophets spoken of in Revelation 11:3. They exercise powers and authority, and seem to act in a political situation similar to that in Ahab's day. Compare Rev 11:4-6. There is another "likeness" here because the "two witnesses" in
Revelation 11 "shall prophesy a thousand two hundred *and* threescore days,
clothed in sackcloth," Rev 11:3 KJV. That would be forty-two months or three
and one half years. That is the same period of time that Elijah asked God to
not let it rain on Israel, and it was so, Jas 5:17-18, 1 Kgs 17:1.

Of course, all of this led to the great confrontation between Elijah and the
prophets of Baal on Mount Carmel in 1 Kings 18 and a clear vindication of the
Lord Yahweh as the only True and Living God, a confrontation which Ahab
personally witnessed. It is a story well worth studying in detail, but it is aside
from the topic here. In 1 Kings 20 the Lord God uses Ahab to defeat and humble Ben-hadad, King of Aram (called "Syria" in some translations but the Hebrew is indeed *Aram* אֲרָם). But even after all of this, Ahab did not repent. Then
in 1 Kings 21 he was involved in the murder of a land owner, and the confisca-
tion of his property when the owner refused to sell his property to Ahab. These
things prompted another confrontation with the prophet.

Then and only then did Ahab come close to true and complete and lasting
repentance. But it must asked here, if Elijah is a "type" of the prophets in Revelation 11; then is Ahab a type of the "beast" of Revelation? Indeed, another of
the "types" of the final rulers of our age, Nebuchadnezzar, also humbled
himself before the Lord our God. This something to think about in a later look
at the final things of our present age. The Lord then responds to Ahab's hum-
bling himself.

> Seest thou how Ahab humbleth himself before me? because he
> humbleth himself before me, I will not bring the evil in his days: but in

his son's days will I bring the evil upon his house. 1 Kgs 21:29 KJV

But a day of reckoning still had to come in 1 Kings 22. A day when the Lord would remove Ahab from his post. As 1 Kings 22 begins it has now been three years without war between Aram and Israel. Ahab remembers at this time "that Ramoth in Gilead *is* ours" KJV, and he asks faithful King Jehoshaphat if he will enter an alliance for them together to retake Ramoth-gilead from the Arameans, 1 Kgs 22:2-3.

Jehoshaphat agreed, "I *am* as you *are*, my people as your people, my horses as your horses." Moreover he asked, "Please inquire for the word of the LORD today," 1 Kgs 22:4-7 NKJV. All of this seems reasonable to Ahab, and he gathered four hundred of his prophets and asked them, "Shall I go against Ramoth Gilead to fight or shall I refrain?" His paid prophets said "Go up, for the Lord will deliver *it* into the hand of the king." The word translated "Lord" here is *adonai* אֲדֹנָי meaning master, perhaps referring to Baal (*baal* בַּעַל) which also basically means master, husband or ruler. Jehoshaphat, who is a worshipper of the LORD God, then asks, "*Is there* not still a prophet of the LORD here that we may inquire of Him?" The word that is translated "LORD" here, in small caps, is a different Hebrew word. It is the name of our God. It is *Yehovah* or *Yahweh*, or *Yaveh* יהוה, the proper name of God. Jehoshaphat is willing for his men of Judah to fight with their brother people, the men of Israel, to recover Ramoth-gilead, but does not buy the corrupt religion of the northern ten tribes.

King Ahab acknowledges that there is one man around of the true prophets of Yahweh, the LORD our God, but he says he hates him because he never says anything good about him. Jehoshaphat says that Ahab shouldn't talk that way, of course implying we should accept whatever the word is from the LORD, and then change our behavior to fit. So they called in Micaiah son of Imlah, a man of God of whom we know nothing else in Scripture, except in this passage. One of the prophets already there, Zedekiah the son of Chenaanah, at this point prophesies in the name of Yahweh (the "LORD") that they will defeat the Arameans. The officers sent to bring Micaiah tell him that all the other prophets are forecasting victory, and that he should be favorable also. Micaiah only says, "*As* the LORD lives, whatever the LORD says to me, that I will speak." 1 Kgs 22:14 NKJV.

Ahab asks him, shall we go battle at Ramoth-gilead or shall we hold back? Micaiah answers tongue in cheek, mockingly giving the king the answer he wants. "Go and prosper, for the LORD will deliver it into the hand of the king!" NKJV. The king is immediately distressed at such, and asks him how many times must he put Micaiah under oath to give the truth in the name of the LORD.

[17] Then he said, "I saw all Israel scattered on the mountains, as sheep that have no shepherd. And the LORD said, 'These have no master. Let each return to his house in peace.' "

[18] And the king of Israel said to Jehoshaphat, "Did I not tell you he

would not prophesy good concerning me, but evil?" 1 Kgs 22:17-18 NKJV

In other words, Micaiah said that Ahab will be killed in battle at Ramoth-Gilead, not an unknown result in ancient warfare. Then Micaiah gives us one of those rare insights into the courts of heaven. There are not very many. One of the clearest is in Job chapters one and two, and there are others, but they are rare. Micaiah then says to listen to the Word of the LORD. The LORD sat on his throne in heaven and all the hosts of heaven (the armies of heaven, the angels of heaven) sat around Him,

> [20] "And the LORD said, '"Who will persuade Ahab to go up, that he may fall at Ramoth Gilead?" So one spoke in this manner, and another spoke in that manner. [21] Then a spirit came forward and stood before the LORD and said, "I will persuade him." [22] The LORD said to him, "In what way?' So he said, "I will go out and be a lying spirit in the mouth of all his prophets.' And the LORD said, 'You shall persuade him, and also prevail. Go out and do so.' [23] Therefore look! The LORD has put a lying spirit in the mouth of all these prophets of yours, and the LORD has declared disaster against you." 1 Kgs 22:20-23 NKJV

The false prophet Zedekiah then slapped Micaiah on the cheek and asks how the Spirit of God went from him to Micaiah. Micaiah says that he will know on the day in which he enters a room to hide himself. Ahab commands Micaiah be put in prison on bread and water until the day he returns from battle, and Micaiah says, "If you ever return in peace, the LORD has not spoken by me. ... Take heed, all you people!" 1 Kgs 22:28 NKJV. And we never hear of Micaiah again in history.

Jehoshaphat, in contrast, was a good man who tried to follow the Lord. The latter part of 1 Kings 22 describes him as conducting himself just as his father Asa had. He did fail to remove all the "high places" of Judah, which were contrary to the Laws of God given through Moses, and which were the incubators of all the immoral religion which was inundating God's people. Still he deported all of what the King James Version calls "sodomites" (the Hebrew is qadesh קָדֵשׁ, the male cult prostitutes) from Judah, 1 Kgs 22:46. It also says that Jehoshaphat made peace with the northern kingdom of Israel, a fact which is reflected in 1 Kings 22. He clearly had respect for the Word of the LORD and sought it. Strangely, in the present story Jehoshaphat hears the Word of LORD but doesn't seem to heed it, so he and Ahab go into battle at Ramoth-gilead.

Ahab tries to disguise himself in battle to avoid being a target. Indeed the Arameans were targeting Ahab as the key to winning their battle. At one point in the battle, the Arameans spotted Jehoshaphat and mistook him for Ahab and pursued him. Jehoshaphat "cried out" it says (I assume to the LORD). When his pursuers saw he was not Ahab they left him alone. But a certain archer of Aram shot at random and struck Ahab. Ahab had his chariot taken out of the thick of the fight but was propped up in his chariot in front of the Arameans as the storm of battle went on all day. As night approached he died, and his blood pooled in the floor of the chariot.

The men of Israel and Judah now cried out, "Every man to his city and every man to his country." They buried Ahab in his capital, and took the chariot to the pool of Samaria to wash out his blood from the chariot, and there according to the Word of the LORD by Elijah, the dogs licked up his blood on the land he had stolen by murder.

The Lord rules in the Kingdom of Men.

> The LORD hath prepared his throne in the heavens; and his kingdom ruleth over all. Psa. 103:19 KJV

> "... That the Most High is ruler over the realm of mankind,
> And bestows it on whom He wishes
> And sets over it the lowliest of men." Dan 4:17 NASB

Ahab, like you and I, received his appointment in history to do, if he would, whatever God has desired. Like you and I, he sometimes did as God *desired*; also just like us, at other times as God *permitted*. When he had served God's purposes in history, he was called to join his fathers and to await judgment of the last day.

I find it strange that, in trying to talk about the nature of Biblical prophecy, it is necessary to recount some of the foundations of a Biblical philosophy of history. But that is what I find I should discuss, and show how these events relate to other prophecies, else when it comes to speak of those things yet to come, there will be no context for thinking over those things.

Another pertinent story is of Josiah who became king of Judah when he was eight years old, around the year 640 BC. His reign was long, thirty one years. Further, "And he did *that which* was right in the sight of the LORD, and walked in all the way of David his father, and turned not aside to the right hand or to the left," 2 Kgs 22:2 KJV.

Then one day you wake up, and find you have been unfaithful!

In the eighteenth year of the reign of Josiah King of Judah, about the year 622 BC, a forgotten copy of the Law of Moses was found in the temple of the LORD. Many things had happened in Judah. The drift from the true religion of Yahweh had been profound, both morally and ritually, with many of practices of true religion as outlined by the Lord for that age being entirely forgotten. The king asked for the book to be read in his hearing. He thought himself a loyal follower of this religion, a faithful adherent to the true religion of God, but when he heard the Law read in 2 Kgs 22:8; he realized how he and his nation were far from faithfulness to the Lord, and he tore his clothes in anguish. Then the king called to the priests of the national religion and told them to ask of the Lord what they should do, for he could clearly see that the anger of God was great against his nation because they had not listened to His Word.

Then Hilkiah the high priest, sought out a prophetess of the LORD to find out what they should do. As strange as it may seem to us today, the priesthood was hereditary but closeness to the Lord wasn't, so Hilkiah the high priest went to the prophetess Huldah, who told him,

> 15 ... "Thus says the LORD God of Israel, 'Tell the man who sent you to Me, 16 "Thus says the LORD: 'Behold, I will bring calamity on this place and on its inhabitants—all the words of the book which the king of Judah has read— ... 18 But as for the king of Judah, who sent you to inquire of the LORD, in this manner you shall speak to him, "Thus says the LORD God of Israel: '*Concerning* the words which you have heard— 19 because your heart was tender, and you humbled yourself before the LORD when you heard what I spoke against this place and against its inhabitants, that they would become a desolation and a curse, and you tore your clothes and wept before Me, I also have heard you," says the LORD. 20 Surely, therefore, I will gather you to your fathers, and you shall be gathered to your grave in peace; and your eyes shall not see all the calamity which I will bring on this place." ' " So they brought back word to the king. 2 Kgs 22:15-16, 18-20 NKJV

Here in other terms is another of those insights into the workings of heaven and its decisions. Desolation has been determined. It is sure, but the Lord is full of compassion and, because of the good heart of the king and his willingness to submit to the Lord, it will be delayed. Josiah will not see this desolation in his day. Then Josiah gathers all the people to Jerusalem to hear the reading of the full text of the covenant. The king listened with the people, and he and they made vows to keep the covenant, and to carry out all it's words.

Josiah, realizing how wrong had been the practices of Judah in approaching the Lord then brought about big changes. In 2 Kings 23 the young king began a campaign and did away with all of the idolatrous priests in the house of the Lord. The priests brought out of the temple all the vessels that were dedicated to the worship of Baal and Asherah and "all the hosts of heaven" (the stars, the angels), and they burned them outside Jerusalem. They brought out the image of Asherah and burned it, and ground it to dust and threw the dust on the graves of the common people who had abandoned the LORD to seek the Baals and the Asherahs. Then they destroyed all the apartments of the cult prostitutes in the temple area, and all the apartments where the women did crafts for Asherah. One can only imagine what things this young king might have taken a part, thinking it all part of the true worship of Yahweh. It is easy to see how ignorant even the high priests were in that day.

Josiah broke down the high places in the gates of Jerusalem. Then the king came to Topheth in the valley of Hinnom, where the people had made burnt sacrifices of their children. (The Hebrew word for a burnt offering is *olah* עֹלָה and the Greek from the Septuagint translation is *holokautōma* ὁλοκαύτωμα, a transliteration from the Hebrew, from which we get the word holocaust). The

Hebrews called this making their children to "pass through the fire." Topheth itself may take its name from drums used in the ceremonies for sacrificing children. Josiah defiled Topheth as a place of worship. He dug up the bones of the priests who engaged in child sacrifice and burned *their* bones on their own evil altars according to 2 Chronicles 34. Topheth in the valley of Hinnom became after this time the city garbage dump of Jerusalem and a type of the eternal place where the trash of the universe will be burned, the valley of Hinnom, or gehenna, *ge-enna* γέεννα, that is "hell." The priests in Judah who had offered up incense to the idols on the high places were no longer allowed in the temple (but evidently not put to death), but at the altar in Samaria he slaughters the priests on their own *altars*; then returning to Jerusalem celebrated the greatest Passover since the days of the Judges. Josiah also took away the mediums and spiritists from the land.

But the Lord did not turn away His fierce anger from Judah in part because of the sins which Josiah's father Manasseh had committed and caused the people to commit, filling the land with innocent blood, 2 Kgs 21:16, 23:26.

Then some strange things happened - things which perhaps throw a light on the many and varied ways in which the Lord may work in our world. At this time also, great events were happening in Babylon. During Josiah's time Nabopolassar came to power in Babylon on November 22, 626 B.C. Then Nineveh and the power of the Assyrians fell to the Babylonians in the summer of 612 B.C. These were earth-shaking events in those times, and the rulers of the east realized that if Babylon was not stopped she would rule over all of the east which was in that time almost all the civilized world. So the Egyptians and others raced north toward Carchemish to face Babylon in battle and if possible to stop her. A message came to the prophet Jeremiah during those days.

> Against Egypt.
> Concerning the army of Pharaoh Necho, king of Egypt, which was by the River Euphrates in Carchemish, and which Nebuchadnezzar king of Babylon defeated in the fourth year of Jehoiakim the son of Josiah, king of Judah: Jer 46:2 NKJV

In other words, Jeremiah says that it is **God's** *will* that the Egyptians go up to Carchemish and **be defeated**. The Lord says He is going to avenge Himself on ⬓ of His enemies.

> For this is the day of the Lord GOD of hosts, a day of vengeance, that he may avenge him of his adversaries: and the sword shall devour, and it shall be satiate and made drunk with their blood: for the Lord GOD of hosts hath a sacrifice in the north country by the river Euphrates. Jer 46:10 KJV

That "land of the north by the river Euphrates" is, of course, Carchemish which is to the north of present day Iraq. God then states the reasons:

> The LORD of hosts,the God of Israel, says: "Behold, I will bring punishment on Amon of No, and Pharaoh and Egypt, with their gods and their kings—Pharaoh and those who trust in him. Jer 46:25 NKJV

So God disciplines not only His own people but *also* the gentiles, the *nations*, even in Old Testament times! In this case Egypt is going to continue as a nation, but God is going to punish Egypt and try to turn her from her idolatry. God says to Judah-to the sons of Jacob, the sons of Israel-do not be afraid of what will happen and assures them they will survive and be cared for.

> Do not fear, O Jacob My servant," says the LORD,
> "For I am with you;
> For I will make a complete end of all the nations
> To which I have driven you,
> But I will not make a complete end of you.
> I will rightly correct you,
> For I will not leave you wholly unpunished." Jer 46:28 NKJV

God had determined to punish Egypt and deliver her into the hands of the Babylonians and has determined to punish (but not destroy) the men of Jacob. At this point we return to good king Josiah in Judah.

In the days of Josiah then, Pharaoh Neco made ready to join his allies in battle against the Babylonians on the river Euphrates. However, geography dictated that to do this he needed to go through the land of Judah. To go around Judah was logistically impossible. To the east of Judah was a huge desert which physically separated Judah from Babylon. This desert was so impassible in normal terms that when anyone went from Babylon to Judah or vice versa, they normally first had to go north, to the area of what is now northern Iraq (in the area of Carchemish or Haran), and then south to whatever was their destination. There was another issue also: it was dangerous to allow a large foreign army to pass through your territory, even if their stated intention was only to pass through and go on and to touch nothing. Israel had more than one problem with these things when they were first coming into their inheritance. Now tense things were happening in Palestine.

> After all this, when Josiah had prepared the temple, Necho king of Egypt came up to fight against Carchemish by Euphrates: and Josiah went out against him. 2 Chron 35:20 KJV

Pharaoh Neco did not really want to fight Josiah. He just wanted to pass through in order to defeat the Babylonians so he might not have to fight them on his own home ground of Egypt! And so Neco sent messengers to Josiah,

> ... saying, What have I to do with thee, thou king of Judah? I *come* not against thee this day, but against the house wherewith I have war: for God commanded me to make haste: forbear thee from *meddling with* God, who is with me, that he destroy thee not. 2 Chron 35:21 KJV

So Neco is saying that **God** wants him to go fight at Carchemish against the Babylonians, which indeed we know is true from the prophet Jeremiah. God *does want it, but it is so that Neco will be **defeated at Carchemish** so that Egypt will be turned over to oppressors*. It should be noted that the battle of Carchemish was indeed an end of Egypt as a first rate power in the world. From this point forward Egypt will still be important but only a second rate power in the ancient world. Then listen to what Scripture says about Josiah and what Neco said. Josiah would not listen to what he was told, but disguised himself and went into battle.

> Nevertheless Josiah would not turn his face from him, ... and hearkened not unto **the words of Necho from the mouth of God**,
> 2 Chron 35:22 KJV (*emphasis added*)

This is all very strange by our standards, that God would use a pagan king to deliver a message to a ruler of God's own people, but that is what we have here. Christians are accustomed to God using men to transmit His messages. Christians are in fact told to carry His message of salvation to the nations.

> [19] Go ye therefore, and teach all nations, baptizing them in the name of the Father, and of the Son, and of the Holy Ghost: [20] Teaching them to observe all things whatsoever I have commanded you ...
> Mtt 28:19-20 KJV

Beyond all of that can be seen here, God in His wisdom may use some very improbable instructors **to try to lead us and get us to do what is right**. This is, of course, one such case, and there are others in Scripture even more striking. When God does such things, this new information will not contradict other plain pronouncements from the Lord. The Word of the Lord is logical and consistent with itself, although it often has some paradoxes in it. This is happening in the year 609 B.C. As was pointed out earlier, Josiah knew that God had already determined punishment on his nation of Judah but would not allow that full punishment to come until after Josiah's day. So Josiah had plenty of reason to know that it *might be* God's will for Neco to meet with his allies at Carchemish! **We often have reason to know the things to which we should pay attention!**

Despite all of this in his background, Josiah will not listen. He prepares to meet Neco in battle at one of the northern mountain passes of Israel on the plains of Megiddo, which is near the mountain of Megiddo. This was in ancient times a common pathway for aggressors to come (either headed north or south) and a common way for invaders of Israel to come, generally from the north by way the mountain of Megiddo, which is in Hebrew *har Megiddo* הַר מְגִדּוֹ or is in Greek *Har-magedōn* Ἁρμαγεδών (Rev 16:16). Armageddon.

Like Ahab much before his time, Josiah took off all of his badges of rank so that he would not be a target for snipers in battle. Also just like with Ahab, it didn't work. Josiah was shot by an archer and carried away from the battle to Jerusalem and died.

God rules the kingdom of men and the hosts of heaven on high, and does as He wishes. **It is foolish not *to listen* and *think*.** God works in history.

The later rulers of Judah had even more problems in dealing with their situation. Among the sorrowful stories of Scripture, there are few more unhappy than the story of Jeconiah, a son born in the declining years of a very long lasting dynasty—that of David son of Jesse. Judah had been steadily declining morally, spiritually, physically, and politically; a*nd yes those things often go together,* not only in Judah, but also among all the nations of the world. Jeconiah's grandfather had been the good king Josiah. Josiah had strengthened the kingdom spiritually, politically, and militarily. But then he had been killed in a foolish battle with Pharaoh Neco of Egypt. At first an uncle of Jeconiah, Jehoahaz, had taken the throne, 2 Kgs 23:31-33, but his rule lasted a mere three months. Then he was deposed by Pharaoh Neco and deported to Egypt where he later died. Then Pharaoh Neco put Jeconiah's father Eliakim on the throne, 2 Kgs 23:34. Neco changed his name to Jehoiakim, and this is the name by which he is known to most of history, including in the genealogy in Chronicles.

Jeconiah's dad also was not much on listening to the Lord. Jehoiakim was still a young man when he came to the throne at age twenty five, but he lived, and reigned long enough to know better than he did. He reigned eleven years as king over Judah, but Scripture also says that "he did *that which was* **evil in the sight of the** Lord **his God,**" 2 Chron 36:5 KJV. It does not make a point as to whether he did what he thought was wrong (but probably he did that also); *rather* he did what **the Lord God *thought*** was wrong, and that is what counts in the final analysis. His reign started in 609 BC. This was the same year that Pharaoh Neco had asked permission to pass through Judah to go fight the Babylonians at Carchemish. Neco had rightly judged that this was the time for united action against Babylon or else they would soon be fighting against Babylon's growing power on their own door steps.

In the fourth year of dad Jehoiakim, Jeremiah had written down all of the Words the Lord God had given to him concerning Judah and Israel, Jer 36:1-2. This was the year 605 BC. It was written down for a special purpose.

> It may be that the house of Judah will hear all the evil which I purpose to do unto them; that they may return every man from his evil way; that I may forgive their iniquity and their sin. Jer 36:3 KJV

So God was planning evil against the nation, just as He does against nations in our own day, *because of their sins,* and the Lord was telling the people all of these things in hopes they would repent. Not a chance in this case! Chronologically, it seems that at this point the prophecy in Jeremiah 46 about the Battle of Carchemish was written.

Then Neco had gone to fight with his allies at the battle of Carchemish in the same *fourth year of Jehoiakim* (Jer 46:2) in the year 605 BC, at a critical crossing on the Euphrates River along the border between modern day Turkey and

Syria. Jeremiah had prophesied about the battle in Jeremiah 46:9-10 which has already been discussed. The result was the downfall of Egypt.

> "The daughter of Egypt shall be ashamed;
>> She shall be delivered into the hand
>> Of the people of the north." Jer 46:24 NKJV

These were world changing events. Babylon was amassing an empire larger than anything the western world had seen to that date. Neco had been right in his political assessment; he had just been wrong in thinking that he and his allies could defeat Babylon, and there was evidently more than one back and forth between Egypt and Babylon over Judah.

It seems then that it was later the same year (605 BC) that crown prince Nebuchadnezzar had laid siege to Jerusalem, and Jehoiakim had evidently surrendered to him, 2 Kings 24. These were without a doubt difficult years for the house of David, trying to hold on to their crown and their country in a war between competing super powers. It was evidently during this first Babylonian capture of the city that Daniel and others were taken captive to Babylon, what was the first of several deportations. There are evidently some issues between different dating systems between 2 Kings, 2 Chronicles, Jeremiah and Daniel here. *I know! I know* that many ancient dates can be linked to precise Assyrian and Babylonian observations of the heavens. Even so there are enough ambiguities between different methods of reckoning time, that if someone assures you they have the the calendar problems of the ancient Middle East all worked out, be skeptical!

The next year (which probably would have been December 604 BC) at a cold time of year when they had the stove fired up for heat and a fast had been proclaimed to the Lord, that the entire scroll of Jeremiah's prophecies were read publicly by Baruch in Jerusalem, Jer 36:8-9. Many state officials heard the reading and ordered Jeremiah and Baruch to go into hiding, and they then took the scroll to the king. The whole thing was read privately to the king (the story is told in Jeremiah 36) and after every three or four columns were read, the king would cut them off with a pen knife and throw them into the fire he was using to warm himself. The king commented,

> ... 'Why have you written in it that the king of Babylon will certainly come and destroy this land, and cause man and beast to cease from here?' Jer 36:29 NKJV

God then commanded Jeremiah to reproduce the scroll word for word, and the Lord said even more.

> 'Therefore thus says the LORD concerning Jehoiakim king of Judah: "He shall have no one to sit on the throne of David, and his dead body shall be cast out to the heat of the day and the frost of the night." '
> Jer. 36:30 NKJV

Thus it was promised in Jeremiah that Jehoiakim would have no son to sit on the throne of David. Jeremiah 25 was evidently written just the year before these things. There Jeremiah had promised Jehoiakim that since he would not listen, God says He will bring Nebuchadnezzar king of Babylon against this land to punish him and all the nation. It was clearly pointed out it was because both the Jewish nation and its leaders had refused to listen to God's holy prophets whom He had sent to warn them. The Lord went on to call the new Babylonian king, "My servant," Jer 25:9. Also it was prophesied in Jeremiah 22 that Jehoiakim would come to a horrible end and not be buried.

> [17] "Yet your eyes and your heart are for nothing but your
>   covetousness,
> For shedding innocent blood,
> And practicing oppression and violence.."
> [18] Therefore thus says the LORD concerning Jehoiakim the son of
> Josiah, king of Judah:
>   "They shall not lament for him,
>   *Saying,* "Alas, my brother!' or "Alas, my sister!'
>   They shall not lament for him,
>   *Saying,* "Alas, master!' or 'Alas, his glory!'
> [19] He shall be buried with the burial of a donkey,
>   Dragged and cast out beyond the gates of Jerusalem."
> Jer 22:17-19 NKJV

After saying that Jehoiakim would have no one rule on the throne of David, his son Jeconiah came to the throne, but it was ever so briefly (2 Kings 24:8-9). It goes on to say that "he did evil in the sight of the LORD, according to all that his father had done," NKJV. The death of Jehoiakim itself is not recorded in Scripture, but is briefly referred to by Josephus, *Ant. 10.6.3.* 2 Kings 24 says Jehoiakim served the king of Babylon three years, and then revolted. 2 Chron 36:6 says that Nebuchadnezzar attacked him, and he evidently surrendered, and it says that Nebuchadnezzar "bound him in bronze *fetters* to carry him off to Babylon" NKJV, and that is the last seen of him in history. Of these and other issues, it should not be supposed that Chronicles is at variance with Jeremiah. The historians are clearly familiar with Jeremiah, hold him to be a prophet, and quote him more than once. Scribal variations are obviously at work in places but at this point the data to sort them out is lacking.

The next part is ambiguous in Scripture. It does not mention an immediate revolt by the young king Jehoiachin/Jeconiah, but it does mention him being besieged by Babylonian armies and the eighteen-year-old surrendering with "... his mother, his servants, his princes, and his officers ..." 2 Kgs 24:10-12 NKJV. It seems this was the third deportation, a much larger one that also included Ezekiel and thousands of others, especially those initially spared of the ruling elite and the craftsmen. Likewise this is noted in the writings of Jeremiah. Jeremiah then commented on Jehoiachin/Jeconiah, or Coniah, as he calls him.

> 24 "*As* I live," declares the LORD, "though Coniah the son of Jehoiakim, king of Judah, were the signet on My right hand, yet I would pluck you off; 25 and I will give you into the hand of those who seek your life, and into the hand *of those* whose face you fear—the hand of Nebuchadnezzar king of Babylon and the hand of the Chaldeans.. 26 So I will cast you out, and your mother who bore you, into another country where you were not born; and there you shall die. 27 But to the land to which they desire to return, there they shall not return." Jer 22:24-27 NKJV

His mom had not been taken in chains to Babylon with his dad, but now the whole bunch go to Babylon. Jeconiah then spent the rest of his life as a POW, a prisoner of war, beginning at age eighteen. He is referred to in 1 Chron 3:15 as "Jeconiah, the prisoner" NASB, and then it tells of his son Shealtiel. Later he was released from prison and allowed to eat at the king's table in Babylon, Jer 52:31-34, 2 Kgs 25:27-29. There have been found in the ruins of ancient Babylon, clay ration tickets for Jehoiachin and his sons in Babylon. (There is little doubt in my mind that the greatest glories of archaeological confirmation of the Bible are yet to come!)

Jeconiah was then replaced by another uncle, Zedekiah, who like-wise had a short and infamous reign over Judah, but by no means as short as the three months of Jeconiah. Here then there is the second prophecy of Jeremiah of neither the father nor the son having any descendant to reign on David's throne! The first was in Jer 36:30, which was quoted above, and now Jeremiah says,

> 28 "Is this man Coniah a despised, broken idol—
> A vessel in which is no pleasure?
> Why are they cast out, he and his descendants,
> And cast into a land which they do not know?
> 29 O earth, earth, earth,
> Hear the word of the LORD!
> 30 Thus says the LORD:
> "Write this man down as childless,
> A man who shall not prosper in his days;
> For none of his descendants shall prosper,
> Sitting on the throne of David,
> And ruling anymore in Judah.'" Jer 22:28-30 NKJV

So it must be asked, how should these two prophecies be taken? In one way you might discount the short reign of Jeconiah as not really happening. How many eighteen-year-old kings are really master of their domain, even if they are a "king"? Not many for sure! Maybe mom or other officials were really the rulers and trying to continue the revolt, thinking dad had surrendered too soon. Perhaps Nebuchadnezzar thought, this boy can not really keep control, and that is why he sent for the boy and the others to be sent to Babylon. Nor is it safe to assume that Jeremiah has forgotten what he said concerning a *king* and his family in a mere six years. Sometimes detractors wish to charge the prophets of God with the most childish of errors. That would hardly be giving the author the benefit of the doubt. Plus, if the authors of the books of Chronicles had thought too much of all of these objections, they surely would not have thought Jeremiah a prophet of God!

However you deal with this apparent discrepancy, you are still left with the emphatic assertions that this line of David will never again sit on the throne of David. But then there is another issue, for you see, Jeconiah/Jehoiachin, is in the genealogy of Jesus the Christ in Matthew.

> [11] Josiah became the father of Jeconiah and his brothers, at the time of the deportation to Babylon. [12] After the deportation to Babylon: Jeconiah became the father of Shealtiel, and Shealtiel the father of Zerubbabel. Matt 1:11-12 NASB

Then come the details. Of the dad, Jehoiakim, it says that he will have no one sit on the throne of David, Jer 36:30. Then of the son Jeconiah it says that "... For none of his descendants shall prosper, Sitting on the throne of David, And ruling anymore in Judah."

But then the Christ does come from the line of Jeconiah, as Matthew well realizes! And He does in fact *now* sit on David's throne. There are many verses that could be quoted, such as from Luke.

> He shall be great, and shall be called the Son of the Highest: and the Lord God shall give unto him the throne of his father David,
> Luke 1:32 KJV

And in Rev 3:21 KJV Jesus says,

> To him that overcometh will I grant to sit with me in my throne, even as I also overcame, and am set down with my Father in his throne.

Clearly the New Testament represents Jesus of Nazareth as a descendant of Jeconiah and as *presently* sitting on David's throne!

So once more, what should be done with the prophecies of Jeremiah have been discussed in detail? Perhaps it is the phrase, "Sitting on the throne of David, And ruling anymore in Judah," Jer 22:30 NKJV. So perhaps Jeremiah is *not* saying that their line will not produce the Christ, but rather saying that their line will never again rule on David's throne *in Judah!*

Now it has been pointed out that Jesus' kingdom was not of this world, not from this realm, depending on your translation of Jn 18:36. It has been pointed out that Jesus is reigning from His throne in heaven and will come again to take the members of His holy kingdom to the New Heavens and New Earth which will come.

However, notice clearly that more than one system of prophecy has God failing to establish His kingdom during the first century and then deciding to come back later; I guess you could say to "try again later." What blasphemy! So many of these systems of prophecy have Jesus coming back a second time, and establishing His kingdom in Judah in Jerusalem, and then ruling the world literally from physical Jerusalem for a thousand years. They are misapplying the prophecies of the conversion of the Jews, and their later glory in this world. But also one should be able see that *if He does*, then **at that point the prophecies of Jeremiah** in **Jeremiah 22 and 36**, WILL HAVE PLAINLY FAILED! To state the case clearly: **Jesus of Nazareth will <u>never</u> rule on a physical throne in physical Judah in this present world!** The pre-millennial theories are in error! The prophet Jeremiah has assured us that this will *never* happen!

He who has ears to hear, let him hear what the Spirit says to the churches! Jesus' kingdom does NOT include a literal "kingdom of God" on this present earth.

A "Post-Millennial" or "Pre-Millennial" World?

Each will sit under his own fig tree, according to Mic 4:4. Is this written of this world or the next? Is it a renewed earth, or a new creation which is called "the new earth"? First of all, let me emphasize that I am <u>NOT</u> post-millennial. Nor do I believe Christ *failed* to establish His kingdom when He first came but will sort of "try again" toward the end of time (blasphemy!). But in Isa 65:17-18 it talks about a new heavens and a new earth, and it is proper to ask: What do you make of the prophecies of Isaiah 65 and 66, and similar passages in other places. Does this describe a heaven on earth as Jehovah's Witnesses, many Seventh Day Adventists and many pre-millennialists say? What is it talking about? Is it really already fulfilled in the church? It cannot fail. Scripture cannot be broken, Jesus says in Jn 10:35.

Also *when* then does this happen? Is it talking about this world or the next? What are our choices? What do we believe, and what does *the Bible* say? The Bible says that **all** Scripture is inspired of God, and is needed to make you complete, 2 Tim 3:16-17. Additionally God says that He will "create" a new heavens and a new earth, Isa 65:17. So let us consider that it says "create" and ask when and where does this happen?

As a side point, it should be noted that *almost all early Americans believed in an earthly millennium,* that there would be a physical millennium here on earth. The occult groups that supported the American Revolution in the 1700's wanted to establish a paradise like "new world order" in America (the documentation is freely available), and viewed domination by distant England as a barrier to their accomplishing their "new order," their "NOVUS ORDO SECLORUM," as is on the back of the American one dollar bill. This became part of the American focusing on this world. Early America, up to the beginning of the 20th century, believed that the world was getting better and better and that one day the whole world would be under true Christianity. Most of the mainline denominations, *and* the churches of Christ believed it. For example, the early American preacher Alexander Campbell's periodical *The Millennial Harbinger* was meant to herald a literal millennium here on earth, in fulfillment of Bible prophecy. It was called *post-millennialism,* that Jesus would come after a literal blessedness here on earth! But how does that fit with evil men becoming worse and worse, 2 Tim 3:13?

You might ask, what changed America's minds? Well it certainly was NOT Scripture, or new in-depth Bible studies, but World Wars I and II, and the rise of communist and fascist dictators, and the propaganda that surrounded their aftermath. It is as if they said (following the media chorus of that day), if we are going to have "world" wars, then things are never going to get better. Then one might ask: where did American's first get these ideas Biblically? *So now let's start at Isaiah 65:18.*

God will "create" Jerusalem rejoicing according to Isa 65:18. But there are two Jerusalems as has been pointed out. There is Jerusalem the holy city, and it is referred to in many passages like Dan 9:16, where Daniel refers to it as "thy city Jerusalem, thy holy mountain" KJV, and it is clear that Daniel is referring to physical Jerusalem.

Ezekiel call Jerusalem the center of the nations in Ezek 5:5, and when he is describing the persecution of God's people in the last days by "Gog and Magog," he describes this persecution as not only occurring in various foreign locales, but also among those "who live at the center of world," Ezek 38:12 NASB. Also the apostle Matthew refers to Jerusalem as "the holy city," even *after* Jesus' death at the hands of the Jews, Mtt 27:53.

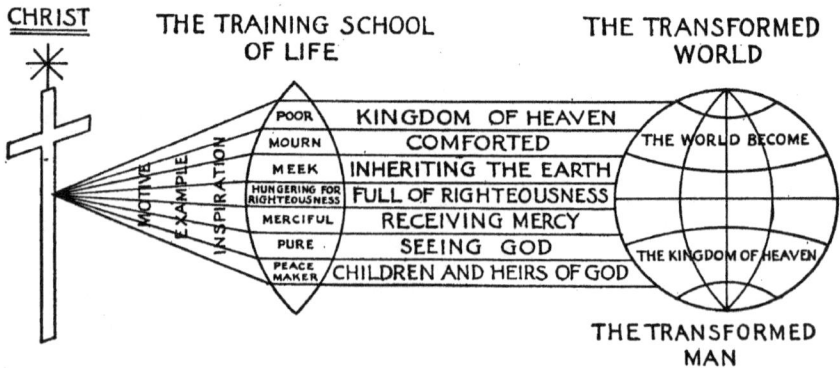

Post-millenialism, as in the above from *Peloubet's Notes* of 1910, often spoke of making "the world" "Christian," and emphasized much we now call "social gospel," but which was originally just a way of looking at Bible prophecy. It was about a paradise "in this creation," **prior to** the Second Coming, which most American churches taught.

But there is both "present" Jerusalem *and* Jerusalem "above" in Gal 4:21-31, as has been pointed out. Paul says

> "25 Now this Hagar is Mount Sinai in Arabia and corresponds to the present Jerusalem, for she is in slavery with her children. 26 But the Jerusalem above is free; she is our mother." Gal 4:25-26 NASB

In addition, as has been noted, Christians belong to the heavenly Jerusalem, the church.

> 22 But you have come to Mount Zion and to the city of the living God, the heavenly Jerusalem, to an innumerable company of angels, 23 to the general assembly and church of the firstborn *who are* registered in heaven, to God the Judge of all, to the spirits of just men made perfect,
> Heb 12:22-23 NKJV

This will be heaven itself in the end.

> 1 And I saw a new heaven and a new earth: for the first heaven and the first earth were passed away; and there was no more sea. 2 And I John saw **the holy city, new Jerusalem**, coming down from God out of heaven, prepared as a bride adorned for her husband. Rev 21:1-2 KJV

For instance, Alexander Campbell's periodical *The Millenial Harbinger* was to herald a literal millenium here on earth, in fulfillment of Bible prophecy, even while acknowleding the kingdom of God was already in existence (Col 1:16, etc.).

We do not belong to the world, Jn 15:19; nor do true believers belong to the present, earthly, Jerusalem below. Jerusalem below is moreover talked about for instance in Isa 1:9-10, where she is called Sodom and Gomorrah, and indeed she is. Furthermore Jerusalem below is talked about in Rev 11:8, where again she is called Sodom and Egypt. So what is "the great city" of the book of Revelation? It is where Jesus was crucified, again as seen from Rev 11:8. It is the city built on blood. It is "present Jerusalem." Look once again.

> 25 For this Agar is mount Sinai in Arabia, and answereth to Jerusalem which now is, and is in bondage with her children. 26 But Jerusalem which is above is free, which is the mother of us all. Gal 4:25-26 KJV

There are two relatively <u>new</u> doctrines about prophecy! One is pre-millennialism, that Christ comes back before the millennium. Despite the straining at gnats, it is really a new view of Scripture, born of Zionist linked groups of the late 19th century, to give their messianic scheming a Biblical twist. The other is the rejection of prophecy, the lamp of *our age*. The idea that prophecy *has nothing to*

do with today. This is really from the so called "Enlightenment," but also it is a new thing, deriving in part from a 20th century *overreaction* to pre-millennialism. (Shall this be called reactionary? Yes.) Neither is part of historical Christianity. Earlier generations knew both that *there was prophecy that had not happened*, and that the kingdom *had* indeed already come in the first century, as can be seen from many Scriptures, including Col 1:13.

> We have also a more sure word of prophecy; whereunto ye do well that ye take heed, as unto a light that shineth in a dark place, until the day dawn, and the day star arise in your hearts: 2 Pe 1:19 KJV

But there is no more crying in this new place, so it says in Isa 65:19. It easy to see this does not fit *this life.* This new "place" is again described in Rev 21:1-2 as coming down out of heaven, and *then* it will be that there are no more tears, Rev 21:4. No longer any death or tears *only* fits *after* this present world is destroyed, 2 Pe 3:11-13. But then on the other hand it says of infants that they will not die **young**.

> "No longer will there be in it an infant who lives but a few days,
>> Or an old man who does not live out his days;
>> For the youth will die at the age of one hundred
>> And the one who does not reach the age of one hundred
>> Will be thought accursed." Isa 65:20 NASB

Babies won't die prematurely, and *most* reach the age of one-hundred! But this also does not fit *our age to date **nor** the new heavens and earth* because there will be NO death in heaven, Rev 21:4. So here this discussion touches on the Scriptural roots of much of both *pre-*millennialism and *post-*millennialism, and Scripture cannot be broken, Jn 10:35. There is a "contradiction" (so it seems) in the prophecies. There are parts that fit only heaven after the end of time, and there are **parts that fit *neither* heaven nor world history to this point!** Isaiah 65 illustrates the basic issues that have caused such splits on prophecy.

But the Jews will recover spiritually. This is very clear from many passages in Scripture. Many Jews and their descendants became followers of Jesus. Many thousands in Jerusalem were baptized in the book of Acts, even though the nation as a whole rejected the gospel. Crispus the leader of the synagogue in Corinth was converted with his family and, of course, the great opponent of the gospel, Saul of Tarsus became Paul the Apostle. Still Christ says to physical Jerusalem, your house is desolate! Your house is desolate *physical* Israel **until** you receive Me, Jesus the Christ.

> [37] O Jerusalem, Jerusalem, *thou* that killest the prophets, and stonest them which are sent unto thee, how often would I have gathered thy children together, even as a hen gathereth her chickens under *her* wings, and ye would not! [38] For I say unto you, Ye shall not see me henceforth, till ye shall say, Blessed is he that cometh in the name of

the Lord. Mtt 23:37-39 KJV

Jesus Christ had wanted better things for the Jews all along. But it is only a partial hardening of Israel, the Jews, that has happened. Paul is telling us of the nations these things so that we will not act arrogantly.

> For I do not want you, brethren, to be uninformed of this mystery — so that you will not be wise in your own estimation — that a partial hardening has happened to Israel until the fullness of the Gentiles has come in; Rom 11:25 NASB

Notice that in context it is talking about physical Israel, the Jews, who are experiencing a "partial hardening" until the full number of the nations come in (the gentiles, literally the "nations" for the Greek word is *ethnos* ἔθνος, from which we get our word "ethnic"). Even the times of the "nations" (*ethnos*) must be fulfilled, Lk 21:24. (Both the word "nations" and the word "Gentile" in Lk 21:24 are translations of the Greek word *ethnos*). That will bring an end to domination of physical Jerusalem by the nations.

> [26] and so all Israel will be saved; just as it is written,
> "THE DELIVERER WILL COME FROM ZION,
> HE WILL REMOVE UNGODLINESS FROM JACOB."
> [27] "THIS IS MY COVENANT WITH THEM,
> WHEN I TAKE AWAY THEIR SINS." Rom 11:26-27 NASB

It is clearly talking about ending the "partial hardening" of the Jews, and of the great majority of physical Israel (as can be seen in verse 25 above) reentering a covenant relationship with God, and God then removing their sins!

So all Israel will be saved, will come to Jesus of Nazareth, the Great Prophet who God was to send! But this will be only after much turmoil!

> And they shall fall by the edge of the sword, and shall be led away captive into all nations: and Jerusalem shall be trodden down of the Gentiles, **until the times of the Gentiles be fulfilled**.
> Lk 21:24 KJV (*emphasis added*)

And it is **physical** Israel (as opposed to the Gentiles, the other nations of this world, as it is also in Rom 11:25). And Israel, physical Israel, will be separated from ungodliness, according to Paul, who is quoting Isaiah when he says,

> [19] So they will fear the name of the LORD from the west
> And His glory from the rising of the sun,
> For He will come like a rushing stream
> Which the wind of the LORD drives.
> [20] "A Redeemer will come to Zion,
> And **to those who turn from transgression** in Jacob," declares the
> LORD. Isa 59:19-20 NASB (*emphasis added*)

At that time, it pictures physical Israel as being faithful. You should look carefully at these passages, *because Paul quotes them and pictures them as **yet to be fulfilled.*** The preaching of the gospel to that point had not fulfilled this, but the physical descendants of Israel *will be turned away from ungodliness.* **And indeed, this has not been fulfilled even to our own day!**

And foreigners will build physical Israel's walls!

> "Foreigners will build up your walls,
> And their kings will minister to you;
> For in My wrath I struck you,
> And in My favor I have had compassion on you. Isa 60:10 NASB

Will "present Jerusalem" Gal 4:25, yet assume importance she has not had? Now Nehemiah built the walls after they came back from the first captivity, but here it pictures a day when foreigners build their walls *and then serve them!*

> 11 "*Your* gates will be open continually;
> They will not be closed day or night,
> So that ı may bring to you the wealth of the nations,
> With their kings led in procession.
> 12 For **the nation** and the kingdom **which will not serve you** will perish,
> And the nations **will be utterly ruined**."
> Isa 60:11-12 NASB (*emphasis added*)

Now what Nehemiah did has only partially fulfilled this prophecy because Isaiah says the nations of the world *have to serve* them! *Did you remember?* God said He would make them the head of the nations if they were faithful.

> 9 **The LORD shall establish thee** an holy people unto himself, as he hath sworn unto thee, **if thou shalt keep the commandments** of the LORD thy God, **and walk in his ways.** ...
>
> 12 The LORD shall open unto thee his good treasure, the heaven to give the rain unto thy land in his season, and to bless all the work of thine hand: and thou shalt **lend unto many nations, and thou shalt not borrow.** 13 And the LORD shall **make thee the head, and not the tail**; and **thou shalt be above only, and thou shalt not be beneath**; if that thou hearken unto the commandments of the LORD thy God, which I command thee this day, to observe and to do them: Deut 28:9, 12-13 KJV (*emphasis added*)

It says that strangers will pasture their flocks.

> And strangers shall stand and feed your flocks, and the sons of the alien *shall be* your plowmen and your vinedressers. Isa 61:5 KJV

And instead of shame they will have a double portion.

> Instead of your shame you shall have double honor,
> And instead of confusion they shall rejoice in their portion.

> Therefore in their land they shall possess double;
> Everlasting joy shall be theirs. Isa 61:7 NKJV

Thus comes another part of the story. In part it was because it did not *seem* **that Jesus would fulfill these things**, that **the Jews originally rejected Him.** The Jews were focusing on such things as Israel looting the Egyptians before they left Egypt and on passages like Haggai chapter 2 where it says,

> And I will shake all nations, and the desire of all nations shall come: and I will fill this house with glory, saith the LORD of hosts.
> Hag 2:7 KJV

The Jews took this in a very this worldly sense, of them looting all the nations of the world. Or on a darker note, the Jews seemed to concentrate on passages like Psalm 58. These things are seldom quoted by Christians because they just do not know what to do with them. I think it pictures the end of time when judgment is executed on those who will not submit to God.

> [10] **The righteous shall rejoice when he seeth the vengeance: he shall wash his feet in the blood of the wicked.** [11] So that a man shall say, Verily there is a reward for the righteous: verily he is a God that judgeth in the earth. Psa 58:10-11 KJV (*bold emphasis added*)

All of which has its place in righteousness (indeed, what have the merciless mass murderers such as Stalin and Hitler and the like deserved?). But the Jews of ancient times and even to this day were often forgetting the foundations of justice and righteousness, and have at times concentrated on *them* literally doing these things to all nations. They have sometimes *tried* to do these things to the nations, thinking that their "day" was near. They have been *forgetting* that in Abraham's seed *all the nations of the earth* **"will be blessed,"** but rather have been thinking of looting or washing their feet in the blood of all nations, which hardly seems to be the blessing to all the nations spoken of!

As has been shown, prophecy caused most Jews to imminently expect the kingdom to come in or around the first century AD. Some tried to do what later Jewish leaders have called "forcing the end." Series of Jewish revolts came over the Roman world. Historian Edward Gibbon says of those times that,

> From the reign of Nero to that of Antoninus Pius, the Jews discovered a fierce impatience of the dominion of Rome, which repeatedly broke out in the most furious massacres and insurrections. Edward Gibbon, *Decline and Fall of the Roman Empire*, Chapter 16, Part 1.

That is a mild but accurate statement of what happened. Gibbon records some of this "fierce impatience" in a footnote in Chapter 16, Part 1. He records that the Jews,

> In Cyrene, ... massacred 220,000 Greeks; in Cyprus, 240,000; ... Many of these unhappy victims were sawn asunder, ... The victorious Jews devoured the flesh, licked up the blood, and twisted the entrails like a

girdle round their bodies. See Dion Cassius, l. lxviii. p. 1145.

There are two observations that should be added here. One is that Gibbon detests the Jews as much as he detests Christians, but Gibbon himself goes on to note that:

> Some commentators ... think that the hatred of the Romans against the Jews has led the historian to exaggerate the cruelties committed by the latter.

Secondly is that none of this is very far from many of the activities of the Jewish radicals in the siege of Jerusalem, which will be discussed later. Many of the most terrible things the Jewish revolutionaries did at that time were carried out **on fellow Jews** who dared to oppose their insanity or dared to even try to eat! Even so, you might go so far as to say that *every* group in history has their share of unworthy episodes, *including* atrocities, as do also the Jews. This is certainly a side of Judaism that most Americans are not familiar with. The noble character and indeed even holy character of so many Jews is apparent from Scripture. And as Rabbi Jesus of Nazareth (Jn 1:38) plainly says, "... salvation is of the Jews," Jn 4:22 KJV.

So why even bring up some of these darker sides of *sections* of Judaism? The masses of the Jews were ready to accept Jesus, as can be seen from much of the histories, as for instance in Jn 7:31. But the radicals and the Jewish leadership swiftly acted to poison the minds of the Jews against Christianity with world shaking consequences. ***The first consequence*** was that this Jewish rejection of *their own* Messiah seemed to make Him even more palatable to the nations of the world, ***and had the unintended result of making the wide and fast spread of Christianity even more sure!***

> I say then, Have they stumbled that they should fall? God forbid: but rather through their fall salvation is come unto the Gentiles, ...
> Rom 11:11 KJV

Then comes ***the second consequence***-that Judaism developed into a massive reactionary group against Christianity with a this world emphasis, much like the ancient Pharisees. They became, in the words of one of their own prophets,

> [14] ... the Jews, [15] who both killed the Lord Jesus and the prophets, and drove us out. They are not pleasing to God, but hostile to all men, [16] hindering us from speaking to the Gentiles so that they may be saved; with the result that they always fill up the measure of their sins. But wrath has come upon them to the utmost. 1 Thes 2:14-16

They have become in the Christian Age a virulent force against every true form of Christianity. They have truly been a world-shaking influence in these activities, the beginning of which you can see in the New Testament and which has not ended even in our own day. Then comes ***the third consequence***. When they finally wake up, it will *once again* be a world-shaking event.

> For if their rejection is the reconciliation of the world, what will their acceptance be but life from the dead? Rom 11:15 NASB

Their eventual conversion will bring a worldwide glory to Jesus the Christ that has not yet been seen in world history! If I have even the least understanding of Scripture, this is not in the least way an overstatement. **The Jews are too pivotal in world history (both in the first century, and for the last two thousand years, and NOW, and in the *FUTURE*) to ignore these events and attitudes and their consequences.**

Although Gibbon notes some of these Jewish atrocities, it must be admitted that he treads as lightly as he can on Roman severity and cruelty (he admires the Romans too much). But he notes with approval the Roman suppression of these Jewish revolts, and he notes the Jewish adaptation to these defeats.

> Awakened from their dream of prophecy and conquest, they assumed the behavior of peaceable and industrious subjects. Their irreconcilable hatred of mankind, instead of flaming out in acts of blood and violence, evaporated in less dangerous gratifications. Chapter 16, Part 1.

I can only take this as an accurate and apropos statement of how these things transpired, and he goes on to note how they turned from such bloody deeds to concentrating on beating the nations in commerce. But when he describes what was really the results of their *misinterpretations* of prophecy, Gibbon calls it a Jewish "irreconcilable hatred of mankind." Ouch! But again, in practical terms, it is not far from the mark.   So when the New Covenant in Christ was opened to the gentiles (the nations), the Jews were disgusted.

> ²⁸ There is neither Jew nor Greek, there is neither bond nor free, there is neither male nor female: for ye are all one in Christ Jesus. ²⁹ And if ye *be* Christ's, then are *ye* Abraham's seed, and heirs according to the promise. Gal 3:28-29

They were surprised, but they understood the tenor of the message. The leaders of the Jews seemed to understand it implicitly even *before* Jesus' death. Then the astonishment turned to anger, and their amazement to rage, and their chagrin to incredulity and stubborn opposition. They had assured themselves that they had every right to abuse the nations, to use them as one might use a cow or a donkey, or even to wash their feet in the blood of the nations. Now the vilest of people, whom they thought only worthy to perish or to be fleeced, these vermin were to be accepted as their equals in the Kingdom of the LORD their God? Damnable! Detestable! Unthinkable! Outrageous! It is plain from their own writings that such epithets were among the nicer things they said about Our LORD and His Christ, Jesus of Nazareth, and about us of the nations!

Ah yes, now a lot of the worldly victory they have had, but still without the crowning triumph. Here then is the incredible thing: that what two thousand years of Talmudism has been unable to deliver to the Jews, the mild prophet from Galilee will deliver. **And it will be a blessing to the world!**

And Israel will have strangers join them (**and it should be added, they will**
clearly need them), and the nations will bring them to their place.

> The peoples will take them along and bring them to their place, and
> the house of Israel will possess them as an inheritance in the land of
> the Lord as male servants and female servants; and **they will take**
> **their captors captive and will rule over their oppressors**.
> Isa 14:2 NASB (*emphasis added*)

So the Jews are *not* pictured as coming to their place on their own, but the
peoples of the world *as bringing them* (physical? spiritual? both?). Then the
nations, the gentiles, *becoming their servants!* Now as a "type" (symbolically)
this happened when the kings of Medo-Persia sent them home after the Babylonian captivity, but Israel ruling over their captors, making their captors
captive! ... *it never happened! But it will happen,* and then will be fulfilled
the other promises. Clearly, if the Jews failure meant the world's riches, what
will their acceptance mean except indeed, **"life from the dead"**! Rom 11:15.

Let me be as clear as I can. The regenerate Jewish nation will become a
world leader *and* it will be a blessing to the world. Does this mean that physical Israel will have influence over the world such as the United States has had
during the twentieth century? Or does this mean that Jerusalem will be the capital of some sort of glorified "United Nations"? I honestly do not know, but
Scripture may tell us. Even so it is clear that Babylon the Great *will build* a
comprehensive world order before the end of time, leading to a final suppression
of Christianity, leading up to the end. But what is the time/distance between
these events? I don't know, but it appears that there is a considerable interlude
between the two. It appears that Babylon the Great is *close* to total control when
the Jews are converted *in what will be for the Jews a time of great* stress, Deut 4:30
NASB.

> And **the LORD** thy God **will** circumcise thine heart, and the heart of
> thy seed, to love the LORD thy God with all thine heart, and with all
> thy soul, that thou mayest live. Deut 30:6 KJV

That is a prophetic statement of fact by Moses. One which clearly **has NOT**
happened. Incredibly, neither the fall of Jerusalem in 586 BC, nor the fall of Jerusalem in 70 AD, nor the Holocaust of the twentieth century of Our LORD were
sufficient. Dear LORD, what will it take? It is mind boggling to think about it!

The Jewish conversion will set imperial time tables back considerably and,
so it appears to me, delay Babylon the Great quite a bit, waiting for the completion of the evangelization of the world.

These things are the two sides of the same coin. That the Jews would reject
their own savior is something this is spoken of in *both* the Old Testament and
the New Testament. Also that the Jews would ultimately accept their Savior
bringing glory both to their Lord, themselves, and the entire world, is likewise

in both Testaments. Some are willing to see half of this equation, but not the other half. Neither side of this coin can be avoided.

But there really is no earthly paradise. They will build houses and vineyards, and they will not labor in vain, Isa 65:21-24; but "NO evil or harm" NASB could only apply to the next universe, Isa 65:25, and Revelation 22. So most of these passages in Isaiah could *only* apply to the new universe without sin and death, 2 Pe 3:10-13. But there are still loose ends, seeming to indicate a "type" that will come in between. **There are additional foretastes of the world to come, "types" if you will, *which are yet to come in history!* God is still act-ing in history. The conversion of the Jews to Christ "as a group," so to speak, will produce some glorious world-wide benefits, and it appears this comes to pass despite evil men and seducers becoming worse and worse. *Remember!* Jesus rules *now* in the **midst** of His enemies, Psa 110:1-2. Then will come in a final surge of lawlessness: Satan will be briefly released from his prison, Rev 20:7.

I think this is the best case for a partial post-millennial position! This has been an examination of the Scriptural foundations of America's earlier beliefs. Cor-rectly understood and received, these events will be aids, not replacements, for focusing on things above, where our life is hidden with Christ, Col 3:1-4. These will be assurances that God is indeed in control of the affairs of men, even to the end of the age, Mtt 28:18-20.

Here also is the crux of the many divisions among men about the things which will happen. The "**pre-milliennialists**" (not recognizing that the king-dom **has** come and believing that Christ will come again before the end), and the **Post-millennialists** (believing that Christ will come *after* a thousand years of "bliss"), both often tend to ignore the clear Scriptures which indicate that the kingdom has already been established and that Christ rules all men *now*. It is Scriptures like Col 1:16 and 1 Cor 15:24-25, Psa 110:1-3, and others. They look for a worldly kingdom which will never come except in deception. Jesus' disciples would have **fought *the first time* IF Jesus kingdom was of this world, Jn 18:36!** We are looking to enter a heavenly kingdom, 2 Tim 4:18. So false systems of prophecy take passages which speak of heaven (the new universe), or symbolically speak of the kingdom as it exists now in this world, and try to apply these verses to a literal kingdom on this present earth. They are confus-ing the symbolic with the literal, and the future world with the present world.

So part of the problem is in confusing Scriptures about the glorious things the Gospel of Jesus Christ is yet to accomplish in this world with the Scriptures about heaven and coming up with a "heaven" on earth. It will not be.

On the other hand the "**A-millennialists**" (there is no literal millennium) often tend to read out all the verses about God's Holy Nation, His Kingdom, and about Heaven as hyperbole, as nearly meaningless symbolism that does not have any "reality." They are willing to read the Gospel parables as symbolic yet meaningful, but not the rest of prophecy. So they often wallow in unbelief.

Don't put on shoes which don't fit you!

> Then he said unto them, O fools, and slow of heart to believe all that the prophets have spoken, Lk 24:25. KJV

The early disciples, like most of the Jews, often failed to understand the Scriptures about the glorious things the Gospel will yet accomplish in history. They sometimes seemed to almost dismiss Heaven as not being real, never seeing that the church is in the beginning stages of this victory over all the nations of this world. They tended to not see that the world itself is now being ruled from Heaven (Psa 110:1-3). The "world to come" (Heb 2:5) will hold an awesome merger of the religious and political for the perfect nation, in the perfect universe which will come after the passing of this one (Isa 66:22, 2 Pe 3:11-13, 2 Tim 4:18, 2 Pe 1:11, Revelation chapters 21 and 22, Isa 11:6-9, etc.). <u>**Everyone**</u> **will see these things with their own eyes,** *but some only from afar.*

What do the Jews need to permanently turn their situation around for good? They need Jesus, and they will finally be converted, but *only in a time of greater stress than they have had so far!* Deut 4:30. *Wow!*

How long then is this period of the glory of the faithful descendants of Jacob here on this present earth? Besides, how would you calculate the beginning of the period, and how would you calculate the end of the period? This author does not profess to know. ***It will be a period which will turn so many of our assurances of "what will be" (both secular and religious) on their very heads!*** Having so many indications in Scripture of the nearness of the end of all things (but what is "near" in eternal terms?), and having so many indications in Scripture of extensive things to be accomplished by conversion of the Jews, I would not attempt to guess. I could, however, be persuaded this ends up being an extended period of time, a time in which Mystery Babylon and the Man of Lawlessness, having thought they had it all "in the bag," are delayed and delayed and delayed. Will this be a handful of generations just before the end? I can not be dogmatic, but I could easily believe, based on what I see in Scripture, that this could be at least a few hundred years. Who knows? Maybe it will even be a thousand years or near it.

We Struggle Against Dark Powers

Eph 6:12

The last things ...
Eschatology,
... and why we study it
... even before the time!

Satan and the Evil Empire

Now let us return to the beginning of our story, at least for a while. Never-theless, that is where it all starts. Now there was much that the man and woman in paradise did not know. The Scriptures indicate that they were naked but were hardly aware of it. They were not ashamed, Gen 2:25. Still there was the other thing about the man and woman in paradise (*paradeisos*, παράδεισος, is the word for a garden in Greek). There was no conscious rejection of what God told them. Whatever God told them, they were doing *at this point*. So in doing what would be inappropriate to us, there was no sin on their part. They were innocent, they were without guilt, without sin! But when we know (or alternate-ly, refuse to "know") and still do wrong, that is much different, as Paul points out.

> [9] For I was alive without the law once: but when the commandment came, sin revived, and I died. [10] And the commandment, which *was ordained* to life, I found *to be* unto death. [11] For sin, taking occasion by the commandment, deceived me, and by it slew *me*. Rom 7:9-11 KJV

So when the man and the woman *know* they should not do something, and do those things, it is very different, and man was given some commands. He was not supposed to eat from the tree of the knowledge of good and evil, and by implication later in Genesis 3, he was also not supposed to eat of the tree of life, and you might surmise there were probably other things, but the text fo-cuses on the item in which there later came an offense.

At this point the serpent appears to man. A powerful spirit appeared as a snake, a serpent. Did he have legs, maybe like a lizard, at first? Is it only after the seduction that the serpent is described as having to crawl on its belly and eat dirt for the rest of its life? We do not really know, do we? The Hebrew word is *nahash* נָחָשׁ, and is a word that is used for all manner of snakes and such. In Isa 27:1 it is used to describe what Isaiah calls a "dragon" or a "monster," and what a modern would probably call a dinosaur. Also *nahash* is used to describe soothsaying, fortune telling, magic or a "spell" (most would call that hypnosis). These black arts were forbidden to the Israelites in Deuteronomy 18 and other places, but such arts were always associated with evil spirits and with serpents. So similarly in Acts 16, when Paul is bothered by a girl who truly has some ability to foretell the future, Scripture says she has "a spirit of divination," and the Greek is that she has the "spirit" of a Python *puthōn* πύθων. Literally then, she had the spirit of a snake. Clearly also the snake was more cunning than any beast, Gen 3:1 NKJV. The *spirit of a puthōn* was also associated with the ancient prophetesses at Delphi.

Now Satan was at one time in heaven. He is pictured as appearing before the Lord God in heaven, with the other angels in Job chapter 1, requesting per-mission to hurt men, and he seems to especially hate good men, any who are faithful to God. So he hates Job, and earnestly desires to hurt him, but he clearly cannot do this without permission, Job 1:6-12. Also it is easy to see that if you are a critter of some kind, and you let an evil spirit possess you, it has serious repercussions. This is a return to the subject of the seed of the Serpent from the beginning of this study.

Satan is called by various descriptive names. Look at the range and inclination of the names and the verses. He is called:

- The serpent Gen 3:4, 14; 2 Cor 11:3, Rev 12:9
- Satan which means "adversary" or "accuser," Job 1:6, etc., as also in a prosecuting attorney
- The devil, "diabolos," meaning a slanderer or a malicious gossip, Mtt 4:1, and this is where we get our word "diabolical."
- The accuser of our brethren, Rev 12:10
- The adversary, 1 Pe 5:8
- The Tempter Mtt 4:3, 1 Thes 3:5
- Our common enemy Mtt 13:39
- The destroyer (Hebrew: Abaddon. Greek: Apollyon), Rev 9:11
- The wicked one, Mtt 13:19, 38
- Belial (from a Hebrew word meaning worthless), 2 Cor 6:15
- The great red dragon, Rev 12:3

Satan is also called various titles which indicate authority and rulership:

- Prince of this world, Jn 12:31
- Beelzebul (ruler of demons), Mtt 12:24
- Ruler of the power of the air, Eph 2:2
- Ruler of the darkness of this world, Eph 6:12
- The angel of the bottomless pit, Rev 9:11
- The god of this world (age), 2 Cor 4:4

All that can be said is, what a daunting list of titles that indicate both great power and malicious evil. It is true Satan is has some rule, but also some limits. It has been pointed out that he is called the god of this world (literally the god of this age). He is called the prince of the power of the air, the prince of this world, the ruler of the darkness of this world. Satan is allowed considerable power in this world. Satan (Rev 12:9) is evidently *allowed* to reward his servants within some limits. When he personally tries to seduce Jesus, it says,

> [5] And the devil, taking him up into an high mountain, shewed unto him all the kingdoms of the world in a moment of time. [6] And the devil said unto him, All this power will I give thee, and the glory of them: for that is delivered unto me; and to whomsoever I will I give it. [7] If thou therefore wilt worship me, all shall be thine Lk 4:5-7 KJV

Where Satan is wrong, Jesus corrects him, but not here. It would seem that he *could* have indeed delivered all of this to Jesus. Many have received it and regretted it. The historian Gibbon records how many men under duress, or very reluctantly, assumed the "honors" of being emperor, knowing full well it was a double edged sword they assumed. Wickedness sometimes reigns, but it consumes its heroes. The Roman Emperor Septimius Severus said he "had been all things, and all was of little value." Jesus already realized these things. He refused.

Further, even the Roman empire has been foreseen in the vision in Daniel 2. It is clearly pictured as the kingdom which is as strong as iron. Those who are unwilling to believe that God would ever speak to us are at pains to prove that the prophecy *had to be* written much later. We have to rule out God as the only *scholarly* way to do it, to *a priori* rule Him out, and if the evidence allows Him, then rule out the evidence? Right? Open-mindedness? Right? Daniel then pictures this kingdom of Rome as being like iron and breaking and crushing and shattering all other kingdoms. However, it is also pictured as having some very basic weaknesses in her foundation, in her feet. Her feet and toes are pictured as being made of both iron and clay, part very strong, and part very brittle and breaking in an instant. What an apt picture of that empire which so long ruled over the Western world. Also how apt a type she makes for the empires of the Christian age. Then comes the New Testament pictures of the Evil Empire of the gospel age.

There is a need to keep some perspective. Clearly one of the central themes of the book of Revelation is "the great city" of this world which opposes "the holy city," the New Jerusalem. First it portrays this city as oppressing the saints and resisting the preaching of the "two witnesses." Then it goes on and paints a picture of the great city in a great earthquake, and the wrath of the nations and times of the end. The narrative then picks up the subject of the great city again, only after discussing the influence of Satan on men, and his special men called "the beast," and the "false prophet." Then it speaks of judgment of the great city, and for the first time calls this city "Babylon the great."

> [7] Saying with a loud voice, Fear God, and give glory to him; for the hour of his judgment is come: and worship him that made heaven, and earth, and the sea, and the fountains of waters. [8] And there followed another angel, saying, Babylon is fallen, is fallen, that great city, because she made all nations drink of the wine of the wrath of her fornication. Rev 14:7-8 KJV

Then it goes back to talking about men and the beast. This is consistent with what will covered later. The church is "conquered" within history. This also will discussed in more detail in the section, "We Hold Fast ...". Then Babylon the great is judged first. Again at the end of chapter 16, it speaks of the destruction of Babylon the great in the general context of the end of time. But there is another key that must be inserted here, an important one. That is the discussion of the principal adversaries of Christianity in our age, and a summary of some key factions in the occult.

Some Age Long Mysteries

What is a "mystery"? It is not the English sense of "I don't know what it is," or "it's a mystery to me." The Greek word is *mustārion* μυστήριον, or "mystery." It is about anything hidden or secret, that you have to be told, or initiated into, to understand. It is about things you *cannot* figure out, things you have to be taught, *something to which you must to have an introduction.*

There are also mysteries in Christianity. Paul talks of the mystery of God's will in Eph 1:9, and the mystery of the gospel, Eph 6:19. The way of salvation is something men have to be told about, it has to be preached. Man cannot figure out what he needs to do by himself. So in the gospels and epistles you have the mysteries of the kingdom of heaven, Mtt 13:10-12. We cannot figure this out, rather we have to be told. We cannot figure out that we must be baptized to be saved, we must be told. We cannot figure out that God wants us to sing to worship Him instead of play a banjo. Rather we must be told. These are, very properly, some of the true "mysteries" of Christianity.

Still, more pertinent to the subject, there are pagan "mystery religions." This is a class of religions that are *both political and religious in nature.* They have some key characteristics.

- They generally claim that some "god" talked to some man or men of old and told them "secrets". They may say that the "god" spoke to Adam, Enoch, Abraham¸ Isaac, Moses, Solomon, or some other patriarch. Or they may say that the "god" spoke to Plato or Pythagoras, or some other ancient. The "gods" then revealed some "secrets" to those honorable ancients.
- These religions then offered a secret knowledge that *you and I* need to be saved.
- But they claim these secrets should not be told to everyone. They are too "holy" to be revealed to "commoners," to the ordinary guy. It was profanity to reveal these secrets to just anyone. Only to the "best" were these "secrets" to be revealed, to those considered "worthy" to receive these "holy" things (or unholy, as the case may be!). So these religions tended to be those of the elite, religions of the rich and famous.

The next part was that these secrets were even too holy to ever be written down, so they were generally transmitted to men through oral traditions handed down verbally from generation to generation. This is what they call "the ancient secret tradition."

So how did these groups operate? They have *initiates* or *novices*, at the entry levels, who are all carefully screened. At the lowest levels they:

- Tell no serious secrets.
- They convince the initiates that the oaths required of them *have been* carried out on those foolish enough to reveal these secrets.

- They are emotionally impressive, but no significant doctrines or "secrets" are revealed.
- They are taught additional "secrets" as they "progress."

So what was the practical effect of these things? They produce a large body of men or women who are trained in keeping secrets. New members are called **"novices."** They generally teach them garbage at first, just to see if they can keep secrets. They teach the true beliefs of the religion only at the very top. The full members are called **"perfects,"** *telios* τέλειος, perfect thus meaning complete or mature or fully trained, as in Col 1: 28, where it says,

> Whom we preach, warning every man, and teaching every man in all wisdom; that we may present every man **perfect** in Christ Jesus: KJV (*emphasis added*)

Paul is saying that men do not need these so called "secrets" to be made complete. We can be complete, perfect, *telios*, by simply following the open teachings of Jesus Christ.

These are religions of the intellectuals, religions of the elite. They do not want the common man in these religions. *The Mystery Religions and Christianity*, by Samuel Angus, is a *pro-mystery religion* treatment of the mystery religions of ancient times, and their battle with Christianity. Angus deals with the organization side of the occult, and shows how such beliefs may manifest themselves organizationally. The _names_ of the organizations and the so-called "gods" change; the _names_ of the doctrines change, but there is an essential unity to the occult. Angus uses a very appropriate "seed" imagery of the mystery religions (page 177), as Christ does in the Word of God in passages like Luke 8. Angus lists seven characteristics of the mystery religions. In the following I am using Angus' main points together with my own comments.

1. They are religions that use "myths," *muthos* μῦθος (made-up stories, tales) and much symbolism to teach their beliefs. The ancient Greek word is '*muthos*', which can be translated as either 'myth' or 'fable'. The mysteries use made-up stories and symbols to hide beliefs that they fear will be rejected. They love to display their "behind the scenes" influence with public symbols. These symbols are constructed so that the "insiders" can recognize each other and can help and support each other's works. But they are also constructed so that if they are discovered and recognized by outsiders, they can be denied, saying, "Oh, you are just misunderstanding," (called "plausible deniability" in the intelligence world). Notice that much of modern fiction falls under such a classification.

They were religions full of symbolism, myth, and allegory. They were religions which were both materialistic and pantheistic. God is the universe, so there is no difference between God and the world. You might well say that they are the ultimate religions of this world, as indeed they are.

2. They are religions that promise "salvation." Through initiation, a person became one with their "god." If they gave the correct formula (knowledge), they could ward off evil spirits and invoke good powers.

3. They are systems of secret "knowledge," *gnosis* γνῶσις. In 1 Tim 6:20 it talks about oppositions of what is falsely called "knowledge," NKJV (The Greek word *gnosis* by the way is the root of our modern English word "know," with the silent Greek "g" sound changing to a silent "k" in the English word "know".) In the lower levels of initiation, the "secrets" are mainly decoys intended to test the secret keeping ability of the initiate. Only those who prove their abilities and prove to be "receptive" are advanced to the "higher" secrets.

4. They had secret "holy" dramas in which they acted out their beliefs. They used powerful ceremonies and dramas to hide beliefs that they fear will be rejected. Even in the most informal and loosely organized setting of the occult (for instance some small covens of witches) drama tends to play a part.

In the more predatory levels of the occult (which Angus does not really deal with), the ceremonies often involve criminal acts in which the initiate must participate, and which effectively bind him or her to the group. This is what I call the "Pinocchio Principle." Like the little boys in the Disney cartoon, if they go to Pleasure Island and make a *complete* "ass" of themselves, then they will never be able to tell what they know. They will not have the "will" to admit these things, so they can then be trusted to be used out in the world as little "donkeys" ("mules"?) in the service of their masters, and can even be sold into the service of others! Heinous acts done in secret often produce cooperation, secrecy, and discipline that an outsider can scarcely imagine—a Satanic lockstep that literally goes beyond the grave ... all the way to destruction!

5. They were religions of the "end of time" things. They were eschatological religions, religions about the "last things" of this world. They were thought to be against agnosticism. To be an agnostic means that you do not really know, or you think you can not know, but those who have this knowledge think they "know." The book of Colossians is among other things specifically written to refute these false claims of knowledge. Baptist scholar A. T. Robertson called his commentary on Colossians, *Paul and the Intellectuals.*

6. They were "personal" religions. In fact they were the only real competition to Christianity in the early centuries of our age.

7. They were cosmic religions dealing with the entire universe.

To all of this I would emphasize some other characteristics, not entirely dealt with by Angus, but which are clear from history:

A. They were "religious" and "political" in nature. The Bauer, Gingrich, and Danker *A Greek-English Lexicon of the New Testament and Other Early Christian Literature,* (Chicago: University of Chicago Press) 1979, describes the word "mystery" (the Greek word '*mustārion*' μυστήριον) as "secret, secret rite, secret teaching, mystery, a religious technical term, applied in secular Greek (predominately plural) mostly to the mysteries with their secret teachings,

religious and political in nature, concealed within many strange customs and ceremonies," (*bold and underline emphasis mine, nf*).

Sometimes they were started for political reasons, and sometimes for religious reasons, but if they formed cohesive units, they almost always ended up being used for political purposes, thus often attracting the attention or the wrath of many nation's native intelligence resources.

B. They are very factional in nature. Various factions within the occult fight between each other (especially for ultimate dominance), and these fights often overflow into nations, religions and political groups that they infiltrate or create. They fight between 'black magicians' and 'white magicians' (the "other guys" are always the "black" magicians), between a "male" faction and a "female" faction (the "male" faction will win, see Revelation chapters 17 and 18), between a "high-tech" faction and "primitive" faction (although they always want the high tech goodies for themselves, and Babylon at the end seems to be selling a little bit of everything to everybody). Of course the personal fights are a trait of any fleshly organization. Their cooperation with each other can be reasonably compared to the cooperation of rival Mafia factions, fighting each other and united against any opposing authority.

C. They creep into other religions to try to change them from inside, that is to say, they are "syncretistic." This is one of the most important traits, and it may be missed if you don't read their literature carefully. They are chameleons. They are masters of deception and intrigue in fighting their religious and political enemies. The *names* of doctrines and gods in the occult change a lot, but essential ideas remain. They adopt the *names* and nomenclature of whatever is the dominant religion, and substitute the content of the mysteries.

This is anticipating the subject a little, but in this process they "create" many "harlots" (Rev 17:5), false religions (factions/denominations) that seem like their "parent" faiths but which really are not. They always try to change the content of other religions without changing the form. They try to draw all other religious activities into themselves. They ignore the original significance of other religions, and try to idealize "what was said into what should have been intended," Angus, pg 50. They are subversive of other religions, all other religions, not just Christianity.

> For certain persons have crept in unnoticed, those who were long beforehand marked out for this condemnation, ungodly persons who turn the grace of our God into licentiousness and deny our only Master and Lord, Jesus Christ. Jude 4 NASB

D. They use what you might call 'guided conflict' to accomplish their aims. That is, they try to infiltrate both sides in any conflict (national, religious, political, educational, etc.), and lead both sides so that they can manage the results and guide events toward their objectives. Stated plainly, they try to make it so that what you might call the 'bad guys', <u>lead *both* sides</u> in any conflict! This is in a way another facet of the 'syncretism' side of the occult. Such techniques have been honed since ancient times, and have often gotten them into much trouble. As the mysteries spread their heresies in their competitors, their heroes have often fought *each other* as "Christian" leaders, then blamed Christianity for being "factional."

For instance several times in the history of the Roman Empire the mystery religions were completely outlawed as subversive to the public good. These techniques pre-date modern mass-media techniques by thousands of years. As they affect Christianity, they are discussed in some detail in the book of Jude and in 2 Peter 2.

Janus, the two-faced "god," from a Roman coin

Lastly under this heading, they often conduct "operations" in their own behalf and also hire out such services to others (such as to deliver the victory in a "war," to the highest bidder). Thus "Mystery" Babylon is described as both a *harlot*, selling herself and her services, and as the mother of harlots (Revelation chapters 17 and 18).

E. They are messianic in character. They reject Jesus of Nazareth, but they intend to offer a substitute. They have a great competition between the groups to see who will provide and prove to be the true 'Beast,' and they use this and other Christian terminology among themselves. The concept of an occult messiah seems to even predate Christianity but has definitely become more important with time.

What I have added in these last comments is often implicit in the reading material, but not always *explicit*. Even so, both Angus' comments and the additional material I have added, are all things which can be seen from the outside and from publicly available material, without dealing with their "secrets."

Some things should be noticed. One is that often times almost all of the leading men of a society are members of whatever is the dominant *mystery* religion of that nation or group. The other is that often they constitute a religion that needs to hide in the dark. Despite their pretensions to great knowledge, the mysteries are intellectually and theologically weak, but emotionally very strong—very vivid. Also they are *often* morally questionable (to say the least). Frequently they must hide in part because they just cannot stand the scrutiny which Christianity does. Lastly, it must be noted that great numbers of men and women have served in these secret orders almost all of their adult lives, often without ever (or too late) realizing the nefarious purposes they were serving. The lower level personnel are never really able to determine the purposes which they are serving. The mystery religions are by their very nature well suited to such duplicity and deception.

The chart on this page of the development of the "mysteries" outlines the general development of the mystery religions.

What I have related here is an awesome picture of religions of the elite. The reality is often very bland. Many down through history have joined these groups as nothing more than social clubs or business groups and never took them very seriously. There are many examples from both ancient and modern history. Of old, Lysander was told during his initiations to confess his sins. (Isn't that a pattern? They always want us to confess our sins to *them*. It is part of the Pinocchio principle.) In our ancient story, Lysander then asked who he should confess his sins to? His initiators (*mustagogi*) said "to the gods." Lysander however was not willing to bear himself to them, and told them,

> "Then if you will go away I will tell them."
> Edwin Hatch, *The Influence of Greek Ideas on Christianity*,
> Harper, 1957, pp 286-287

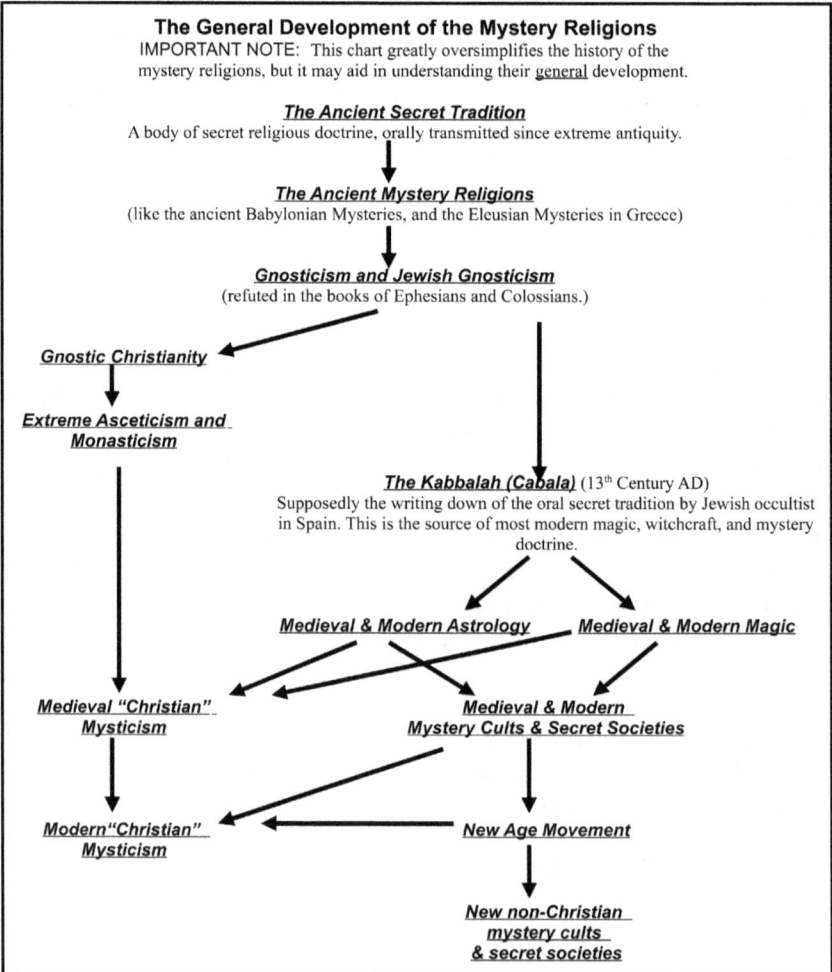

The General Development of the Mystery Religions

IMPORTANT NOTE: This chart greatly oversimplifies the history of the mystery religions, but it may aid in understanding their general development.

The Ancient Secret Tradition
A body of secret religious doctrine, orally transmitted since extreme antiquity.

The Ancient Mystery Religions
(like the ancient Babylonian Mysteries, and the Eleusian Mysteries in Greece)

Gnosticism and Jewish Gnosticism
(refuted in the books of Ephesians and Colossians.)

Gnostic Christianity

Extreme Asceticism and Monasticism

The Kabbalah (Cabala) (13th Century AD)
Supposedly the writing down of the oral secret tradition by Jewish occultist in Spain. This is the source of most modern magic, witchcraft, and mystery doctrine.

Medieval & Modern Astrology　　*Medieval & Modern Magic*

Medieval "Christian" Mysticism

Medieval & Modern Mystery Cults & Secret Societies

Modern "Christian" Mysticism

New Age Movement

New non-Christian mystery cults & secret societies

Many have enjoyed the fellowship, business ties, advancement, or parties, viewing the ritual as just mumbo jumbo foolishness. Clearly such is not possible with some of the groups. Many only vaguely realize the religious nature of some of the groups, and how blasphemous parts of the ritual are. More surely than most, many of these become captives (2 Tim 2:25-26) of the devil.

Also not a small number down through history have sneaked away from such groups as stupid, shameful, or dangerous; often pursued by threats to keep quiet about what they have seen. My friends, do not swear allegiance to iniquity before you have even heard it!

Their influence in history has been great. So much so that the true account of history often bears little relationship to popularly circulated accounts. A specialist in a small phase of history may know and write about the details here and there, but the generalists seem to never know, or disclose, the hidden hand of these societies. Richard Deacon in his *A History of the British Secret Service*, Taplinger, NY, 1969, discusses the role of famous British occultist and Satanist Aleister Crowley in British Intelligence in World Wars I and II. Crowley, though he is widely acclaimed in certain circles, was unsavory in the extreme and proudly declared himself to be "the Great Beast"! Deacon comments,

> There has been from time immemorial a strange union between occultism and espionage, probably because occultist tend to go underground and therefore make good agents. pg 311

So the connection is nothing new. The dubious honor roll of those involved in the occult and politics and espionage is both lengthy and legendary. Their greatest "hour" (almost literally) is yet to be felt.

The gospel of Jesus Christ is different from these groups in several particulars. The truths of Jesus Christ are for everyone. Christianity is not just for the intelligent, the rich, the powerful, the smart. It is not just for "men" or just for "white men" or "free men". Christianity is for *everyone*. Once again let us look near the end of Colossians chapter one.

We proclaim Him, admonishing **every** man

and teaching **every** man with **all** wisdom, so that

we may present **every** man complete in Christ.

Col 1:28 NASB (*emphasis added*)

Christianity claims superiority to all such pretensions of "inside knowledge," and Christianity claims to teach *ALL* men with *ALL* wisdom. And it does, but to some the gospel is hidden (Mtt 13:13), but not because it is withheld.

Finally, let's notice that the word "mystery" *can mean the secrets* of the group, or it *can mean the entire organization*, the whole "secret religion." Then comes a couple of key passages. First, in 2 Thessalonians 2 that it describes a powerful deceiver who pretends he is God and has the entire world worship him—all the world that is except the saved. This man is also personally destroyed by the second coming of Christ. Further, this man is backed and produced by "the mystery of lawlessness," which existed even in the first century.

> For the **mystery** of lawlessness **is already at work**;
> only he who now restrains *will do so* until He is
> taken out of the way. 2 Thes 2:7 NKJV
> *(emphasis added)*

So (written around 51 to 52 AD) what is described is a religion that is in operation in the first century and which will operate until it produces this "man of lawless," 2 Thes 2:3. It **works by the power of Satan**, 2 Thes 2:9-10, and will work in history until it produces the worldwide worship of one Satanic individual. MAYBE the text indicates *organizational* unity and continuity down through history to our present time. *Many* divergent mystery groups claim such organizational unity, some of them even claiming organizational unity that goes back to the likes of Solomon, Moses, or Enoch or even all the way back to Adam! (So they claim!) But at a *minimum* the wording in 2 Thessalonians 2 indicates *doctrinal* unity throughout the Christian age. The New International Version translation is "the secret power of lawlessness," which is not far of the mark, and Paul says that you know what holds him back, 2 Thes 2:5-6.

Although many branches of the occult claim a unity that goes back to ancient Babylon or before, passages like 2 Thessalonians 2 leave it as an open issue whether the continuity is *spiritual, doctrinal,* or *organizational*, **with either or both or *all* fitting the text**. Zechariah 5, written about 520 BC, pictures mystery Babylon as being prepared, but as being at that point still in the future. 2 Thessalonians 2 and Revelation pictures it as a first century reality.

Then comes the dazzling pictures of Babylon the Great, which can be seen in Revelation chapters 16 and 17. The angel tells the apostle John in Revelation 17 to come see the judgment of the great prostitute, the one who sits on many waters, the one with whom the rulers of the earth have committed fornication, and the one who had made all the people of the earth drunk with the wine of her fornication. This is talking about some **entity**, a "woman" it indicates, **who renders the whole world unable to think clearly**, makes them intoxicated. Then the angel carried John away into a "wilderness." The Greek word is *érāmos* ἔρημος; a word that is frequently used to name what most would call a desert, but it is also used to describe any deserted or unpopulated place. In a way it is the opposite of one of the words for "world," *oikoumenā* οἰκουμένη in the sense of the "inhabited world" or the "civilized world." The angel is taking us to a desolate place, an abandoned place, where people do not live, from where such a one as this whore may reign. I think, among other things, it is speaking of Babylon's need to hide.

Then John sees the "woman" sitting on a scarlet "beast." The word beast here is the Greek *thārion* θηρίον, and it is the regular word for a wild "beast"-to use the modern term, a wild animal, a creature—although I cannot help but think of this as more in the way of what could be called a "monster." It does appear like a monster to me. The monster has seven heads and ten horns. It seems to be the same monster which is described in the first few verses of Revelation 13 as coming up "out of the sea" from Satan, the dragon, Rev 12:9. It is there described the same way: seven heads, ten horns. A monster! One "head" is said to be full of blasphemous names. The prostitute is very rich and very nasty. She is clothed in the expensive clothing of scarlet and purple, which few but the very rich could afford, and she is wearing all sorts of jewelry and is drinking from a gold cup filled with the filthy fluids of fornication. Then John sees that the woman has a name written on her forehead,

> ... **MYSTERY**, BABYLON THE GREAT, THE MOTHER OF HAR-LOTS AND ABOMINATIONS OF THE EARTH.
> Rev 17:5 KJV (*bold emphasis added*)

I think the punctuation is more logical in the King James Version and the New International Version. It would appear from context that she is at least partially hidden, to at least some degree unrecognized, and it does seem to speak of her as if she is in existence in the first century (which to the side, would fit Rome). The apostle John does not write as if he has seen her before. He goes into "the wilderness" to see her. Is she "Mother Earth"? Isis, Asherah of the Old Testament Canaanites (Deut 16:21, etc.)? That would fit, but Revelation at any rate is not specific. She is a "Mystery," again the word *mustārion* μυστήριον. Remember, "**mystery**" in Greek is not really like the English word. Remember, it is primarily **a religious technical term** in the first century, describing either **1.** the secrets of the hidden or semi-hidden cult, or **2.** it describes the cult itself, *organizationally* you might say. Paul assures us in the second chapter of 2 Thessalonians that there is "mystery" already at work that is characterized by "lawlessness." Are they one and the same? It is not plain, but it appears they are at least associated mysteries. Go back and read the section on following types and patterns in Scripture. The beast will later be seen to hate the prostitute, but he seems in a way to be produced by this same prostitute, the Great Harlot, and they seem to share the same loathing of the gospel. Then it describes the prostitute as drunk, losing her bearings, drinking the blood of Christians!

The angel then says she will tell John about the "monster" and the "prostitute." Notice it says in Rev 17:7 that the ***monster / beast*** carries ***her***, *the prostitute!* The monster carries the Great Prostitute!

In Rev 17:8 that Babylon sits on seven mountains and seven kings. Kings we understand. Mountains are more ambiguous, and the subject of "mountains" in Scripture was in the section on "The Lord Our God will Reign," and it was pointed out that "mountains" are often symbolic of the center of some cult or religion. The Greek word in Rev 17:9 once again, really is the word "mountain," *oros* ὄρος, not the word for "hill." Many associate this with the "seven hills of Rome," but that seems a stretch. Rome is close but not quite the fulfillment. The word is mountain.

Religious aspirations are often associated with "mountains," even today. Like the ancients, people today tend to feel "closer" to God on a high mountain. When the Jews apostatized from the Lord and sought other gods, they went to what the Old Testament calls "the high places" to seek them. In Isaiah 2 it says that the "mountain" of the Lord's house is to be established as higher than any other "mountain." Later on Isaiah says that all nations,

> ... shall worship the LORD in the holy mount at Jerusalem. Isa 27:13 KJV

It is speaking in the religious sense of a dominating mountain. You can go on and on. The Samaritan religion is based on the mountain of Samaria. Jesus comments on these things to a Samaritan woman and speaks of the Old Testament Religion and the Samaritan religion under the figure of "mountains."

> Jesus saith unto her, Woman, believe me, the hour cometh, when ye shall neither in this mountain, nor yet at Jerusalem, worship the Father. Jn 4:21 KJV

Revelation 17 seems to be using "mountains" in this religious sense. That would go along with the word *mystery* in the religious sense. This would go along with hatred of Christianity as religion. Money itself is not opposed to Christianity. The woman is very broadly based. Rev 17:15 says that the waters on which the woman sits "are peoples, and multitudes, and nations, and tongues," KJV. She is seated on a monster with seven heads and ten horns, and **John seems to be telling us the prostitute is seated on seven different religions!**

But the prostitute has offended the Lord of Hosts. She has abused and destroyed the saints, and the saints have been pictured earlier in Revelation as having been sacrificed on the altar, and asking the Lord, How long, O Lord? How long? And the angels tells John,

> [16] And the ten horns which thou sawest upon the beast, these shall hate the whore, and shall make her desolate and naked, and shall eat her flesh, and burn her with fire. [17] For God hath put in their hearts to fulfil his will, and to agree, and give their kingdom unto the beast, until the words of God shall be fulfilled. [18] And the woman which thou sawest is that great city, which reigneth over the kings of the earth. Rev 17:16-18 KJV

The prostitute is "the great city," which rules over kings! There are two things to remember here. One is that she is "a city" or is located in "a city." The second is that she is not really government. Many tend to think of Babylon the Great as government, large world-wide government, often associated with the Roman empire. There is some merit here, and that will be covered later. Rome did rule over many "kings," so in that sense it seems to fit. On the other hand, it seems to not actually picture the prostitute as "government," but as ruling over governments. That be seen more clearly later, while still putting "Rome" in perspective. At this point, just remember the basic point. She is not government, rather she rules over governments. She by implication comes to rule over *ALL* the kings of the earth, and she is hated by many of those kings, and a coalition of those kings destroy her *completely*, within history.

Then there are details to notice. Then John sees another angel coming down from heaven, an angel with a lot of authority, and the angels are saying,

> ² ... Babylon the great is fallen, is fallen, and is become the habitation of devils, and the hold of every foul spirit, and a cage of every unclean and hateful bird. ³ For all nations have drunk of the wine of the wrath of her fornication, and the kings of the earth have committed fornication with her, and the merchants of the earth are waxed rich through the abundance of her delicacies. Rev 18:2-3 KJV

Look again at this passage. Once more there is a contrast between Babylon and kings/government. Babylon is a religious evil, a place where demons live and the unclean spirits live and vultures linger, and she has committed fornication with all the kings of the earth and gotten them drunk.

Then there is a plea to the people of God: Come out of her My people, lest you take part in her sins and get caught in her punishment. It is pictured as if you could be part of Mystery Babylon for many years and not know it. We are warned, that if you know, if you see and understand, you are to have the good sense to come out. Like Sodom of old, if you stay there, you will perish with her.

It is interesting how things often work. How men can be part of a religion, business, or a society and faithfully work for it, think their service good and healthy and beneficial to the world, and only after many years have the truth "pierce the void," as some comedians have termed it. These are facts of both some religions and some businesses. Sometimes we accept too uncritically the facades we are given to believe, and do not look with understanding on the evil which is often right before our eyes. If you are there and wake up, the injunction applies you: Come out of her My people ... lest you share in her punishment. The Lord wants Babylon to be paid back double for her sins. They are as high as the heavens. Babylon has lived in evil pleasure. She says that she sits as a queen, not a widow, and she will never see sadness, Isa 47:7ff, Rev 18:7.

So it will be that she will be destroyed in a single *day*. She will be burned up because *God is the One Who judges her* and He is strong. He can make some of the kings destroy her, God can *put it into their hearts to do such a thing!* Still, notice that most of the kings are sad over her passing because she was the strength behind them. She is the one who put them in place and supported them. Also the merchants weep and are sad. Babylon was the source of their sales, and she sold everything: gold, silver, pearls, linen, purple, silk, bronze, iron, marble, cinnamon, spices, perfume, wheat, cattle, sheep, horses, chariots, slaves, and literally the "souls of men." You name it, the list goes on for several verses. Even so there is more to observe here. What is seen here does not seem to be so much of a political entity as a *commercial entity*. Clearly there are political implications to what can be read, but taking the reading over all, it seems more to be describing **a religio-commercial empire** than what one would normally call government. In an overdrawn way you might say this describes Rome, but in Revelation 18, and in some of the Old Testament parallels which will be looked at, it seems more to be describing an extended commercial empire. Commerce, immorality, evil religion and hostility to Christianity seem to be the defining characteristics. But was this the central and defining characteristics of ancient Rome? It is not seduction or commerce that is the defining characteristic of ancient Rome; rather it is iron, just as in Daniel 2 and Daniel 7. It is legions and the generals of Rome, not the commerce, great though its commerce came to be. *Rome was not "really" the commerce, but instead it was the iron spiked boot of the conqueror*, and when her armies failed, then she also failed.

Also ancient Rome's forte was not illusion or magic, but brute strength and endurance, ah that endurance! Her religions were crude and really unbelievable even in the paganism before emperor cults. But there was no sophisticated seduction. Saying "Caesar is Lord" was just a formality, like saluting the flag, like the pledge of allegiance; not ever a sorcery to deceive the whole earth. But Babylon the Great is different, and her power is in religion and her seduction to iniquity. Rome's power was military, and she was good at administration. Babylon's power is seduction, and she is good at business; selling most *anything*!

Still, in one hour such wealth has been laid waste, and it seems to imply that such luxury will be *permanently* lost. If so, that also implies that the events spoken of are very close to the end, and there will appear other indications of these things happening very close to the end. The businessmen and the shippers and the kings are weeping. However, the Scriptures say,

> Rejoice over her, *thou* heaven, and ye holy apostles and prophets; for God hath avenged you on her. Rev 18:20 KJV

The church will be happy, and she is told to rejoice. This will be a happy day. Babylon has been the enemy of Christianity. It is implied in Scripture that she had been a partner with the beast in once for all suppressing the church, a subject to be addressed later. Then comes one more defining characteristic of Babylon the Great in the book of Revelation.

> And a mighty angel took up a stone like a great millstone, and cast it into the sea, saying, Thus with violence shall that great city Babylon be thrown down, and shall be found no more at all. Rev 18:21 KJV

So after she falls, Babylon will no longer exist ... *at all*. It is as if she disappears. How complete is her disappearance? Never again will there be *ANY* human activity in her after her fall, *NOT OF ANY TYPE!* Just as Scripture was very specific about Babylon the Great selling everything, so also Scripture is very specific *that no human activity will occur in her after her fall.*

> ²² And the voice of harpers, and musicians, and of pipers, and trumpeters, shall be heard no more at all in thee; and no craftsman, of whatsoever craft *he be*, shall be found any more in thee; and the sound of a millstone shall be heard no more at all in thee; ²³ And the light of a candle shall shine no more at all in thee; and the voice of the bridegroom and of the bride shall be heard no more at all in thee: for thy merchants were the great men of the earth; for by thy sorceries were all nations deceived. Rev 18:22-23 KJV

I think this is talking about the greatest city the world will *ever* see, and greater than anything you and I have seen yet, but after she is destroyed there is nothing there, and she is destroyed root and branch. Wars are there and murder, for in the prostitute were found the blood of the saints, and of ALL who have been killed upon the earth, Rev 18:24. Also you see again here the commercial nature of this Babylon. She has her own "merchants," and her CEO's and her Heads of the Board were "the great men of the earth." These are the men who dominate the world through commerce, without rule or conscience or sympathy or condescension, but for coercion, to exploit. Mammon is their god, and damnation their destiny. The Hebrew prophet James says of such men,

> ¹ Go to now, ye rich men, weep and howl for your miseries that shall come upon *you*. ² Your riches are corrupted, and your garments are motheaten. ³ Your gold and silver is cankered; and the rust of them shall be a witness against you, and shall eat your flesh as it were fire. Ye have heaped treasure together for the last days. ⁴ Behold, the hire of the labourers who have reaped down your fields, which is of you kept back by fraud, crieth: and the cries of them which have reaped are entered into the ears of the Lord of sabaoth. ⁵ Ye have lived in pleasure on the earth, and been wanton; ye have nourished your hearts, as in a day of slaughter. ⁶ Ye have condemned *and* killed the just; *and* he doth not resist you. Jas 5:1-6 KJV

There is indeed judgment to come, but there is also much judgment even in this life, for Jesus rules, not Satan. For by the sorceries this incredible Mystery Babylon the Great, all the nations were deceived. It speaks here as if it were some sort of "magic," and so it does in the Old Testament. It seems to speak of a world-wide hypnotism, a global mind control, international mental chains of darkness, forged by money and pleasure. It would almost seem to be a level of mental control not possible in primitive society, still it may just be speaking of Babylon the Great at her height toward the end. Many view big government as the problem, but that is not what Revelation says. **The problem is not Big Brother, but rather the problem is Big Mother ... a whore.** The nations are "charmed," "seduced." The prostitute has been "corrupting" the nations with her fornication, Rev 19:2; and deceiving them with her "sorcery" (the Greek word is *pharmakeia* φαρμακεία, which is a Greek word for casting "spells" by drugs and other means), Rev 18:23. The incantations of her selling has brought about "all" the slain of the earth. The fascination of her sensuality has drawn a multitude, indeed all who have not turned to God.

The prostitute rides on Satanism. Satan has been thrown from heaven in Revelation 12, and stands on the sands of the seashore in Revelation 13. Out of the sea comes a monster of Satan in Rev 13:1 and the verses following. This sea, the waters, are tribes and languages and nations, Rev 17:15, on which the prostitute sits, and out of which Satanism comes. Then the dragon, Satan Rev 12:9, gives his authority and a throne to the monster, Rev 13:2. The prostitute rides this Satanic monster, and you might say, as the rider brings the horse to the point of victory, so the prostitute brings the monster to victory. She is the key to Satan's victory, the dominance of the Mystery. But the monster hates the prostitute, and Babylon the Great is destroyed because God wanted it.

> And the ten horns which thou sawest upon the beast, these shall hate the whore, and shall make her desolate and naked, and shall eat her flesh, and burn her with fire. Rev 17:16 KJV

They will "eat her flesh." Whatever your theory is of "Babylon the Great," these are some of the most powerful obstacles you face to secure your theory. There is in the goddess cults a vague and moving dread of these things. How often they have ceremonially been the victim. And this will be the final end in history. Not after the end of history, rather within history.

Do you think it is ancient Rome? There are lot of similarities. Clearly the book of Revelation was written for early Christians **and** later Christians. Clearly also the early Christians thought of Rome as if she was this Babylon the Great, and much of the evidence can and has been deduced. Ancient Babylon fell in a single day, really a single night, as the Greek historian Herodotus describes in detail, BUT Babylon the Great falls "in one hour," Rev 18:17, 19. Rome? Gibbon's *Decline and Fall of the Roman Empire* covers Rome's fall in about *fifteen hundred years*, not a day, not an "hour," not even in an extended sense. And there are still in the city of Rome today: orchestras, musicians, craftsmen, weddings, the light of a lamp, and so on. Rome is still there, and is still an active city. She is not like Babylon of old which is no longer inhabited. But Babylon the Great, when she falls, will no longer be a city, will no longer be inhabited, *at all! She will follow here the type of ancient Babylon of history and of ancient Sodom of history!* **Were the early Christians wrong? NO!** But Rome is only a type. Only one of several "types," "symbols," of the final evil empire of money and sex and perverted religion. Remember the earlier lessons on "Type and Anti-type"?

Don't ignore facts which "don't seem to fit!" These
are often the signal that you are dealing with
a model, not a fulfillment.

So what is the type (symbol) and the anti-type (the fulfillment)? In a way both are. So as noted under "Type and Anti-Type," Scripture says of 2 Sam 7:12-15 that **both** Solomon fulfills it (as noted in 1 Kgs 8:17-20), **and** *also* Jesus fulfills it (Heb 1:5). *The type, the shadow, came soon after the prophecy* (Solomon), and what we might call the ultimate fulfillment is Jesus, (about a thousand years later), and **both** are in the prophecy. The things in 2 Samuel 7 that do not fit Solomon *are the tip off that Solomon is really symbolic of someone else who would come.* So it is with the Book of Revelation. *Ancient Rome is in one sense a "ful-fillment," but not the ultimate one. Ancient Rome is just a type.*

In one way this is one litmus test of many theories. Is the Catholic church the "real" Babylon the Great? This has been a popular theory with many Protestants for some five hundred years. Once again, there are many little things which do not fit, and there are today (just like for ancient Rome) weddings in Rome and craftsmen and musicians, and so on. Incomplete at the very least! London has been proposed for these honors (?), and so has New York, and Paris (Napoleon as the anti-christ) and likewise for many theories. At best these are all incomplete theories. If you could marshal enough evidence, you might say you made the case for another "type" in history; but most of these fall well short of the ultimate fulfillment. And so it is with ancient Rome. She did not prove to be the final item of Scripture.

Religion, Babylon, and Effective Rule

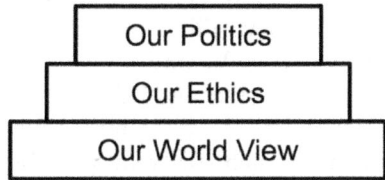

It is time for us to look at how ideas make an impact on society. Many things came out of the ancient discussions of Socrates, and his debates about reality have continued down to our own time. It is clear though from the things he said that ideas are important, and that the foundations of our actions are in how we view the world. Did God make it? Did it just happen? Is man just a glorified animal, or is he really in the image of God? Whatever your decisions are, your decisions then determines your ethics. How should you act if you are just an animal, or descended from amoebae? Or how should you act if you are a special creation in God's image? How should you treat other men or the creation? Your view of the world, how you judge reality, determines your ethics. Then your ethics will determine your politics. Those are some of the basics which Socrates (Plato if you will), demonstrated in his extensive discussions. If man is but an animal, then animal-like conduct should be approved by law. Or if man is a special creation in God's own image, then the murder must be punished. But whatever your view, your world view will determine your ethics, and your ethics will then determine your politics!

An example of "right and wrong" from the mechanical world is perhaps a good way to start. Generally speaking, it is "wrong" to use a regular knife blade as a screw driver. A regular knife blade was not *designed* (reality) to loosen or tighten screws. The further "reality" (as everyone knows) is that if you use your good knife blade to try to tighten or loosen screws, instead of making sure that you have the correct tools on hand, you will very likely break that fine tip off your knife blade, ruin it for further use and fail to get the screw tightened or loosened, and perhaps ruin the screw head. So the "right or wrong" (the mechanical "morality" if you will) of using a knife blade as a screwdriver is firmly based in reality.

Socrates

Actually, the same is true of the rest of our "rights and wrongs." They are in the end based on reality. *Our ethics (the morality, the **right** or **wrong**), are based on our world view* (what we think is **reality**). Change the supposed world view, and your ethics end up being changed with them. Sometimes someone's sense of "reality" doesn't *seem* to be there, but it is (although it is at times hard to see) and its presence is always implied. Sometimes we do not understand this reality, but that shouldn't stop us from correctly acting on it. For instance, we may not understand AC electricity but may be told to "never touch a 240 volt AC line" (an *electric morality*, an *electric wrong*, if you will excuse the expression). This *electric morality* is based on an *electric reality*. Violate the volts and you will fry yourself. But you don't really have to *understand* "AC theory." The same is true in religious matters. Our morals are based on our world view (*reality*). If your world view of reality is distorted, then your ethics will be distorted.

Take ethics concerning man, for instance. The truth (*reality*) is that man is a special creation of God, made in God's own image, and he is not just another animal. Furthermore, *God* has given man dominance over the earth (all of which is related to us in the book of Genesis). **If** instead man was rather a chance blob of matter, then how we treat man changes. If he is just a blob, there is no wrong in treating him like a blob. You can throw him around, smash him, beat him, trash can him, because he is only a blob. This is the foundation of a pornographic view of man. You can not do anything "wrong" with man (or woman) because they are just blobs anyway. If man was not really created in God's image and given dominance, there may be no reason for man to *have* dominance (the "Green" or "ecological" view of man). Different world views (correct or incorrect) produce different ethics.

On the other hand, our ethical statements reflect some supposed view of reality, whether right or wrong. If that world view is correct, *and if we reason from it correctly,* then the ethics—the rights and wrongs we declare—are indeed true. If our world view is incorrect, *or if we reason incorrectly from the correct world view (beg your pardon, but there is indeed a reality), then our ethics will be wrong or distorted. So when the Pope, for instance, declares that abortion is wrong, his declaration is based upon a supposed reality; that the fetus is indeed a "human being", a man. If the Pope is right in his presumption of reality, then the ethic he declares is "right." If the supposed "reality" is incorrect, however, then the ethic is also incorrect. Morality and Reality are inseparable. Solomon spoke of the hope of Scripture as a basis for conduct.

> For surely there is a hereafter,
> And your hope will not be cut off. Prov. 23:18 NKJV

There is no separating the two. There is no separating between the "moral claims" of Jesus, and His claim to have been raised from the dead. They are inseparable. There is *no qualifier at the bottom of the page* which says,

> The above statements have nothing to do with reality, or any fact or item of knowledge that may be in anyway verified. Other restrictions may apply.

Whatever God says is true. All of it. *Even statements concerning what you might call covered by "science."*

> for prophecy never came by the will of man, but holy men of God spoke as they were moved by the Holy Spirit. 2 Pe 1:21 NKJV

These men spoke from God as they were "carried along" by the Holy Spirit. When it says in Scripture that there are paths in the sea, that means there are. So when God inspires a man, whatever he tells him is true. All of it. God knows the reality of man and this earth, and this universe, and whatever he tells man about "reality" is true, and without error. Test it all you want. It will in the end prove to be true.

How would you tell that something is not inspired? It is very simple. It ends up not being true.

> [21] And if thou say in thine heart, How shall we know the word which the LORD hath not spoken?' [22] When a prophet speaketh in the name of the LORD, if the thing follow not, nor come to pass, that *is* the thing which the LORD hath not spoken, *but* the prophet hath spoken it presumptuously: thou shalt not be afraid of him. Deut 18:21-22 KJV

This is not cryptic. If what is said is false, it is not from God.

> Every good gift and every perfect gift is from above, and cometh down from the Father of lights, with whom is no variableness, neither shadow of turning. Jas 1:17 KJV

So political conflicts end up trying to change the religious views of the nations. This is why large and powerful intelligence agencies infiltrate religions and philosophies of all types. This is why King James I of England sponsored a government translation of the Bible, approved for public worship in England. The big movers and shakers realize that to change the politics of a nation, they must first change the ethics, and to change the ethics, they must first change the religious views of a nation. It is all about power and money.

Then we come to one of the major mistakes of the Roman empire. Yes, they had the strength of iron, as prophesied in Daniel 2. But their feet and legs were iron mixed with clay. Amidst great cultural and religious diversity the Romans succeeded in creating an enduring multinational government, where others had failed. But they realized too late their greatest weakness: there was no unifying principle for the Empire, nothing to fuse together her diverse subjects, cultural-ly you might say. There was nothing that gave a single vision for dealing with problems. If there is no unifying "truth," then there is no "true" way to behave.

Too late they tried to impose a cult of emperor worship on the empire to create that unified vision. At first it seems to have been the pagan provinces who wished to flatter their masters with divinity. The first emperors were in fact not a little embarrassed with such claims, and while accepting such fawning, did not make such claims for themselves. Over time both the emper-ors and the Senate came to fully realize the advantage of these things, and grad-ually began to both accommodate and to use such adulation, even if it had at first been offered maybe in part, tongue in cheek. The pagans, both Greek and Roman, had more than one level of "gods." At the top were the fullest "gods" like Jupiter and Venus (whom Paul says by nature are not gods, Gal 4:8). Below them were those orders of "gods" which the pagans called "demons." The Greek word was *daimonion* δαιμόνιον, and yes, it is the same word used in the New Testament. Everyone realized that demons were like men, a mixture of good and evil, maybe at times even more evil than good, but so what? That was also true of the higher "gods," all of whom Paul calls demons in 1 Cor 10:20.

> No, but I say that the things which the Gentiles sacrifice, they sacrifice to demons and not to God; and I do not want you to become sharers in demons. NASB

So goodness, or the lack of it, was never a barrier to being a so-called "god." Then just below the demons in the pagan pantheon were exalted men, who had done great deeds, and had ascended into the order of the "gods." Yes, even a man could perhaps become a "god," and this order of "gods" was called heroes. None of this was outside of normal pagan foolishness, but the Romans would be embarrassed to claim such foolishness for themselves. So, reluctantly at first, they bought into the system.

Diversity (your religion) was to be tolerated, but only under the banner of Caesar is Lord, and each was as a minimum to offer their pinch of incense, and say Caesar is Lord. It was to Rome just an indication of patriotism. It was to them much like giving an oath of allegiance, like giving the pledge to the flag. **But there never was a "mark" for this, as in Rev 13:16-17.** A few of the fool-ish may have tattooed such on their hand or their forehead, but it was not required by law. **Neither was it** necessary **to bear Caesar's name or the number of his name in order to buy things or sell things.** In Latin as in

Greek and Hebrew, the letters all have numeric values (remember Roman numerals), and you can use the letters to write down numeric values. On the other hand, you might add the numeric values in your name. So a Roman lad might carve in a tree, "265 loves 374." Yes, these things do say something, but this would be chiefly an additional check on our ideas when all the rest of the prophecy seemed to be being fulfilled. **But there was no such legal requirement in the first centuries after Christ to bear the number or the name of the Caesar!** All you needed was to grab a pinch of incense (which the authorities would supply), throw it into the fire, and say, "Caesar is Lord." That was all. They gave you a certificate that you have performed the required "sacrifice." **It was only a certificate, and it was not required for buying and selling.** That once again is an indication that ancient Rome is only a "type," not the ultimate fulfillment. At sometime in the future though, it will be required.

> [16] And he causeth all, both small and great, rich and poor, free and bond, to receive a mark in their right hand, or in their foreheads: [17] And that no man might buy or sell, save he that had the mark, or the name of the beast, or the number of his name.
>
> Rev 13:16-17 KJV (*bold emphasis added*)

An ancient certificate of proof of offering incense in worship to Caesar. There was no official "mark" for buying or selling in early centuries after Christ. That is for the ant-type, the fulfillment, later in history.

But that will only be in later times, and there will be plenty of time to look at the details of *other* things way before there is a need to start trying to calculate "the number of his name."

Now to the Romans this was all a nominal matter, of no great significance. The average resident of the empire already regularly worshiped perhaps several "gods," and to add one more did not make much difference. However, this was a bloody battle to the Christians to whom only Jesus was Lord. Still, the Christians won in the end and crushed the pagan world order with the Christian faith, as prophesied in Dan 2:44. Here also is another indication that ancient Rome was not the ultimate "Babylon the Great." Because you see, the beast who is yet to come, the ultimate one, not the monsters of the Roman empire, will "make war with the saints, and to **overcome them**," in Rev 13:7 KJV and other passages. *However, the saints of old overcame the Roman empire, INSTEAD OF the Roman empire overcoming them!* Ancient Rome was only symbolic of the ultimate Mystery Babylon of history, the anti-type. The "real" Mystery Babylon (if you want to put it that way) will

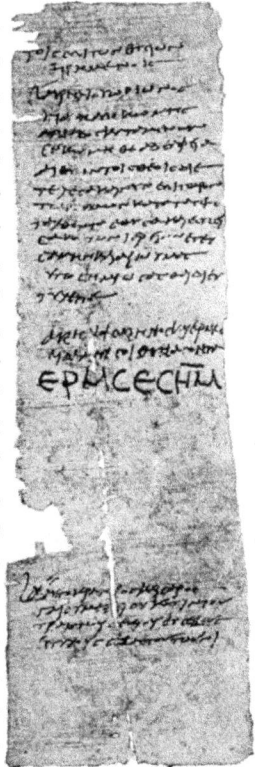

be in some ways "like" the ancient Roman empire.

Then Rome tried a Christian Empire. If paganism had not proved a sound foundation for rule, maybe Christianity could. But there were problems. Christianity had from the first been aggressively infiltrated by the occult (Mystery Babylon/ the Mystery of Lawlessness) and had "caught" a variety of heresies contrary to Scripture. Oh how often it is that the enemies of the Cross blame Christianity for the heresies they have planted!

> [24] Another parable put he forth unto them, saying, The kingdom of heaven is likened unto a man which sowed good seed in his field: [25] But while men slept, his enemy came and sowed tares among the wheat, and went his way. [26] But when the blade was sprung up, and brought forth fruit, then appeared the tares also. Mtt 13:24-26 KJV

So it comes that they both grow side by side, and how frequently the secular historian confuses one with the other, frequently treating the heretic as the faithful servant, and the faithful servant as the heretic. What is to be done with the kingdom? Here are the words of the Master.

> Let both grow together until the harvest: and in the time of harvest I will say to the reapers, Gather ye together first the tares, and bind them in bundles to burn them: but gather the wheat into my barn. Mtt 13:30 KJV

The Emperor finally had enough of this. They needed a unified world view. He called the great churchmen of the empire together, and said in effect, "Okay, you guys fight it out, and whatever you tell me is 'right' (orthodox), I <u>will</u> enforce, and <u>we will have unity</u>!" And they did, and he did, and so came the first church councils, and a measure of unity in a revised Roman Empire. **Political unity cannot be separated from a unified world view.**

Now in the past few hundred years there has been a conflict for a "New World Order." The rulers of our New Age are irritated at being subject to God. For in our age Christ rules, so,

> Let every soul be subject to the governing authorities. For there is no authority except from God, and the authorities that exist are appointed by God. Rom 13:1 NKJV

Many world rulers realize this. They are anxious to cast away bonds to God.

> [2] The kings of the earth take their stand
> And the rulers take counsel together
> Against the LORD and against His Anointed, saying,
> [3] "Let us tear their fetters apart
> And cast away their cords from us!" Psa 2:2-3 NASB

They want man to rule, not God, and they speak of true religion as being an ideology of liberation. What do you want to do? *Everything?* Then *everything* must be accepted. *Anything?* Then *anything* must be accepted in this ecumenism.

The new gods are those of a democratic collective will, not of Jehovah. As the old saying goes, The voice of the people has become the supposed voice of God. We consult opinion surveys, instead of the LORD Jesus Christ. Jesus of Nazareth is not acceptable to this Age. The New World Order is in fact indulgent of every evil, but will not tolerate the exclusiveness of the one and only God, the One who says "No one comes to the Father except through Me," Jn 14:6 NKJV, of whom it is said "Neither is there salvation in any other," Acts 4:12 KJV. Jesus **is** THE answer, but to a world with many diverse sins, this is in itself an offense. Still, distressing as all of this is and as foreign to the truth and to the gospel, these compromises are not the end.

THIS CONFLICT WON'T GO AWAY. Either we stick with a nation based social order as God instituted with the confusion of tongues (in Genesis 11), with Jesus as King of Kings and Lord of Lords, **or** for a new order, we must have a new world view. If men are to be freed all from the "burdens" of past beliefs, then like militant Islam, also traditional Catholicism, and simple biblical faith must also perish, and any other power that represents any authority or rule or limitation on man. Chaos, religious and political, must come first.

> "... that day will not come until the rebellion occurs and the man of lawlessness is revealed ..." 2 Thes 2:3 NIV

But diversity itself only leads to the Roman Empire's stalemate. It only gives us variety (or rather confusion), without principles for united action, without *order* for the New World *Order*. While diversity may be necessary for a swishing, shifting world society, it is a political foundation for nothing but chaos. The New World Order is not safe without a *religious/philosophical* consensus. The council of the wise of the New Age will never buy such a dead end; they know history too well. A new unifying principle must come, a new basis for stable government, a new emperor cult which will endure, a new god. It is a *political* necessity for a world without Jesus of Nazareth, and in the end this consensus must be enforced. *Yes, that is right, the end of all this liberality,* **will not be liberal, but rather despotic, and oppressive, and illiberal.** But all the New Order has is the world, and it is all in the power of the evil one, 1 Jn 5:19, so no one but the god of this world 2 Cor 4:4, is acceptable. Scripture speaks of one,

> "who ... exalts himself above every so called god or object of worship," 2 Thes 2:4 NASB

A new focus must finally come, one far beyond this acceptance of everything and anything. His authority comes from Satan, Rev 13:4; and God Himself will help him deceive the nations, 2 Thes 2:9-12. He will bring a corrupted church persecution, and a corrupted world much trouble from God, Psa 2, and Rev 19. He will be destroyed by the second coming of Jesus Christ, 2Thes 2:8; and with his false prophet will be thrown *alive* into hell, Rev 19:20.

British occultist W. B. Yeats pictures *the Spiritus Mundi* (literally the spirit of the world) as personified in this man, the beast, who will come **back** *after a* *long sleep*, in his widely quoted poem "The Second Coming."

The Second Coming

W. B. Yeats

Turning and turning in the gyre
The falcon cannot hear the falconer;
Things fall apart; the center cannot hold;
Mere anarchy is loosed upon the world,
The blood-dimmed tide is loosed, and everywhere
The ceremony of innocence is drowned;
The best lack all conviction, while the worst
Are full of passionate intensity
Surely some revelation is at hand;
Surely the Second Coming is at hand.
The Second Coming! Hardly are those words out
When a vast image of Spiritus Mundi
Troubles my sight: somewhere in sand of the desert
A shape with lion body and head of a man,
A gaze blank and pitiless as the sun,
Is moving its slow thighs, while all about it
Reels shadows of the indignant desert birds.
The darkness drops again; but now I know
That twenty centuries of stony sleep
Were vexed to nightmare by a rocking cradle,
And what rough beast, its hour come round at last,
Slouches toward Bethlehem to be born.

Once again, notice carefully, Yeats is speaking of the "second coming," *not* of Jesus the Christ, but of the "beast." The beast will be discussed in the later section, "We Hold Fast in the Great Conflict."

There are many other things to tell about the literary hero William Butler Yeats. Among other things he was a member of the occult society the "Order of the Golden Dawn," (of which Aleister Crowley, who was mentioned earlier, was also a member). An offshoot of this "Order" was the German "Thule Society" which was instrumental in producing Adolph Hitler. Yeats says, "Things fall apart; the center cannot hold." "Mere anarchy," is the preliminary chaos that ushers in "the man of lawlessness," the special rebellion. "A blood-dimmed tide is loosed ... everywhere." Innocence disappears, and there is lack of conviction. Written in 1919, Yeats seems to write as if he expects the confusion following World War I to lead to the appearance of the "beast." Should we think here of Hitler and Mussolini and Stalin, and pre-World War II apocalyptic-prophecy literature? The "Spiritus Mundi" appears. This is Latin for "the spirit of the world." You might compare 2 Cor 4:4 about Satan being "the god of this world," or literally, "the god of this age." Yeats capitalizes this "Spiritus Mundi," as if a name, a title, a person. Yeats is talking about the same things written about in these last sections of this study, but from an opposite point of view. Yeats also says that this spirit of the world arises in the "desert" after "twenty centuries of stony sleep." How telling! Does Yeats mean that the "was" of the beast in Rev 17:8, occurred in the first century? There will be more of this later. Yeats seems to be saying that he expects him soon! He knows about him from another point of view than most of us do. Jesus Himself said,

> I am come in my Father's name, and ye receive me not: if another shall come in his own name, him ye will receive. Jn 5:43 KJV

If we will not accept Jesus Himself, we will end up accepting someone else. This is built into the nature of things. Christianity can survive in a pagan world. In ancient Babylon, the righteous Daniel rose to a position of trust and power in the middle of great corruption. In ancient Rome, Christianity finally conquered that empire. It will also survive the greatest trials of all time. The church at that time will be the,

> "heavy stone for all the peoples; all who lift it will be severely injured. And all the nations of the earth will be gathered against it," Zech 12:3. NASB

What a shock to the New Order, when Jesus appears with flaming fire to rescue His church, 2 Thes 1:7-9, Rev 20:9!

> But though we, or an angel from heaven, preach any other gospel unto you than that which we have preached unto you, let him be accursed. Gal 1:8 KJV

Still there seem to be other types of this world wide empire. Just as Babylon is a type of the great land empires of the world, so Tyre is the type of the great maritime empires of the world, those who trade and dominate by ships. The people of Tyre were the descendants of Noah through Canaan, Gen 10:15, so it can be clearly said that the Phoenicians were Canaanites. It is curious about some of these things. The word for Canaan, *kenaan* כְּנַעַן, is also one of the Hebrew words for a merchant, as in *kenaani* כְּנַעֲנִי, as in Hos 12:7.

These guys were sailors, and very good ones, in a time when sailing was a very difficult and dangerous business. Tyre was by the time of David the main Phoenician city, and it was a vast empire of trade and commerce. The Phoenicians traded from one end of the Mediterranean to the other. It mentions (in Isaiah) ships from Tarshish, and which seems to be referring to Tartessus in Spain on the far end of the Mediterranean. Also it was the Phoenicians who established the mighty empire of Carthage around 800 BC, the only nation that was able to seriously challenge Roman growth.

Tyre was very hard to fight. She had an island fortress, just off the coast of Palestine. The water was only about eighteen feet deep, but it was several hundred feet offshore, so they had quite a moat around them. However, when you read about Tyre in Isaiah 23 she is in trouble. The ships come back wailing, crying! This is an "Burden" it says in the King James Version. The NET Bible says, "Here is a mess about Tyre. Wail!" Isa 23:1. Interesting. It talks about Tyre being destroyed. The money is all being dried up. Their source of trade is all disappearing. The last leg of the journey from Spain would be Cyprus, so the sailors have just landed at Cyprus and heard that Tyre has fallen in Isa 23:1.

Now Tyre was the principal city of the Phoenicians, the strongest, the most secure, so the rest of you cities on the coast land should be quiet, Isaiah says. Sidon, about 24 miles north of Tyre, should be quiet, Isa 23:2. Like America of the twentieth century or Britain of the nineteenth century, Tyre was "the market of the nations." The Egyptians sold their wheat all across the Mediterranean through the Phoenicians, the men of Tyre. The prophet says, you merchants of Sidon should be ashamed. The grain of Egypt was Tyre's revenue, Isa 23:3. So many were to be killed in Tyre's fall that it was just as if she had never given birth to any children, Isa 23:4. This in turn causes anguish all across the world. Even Spain/Tarshish, along with Egypt will be in anguish, Isa 23:5-6. Who planned this against Tyre? It was the Lord of Hosts who planned this, Isa 23:8-9.

It speaks of Tyre's businessmen as if they were princes, "the honourable of the earth," KJV. This is very reminiscent of modern western Europe and America, where the preeminent businessmen and bankers often have more power and influence than presidents or prime ministers. These are men who can command petty despots to roll over and bark, and woe to them if they fail to obey. That is what it was like also in the sixth and seventh centuries before Christ, and that is what it is often like when huge commercial empires dominate peoples, or the like the East India Company of earlier centuries, sometimes even sub-continents.

So the Lord had planned this destruction. The Lord has stretched out His hand and made the kingdoms quiver in fear and gives a command that the fortresses be destroyed. However, who is to conquer Tyre? It is Babylon of old according to Isa 23:13!

Tyre is to wail and cry, Isa 23:14. It clearly indicates that their little island refuge is to be taken, "For your stronghold is destroyed," Isa 23:14 NASB. That is the way it was a couple of times before she ceased to exist. There was built land causeways out into the ocean to assault the walls of Tyre. It was done once by Babylon as seen here in 573 BC, a few years after the end of second Kings and the fall of Jerusalem, and later on by Alexander the Great. Tyre was so rich in ships, that many of the people just left the city in ships when it was about to be conquered, and fled to other nations. Overflow your banks like the Nile, it says in, Isa 23:10. So just like the Nile floods all over Egypt, Tyre will flow out of her city, all over her land of commercial trading, to Egypt, even to Spain. The further away the better. There is no longer strength to hold on, or any way to dominate her colonies. She is to be forgotten for seventy years according to, Isa 23:15a.

I think it is striking that this is the same period of time as for the punishment of Jerusalem, 2 Chron 36:21.

Consider also that there is definitely a dark side to Tyre! They had basically the same religions as the rest of the Canaanites. They had the horrible Baal worship. They had the immoral worship of mother earth as Asherah. They had the human sacrifices of the rest of the Canaanites, and this was passed on to Carthage and other colonies. The infamous and immoral Jezebel was a Phoenician, 1 Kgs 16:31. Jezebel is a type of all that is evil in religion in the book Revelation. Religion that is so evil that it includes fornication, Rev 2:20-23.

So what is seen here is that Tyre also is described as a harlot in Isa 23:15b-16. She is described as an ancient Mediterranean prostitute who dresses up in brightly colored clothes and walks up and down the city strumming on a lyre and looking for the gullible, to make an immoral trade. Now commerce, selling or trading, is not evil in itself. But the desire for wealth can lead to all sorts of foolish and hurtful things.

> [9] But those who desire to be rich fall into temptation and a snare, and *into* many foolish and harmful lusts which drown men in destruction and perdition. [10] For the love of money is a root of *all kinds of* evil, for which some have strayed from the faith in their greediness, and pierced themselves through with many sorrows. 1 Tim 6:9-10 NKJV

Not that money is evil. The love of it, however, is what can lead to every kind of sin. Tyre is clearly accused of double dealing, of immoral dealing, in order to make more money—of doing almost anything for anyone in order to make money and set up a money making empire. She will play the harlot with all the kingdoms (that is the way it is translated in the NASB, NIV, NKJV, and KJV). Then after seventy years of fleeing, she will go back to trade as a prostitute, Isa 23:17.

Many of the details of the destruction are not known. Keil and Delitzsch's commentary gives a good account of the historical issues.

> Hitherto, therefore, these have been only preludes to the fulfilment of the prophecy. Its ultimate fulfilment has still to be waited for. But whether the fulfilment will be an ideal one, when not only the kingdoms of the world, but also the trade of the world, shall belong to God and His Christ; or *spiritually*, in the sense in which this word is employed in the Apocalypse, i.e., by the true essence of the ancient Tyre reappearing in another city, like that of Babylon in Rome; or *literally*, by the fishing village of *Tzur* actually disappearing again as Tyre rises from its ruins-it would be impossible for any commentator to say, unless he were himself a prophet. *Commentary on the Old Testament,* Keil and Delitzsch, *Vol VII, Isaiah,* by F. Delitzsch, (Two Volumes in One), Eerdmans, Grand Rapids, Michigan, 1988 pg 421.

So these German scholars speculated about Tyre as only a "type." It brings up some considerable thoughts. The key issue is that this seems to be a type, symbolic of some future fulfillment! In this way it comes about that we must compare ancient Tyre with the New Testament Babylon the Great in Revelation. Babylon the Great is a mother of prostitutes in Rev 17:1-6. Look at the description of her fall, Rev 18:9-19. Look at how eerily this is like the description of the fall of Tyre that was read earlier in Isaiah 23. In addition here is another strange thing. The king of Tyre is also spoken of in another "oracle" against the king of Tyre in Ezekiel 28, as if he is Satan. This is in a passage that starts by saying that all of this is because the heart of the king of Tyre has been proud, and he has said he is a "god," Ezek 28.2

> [12] "Son of man, take up a lamentation for the king of Tyre, and say to
> him, "Thus says the Lord GOD:
>> 'You were the seal of perfection,
>> Full of wisdom and perfect in beauty.
> [13] You were in Eden, the garden of God; ...""" Ezek 28:12-13 NKJV

A "god" he thinks he is, but he is not; however, he was in the garden of Eden. Strange that a knowledgeable man and a prophet, like Ezekiel, would speak of a contemporary king as being in the garden of Eden. What is more, the king of Tyre was also an angel, a cherub who was in heaven.

> [14] "You *were* the anointed cherub who covers;
>> I established you;
>> You were on the holy mountain of God;
>> You walked back and forth in the midst of fiery stones.
> [15] You were perfect in your ways from the day you were created,
>> Till iniquity was found in you." Ezek 28:14-15 NKJV

Notice the contrasts. The king of Tyre only *thinks* he is a "god," but he *was* in the garden, and he *was* in heaven, on the mountain of God (the real Mount Zion in heaven). Also he was a "covering cherub." A cherub is one of the highest orders of angels, among those who are closest to God, and it was cherubim who guarded the garden of Eden from entry after the fall of man in Genesis 3. The plural of cherub is cherubim, and, no, they do not look like naked little baby boys. The most detailed descriptions we have of cherubim are in Ezekiel 1, and in Ezekiel 10. Compare Ezek 10:1. These are no doubt symbolic descriptions intended to give us an idea of the awesomeness and power of these creatures, and all you can say is "Wow!" Now to say that one of these is a "covering cherub" seems to indicate that he was one of those angels that actually "covered" or hovered over the very throne of the LORD our God in heaven. Such is what seems to be pictured in the plan for the ark of the covenant. The lid of the ark represented the throne of God itself, called the "mercy seat" in passages like Ex 25:17 and Heb 9:5. And over the mercy seat are pictured two angels, cherubim, spreading their wings over the throne of God, covering it. Compare picture of the ark of the covenant on page 4.

So what is this? The King of Tyre is evidently a type, symbolic of Satan. So how would you know this? Mostly by things that do not fit "the type." For instance: saying he was in the garden of Eden, "the garden of God," it calls it, Ezek 28:13. Satan was in the garden of Eden, but the king of Tyre was not! *In fact he was further away from Eden in time, than we are from Christ's birth!* It says he was an angel, a "cherub," Ezek 28:14. Still the King of Tyre was not a "god," but only a man.

Cherubim?

A more of less "human" form for the angels on the ark of the covenant (as on page 4), may be right, aside from the effeminancy of the angels, which is traditional in Western art.

... "Because your heart *is* lifted up, And you say, 'I *am* a god, I sit *in* the seat of gods, In the midst of the seas,' Yet you *are* a man, and not a god, Ezek 28:2 NKJV

Does part of Ezekiel 1 look something along this order?

Josephus said in the first century that no one knew what the cherubim in Solomon's temple looked like, Antuquities 8:3:3. Others have taken the human winged bull and lions from Nineveh (above right) as cherubim. The descriptions in Ezekiel chapters 1 and 10 are awesome. Even so, these are everywhere acknowledged as symbolic of the tremendous power, strength, ferocity, intelligence and sight of these daunting creatures of God's creation.

Here is another strange thing. Not a "god," but he is an angel that was in heaven, and that he is "a man not God." Also there are *two very different deaths* described in Ezekiel 28. The king of Tyre will be killed (should we say assassinated?), by foreigners.

7 "Behold, therefore, I will bring strangers against you,
   The most terrible of the nations;
   And they shall draw their swords ...

10 "... You shall die the death of the uncircumcised
   By the hand of aliens; ...' Ezek 28:7, 10 NKJV

But a different death is described later in Ezekiel 28 for the "cherub,"

Therefore I brought fire from your midst;
   It devoured you,
   And I turned you to ashes upon the earth

In the sight of all who saw you. Ezek 28:18 NKJV

So they die different ways. The cherub seems to die by having fire come out *from* **within** *him! There are dual (or maybe even triple) subjects in Ezekiel 28, perhaps more clearly than in any other passage of Scripture.* The king of Tyre must have been one conceited and haughty little weasel. If the king of Tyre himself claimed to be a god, though such was not unknown in the ancient world, then it has been lost to me from ancient history. He seems to be a type of both Satan, and some special merchant prince who thinks he is god. Both! These are *typical inconsistencies or exaggerations* such as can be seen in a passage, when one thing is a type or symbol of another, when there are *dual subjects.* Sometimes the contrast between type and anti-type is subtle and sometimes it is glaring, as in Ezekiel 28.

What then can be learned about Satan here? Satan was at first created both beautiful and good, Ezek 28:13, and blameless, Ezek 28:15. He was evidently lifted up with pride, Ezek 28:17. Clearly there was a revolt in heaven before there was a revolt on earth. Satan was cast out of heaven, Ezek 28:17. Satan, by his lies and half-truths, spread that revolt to mankind. Likewise in Revelation 12 Satan is pictured as being cast out of heaven to the earth, Rev 12:7-13.

My friends, this Book is a unity, from one end to the other. In the tasks of working for a living, making money, and ordinary corporate and government dealings and the business world, you may make you run into Babylon before you know it. The drug business, the slave trade, dirty dealing, even out and out murder, theft, and blackmail are often just below the surface of the shiny facade that all see. We need to be alert. Many of us have at one time or another worked for Mystery Babylon. If you find yourself there, the New Testament and the Old Testament command is to flee!

There is more to say about this god-king from the Old Testament prophets, but for now let's content ourselves with seeing more of the parallels of Scripture between Babylon the Great, ancient Babylon, and ancient Tyre.

ANCIENT TYRE AND	MYSTERY BABYLON THE GREAT
(All from the KJV)	
Ezek. 27:3 And say unto Tyrus, O thou that art situate at the entry of the sea, which art a merchant of the people for many isles, Thus saith the Lord GOD; O Tyrus, thou hast said, I am of perfect beauty.	Rev. 18:7 How much she hath glorified herself, and lived deliciously, so much torment and sorrow give her: for she saith in her heart, I sit a queen, and am no widow, and shall see no sorrow.

Ancient Tyre

Ezek 27:29-32   29 And all that handle the oar, the mariners, and all the pilots of the sea, shall come down from their ships, they shall stand upon the land;   30 And shall cause their voice to be heard against thee, and shall cry bitterly, and shall cast up dust upon their heads, they shall wallow themselves in the ashes: 31 And they shall make themselves utterly bald for thee, and gird them with sackcloth, and they shall weep for thee with bitterness of heart and bitter wailing. 32 And in their wailing they shall take up a lamentation for thee, and lament over thee, saying, What city is like Tyrus, like the destroyed in the midst of the sea?

Ezek. 27:12-15 12 Tarshish was thy merchant by reason of the multitude of all kind of riches; with silver, iron, tin, and lead, they traded in thy fairs. 13 Javan, Tubal, and Meshech, they were thy merchants: they traded the persons of men and vessels of brass in thy market. 14 They of the house of Togarmah traded in thy fairs with horses and horsemen and mules. 15 The men of Dedan were thy merchants; many isles were the merchandise of thine hand: they brought thee for a present horns of ivory and ebony.

Ezek. 27:16 ,17 ,18, 19, 20, etc,

Mystery Babylon the Great

Rev. 17:4 And the woman was arrayed in purple and scarlet colour, and decked with gold and precious stones and pearls, having a golden cup in her hand full of abominations and filthiness of her fornication:

Rev. 18:9-11 9 And the kings of the earth, who have committed fornication and lived deliciously with her, shall bewail her, and lament for her, when they shall see the smoke of her burning, 10 Standing afar off for the fear of her torment, saying, Alas, alas, that great city Babylon, that mighty city! for in one hour is thy judgment come. 11 And the merchants of the earth shall weep and mourn over her; for no man buyeth their merchandise any more:

Rev. 18:15 The merchants of these things, which were made rich by her, shall stand afar off for the fear of her torment, weeping and wailing,

Rev. 18:19 And they cast dust on their heads, and cried, weeping and wailing, saying, Alas, alas, that great city, wherein were made rich all that had ships in the sea by reason of her costliness! for in one hour is she made desolate.

Rev. 18:12-13 12 The merchandise of gold, and silver, and precious stones, and of pearls, and fine linen, and purple, and silk, and scarlet, and all thyine wood, and all manner vessels of ivory, and all manner vessels of most precious wood, and of brass, and iron, and marble,

13 And cinnamon, and odours, and ointments, and frankincense, and wine, and oil, and fine flour, and wheat, and beasts, and sheep, and horses, and chariots, and slaves, and souls of men.

Then compare Tyre and Babylon as Prostitutes. (Also from the KJV.)

Tyre as a Prostitute	Mystery Babylon as a Prostitute
Isa 23:15 And it shall come to pass in that day, that Tyre shall be forgotten seventy years, according to the days of one king: after the end of seventy years shall Tyre sing as an harlot.	Rev 17:1 And there came one of the seven angels which had the seven vials, and talked with me, saying unto me, Come hither; I will shew unto thee the judgment of the great whore that sitteth upon many waters:
Isa 23:16 Take an harp, go about the city, thou harlot that hast been forgotten; make sweet melody, sing many songs, that thou mayest be remembered.	Rev. 17:2 With whom the kings of the earth have committed fornication, and the inhabitants of the earth have been made drunk with the wine of her fornication.
Isa 23:17 And it shall come to pass after the end of seventy years, that the LORD will visit Tyre, and she shall turn to her hire, and shall commit fornication with all the kingdoms of the world upon the the face of the earth.	Rev 17:5 And upon her forehead was a name written, MYSTERY, BABYLON THE GREAT, THE MOTHER OF HARLOTS AND ABOMINATIONS OF THE EARTH.

Now let's do some comparisons with ancient Babylon. Babylon was at the height of her powers in Jeremiah's day. Every nation had been handed over to her by the Lord our God,.

> [37] "You, O king, are the king of kings, to whom the God of heaven has given the kingdom, the power, the strength and the glory; [38] and wherever the sons of men dwell, or the beasts of the field, or the birds of the sky, He has given them into your hand and has caused you to rule over them all. You are the head of gold." Dan 2:36-38 NASB

Babylon had existed for a long time. However, she rose quickly to her fullness of power. Perhaps that is significant for Babylon as a type. Now she is dominate. Still at the height of her powers, while Jeremiah is no more than a citizen of a nation ruined by Babylon, or a fugitive in Egypt, he announces that Babylon also will fall, Jer 50:2.

Her fall will be by a nation that will come from out of the north. She will be ruined, and no one will live there after it is over, Jer 50:3, 9, 41-42. Earlier it was pointed out that actually happened, and how Babylon is desolate to this day, desolate despite Saddam Hussein's late 20th century attempt to revive her. It was a coalition of Medes and Persians who ruined her, and Jeremiah says that will happen, though not be until long after he was dead, Jer 51:11, 28-29. God is against Babylon, Jeremiah says! Yes, He has used Babylon to punish other nations. She is God's war-club, a destroying mountain, "the hammer of the whole earth," Jer 50:23-24

This fall of Babylon happened. The Medes and the Persians laid siege to Babylon but no one expected them to actually capture the city. They diverted the river that flowed through the center of the city. As Herodotus tells, and also Daniel pictures in Dan 5:1-4, on a particular night, all of Babylon was in a big drunken party. God had told this by Jeremiah over seventy years before it happened, Jer 51:57.

Then it was that they saw the handwriting on the wall, Dan 5:5-6. So, as recorded by the historian Herodotus, on a night of general partying, when the city felt secure, and the interior walls by the river with its bridges, were not adequately guarded, the invading armies entered the city on the now dry river bed and entered the city almost bloodlessly, and Babylon fell as was foretold, Jer 51:30-32. Babylon will be completely desolate, like Sodom it says.

> As God overthrew Sodom and Gomorrah and the neighbour cities thereof, saith the LORD; so shall no man abide there, neither shall any son of man dwell therein Jer 50:40 KJV

Here is another key point. Babylon is ruined because she has ruined the people of God. In Revelation she has evidently participated with the beast in the suppression of the church, has been a part of making "war with the saints and" overcoming them, Rev 13:7; and then she is demolished and burned. Interestingly enough, the beast evidently considers the church the primary adversary, and Babylon after that, in his scheme to be worshiped (Rev 13:12), above every "god" or thing which may be worshiped (2 Thes 2:4). So for smashing the saints, she must be punished.

> [35] Let the violence done to me and my flesh be upon Babylon,"
>> The inhabitant of Zion will say;
>> "And my blood be upon the inhabitants of Chaldea!"
>> Jerusalem will say.
> [36] Therefore thus says the LORD:
>> "Behold, I will plead your case and take vengeance for you.
>> I will dry up her sea and make her springs dry.
> [37] Babylon shall become a heap,
>> A dwelling place for jackals,
>> An astonishment and a hissing,
>> Without an inhabitant." Jer. 51:35-37 NKJV

Just like with ancient Babylon, the church falls first, then Babylon the Great, all within history.

We are to get out of Babylon! Flee! Come out of her, we are told in Jer 50:8, Jer 51:6-8, and Jer 51:45-46. These words are repeated in Rev 18:4-5. However, they seem to apply more particularly to Babylon the Great. Young women, young men, do not ever take a job that you can never afford to walk away from. Do not ever take on so much debt, that you cannot afford to walk away from your job! If you wake up one day, and find yourself in Babylon ... get out! Babylon will fall, all because she has killed God's elect, his holy people, Jer 51:49. Even if she reaches the sky, even if she reaches the stars, she will fall. The destruction is no accident, nor from men. "From Me destroyers will come to her," Jer 51:53 And heaven and earth will rejoice over her fall, Jer 51:48. And when Babylon falls, God's people will return to God and to "Zion."

> ^{4} In those days, and in that time, saith the LORD, the children of Israel shall come, they and the children of Judah together, going and weeping: they shall go, and seek the LORD their God. ^{5} They shall ask the way to Zion with their faces thitherward, saying, Come, and let us join ourselves to the LORD in a perpetual covenant that shall not be forgotten. Jer 50:4-5 KJV

Earlier it was noted that Jews return to Palestine, we might say to Zion; and then turn to the Lord. But in this passage they turn to the Lord, and then go to "Zion."

Now "Zion" is what you might call capital hill in "present Jerusalem" Gal 4:25. It is where the temple of old was, and where the king's palaces were, and where the Mohammedan "Dome of the Rock" is today. Also "Zion" is God's throne, where He lives *in heaven*, in Psa 11:4.

> Then the moon shall be confounded, and the sun ashamed, when the LORD of hosts shall reign in mount Zion, and in Jerusalem, and before his ancients gloriously. Isa 24:23 KJV

The "true" Zion is in heaven, and the earthly Zion is only another type; and so when all the earth falls to never rise again, and the sun and the moon are ashamed to shine, the Lord of Hosts will reign from the true Mount Zion in heaven. So it is that the Hebrew prophet says,

> ^{22} But you have come to Mount Zion and to the city of the living God, the heavenly Jerusalem, to an innumerable company of angels, ^{23} to the general assembly and church of the firstborn *who are* registered in heaven, to God the Judge of all, to the spirits of just men made perfect, ^{24} to Jesus the Mediator of the new covenant, and to the blood of sprinkling that speaks better things than that of Abel.
> Heb 12:22-24 NKJV

Notice that the Old Testament and the New Testament are consistent on this. So Babylon falls, *and it is **after this** that God's people go to Zion.* That is indeed the way it was and will be. When physical Babylon fell, the Jews returned to Palestine under Cyrus the Mede, as you read in the books of Ezra and Nehemiah. So it is near the last day that Babylon will fall and God's people will repent, and they will be taken to heavenly Zion. Heaven! The reign of the beast lasts only three and a half years. So evidently this deliverance follows very soon, not many years off, after the fall of Babylon the Great.

There are other types also in the Old Testament of this final ghastly empire of money and debauchery. Included is that great enemy of God's people, a brother-people who should have been friends of the holy people, Edom. Also Assyria is so used as a type of these things in places. There is no need to go through all of this. You can see it for yourself if you have listened.

Two Shepherds

Now we will look at a story of two shepherds, from one of the most complex books in Scripture, the book of the prophet Zechariah. You don't need the book of Zechariah to know that there are two shepherds, one good, one bad; but they are in the book of Zechariah. There is much of it which will only be understood by the faithful very near to the end. But the two shepherds are there, along with some important information.

Turn to the prophet Zechariah. He and the prophet Haggai had arisen together in the time of Ezra. The date given in Zech 1:1 figures as October and November of the year 520 Before Christ. There is more to talk about in the Book of Zechariah than can be covered in any single book. This is in spite of its brevity, and relative neglect by both the scholarly world and preachers of the gospel. A good place to introduce this present discussion is by looking at Zechariah chapter 5. This is written *after the Babylonian captivity of the Jews, and after Babylon has fallen, and they have returned to Palestine.* Zechariah sees a flying scroll, and the angel tells Zechariah that this is the curse that is going "over the face of the whole earth," Zech 5:3 KJV. The word here is the Hebrew *erets* אֶרֶץ, and can mean either a land or country, or it can mean the earth, as in the King James Version, which I think makes more sense. If we take it that way, the next section about a basket makes more sense. This basket is seen as going "through all the earth," Zech 5:6 in the King James Version.

The basket is called an ephah, a unit of measure. It seems to be referring to a basket big enough to hold a small person. The basket has a lead cover to hold something down in it. The Greek Septuagint says the lead cover weighs a talent, which is about ninety-four pounds. The angel lifts the lead lid, and there is "a woman" inside. The angel says, "This *is* wickedness," Zech 5:8 KJV, and then closes the lid. Then the basket is taken up by "two women" with wings (like angels?), and they hold the basket between heaven and "earth" (yes, its the same word, *erets*). Zechariah in the vision asks the angel where the basket is being taken and he is told it being taken to Shinar (that is the plains of Babylon), to build a house/temple for her there (Zech 5:11), and set her on a pedestal.

So what is presented to us is a "woman" who is by implication a "god." She is later to be worshipped and so it is implied to have a temple built for her. In

Zechariah's time she is restrained in a basket, and later will be seated in the land of Babylon. Is this the great whore of Revelation? Time, notice the time. "The mystery of lawlessness" in 2 Theses 2:7 is clearly already in operation in the first century of Our Lord Jesus Christ, according to that verse. It is "already at work." It is implied that Mystery Babylon is already in existence by the book of Revelation, and is already drinking the blood of the saints. (Are they the same? No! But it seems they are out of self-interest allied "mystery religions," but the beast thoroughly hates the whore who rides him, Rev 17:7, 16.)

The major mystery religions of the Gospel Age seem to already exist in the first century AD. Is Zechariah telling us *when* "the woman" of Revelation will be established? Perhaps. Zechariah begins his prophecies in 520 BC. If this is a correct reading, then the great whore is established on the plains of Shinar sometime soon after this prophecy and clearly before the first century AD. If then you take your cue from Babylon of old, then Babylon the Great (like the Babylonians of old) has existed for a long time. Also perhaps like Babylon of old, she comes to her fullness of power near the end of our age, and perhaps only enjoys her fullness of power a short period of time.

Then there is a wandering discussion of two particular shepherds in Zechariah chapters 11 through 13. The discussion does not seem to be either symmetrical nor chronological.

The Lord now says that He will no longer have pity on the earth (*erets*). It has been mentioned and will be discussed later on that the beast is revealed after a wave of lawlessness, what the NIV correctly calls a "rebellion." That is so, but the end of all these things will be the most absolute despotism the world has ever known. The Lord will deliver men into each others power, "and into the hand of his king," Zech 11:6, "and they will smite the" earth (*erets*), although here the NASB the KJV and the NKJV use "land." Figure that one out!

Then it seems Zechariah starts acting out before the men of Judah the role of the two different shepherds. Significantly, shepherd in the Old Testament is a symbolic term that is also used for governmental rulers. God says that when Saul becomes king over Israel he was to "shepherd my people," 2 Sam 5:2. Later the prophets say that the greater David will "be their shepherd," Ezek 34:23. The rulers of a country according to the Old Testament concepts are to be those who shepherd the flock.

> So I pastured the flock *doomed* to slaughter, hence the afflicted of the flock. And I took for myself two staffs: the one I called Favor and the other I called Union; so I pastured the flock. Zech 11:7 NASB

Then Zechariah says that, as a shepherd, he kills three shepherds in one month. They were tired of him, and he was tired of them. Then the LORD says to cut his staff called Favor (NASB)/Beauty (NKJV and KJV) to pieces, to break "my covenant which I had made with all the people," KJV. All you can say is, "Wow!" Zechariah then says that the afflicted who were watching him realized that this was the word of the LORD. So it is speaking of ending a covenant, and then in context it relates this with the death of one the two shepherds.

> And I said unto them, If ye think good, give *me* my price; and if not, forbear. So they weighed for my price thirty *pieces* of silver.
> Zech 11:12 KJV

This is price for which Jesus was sold by the traitor Judas, Mtt 26:14-15. Then it speaks of the destiny of that silver, the wonderful price for which Jesus was betrayed.

> And the LORD said unto me, Cast it unto the potter: a goodly price that I was prised at of them. And I took the thirty *pieces* of silver, and cast them to the potter in the house of the LORD. Zech 11:13 KJV

Of course, all of this happened with Judas, including the purchase of a potter's field with the money from the betrayal, Mtt 27:3-10, Acts 1:10-20. Remember also that Zechariah is precisely dated, as "The eighth month of the second year of Darius," which translates to October/November of 520 BC, over five hundred years before the death of Jesus the Christ. So the covenant which is ending is that of the Mosaic Covenant with Israel, the "Old Law." And "the afflicted" realize this. The special covenant with the Jews was ended at the cross, from the betrayal of Judas. This is the same thing said in Colossians.

> [13] When you were dead in your transgressions and the uncircumcision of your flesh, He made you alive together with Him, having forgiven us all our transgressions, [14] having canceled out the certificate of debt consisting of decrees against us, which was hostile to us; and He has taken it out of the way, having nailed it to the cross. Col 2:13-14 NASB

I warned you that Zechariah's discussion of the two shepherds wandered back and forth. Of this good shepherd who will come, he says later,

> [6] "And one will say to him, 'What are these wounds between your arms?' Then he will say, '*Those* with which I was wounded in the house of my friends.'
>
> > [7] "Awake, O sword, against My Shepherd,
> > And against the man, My Associate,"
> > Declares the LORD of hosts.
> > "Strike the Shepherd that the sheep may be scattered;
> > And I will turn My hand against the little ones."
> Zech 13:6-7 NASB

Clearly Zechariah views the Christ as being killed, indeed of being killed by His own people. He received His wounds "in the house of my friends." Notice that he speaks of this good shepherd *as receiving these wounds and yet living.* Then He says, "Awake, O sword, against My Shepherd, and against the man, My Associate," Zech 13:7, "my fellow" in the King James Version, "the man who is close to me," in the NIV. He says that the sword is to awake against the good shepherd. Take a look and you will see that the "sword" is here a symbolic term for violent death. It means that Jesus died violently. It means that Jesus did die, but as has been pointed out, after His death He is able to talk about His wounds received in the house of His friends. Now Jesus did not die literally by a sword. As far as we know, a sword itself never touched Him. He finally died of a ruptured heart. A spear did pierce His side, but that was only after He had died, Jn 19:20. **So notice clearly, "sword" is used metaphorically of a violent death, just as in Psalm 22 which was covered earlier!** *Remember these things!* After His death, it has happened that "Strike the Shepherd that the sheep may be scattered," and God turns His hand against the disciples to scatter them, "the little ones." Of course this is quoted in Mtt 26:31 and the passage following about the scattering of the disciples at Jesus death. There is much more to this passage in Zechariah, and much more in Zechariah about the death of Jesus of Nazareth. But now back to Zechariah 11. Then the prophet says,

> Then I cut in pieces my second staff Union, to break the brotherhood between Judah and Israel. Zech 11:14 NASB

It is the same as was declared to you earlier. Any union between earthy Jerusalem and Jerusalem above (Gal 4:25-26), between the Jews and the Israel of God (Gal 6:15-16), is dissolved. Why? Because the Jews refused to listen.

> [11] But they refused to hearken, and pulled away the shoulder, and stopped their ears, that they should not hear. [12] Yea, they made their hearts as an adamant stone, lest they should hear the law, and the words which the LORD of hosts hath sent in his spirit by the former prophets: therefore came a great wrath from the LORD of hosts. [13] Therefore it is come to pass, that as he cried, and they would not hear; so they cried, and I would not hear, saith the LORD of hosts;
> Zech 7:11-13 KJV

So Zechariah in these passages is talking about the things leading to the next captivity in Zech 8:7-8 (because they have just returned from the Babylonian Captivity), and he is going on to talk of another shepherd who will come who cares nothing for the sheep.

Notice that in this discussion Zechariah first talks about the death of Jesus in the context of Judas, and that also is an interesting link in this discussion. Before Jesus went to heaven He prayed to the Lord that He had lost none of His disciples except Judas, whom He calls "the son of perdition," Jn 17:12. The Greek word used there is *apōleia* ἀπώλεια, which means destruction or to perish. Then in 2 Thes 2:3 Paul tells us that the man of lawlessness is also "the son of destruction," and it is exactly the same Greek phrase "*ho uios tas apōleias*," ὁ υἱὸς τῆς ἀπωλείας, What is Paul telling us here? Only that "the lawless one," just like Judas of the gospels, is characterized by destructive behavior. He is destruction personified, and like Judas, "it had been good for that man if he had not been born," Mtt 26:24. Of this greater person of treachery he speaks, and Zechariah basically indicates then that he puts on again the costume of the foolish shepherd. That is what both Judas and the man of lawlessness are—foolish shepherds—men without a lick of sense. Zechariah has already spoken of the death of the true shepherd, and now listen to the oracle.

> For indeed I will raise up a shepherd in the land *who* will not care for those who are cut off, nor seek the young, nor heal those that are broken, nor feed those that still stand. But he will eat the flesh of the fat and tear their hooves in pieces. Zech 11:16 NKJV

This is a gruesome picture. The false shepherd is so savage and merciless that he not only does not care for the people enough to protect them, but he even devours the sheep, not just for the wool, but down to tearing off their hoofs. What will happen to this despicable character?

> "Woe to the worthless shepherd,
>> Who leaves the flock!
>> A sword *shall be* against his arm
>> And against his right eye;
>> His arm shall completely wither,
>> And his right eye shall be totally blinded." Zech 11:17 NKJV

Do you remember what was said about what the "sword" represents in the book of Zechariah and in Psalm 22, and Romans 13? It was symbolic of a violent death. So notice what it says about the foolish shepherd, the worthless shepherd. Observe that there is implicit conflict in the narrative. On one hand it seems to say he dies, if you make the comparison with the good shepherd in chapter 13, who is clearly represented as killed. On the other hand, it seems he is alive. The sword is on his arm and his right eye. He will survive being killed, but they won't be able to repair some of this. "His arm shall completely wither, And his right eye shall be totally blinded."

This is speaking of the beast. This same paradox is in the book of Revelation. He is the head "whose fatal wound was healed," Rev 13:12. There is the same contradiction. If it is really a fatal wound, it cannot be healed. And if is healed, it really was not fatal. Lastly, a chart of comparisons may be useful.

The Worthless Shepherd Matrix

Zechariah 11, Called the "idol shepherd" KJV
"Worthless" (Hebrew elil אֱלִיל) = an idol in Isa 2:8, 18, 20, etc
In the NASB it is translated futility (1 time), idols (16 times), images (1 time), worthless (twice)

"Shepherds" often = rulers.   And "horns" often = rulers
See especially: Jer 6:3-6, Jer 23:4-6, Ezek   Dan 8:21, Dan 7:24
43:15, 23, Ezek 37:24,
Isa 44:28, 2 Sam 5:2

Zechariah 11	Daniel 7	Revelation 13
	Ten horned beast, vs 7, 20, 24	Ten horned beast, vs 1
Bad shepherd vs 17	A little horn vs 8, another king vs 24, imposing and boastful vs 20, 25	One of the heads vs 3, proud words, blasphemes vs 5-6
Got rid of 3 shepherds vs 8	3 horns uprooted vs 8, 20, 24	
Destroys the flock vs 9, 15-16, eats the meat, tearing off the hoofs vs 16	War on the saints and defeating them, vs 21, 25	Makes war on the saints and conquers them, vs 7
	For a time, times and half a time, vs 25	For 42 months vs 5
Stricken by the sword vs 17 (which = death, cf. Zech 13:7) Arm withered, right eye blinded, vs 17	Slain vs 11	Wounded by the "sword" vs 14, fatal wound, vs 3, 12 Yet lives, vs 14, fatal wound healed vs 3
"idol" shepherd vs 17 (KJV)		Breath to an image vs 15

"For the vision is yet for the appointed time;
It hastens toward the goal and it will not fail.
Though it tarries, wait for it;
For it will certainly come, it will not delay. "

Habakkuk 2:3 NASB

[19] Do not quench the Spirit;
[20] do not despise prophetic utterances.
[21] But examine everything *carefully*;
hold fast to that which is good;
[22] abstain from every form of evil.

1 Thes 5:19-22 NASB

So we look closer at the special king,
the special seed,
who opposes God.

The sinful nations will ALL be
delivered into his hand.

The same principles
in reading apply.

We Hold Fast
in the Great
Conflict

God Wins the Battle,
but we must hold fast until the end!

Most of us are only in the
preliminary skirmishes
of this battle.

What will happen to "Jerusalem"

"Where there is no vision, the people perish ..."
Prov 29:18 KJV

Both in Luke 21 and Matthew 24 and in the parallel passages, there are obviously dual subjects or more, as shall be shown. Much of the issue is NOT whether there is more than one subject, but it is instead similar to that of discussing the Book of Revelation, or 2 Samuel 7:12-16, Where does one subject stop and the other subject begin?

Jesus has just entered Jerusalem. He has cleansed the temple. He has silenced the Pharisees, Sadducees and Herodians, and has denounced their evil practices. They have no real answer for Jesus, but they refuse to believe the signs he offers. Then in Luke 21 Jesus and His disciples are walking out of the temple compound, and they took note of the beautiful stones and overlays of the temple in Lk 21:5. Now the temple area was built on some huge stones. According to Jewish historian Josephus, some of these stones were 38 feet long, 12 feet high, and 18 feet wide, and others were more than 68 feet long, 7-1/2 feet high, and 9 feet wide. (Josephus gives the dimensions in cubits, *Antiquities, XV, 392; Wars, V, 189 and 224*. These figures are with an eighteen inch cubit.) The temple in Jerusalem was also at this time fabulously rich. The temple was covered with so much hammered gold plate and costly stones, that at a distance it looked like a brilliant snow covered mountain shining in the sun (Josephus, "Wars" V, 223). And Jesus once again tells His disciples that not one of these stones will be left standing on another, Lk 21:6. That is an incredible prediction, and as is known from history, that is exactly what happened in 70 AD.

The Three Questions: One of the things that Jesus prophesies specifically in the gospels is the destruction of Jerusalem. That brought up more than one question from His disciples. Questions such as: *When will the temple be destroyed? What are the signs of Jesus coming? What are the signs of the end of the age?* From a more detached perspective it is easy to see,that this was more than one question, but it was not plain to the disciples. Luke 21 relates them asking when one stone will not be left standing on another. Mtt 24:3 has the disciples asking all three questions, and, by implication, has Him relaying all three answers. Luke in partial contrast has them asking about the stones, but still shows Jesus' discussion drifting from these things to some of the things of the end, *as if these events are in their very happening meant to be "types"/"symbolic" of the end of time!*

Jesus plainly says to not be misled about these things. Many men will come in Jesus' name, saying they are the Christ, and that the time is near, Lk 21:7-8. In many periods in history, there has been a new false christ or a new false prophet almost every year. Jesus then tells us how to sort these things out. Some view these aberrations as proving there is not a real second coming, but the Hebrew prophet Jesus of Nazareth up front, from the very beginning, says that "many shall come in my name, saying, I am *Christ*;,' and, 'the time draweth

The future fall of Jerusalem in 70 AD is used by Jesus in the gospels as symbolic of the end of the world. The "type," the symbolic, often comes soon after a prophecy, and the anti-type, the ultimate fulfillment, often comes long after the prophecy.

near,'" Lk 21:8 KJV. It was never to be that less than "many" who would come in His name, claiming to be Him, and teaching that the time of the end was near ... well before the real end of all things in this universe.

Jesus says that wars and disturbances *are not* a sign of "the end," Lk 21:9. If you listen to the radio or watch the TV preachers, they continually declare that the wars and rumors of wars are proof that we are close to the end, *but Jesus says no!* "The end" does not come immediately! Rather it is when they think it is peace and safety that Jesus comes again, according to 1 Thes 5:3-5. You may chose who best to believe.

So there two subjects in Luke 21 (and similarly in Matthew 24). The two deliberate subjects are: (1.) the destruction of Jerusalem in 70 AD. **Look carefully.** War and disturbance *is a sign that the destruction of Jerusalem in 70 AD "is near."*

> And when ye shall see Jerusalem compassed with armies, then know that the desolation thereof is nigh. Lk 21:20 KJV

The Jewish revolt started in 66 AD, and the war continued until Jerusalem was completely destroyed. So *war is **clearly** a sign* of the second destruction of Jerusalem in 70 AD, and it is treated that way in Lk 21:20-24. But it is not a sign of the Second Coming, because (2.) "when you hear of wars and commotions, do not be terrified" is also in Luke 21,

> "But when you hear of wars and commotions, do not be terrified; for these things must come to pass first, but the end will not come immediately." Lk 21:9 NKJV

It is when they are saying peace and safety that Jesus comes again.

> For when they shall say, Peace and safety; then sudden destruction
> cometh upon them, as travail upon a woman with child; and they shall
> not escape. 1 Thes 5:3 KJV

So from the first look there are dual subjects which are intertwined and
which do have some relationship to each other. Multiple intertwined subjects
are of course common in prophecy, for instance in 2 Sam 7:12-16 *and many others*,
as has been shown. In 2 Samuel 7 the subjects are both Jesus and Solomon. Go
back to the lesson on "Type and Anti-Type" to review the discussion and analysis. In Luke 21 the two subjects are, 1.) the 70 AD destruction of Jerusalem,
and 2.) the end of the world, and they are similarly intertwined.

When there are two subjects in a prophecy, one is normally a type, a symbol, a model, a shadow, of the other. This is the normal way prophecies work.
For instance, in 2 Samuel 7, Solomon, who is clearly in the prophecy, is a type
of the Christ, who is also clearly in the prophecy, *and both subjects are intertwined
in the passage.* This is a normal way that many prophecies are written! In the
present text, it means the fall of Jerusalem in 70 AD is also a *"type," is a model of,
the end of this world.* That is to say, the end of this world will be *"like"* the destruction of Jerusalem in some ways. Consistently, the signs symbolism are the
little bits of information which were not really fulfilled in the symbol.

Now nation will rise against nation, Jesus says in Lk 21:10. That is a sign of
the second destruction of Jerusalem in 70 AD, but *not* of the second coming, according to Lk 21:9!

But earthquakes and plagues and famines will come, Lk 21:11. Now some
of the things listed will accompany both the 70 AD destruction of Jerusalem
and the second coming, but the big plagues, famines, and earthquakes will come
near the end of this world, when every mountain and island will be moved, Rev
6:12-14. *Every* island and *every* mountain being moved will only happen at the
second coming.

Also, it appears to be plain that, despite many medical and scientific advances, the big plagues (disasters) occur near the end, when for instance a third
of the fish in the sea die, Rev 8:8-9. Jesus clearly says there will be great signs
from heaven, Lk 21:25, and that will be discussed later. However, it is in some
ways just like knowing that snow is "near," which does not also mean you know
the day or hour it will fall. For heavens' sake, even when the weather man
knows snow is near, he can never give us the hour, and often cannot for sure
even give us the day. We won't know the exact time (Mtt 24:36), but "there shall
be signs," Lk 21:25 KJV; **and that is why this chapter in Luke is being written,** *so that men can know when both the destruction of Jerusalem, and the second coming
are "about to take place" or are "near,"* Lk 21:7-9! The faithful will "see the day
approaching," Heb 10:25 KJV. The rest will be blinded by their sins. But Jesus
says persecution comes first.

> [12] "But **before** all these, they shall lay their hands on you, and persecute *you*, ... [13] And it shall turn to you for a testimony.
> Lk 21:12-13 KJV (*emphasis added*)

Indeed, persecution comes before both events. All know of the persecutions of early centuries, during which the church won, and finally overcame the Roman Empire, as predicted in Dan 2:44.

Jesus warns that Christians will be "hated by all *men*" KJV, even our own relatives, Lk 21:16-17. But "hated by all *men*" (emphasis added) only applies to the end of time. Hated by "all" never happened in the early centuries, for many were sympathetic with the patiently suffering Christians. This can be seen from Tacitus' description of the persecution by Nero. In fact, in the early centuries the church was steadily gaining ground despite persecution. It was said of the early centuries that "the blood of the saints is the seed of the church." However, this will not be so in the final persecutions the church will face, and "all men" will hate us. *There is a difference between these two periods of persecution!* In the persecutions at end of this age "the beast" will "overcome" the church, Rev 13:4-7 KJV, for *forty two months*, during which *all* of the saved will not be able to buy or sell **anything**, Rev 13:5, 16-17. *For three and one half years (which is also called "time, times, and half a time" or 1260 days)!* This never happened during the early persecutions; they are only symbolic. So parts of Luke 21 fit one thing, and parts other things.

Even so there is persecution before both events, and Jesus tells us how we should act, not making up our minds ahead of time what to say, Lk 21:13-15. Jesus says persecution will bring an opportunity for our testimony, and that He will help us know what to say. He commands us: do not plan what you are going to say. That is a command!

> [18] But there shall not an hair of your head perish. [19] In your patience possess ye your souls. Lk 21:18-19 KJV

Jerusalem will be surrounded by armies, Lk 21:20. That applies literally to the second destruction of Jerusalem in 70 AD. From secular history it is known that the Christians of first century Jerusalem believed these prophecies, and got out *as the Romans were surrounding the city.*

> [21] Then let them which are in Judaea flee to the mountains; and let them which are in the midst of it depart out; and let not them that are in the countries enter thereinto. [22] For these be the days of vengeance, that all things which are written may be fulfilled. Lk 21:21-22 KJV

There is a secondary sense in which spiritual Jerusalem (the church, see Heb 12:22-23) is surrounded by armies in persecution **before** the *last day*. There is not enough time to discuss this here, but it is spoken of in Rev 20:7-9, and Ezekiel 38, and many other passages, which will be looked at later. It will not be physical war, but part of a spiritual war. It will be a round up by the police and military forces of the beast of unwanted people, whom the world will no longer be able to tolerate: *the saints of the Most High God*, to try to exterminate Christianity once and for all. The church will only be rescued from these persecutions by Jesus' Second Coming, Deut 32:36, Lk 21:27-28. In contrast, the second destruction of physical Jerusalem in 70 AD, has led to Jerusalem being trampled under foot "until the times of the Gentiles are fulfilled," Lk 21:24.

But the powers of the universe will shake at Jesus' Second Coming. "There shall be signs," Lk 21:25 KJV; and the powers of the heavens will shake, Lk 21:26; and *then* men will see Jesus Himself, Lk 21:27. This is a consistent picture of the second coming. He will be revealed with His mighty angels in flaming fire, taking revenge on those who know not God and who will not obey the gospel, 2 Thes 1:7-8, and this present universe will be destroyed, 2 Pe 3:10-11. Jesus' appearance in the heavens will come suddenly, but men will have time to run to the hills and hide themselves "in the caves and among the rocks," and they will say to the mountains, "Fall on us, and hide us from the face of him that sitteth on the throne, and from the wrath of the Lamb:" Rev 6:16 KJV

Even so, many stumble at the place where it says "This generation shall not pass away, till all be fulfilled," Lk 21:32.

But the whole passage is contradictory unless you recognize the dual subjects! For instance Jesus says,

> And when these things begin to come to pass, then look up, and lift up your heads; for your redemption draweth nigh. Lk 21:28 KJV

However, this makes no sense of the destruction of Jerusalem in 70 AD. The destruction of Jerusalem brought punishment on a sinful and unbelieving nation, but did not rescue either Jews or Christians from persecutions.

Take for instance also the fact that **all** men will *literally* see Jesus at His Second Coming, Rev 1:7, Lk 21:27. But *it is a stretch* to say that **all** men really saw Jesus in the clouds in 70 AD. At best such is a metaphor, a type, symbolic of the Second Coming! Then in Lk 21:34-35 Jesus says,

> [34] "... that day ... [35] For as a snare shall it come on **all** them that dwell on the face of the whole earth. Lk 21:34-35 KJV (*emphasis added*)

However the destruction of Jerusalem in 70 AD came only upon Judea and Galilee.

Dual meanings are common in prophecy. As has been pointed out, a son of David building "a house for My name" in2 Sam 7:13 means one thing for Solomon (the physical temple, 2 Chron 6:10), and another thing for Jesus (Jesus builds the spiritual temple, the church, Mtt 16:18, 1 Cor 3:16, etc.).

Similarly the word "generation," *genea* γενεά in Greek, has a dual Greek meaning of 1.) a race (the primary meaning), or 2.) a generation (the secondary meaning used in many translations). It might be cute to say that "this generation shall not pass away" applies to all that went before it, but it has already been pointed out that Lk 21:9 and many other passages before Lk 21:32 do not make sense of the 70 AD siege of Jerusalem! So that "this generation will not pass away" might mean that Jerusalem will be destroyed in that generation (which did happen), and the end of time will come before the Jews as a "race" pass away (which seems to match what is happening). A typical double meaning in prophecy.

This section has used Luke 21 as the primary base in discussing these things. You can also use Matthew 24 as a base and show the same things. These are not completely equal sections, but the range of discussion is very similar.

Part of the problem is the astounding nature of the things which will happen. Jesus wants to prepare us for the severe nature of the last things by comparing it to the terrible destruction of Jerusalem in 70 AD. **So Jesus is also telling us in particular:** the destruction of Jerusalem in 70 AD is **symbolic of the end of the world**. It is a type, pattern, of the end of the world. So then comes the next part of the discussion. The Jews have been a rebellious people from ancient times—rebellious against all authority, even God's. Moses said it well.

> For I know thy rebellion, and thy stiff neck: behold, while I am yet alive with you this day, ye have been rebellious against the LORD; and how much more after my death? Deut. 31:27 KJV

The enemies of the rebuilding of Jerusalem in 6th century BC, rightly noted that Jerusalem is

> ... a rebellious city, and hurtful unto kings and provinces, and that they have moved sedition within the same of old time: for which cause was this city destroyed. Ezra 4:15 KJV

Down through history, the Jews have been a bitter, contentious, and obstinate people; always ready to make trouble, or to form a mob to achieve what they could not achieve legally, as can clearly be seen in both the Gospels and Acts. These traits led to such things as the Jewish expulsion from Rome during the reign of Claudius, Acts 18:2. Their obstinate behavior has often made it hard for others to deal with the Jews, *or for the Jews to deal with each other!* Many have heard them complain of each other in these respects.

Since the days of the Roman General Pompey, the Jews had been under Roman rule. The Jewish historian Josephus describes the way that Roman rule came in.

> Was it not derived from the seditions that were among our forefathers, when the madness of Aristobulus and Hyrcanus, and our mutual quarrels, brought Pompey upon this city, and when God reduced those under subjection to the Romans, who were unworthy of the liberty they enjoyed? (*Wars.* V, 396)

From that time forward, revolt against the Romans was always simmering, just below or sometimes even on the surface. Revolution's most radical political form was in what was called Zealots and "the Assassins" (literally "the daggers"), and there was an "Egyptian who some time ago stirred up a rebellion and led the four thousand assassins out into the wilderness?" Acts 21:38 NKJV. The Zealots had a lawless, unforgiving, uncompromising, and one might even dare to say an irrational rejection of submission to *anyone*, especially of the nations, but really even to other Jews. They well represent the spirit of all the Jewish revolutionaries of the Christian age. When these cultic elements have influenced Western revolutions, this irrational spirit of rebellion to anyone reappears. Their lawless and negative impact is not seen any more clearly than in 70 AD. Gibbon notes,

> "From the reign of Nero to that of Antoninus Pius, the Jews discovered a fierce impatience of the dominion of Rome, which repeatedly broke out in the most furious massacres and insurrections."
> *Decline*, Chapter 16, Part 1

It has been demonstrated that there were dual/overlapping subjects in Luke 21 and in Matthew 24. *So there were signs in the heavens before the destruction of Jerusalem*, and other signs *the Jews themselves recorded*. Josephus noted several strange occurrences.

> So before the Jews' rebellion, and before those commotions which preceded the war, when the people were come in great crowds to the feast of unleavened bread, on the eighth day of the month Xanthicus [Nisan], and at the ninth hour of the night, so great a light shone round the altar and the holy house, that it appeared to be bright day time; which light lasted for half an hour. *Wars*, V, 289-290

> Moreover, the eastern gate of the inner [court of the] temple, which was of brass, and vastly heavy, and had been with difficulty shut by twenty men, and rested upon a basis armed with iron, and had bolts fastened very deep into the firm floor, which was there made of one entire stone, was seen to be opened of its own accord about the sixth hour of the night. Now, those that kept watch in the temple came hereupon running to the captain of the temple, and told him of it: who then came up thither, and not without great difficulty, was able to shut the gate again. *Wars* V, 293-294

Then Josephus tells us of an ordinary farmer whose name was Jesus (the Greek form of the name Joshua).

> who, four years before the war began, and at a time when the city was in very great peace and prosperity, came to that feast whereon it is our custom for everyone to make tabernacles to God in the temple, began on a sudden cry aloud, "A voice from the east, a voice from the west, a voice from the four winds, a voice against Jerusalem and the holy house, a voice against the bridegrooms and the brides, and a voice against this whole people!" This was his cry, as he went about by day and by night,

in all the lanes of the city.

However, certain of the most eminent among the populace had great indignation at this dire cry of his, and took up the man, and gave him a great number of severe stripes; yet did not he either say anything for himself, or anything peculiar to those that chastised him, but still he went on with the same words which he cried before.

Hereupon our rulers supposing, as the case proved to be, that this was a sort of divine fury in the man, brought him to the Roman procurator; where he was whipped till his bones were laid bare; yet did he not make any supplication for himself, nor shed any tears, but turning his voice to the most lamentable tone possible, at every stroke of the whip his answer was, "Woe, woe to Jerusalem!"

And when Albinus (for he was then our procurator) asked him who he was, and whence he came, and why he uttered such words; he made no manner of reply to what he said, but still did not leave off his melancholy ditty, till Albinus took him to be a madman, and dismissed him.

Now, during all the time that passed before the war began, this man did not go near any of the citizens, nor was seen by them while he said so; but he every day uttered these lamentable words, as if it were his premeditated vow, "Woe, woe, to Jerusalem!"

Nor did he give ill words to any of those that beat him every day, nor good words to those that gave him food; but this was his reply to all men, and indeed no other than a melancholy presage of what was to come.

This cry of his was the loudest at the festivals; and he continued this ditty for seven years and five months, without growing hoarse, or being tired therewith, until the very time that he saw his presage in earnest fulfilled in our siege, when it ceased; for as he was going round upon

Roman soldiers on the march. From Trajan's column in Rome.

the wall, he cried out with his utmost force, "Woe, woe, to the city again, and to the people, and to the holy house!" And just as he added at the last, — "Woe, woe, to myself also!" there came a stone out of one of the slings, and hit him, and killed him immediately; and as he was uttering the very same presages, he gave up the ghost. *Wars*, V, 300-309.

There were false prophets leading up this time. Gamaliel mentions a couple.

> [35] And said unto them, Ye men of Israel, take heed to yourselves what ye intend to do as touching these men. [36] For before these days rose up Theudas, boasting himself to be somebody; to whom a number of men, about four hundred, joined themselves: who was slain; and all, as many as obeyed him, were scattered, and brought to nought. [37] After this man rose up Judas of Galilee in the days of the taxing, and drew away much people after him: he also perished; and all, even as many as obeyed him, were dispersed. Acts 5:36-37 KJV

Let's bear in mind that these are Jewish accounts of those times. We may or may not like them, but they are not Christian accounts. The Roman historian Tacitus also records many of these same extra-Biblical signs, Tacitus *Histories*, V, 13. However, revolution drew strength in 66 AD. They were able to seize Jerusalem and to ambush and defeat a Roman relief column from Syria. Then drawing their strength together, they were able to throw all the Romans out of Galilee. Rome first vacillated, then sent the Roman general Vespasian to Palestine with an army. Many things happened, and many tried to talk some sense into the Jews. When Paul was on trial, he had to appear before King Agrippa, and Paul said to him,

Vespasion, the Roman general who began the reconquest of Palestine, and later became emperor of Rome.

> [2] I think myself happy, king Agrippa, because I shall answer for myself this day before thee touching all the things whereof I am accused of the Jews: [3] Especially because I know thee to be expert in all customs and questions which are among the Jews: Acts 26:2-3 KJV

Agrippa vainly tried to get the Jews to use their heads during the revolt.

> "What are you pretending to be? Are you richer than the Gauls, stronger than the Germans, wiser than the Greeks, more numerous than all men upon the earth? — What confidence is it that elevates you to oppose the Romans?" *Wars*, II, 364.

For it was indeed God who had made the Romans to rule because the third kingdom of bronze (the Greeks), "which shall bear rule over all the earth," (Dan 2:39 KJV), was to be followed by the Romans who will be a fourth kingdom "strong as iron: forasmuch as iron breaketh in pieces and subdueth all things: and as iron that breaketh all these, shall it break in pieces and bruise," Dan 2:40 KJV. All of these things were such things that the Jews *already* knew and to which they should have paid attention. Some of King Agrippa's counsel to the Jews may remind us of what many call "impractical" in Jesus. But Agrippa, warning of coming Roman punishment advised the Jews that,

> "Now nothing so much damps the force of beatings as bearing them with patience; and the quietness of those who are injured, diverts their enemies from further afflicting them." *Wars*, II, 352.

But all of this good counsel came to nothing. The Roman General Vespasian first retook Galilee, and in the process captured the Jewish general Josephus, who had been in charge of Galilee. Josephus then became an advisor to the Romans on Jewish affairs. Josephus was an intelligent but also a very self-seeking man. Although most Jewish writers despise him, in a real way he illustrates the survivability of the Jews when in a pinch. To him we owe our best eye witness account of the Jewish revolt, a full seven volumes. Jewish writers often view him as if he was anti-Jewish, but that is not so. He tried to help the Jews when he could, but he had simply come to see the revolt for what it was: senseless.

Josephus makes many damaging admissions against the Jews, verifying the lawless character of many Jews and the Bible prophecies of their revolt, admissions which the Jews find irritating to acknowledge to this day.

A late first century/ early second century AD, Roman soldier, from Trajan's column

A stand was finally taken in Jerusalem. It was a big war, and the Romans, under Vespasian and Titus, did whatever was necessary to bring the lawless Jews to justice. An example is Masada, a fortress on a 1500 foot high mountain near the Dead Sea. The Romans just built an earthen ramp to the top of the mountain and then took it. At Jerusalem, trenches were built all the way around the city, as it is called in Luke, an embankment. The whole Roman army bent their backs to the work, and finished it in an incredible three days, *Wars* V.508-511. As the Christians saw the Romans under Titus encircling the city, they quickly got out of the city, recognizing the prophecies of Jesus in 33 AD,

> [20] And when *ye* shall see Jerusalem compassed with armies, then know that the desolation thereof is nigh. [21] Then let them which are in Judaea flee to the mountains; and let them which are in the midst of it depart out; and let not them that are in the countries enter thereinto. Lk 21:20-21 KJV

So *"war" **was** a sign of the 70 AD destruction of Jerusalem!* But being the feast of the Passover, many of the Jews, thinking of safety only in Jerusalem, fled to the city. It was a time of lawlessness, and groups of guerrilla bands took over Jerusalem and competed for overall control. As in many revolts, this was especially to the detriment of the native population, in this case of Jews. So during the revolt it was war outside against the Romans and civil war inside, each individual guerrilla faction against everyone else. Now Jerusalem was usually a comparatively small city, but during the Passover, huge numbers came into Jerusalem for the feast. At the time that the Romans came, practically the whole nation was in Jerusalem. Josephus gives a figure of *approximately two million seven hundred thousand people celebrating a Passover*, so hundreds of thousands of Jews were shut up in the city, and the city was very rich, with all of the offerings that had been brought to the temple. Josephus, *Wars* VI, 422-426.

Titus, Vespasian's son and later emperor, who completed the conquest of Jerusalem. Both father and son were level-headed, fair-minded men, not vindictive.

The revolutionaries then spent as much time fighting each other and other Jewish citizens as they did fighting the Romans. Anyone who opposed their suicidal plans was murdered, although many of the rich were able to buy their way out of the city to surrender to the Romans. **The revolutionaries killed more Jews inside the city than the Romans did outside.** Almost all the **poor** were **murdered**. About 600,000 of their bodies were thrown outside the gates of the city, and the rest of the dead were piled into houses that were then shut up. (*Wars*, V, 569-570). The revolutionaries always managed to stay in food, but the famine was so severe that many ate old cow dung (V, 571), some cannibalism occurred, and Josephus especially notes the eating of infants, *Wars* VI, 205-219. The same things were prophesied by Moses.

> And thou shalt eat the fruit of thine own body, the flesh of thy sons and of thy daughters, which the LORD thy God hath given thee, in the siege, and in the straitness, wherewith thine enemies shall distress thee: Deut 28:53 KJV

But the revolutionaries refused to surrender, and false prophets kept them going, *Wars*, VI, 285-286. Josephus commented,

> "Now this was the work of God ... that he might bring on the destruction of Jerusalem." *Wars*, IV, 104.

And many signs occurred. Josephus says,

> Thus there was a star resembling a sword, which stood over the city, and a comet, that continued a whole year. *Wars*, V, 289.

And there were signs in the clouds,

> and were not the events that followed it of so considerable a nature as to deserve such signals; for, before sunsetting, chariots and troops of soldiers in their armor were seen running about among the clouds, and surrounding of cities. Moreover at that feast which we call Pentecost, as the priests were going by night into the inner [court of the] temple, as their custom was, to perform their sacred services, they said that, in the first place, they felt a quaking, and heard a great noise, and after that they heard a sound as of a great multitude, saying, "Let us remove hence." Wars, V, 298-300

The Roman General Titus asked what these events showed but "God's anger against them, and of his assistance to us?" (VI, 40) So men sensed that these things were from God! Titus said God himself helped the Romans, for,

> "We have certainly had God for our assistant in this war, and it was no other than God who ejected the Jews out of these fortifications; for what could the hands of men, or any machines, do towards overthrowing these towers!" Josephus, Wars, VI, 411.

And finally the city fell. There had been no intention among the Romans to destroy the temple, but Josephus comments

> but, as for that house, God had for certain long ago doomed it to the fire; and now that fatal day was come ... Wars, VI, 250.

The temple itself was made of huge stones, which were then overlaid with cedar planking, which were then overlaid with hammered gold plate. Once the fire started, it was unstoppable, *melting the gold down into the crevasses of the stone*

Roman soldiers parading booty from the Jerusalem temple in Rome, including the golden lampstand from the Holy Place. From the Arch of Titus in Rome.

Titus in his chariot leading the victory parade in Rome after conquering Jerusalem. From the Arch of Titus in Rome.

foundations, ***so that literally every stone had to be overturned to get the melted gold.*** All of which was to fulfill what Jesus said when He prophesied in 30 AD,

> "Do you not see all these things? Assuredly, I say to you, not *one* stone shall be left here upon another, that shall not be thrown down."
> Mtt 24:2 NKJV

The casualties were frightful. Josephus estimates that during a feast time there were over two million five hundred thousand people in Jerusalem. But at the end of the siege **only 97,000 captives were taken**, and **an estimated one million-one-hundred-thousand had been killed**, *Wars*, VI, 420ff. The very old and the very young ended up being killed. The prisoners were sold into slavery or fought to the death in the arena, *Wars* VI. 382-384, and VII. 37-38.

But the Christians escaped. The ancient historian Eusebius (*Histories*, III. v.) tells us that when the Christians saw the Roman armies coming and knew Jerusalem's desolation was near, as they were told in Lk 21:20-21; and went to Pella before they were trapped in the city.

Some of the Jews ended up in a victory parade in Rome, a "Triumph", and the arch of Titus was built in Rome to commemorate this victory. Pieces from the temple are pictured there (see page 215). *So this is the story of how the temple was*

Roman "standards," their equal to our flags, but often containing idolatrous images, like the eagle above which represented the Roman "god" Jupiter.

destroyed! Josephus clearly lays the blame for all of this on some of the sects of Judaism. "a city otherwise of great magnificence, and of mighty fame among all mankind." *Wars*, VII, 4.

After taking the city with a long siege, idolatrous images were set up in the temple area. Idols **are** *an abomination to God!* The Roman standards were set up, and sacrifices were made to them. So much gold was taken as loot, that the money supply became inflated, and a pound of gold sold for half price in the eastern empire, Josephus *Wars* VI. 316-317. Then they dismantled the entire city. The wall and the temple was razed to the ground, Josephus Wars VII. 1-3; and the stones were dug up to get the silver and gold, Josephus *Wars* VII. 113-115.

So what was accomplished? A time of punishment, Lk 21:22. A people who resisted and killed the Christ and tried to prevent the spread of the gospel were severely punished. Literally there was not left one stone on another. The unneeded system of animal sacrifice was put out of the way. As the author of Hebrews wrote about it in the 60's AD,

> In that He says, *"A new covenant,"* He has made the first *obsolete. Now what is becoming obsolete and growing old is ready to vanish away.* Heb 8:13 NKJV

Indeed it did "soon disappear." But look what did not happen! After the conquest, the Romans did bring their idolatrous standards into the temple area, and offered sacrifices to pagan gods, Wars, VI, 316-317. This surely was an abomination to God, yet Jesus says,

Roman soldiers with their Emperor Trajan celebrating a victory of capturing a city. Note their pagan standards, and the preparation of a sacrifice of a ram and a pig. From Trajan's column in Rome.

> [15] When ye therefore shall see the abomination of desolation ... stand in the holy place, ...
> [16] Then let them which be in Judaea flee into the mountains Mtt 24:15-16 KJV

But this was too late to flee the desolation of Jerusalem! So Jesus' prophecy was a failure, or He speaks of *another* abomination, *another* time to flee. Also the siege did not mean either the Christian's or the Jew's "redemption is drawing near," Lk 21:28, and worst persecutions were yet to come for Christians and Jews. But Jesus said,

> when ye see these things come to pass ... the kingdom of God is nigh at hand. Lk 21:31 KJV

However the 70 AD destruction did not bring the kingdom of God near either in the sense of the church (for the kingdom was already here in this sense, as has been shown from Col 1:13 and other passages), or heaven (2 Tim 4:18). And Jesus' angels did **not** come with a great trumpet and,

> ... gather together his elect from the four winds, from one end of heaven to the other. Mtt 24:31 KJV

So these and other loose ends are showing, although *many liberal scholars would have us believe that Matthew 24 was written **after** the event.* Hardly! Mtt 24:31 would never have been written in retrospect about Jerusalem in 70 AD. But as long as the Jews continue in their obstinate unbelief, it is still true that they

> [15] who killed both the Lord Jesus and their own prophets, and have persecuted us; and they do not please God and are contrary to all men, [16] ... but wrath has come upon them to the uttermost. 1 Thes 2:15-16 NKJV

Isaiah was right about the Jews.

> ... In returning and rest shall ye be saved; in quietness and in confidence shall be your strength: and ye would not. Isa 30:15 KJV

Another day is coming for the Jews, a better day for the nation both spiritually and physically. The change will begin to occur,

> "When you are in distress and all these things have come upon you, in the latter days you will return to the LORD your God and listen to His voice," Deut 4:30 NASB

The conditional "if" of the promise as translated in the KJV, is not really there, it is really a human surmise. Most newer translations show Deut 4:30 as a statement of fact, as above, and indeed, many prophecies speak of Israel becoming faithful *after* a time of stress. For instance, Zech 10:9-11. But that did not happen in the wars of the Jews in 586 BC or 70 AD, nor in the Nazi Holocaust. Instead the first prophecies of Jesus came to pass in 70 AD.

> "they will level you to the ground and your children within you because you did not recognize the time of your visitation." Lk 19:44 NASB

Idols in the Temple

Earlier from Daniel 8 Alexander the Great was discussed and how he conquered most of the then known world. It was discussed how Alexander's kingdom was split up four ways at his death, and how the book of Daniel talks about these kingdoms as the four horns in Dan 8:22 and as four kingdoms in Daniel 11. (See the earlier section on "Daniel's Visions.")

The Kings of the North and the Kings of the South were discussed in Daniel 11. The Seleucids are called "kings of the North" (they were "north" of Judah, the land of the Jews), and the Ptolemies were called the "kings of the South" (they were "south" of Judah, the land of the Jews). Now the subject falls on some of these particular kings, who are also mentioned in Daniel chapter 11. One of these was a very ambitious king, Antiochus the Great. He tried to increase his territory. First, he attacked toward the south. After a series of events, he gained control of Palestine, the land of the Jews. There was some back and forth during those years, and some of the Jews changed sides back and forth, siding first with the kings of the South and then with the kings of the North until it was finally settled. This is in Dan 11:14-17. Interestingly enough, Antiochus the Great established his own emperor cult in which he was worshipped as god. Such things were far more common in the East, and such things are reflected in many of the names of both the kings of the North and the kings of the South, as you can see from the lesson on Daniel's Visions. (See the chart on as 124.)

Seleucus IV Philopater

Then Antiochus the Great tried to gain a foothold in Europe. After a series of battles he was defeated by the Roman Armies at the Battle of Magnesia in 190 BC. The Romans had been outnumbered more than two to one in the battle, but had still whipped Antiochus the Great. They then imposed huge penalties on him, Dan 11:18. These were war reparations to use the modern term.

The next king of the north was his son Seleucus IV Philopator. He had to finish raising the money for this huge fine to the Romans to pay for the war, and so he tried to raid the temple in Jerusalem. This was the first time that the kings of the north tampered with the temple in Jerusalem. The new king's tax collector, a man named Heliodorus, came to Jerusalem to rob the temple. It would take some time to tell the details, but he was unsuccessful, Dan 11:20.

Then another king came to the throne, *Antiochus IV Epiphanes*. His title "Epiphanes," which means Illustrious. Many in his own times called him "Antiochus Epimanes," that is to say "Antiochus the Crazy." He knew and understood the Romans because he had been a hostage in Rome and was partly raised in Rome. He is talked about in both Daniel 8 and Daniel 11. He is called a "despicable person" in Dan 11:21 NASB, and he came to power in 175 BC by flattery and intrigue. He was not supposed to be the ruler, but by a series of plots and intrigues he became king and had the infant son assassinated who was supposed to become king. He also had the High Priest in Jerusalem, a man by the name of Onias III, assassinated. So he came to power and made his first invasion of Egypt, as recorded in Dan 11:21-24, and 1 Mac 1:16-19.

Then on the way back from his second war against Egypt, in the flush of victory and needing money to pay his debts, he robbed the temple in Jerusalem. Temples often acted in those days as banks. A "safe" place for people to store their money. He came to Jerusalem, entered the Holy of Holies, and took some more treasure in 169 BC . He took 1,800 talents of silver according to 2 Mac 5:21, and 1 Mac 1:20-26. This is further described in Dan 11:25-28.

Then came *his final invasion of Egypt,* Dan 11:29, 2 Mac 5:1; but it was different this time. He was winning the battles and was generally successful. He was successful that is until the Romans intervened. The story is told by the Greek historian Polybius (*Histories,* 29.27.1-10), and

Antiochus IV Epiphanes

what a story it is. The Roman Senate had decided that they *did **not*** want Antiochus Epiphanes taking over everything. In July of 168 BC, a Roman envoy by the name of Popillius Laenas, with but a handful of men met Antiochus, surrounded by his troops, outside of Alexandria Egypt in a place called Eleusis. Popillius told him to withdraw and to leave Egypt alone. Antiochus gave an evasive answer indicating that he would think about it. Popillius took his staff and drew a circle around Antiochus in the sand, and told Antiochus that he was to give an answer *before* he walked out of that circle or he would be at war with the Romans. He knew the Romans well and greatly respected their power because of his time as a hostage in Rome. He did not dare openly oppose the Romans. So Antiochus stuttered and stammered, and then, *in front of all his servants and commanders,* said he would return home! What can you say, but what courageous envoys the Romans had, and what a story! But some other things were happening back home in Palestine.

Antiochus Epiphanes had started what had turned into a great culture war in Palestine. He needed a way to unite his ethnically diverse kingdom, and so the way he proceeded to try to do this was by promoting Greek culture as a unifying influence for all. Greek culture was indeed dominating the world. Everybody lived the way the Greeks did. *Nobody* worshiped just *one* god, and in just *one* way. The Greeks had athletic contests in which the contestants wore no clothes, and they ate pork, enjoyed good drama and theater, and homosexuality was rampant among both the Greeks and those whom they "converted" to their culture. *Everyone was doing it!* Literally *no one* (so to speak) was living by the books of Moses. It was really a "culture war," especially from the viewpoint of Antiochus IV, and Greek culture was dominant in those days, as indeed it is even today in the West. Some ambitious Jews were willing to violate Moses law to win power and gain the favor of Antiochus Epiphanes. They offered Antiochus a great deal of money to become high priest and to build a Greek style gymnasium. They adopted Greek customs and began wrestling and running naked in public, as the Greeks did in the Olympics in ancient times, 1 Mac 1:11-15. According to 2 Mac 4:18-20, even collecting offerings for pagan gods!

Of course, the faithful resisted all of this, and Antiochus, *who was not normally a narrow minded person*, was persuaded to try to **force** Greek customs on the Jews, Dan 11:29-30. So in this way persecution came to the Jews. **However the finger seems to point toward those** inside **God's people** (the Jews of that time)**, who seemed to think that force was the solution.** Terrible persecution then came, persecution that was brought on in part because some of God's people really wanted to move away from Scripture, Dan 11:32-33.

A general by the name of Apollonius was sent, 2 Mac 6:24-26. They stopped the Old Testament sacrifices commanded by Moses and made them stop following Moses' law. Baby boys who had been circumcised were killed, and then the dead babies were hung around their mothers' necks. Then the mothers were paraded around town and thrown off the city walls to their death, 2 Mac 6:10. Whenever a copy of the Bible was found, it was destroyed, Josephus *Ant.* XII, 256. 2 Maccabees tells of the courage of an old scribe by the name of Eleazar. First they forced pig meat into his mouth, which of course is forbidden to Jews under the old law, 2 Mac 6:18-20. They then tried privately to persuade him (and he still refused), and then tried to get him to *pretend* to eat some pork. He still refused and he told them to kill him. So they tied him to a rack, and beat him to death.

A bust of the "god" Zeus.

Then comes what is in Scripture the first "abomination that maketh desolate." The book of Daniel says that an abomination that causes desolation will be set up, Dan 11:31. An abomination? What does that mean? It is the word *shiqquts* שִׁקּוּץ, and it means something *detestable* (and it is often translated *detestable*), something that is repulsive, and disgusting. What are some examples from the Old Testament of an abomination? Well, murdering children as a sacrifice to idols is an abomination to God in Deut 18:9-12. Homosexuality is detestable to God according to Lev 18:22-23, and this particular word is often used to refer to pagan idolatry as detestable to God, Deut 29:17, and all of this is the same word as Dan 11:31.

Daniel says that this is something so bad that it makes everything desolate, *shamem* שָׁמֵם, like a desert, a place that will not grow anything and a place where no one can live. It is sometimes translated 'destroyed,' or something that is made a "waste" when it is polluted or ruined.

This was fulfilled in 167 BC by Antiochus Epiphanes. They polluted the temple. They set up an idol of Zeus Olympus in the temple, 2 Mac 6:1-2. Again it is described in 1 Mac 1:52-64, "and very great wrath fell on Israel"; it was an abomination that makes desolate! *And this was on our Christmas day, the Jewish month Kislev (December) 25, 167.* Some express hesitation in confirming the statue of Zeus in the temple of Jerusalem, but most take it at face value.

> In the Temple an altar to Zeus Olympios was erected, and sacrifices were to be made at the feet of **an idol in the image of the King**. "Antiochus IV Epiphanes." (*emphasis added*)
> *Encyclopedia Britannica*. Standard Edition. Chicago, 2010.

Fortunately, this is not the end of the story. A faithful Jewish priest by the name of Mattathias was asked to sacrifice in his little village of Modein, and the story is told in 1 Mac 2:15-28. This began many years of guerrilla warfare on the part of the Jews, called the Maccabean Wars, which ended in the Jews winning their independence. The temple was re-dedicated on Kislev (December) 25, 164, after the Jews had cleansed the temple. This is the modern Jewish feast of Hanukkah, or what we of the nations sometimes call 'Jewish Christmas', when the temple was finally cleansed from idolatry. It is called the Feast of Lights, or the Feast of Dedication in Jn 10:22 (also see 1 Mac 4:47-59). There are two things to point out here:

1. Not all of what is said in Daniel matches Antiochus Epiphanes! For example Dan 11:36 to the end of the chapter, does not fit what is known about Antiochus Epiphanes, or any king from ancient times. Daniel 8 says,

An ancient coint depicting Zeus. The statue erected in the temple of the Lord in Jerusalem might have been much like this. Notice the eagle which he holds in his hand, which is symbolic of Zeus.

> And it grew up to the host of heaven; and it cast down some of the host and *some* of the stars to the ground, and trampled them. Dan 8:10 NKJV

At the least this seems hyperbole of Antiochus IV. It seems to point to a greater evil than him. Such are the signs of a type in Scripture. In Daniel 8 it says,

> And his power shall be mighty, but not by his own power: and he shall destroy wonderfully, **and shall prosper, and practise**, and shall destroy the mighty and the holy people. Dan 8:24 KJV (*emphasis added*)

Antiochus IV did do a lot of damage, but he definitely did not "destroy ... the holy people." It would appear that in part because Rome was looming from the west. Perhaps this was a major factor in the Jews being able to successfully revolt. They definitely were not destroyed, even in human terms, and anyone writing *at that time or more especially **following** that time*, would have known this. Even so it has been shown and will be apparent that there are other prophecies of one who does "overcome" the holy people. It also says in Daniel 8,

"In the latter period of their rule,
When the transgressors have run *their course*,
A king will arise,
Insolent and skilled in intrigue." Dan 8:23 NASB

This seems to fit Antiochus IV in part, but can it really be said that "transgressors had run their course"? Maybe or maybe not. It can definitely be taken more than one way. It does seems that Antiochus brought the transgressors to their height, rather than him coming to power when they had already run their course. Then it says,

"And through his shrewdness
He will cause deceit to succeed by his influence;
And he will magnify *himself* in his heart,
And he will destroy many while *they are* at ease.
He will even oppose the Prince of princes,
But he will be broken without human agency. Dan 8:25 NASB

Antiochus Epiphanes died of an illness or an accident. Interesting. It seems to coincide with other patterns that show up, and it does looks like Antiochus Epiphanes is a 'pattern' Still a lot of this seems at best to be hyperbole. The key here would be Dan 8:24 which was discussed above. Another, greater Crazy Man will come who will fit the pattern and supply what is missing. Another and greater one who is "a man and not God," as has been shown.

2. All of us need to see for ourselves personally that we can "go too far!" We should be careful. We can do something vile and detestable enough, that it will ruin everything, make it *desolate* and make it unusable. The Scriptures warn about being like Esau.

> [15] See to it that no one comes short of the grace of God; that no root of bitterness springing up causes trouble, and by it many be defiled; [16] that there be no immoral or godless person like Esau, who sold his own birthright for a single meal. [17] For you know that even afterwards, when he desired to inherit the blessing, he was rejected, for he found no place for repentance, though he sought for it with tears.
> Heb 12:15-17 NASB

In 1 Jn 5:16 it says there is a sin that leads to death, and do not pray about that! We need to seek God while we can.

Seek the LORD while He may be found,
Call upon Him while He is near. Isa 55:6 NKJV

Now look at the abomination of desolation in Mtt 24:15-17. In talking about what would happen to "Jerusalem," it was clear in the opening verses of Matthew 24 that Jesus' disciples asked him three questions: *1.) When will the temple be destroyed? 2.) What are the sign of Jesus coming? 3.) What are the signs of the end of the age?*

Now we turn to the abomination of desolation. It has been discussed how the Greek king Antiochus Epiphanes fulfilled many prophecies in both Daniel 8 and Daniel 11. He *did* enter the Holy of Holies where only the High Priest was allowed to go, and that was a symbol of God's only special dwelling place. (1 Mac 1:20-21, 2 Mac 5:15-17). He robbed things that belong to God Himself.

> Then shall he return into his land with great riches; and his heart *shall be* against the holy covenant; and he shall do *exploits*, and return to his own land Dan 11:28 KJV

So here was a mere man who entered a place where only God belongs, and where a man was worthy of death if he dared to enter it uninvited. He had persecuted God's people for following the true religion of God. There are many stories like the one of the faithful mother and her seven sons in 2 Maccabees 7, who were tortured and killed for not eating pork. Many, while trying to warn others, fell in the persecution, Dan 11:33-35.

Now Daniel 11 (up to verse 35) does seem to fit Antiochus and what is known of this history. Still, not all of this matches Antiochus Epiphanes! Parts of both Daniel 11 and Daniel 8 do not fit. Well exactly what is it? What does not fit? Look at Dan 11:36 which says the king will "do according to his will" KJV. First of all, it is clear that Antiochus Epiphanes did not do just whatever he pleased. The story was covered about the Roman envoy by the name of Popillius Laenas and how he faced Antiochus in the desert and turned him back to his own land, forced him to abandon his conquests in Egypt. So the first part of Dan 11:36 is not true of Antiochus Epiphanes.

In Dan 11:40 it talks about the end: "At the end time the king of the South will collide with him ..." NASB. But Antiochus Epiphanes time was **not** the *end* of **anything**. He **was not the end** of the Law of Moses! He **was not the end of the kings of the North or of the South**, the Seleucid kings of Syria or the Ptolemaic kings of Egypt! He **was not the end of the nations' rule over Palestine. Nor was it the end of time!** (But Jesus **IS** talking about the end of time in Matthew 24.) So the time of Antiochus Epiphanes was not the end of anything. Period!

In Dan 11:41 it pictures Antiochus Epiphanes as invading the land of Israel: "He will also enter the Beautiful Land, and many countries will fall; but these will be rescued out of his hand: Edom, Moab and the foremost of the sons of Ammon," NASB. But in fact, he already had Israel, as was seen earlier! He had no need to *invade* Israel!

In Dan 11:42 it pictures him as conquering Egypt: "He shall stretch forth his hand also upon the countries: and the land of Egypt shall not escape," KJV. But Egypt did escape. He was never able to conquer and keep Egypt; the Romans would not permit him to keep his conquests!

Notice again in Dan 11:36 that it says that He will exalt and magnify himself above every god. That does not really fit Antiochus Epiphanes. Remember that he introduced an idol of Zeus Olympus into the temple in Jerusalem, and he in fact built a significant temple to Zeus in Greece, the ruins of which still stand. As you can see, that is another *god* that he *promoted and worshipped*. It is true he entered the Holy of Holies, but in general he had the same open minded attitude about worshipping a variety of different gods that all of the Greeks had. Was he willing for men to call him **a** god? The answer is 'yes he was'. But did he exalt and magnify himself above every god? The answer is NO! He accepted, both implicitly and explicitly, many so-called "gods."

Similarly in Dan 8:10: "And it grew up to the host of heaven; and it cast down *some* of the host and *some* of the stars to the ground, and trampled them," NKJV. The "host of heaven" is literally the armies of heaven (as was shown earlier), and the "stars" represent angels, as can be seen from both Job 38:7, and also from Rev 12:4, 7-9. Can it really be said that Antiochus' actions caused some angels to fall? It does not seem like it! It seems like exaggerated language! Remember, as has been repeatedly pointed out, that exaggerated language is often an *indicator* of a *pattern or symbol.*

Dan 11:45 implies that he will die near Jerusalem: "He will pitch the tents of his royal pavilion between the seas and the beautiful Holy Mountain; yet he will come to his end, and no one will help him," NASB. But as opposed to this, Antiochus Epiphanes died at Tabae in Persia in 164 BC.

Notice that the things covered here would never have been written by someone writing later, trying to retrofit their account to make it look like prophecy. Only a fool of a charlatan would try to fake *this* prophecy in *this* way after it happened or would have put in these many lines which were not true of Antiochus Epiphanes. If the book had *first* appeared *in the time of* Antioch Epiphanes and the people had been looking for these extraneous statements to happen at that time, they would have quickly dispensed with the book as a fraud. *Only if the book had been around for a while, like for instance from the time of Daniel! (I jest!), **then**, it would have been significant enough to take notice of it!*

My friends, this is not secret knowledge or something you can only read about in sermon books or in the Bible. Antiochus Epiphanes was a public figure, and these things are told about in secular history, both ancient and modern.

Now notice what Jesus said in Mtt 24:15-18.

> [15] When ye therefore shall see the abomination of desolation, spoken of by Daniel the prophet, stand in the holy place, (whoso readeth, let him understand:) [16] Then let them which be in Judaea flee into the mountains: [17] Let him which is on the housetop not come down to take any thing out of his house: [18] Neither let him which is in the field return back to take his clothes. KJV

First of all it is clear that Jesus is saying that the prophecies in Daniel about the abomination of desolation *have **not** been completed!*

Indeed, as the discussion has shown, much of this does **not** fit the time of the Maccabees! Matthew was written over 200 years after all this happened.

Thus, Jesus is saying that although much of Daniel 11 has been fulfilled in Antiochus Epiphanes, he is just a *'pattern' or a symbol* for the final abomination of desolation. So as was pointed out earlier, the final abomination of desolation has not been fulfilled, so Jesus in essence says, "that's right, it hasn't been fulfilled.'" So when it appears in the holy place, "the abomination of desolation ... stand in the holy place, (whoso readeth, let him understand:)," Mtt 24:15 KJV, we need to take action!

Remember what was said about the destruction of Jerusalem and the temple in 70 AD? Idolatrous images were set up in the temple area, the Roman standards; and sacrifices were made to those images. Such images are detestable, are abominable to God, and this is in many places in Scripture.

Now some say that this (the Roman standards being raised in the temple itself) is the abomination of desolation. But look again at what happened at the Destruction of Jerusalem. Remember that the Romans surrounded Jerusalem and trapped over a million people inside the city. Remember that the Christians saw the armies coming to surround Jerusalem, and they remembered the prophecy in Luke 21. So all the Christians escaped. When the Christians saw the Roman armies coming, they knew that its desolation was near, and they got out of town and went to Pella before they were trapped in the city, Lk 21:20-24. *So the armies coming to surround Jerusalem* was sufficient notice to save the Christians of the first century from destruction in Jerusalem! War was a sign to flee!

But remember, Jesus is answering three questions:

1.) When will the temple be destroyed? **2.)** What are the signs of Jesus coming? and lastly **3.)** What are the signs of the end of the age?

Thus, if you look closely, you can see that the Roman standards being raised in the temple does not fulfill Mtt 24:15! First, it *was* abominable, but *it was **not** really a public event* that all of God's people could see, witness, and from which take warning. It was a minor act, toward the end of the war, witnessed by only a few soldiers and officers who were in the ruins of the temple and Jerusalem. Second, *it was too late to be a warning for Christians **or any one else** to run for their lives!* If the Christians had waited for the Roman standards to be raised in the temple area, it would have been too late, and they would have been destroyed in Jerusalem along with the unbelieving Jews.

So what can be seen? That the last part of Daniel 11 is yet to be fulfilled. It was not fulfilled in the second century BC, and it was not fulfilled in the destruction of Jerusalem in 70 AD. **So it is still to come.** The abomination of desolation in Mtt 24:15 has **not** happened yet. Another apostasy of God's people has to come, greater than what has been seen in history so far. Another "king of the North" has to come. Another image has to be set up, another idol, in what Scripture calls "the temple of God" (2 Thes 2:4). It is evidently in connection with some of these other things which are told in Matthew 24.

My friends, I do not think that the great image of Daniel 11 has come yet.

Still the church of our Lord is very much full of idols which His people have put before the Lord of Hosts. What is idolatry anyway?

> [5] Therefore consider the members of your earthly body as dead to immorality, impurity, passion, evil desire, and greed, **which amounts to idolatry**. [6] For it is because of these things that the wrath of God will come upon the sons of disobedience, [7] and in them you also once walked, when you were living in them. Col 3:5-7 NASB (*emphasis added*)

In ancient times Israel was made desolate because idols were put in the place where only God belongs. Still have we my friends, *put other things before God in our lives?* Have we put television where God belongs? Have we put sports where God belongs? Have we put our comfort where God belongs? Have we put entertainment and pleasure where God belongs? What have we put where only the LORD our God belongs? And what will we do about it?

A Special Man of Lawlessness

"But limitation is the essence of liberty, for as soon as
liberty is complete it dies in anarchy."
Will Durant, *Rousseau and Revolution*. pg 472

Many associate these prophecies with pre-millennial errors and ignore them. Liberal theology thinks this all refers to ancient Rome. The basics do not rest on obscure prophecies or murky language, but on some very clear texts.

> But the Spirit explicitly says that in later times some will fall away from the faith, paying attention to deceitful spirits and doctrines of demons, 1 Tim 4:1 NASB

This passage speaks specifically of some in the church rebelling against God's authority, but the rebellion will actually go further than that.

> For the time will come when they will not endure sound doctrine ... 2 Tim 4:3 KJV

> [1] This know also, that in the last days perilous times shall come. [2] For men shall be lovers of their own selves, covetous, boasters, proud, blasphemers, disobedient to parents, unthankful, unholy, [3] Without natural affection, trucebreakers, false accusers, incontinent, fierce, despisers of those that are good, [4] Traitors, heady, highminded, lovers of pleasures more than lovers of God; [5] Having a form of godliness, but denying the power thereof: from such turn away. 2 Tim 3:1-5 KJV

In 2 Thes 2:3 it says,

> Let no one in any way deceive you, for it *will not come* unless the apostasy comes first ... NASB

And the word "falling away" (KJV) or "apostasy" in Greek is *apostasia* ἀποστασία, is stronger than just "falling away." It is a normal word for a civil rebellion, a revolt, as can be seen from the lexicons quoted below.

> "defection, revolt"
> (*A Greek - English Lexicon of the Septuagint*, Second Edition, Lust, Eynikel, and Hauspie 2003)

> "apostasy, rebellion"
> (*A Concise Greek-English Dictionary of the New Testament*, Newman, United Bible Societies, 1993)

> "39.34 ... to rise up in open defiance of authority, with the presumed intention to overthrow it or to act in complete opposition to its demands — 'to rebel against, to revolt, to engage in insurrection, rebellion.'"
> (*Greek-English Lexicon of the New Testament Based on Semantic Domains*, Louw and Nida, 1989, United Bible Societies.)

> "... rebellion, abandonment in religious sense, apostasy ... Of the rebellion caused in the last day 2 The 2:3."
> (*A Greek-English Lexicon of the New Testament and Other Early Christian Literature*, Arndt, and Gringrich, University of Chicago, 1957)

> "1. a defection, revolt, ...
> 2. departure from, ...
> 3. distance, interval, ..."
> (*An Intermediate Greek-English Lexicon founded upon The Seventh Edition of Liddell and Scott's Greek-English Lexicon.* Oxford, At the Clarendon Press, 1889. Yale University Press.)

Thayer's Lexicon (put together before the discovery of so many of our Greek papyri) neglected this sense of the word, but in a political context it definitely has these meanings. And the man of lawlessness in 2 Thessalonians 2 definitely has political overtones, which would be absolutely necessary for any sort of imposing anyone who puts himself forward as the exclusive "God." The NIV really gives the sense of the passage:

> Don't let anyone deceive you in any way, for that day will not come until the rebellion occurs ... 2 Thes 2:3 NIV

Apostasia would of course include defection from the true and living God, but "apostasy" goes further. In context it has the idea of shaking your fist in the face of God's authority. It is like the man in the Law of Moses who despises to follow God's ways, the man who,

> "... will boast, saying, 'I have peace though I walk in the stubbornness of my heart in order to destroy the watered *land* with the dry.'"
> Deut 29:19 NASB

So he says, "I will do whatever I want to do." Or to put it in clearly Satanic terms, "Do what you will." This great rebellion is described in many places and in many ways in Scripture, but 2 Thes 2:3 says that it has to happen before Christ comes again.

**There is <u>much</u> we cannot or will not know, however
the outlines of these events are not obscure.**

Also some things pointed out in Matthew 24 did not happen. As everyone knows, Jesus did **not** gather his elect from one end of the heavens to the other, Mtt 24:31. It just did not happen. So some of Matthew 24 has to do with the end of time, not 70 AD. Remember the three questions Jesus is answering? The stars did not fall from the heavens as predicted in Mtt 24:29. It did not happen. But it will happen later, as Peter tells us in 2 Pe 3:10.

> But the day of the Lord will come as a thief in the night; in the which the heavens shall pass away with a great noise, and the elements shall melt with fervent heat, the earth also and the works that are therein shall be burned up. KJV

So a great "rebellion" and "apostasy" will occur, and then a special false messiah will appear. But many false christs will come *first*. The "special" man of lawlessness will come on the heels of the general rebellion, and he will advance the rebellion against God. He is called the "man of sin" KJV, or(the better reading is) "the man of lawlessness" in 2 Thes 2:3. This is to say, his main characteristic is lawlessness. He sets himself up "shewing himself that he is God.," 2Thes 2:4 KJV. He seems to be a replacement christ, and in fact that is what the word "*anti*" ἀντί in "anti-Christ" suggests. The Greek word "*anti*" is used in passages like Mtt 2:22 where it speaks of Archelaus reigning "in place of" (*anti*) "his father Herod." It is similarly used in other passages, for instance, where Jesus says "Now suppose one of you fathers is asked by his son for a fish; he will not give him a snake instead" (anti) "of a fish, will he?" Lk 11:11 NASB.

An example of the secular use of the word anti will be useful. A contract is often called a writing, a "graphon," and a "copy" of the contract is an "antigraphon." This can be seen in a marriage contract in Nero's 13th year, A.D. 66, *Loeb Classical Library, Select Papyri, I, Non-Literary Papyri, Private Affairs*, Hunt and Edgar, Harvard Press, 1988, pg. 12.

Man of Lawlessness, 2 Thessalonians 2	Anti-christ, 1 John
1. Is the product of rebellion, 2 Thes 2:3	1. Is the product of a departure, 1 Jn 2:18-19
2. Exalts himself above God, 2 Thes 2:4	2. Denies the Father and the Son, 1 Jn 2:22-23
3. The Mystery of Lawlessness is already at work, 2 Thes 2:7	3. The spirit of the anti-Christ is already in the world, 1 Jn 4:3
4. The man of lawlessness is a deceiver, 2 Thes 2:9-12	4. The anti-Christ is a deceiver, 1 Jn 2:22

Thus, in the full sense, an "anti-christ," is a replacement christ, a pseudo messiah, a false Christ; and not just someone who is "against" Christ. How can a mere man, who claims exclusively to be God, not be considered "anti-Christ"? Here is a comparison of the man of lawlessness and the anti-christ.

Now all of this is associated with an "abomination." A great culture war in the second century BC, in Palestine has been reviewed. How King Antiochus IV of Syria (the king of the North, Dan 11:21ff) tried to force Greek culture (along with paganism) on those Jews who wished to stick by God's Word. With Antiochus, it was a political issue necessary to unite his kingdom. He even went so far as to put an idol of Zeus-Jupiter in the temple and offered unclean sacrifices (2 Maccabees 6, etc.). The Jews revolted against this "abomination" and won. The story is prophesied in the book of Daniel and described in several non-biblical books of history, such as Josephus, and 1 and 2 Maccabees.

But a much later "abomination" will be put in the "temple of God" (Mtt 24:15-16, 2 Thes 2:4), with far worse results for sinful men, and "All who dwell on the earth will worship him ..." Rev 13:8!

The **whole** world will worship him. Many have come and will come with partial success, but this one will come with special power and authority from Satan. In Rev 13:2 it says "... and the dragon gave him his power, and his seat, and great authority" KJV, and the dragon is identified in Rev 12:9 as Satan. Then in 2 Thes 2:9 it says that his coming is "... after the working of Satan with all power and signs and lying wonders," KJV. This is no ordinary opponent of God. He will come with demonic signs and wonders. What is called "another beast coming up out of the earth" (Rev 13:11 KJV), or is later called the "false prophet," performs great signs and wonders and even causes fire to come down from heaven to earth in the sight of men. And because of the signs he is able to give, he deceives those who dwell on the earth, Rev 13:13-14.

> [24] For there shall arise false Christs, and false prophets, and shall shew great signs and wonders; insomuch that, if it were possible, they shall deceive the very elect. [25] Behold, I have told you before Mtt 24:24-25 KJV

So extraordinary powers and signs accompany this particular man spoken of in Revelation 13 and 2 Thessalonians 2. Still beyond all that has been said, this particular false "god" will be killed and then raised from the dead. The Scriptures says he is "the beast, which had the wound by a sword, and did live." Rev 13:14 KJV. He received a fatal wound,

> I saw one of his heads as if it had been slain, and his fatal wound was healed. ... Rev 13:3 NASB

The beast will be killed and raised from the dead, and he will amaze the entire world. **Look carefully**: it is not the "empire" in the sense of Mystery Babylon which is described here as dying. It is one of the "heads" of the empire that dies. The term "beast" is used in Daniel of an empire, and in Revelation of both an empire and also one of it heads in particular is also called a "beast."

And the dragon stood on the sand of the seashore.

Then I saw a beast coming up out of the sea, having ten horns and seven heads, and on his horns *were* ten diadems, and on his heads *were* blasphemous names. Rev 13:1 NASB

And the particular "beast" who is "slain, and his fatal wound was healed," is one of the "heads" on this beast, Rev 13:3. It is true, as was pointed out, that Mystery Babylon "rides" this beast, this monster.

Here is a chart comparison of descriptions:

Antiochus IV Epiphanes	The Man of Lawlessness	The beast
Because of rebellion Dan 8:12		
The rebellion that causes desolation, Dan 8:13	The rebellion comes first, 2 Thes 2:3	
Exalts and magnifies self, Dan 11:36-37, 7:20	Exalts himself, 2 Thes 2:4	Blasphemes and slanders God, Rev 13:6
	Over everything called God or worshipped, 2 Thes 2:4	Everyone must worship him, Rev 13:12
Abomination that causes desolation set up in temple, Dan 11:31	Sets himself up in the temple of God as God, 2 Thes 2:4	Breath to the image, all worship, Rev 13:14-17
	Comes by the work of Satan, 2 Thes 2:9	Comes by Satan's power and authority, Rev 13:2
	Counterfeit miracles, 2 Thes 2:9	Miraculous signs, Rev 13:13, 16:14, 19:20
War on the saints and defeats them, Dan 7:21, 25, Dan 8:24, 11:33-35		War on the saints and conquers them, Rev 13:7
Against the prince of princes, Dan 8:25	Opposes ... God, 2 Thes 2:4	Makes war on Jesus, Rev 19:19
	All of the lost worship him, 2 Thes 2:11-12	All the lost of the world worship him, Rev 13:8
Destroyed not by any human power, Dan 8:25	Destroyed by Jesus second coming, 2 Thes 2:8	Thrown alive into hell, Rev 19:20

So he carried me away in the spirit into the wilderness: and I saw a woman sit upon a scarlet coloured beast, full of names of blasphemy, having seven heads and ten horns. Rev 17:3 KJV

This particular head/beast, later completely destroys Mystery Babylon.

And the ten horns which thou sawest upon the beast, these shall hate the whore, and shall make her desolate and naked, and shall eat her flesh, and burn her with fire. Rev 17:16 KJV

Other passages also speak of this princely opponent, such as in Habakkuk:

[13] You went forth for the salvation of Your people,
For the salvation of Your anointed.
You struck the head of the house of the evil
To lay him open from thigh to neck.   Selah.
[14] You pierced with his own spears
The head of his throngs.
They stormed in to scatter us;
Their exultation was like those
Who devour the oppressed in secret. Hab 3:13-14 NASB

It was earlier noted what Zechariah says,

"Woe to the worthless shepherd,
          Who leaves the flock!
          A sword *shall be* against his arm
          And against his right eye;
          His arm shall completely wither,
          And his right eye shall be totally blinded." Zech 11:17 NKJV

This is no ordinary false Christ, whose "deadly wound was healed," Rev 13:12 KJV. The verse itself presents the contrast: if it is "deadly"/"fatal" **then it cannot really be healed**, and **if it is healed**, then **it wasn't really deadly**, but this "man" is killed and is brought back to life. It is a special opponent, a special pseudo-messiah, a son of Satan who comes with incredible powers and signs, very near the end of time. In a very way, the exact antithesis of Jesus Christ.

So what holds all of this back? History is full of people who have been able to accomplish their plans, *but it didn't produce what they really wanted.* In a way it is like us in our day to day ambitions. We think that if we could get this or that or the other, we would have what we need. We scheme and work and plot and save and stand, and get it ... *but it doesn't produce what we thought it would.* And that has been the way it is with many in "the mystery of lawlessness."

[5] Do you not remember that when I was still with you I told you these things? [6] And now you know what is restraining, that he may be revealed in his own time. 2 Thes 2:5-6 NKJV

Following is a chart comparing the Christ and the man of lawlessness

Christ	Man of Lawlessness
1. The Holy and Righteous One, Acts 3:14	1. Characterized by lawlessness, 2 Thes 2:3
2. Author of Life, Acts 3:15	2. Literally "the son of destruction", 2 Thes 2:3
3. Humble and obedient to God, even to death on the cross, Phil 2:5-11	3. Proud and exalts himself against God, 2 Thes 2:4
4. Was hidden in a Mystery for ages, Rom 16:25-26	4. Is hidden in a Mystery until his revealing, 2 Thes 2:7
5. Had, and still has, a revealing, Gal 4:4, Acts 1:6-7	5. Still has a revealing, 2 Thes 2:6,8
6. Had, and has, a coming	6. Has a coming, 2 Thes 2:9
7. Came by the Power of God, Acts 2:22	7. Comes by the power of Satan, 2 Thes 2:9
8. Came with miracles, signs and wonders, Acts 2:22	8. Comes with counterfeit miracles, signs and wonders, 2 Thes 2:9
9. By all this men are saved, 1 Jn 4:14	9. By all this men are doomed, 2 Thes 2:10-11

There are four things key things of which we need to take note.

1. There is a mystery *mustārion* μυστήριον which has been in existence at least since the first century of our age. Paul says it is "already at work," NASB. As was discussed in the chapter on "Some Age Long Mysteries," the word mystery can refer either to a religious organization overall, or it can refer to the "secrets" of the organization. The NIV translates this as **"the secret power of lawlessness."** A very appropriate paraphrase.

2. This mystery Paul says is characterized by "lawlessness." The Greek word is anomia ἀνομία which is the negative of the word for law. (*Nomos* νόμος is the word for law, and the "*a*" sound is a negative in Greek, like "un" is a negative in English, so "*a-nomia*" means lawless.) "Sin is lawlessness" according to 1 Jn 3:4. So there is a mystery religion which is characterized by sin/lawlessness. This would fit with it bringing about a rebellion against God and all that He has established.

3. This "mystery of lawlessness" will work until it produces its great "god," the "man of lawlessness," who will be worshipped by the entire world (excepting a handful of Christians), and who will come by the power of Satan, as can be seen in both 2 Thessalonians and in Revelation. The truth is that *for over two thousand years the Mystery of Lawless has always had it "in the bag,"* as if it were a done deal. **This mystery of lawlessness has always been successful, but has never quite "won."**

4. Something is holding back this mystery, this secret power. The Thessalonians as you can see, knew who this was. We are not told who this is, at least not explicitly so far as I can see, but he will finally be taken out of the way (it seems to imply he is taken out of the way by the Lord God). When this barrier to Satan's ultimate success in this world is taken out of the way, then this monster will be revealed.

<u>*All*</u> *"that receive not the love of the truth"* will think that he is really **<u>God</u>**, 2 Thes 2:4, 11-12. "All" is something that happened with no Roman Emperor, Pope, anti-Pope, dictator or *any* "type" or great champion of Satan in the Christian age. This is a special character, a special case, never to be duplicated, and *which does not really fit any historical figure to date.* He will make people <u>*think*</u> *that he really is God*, and he will "fulfill" many "prophecies." In fact he will overcome all human opposition. He will rule the entire world.

> [7] And ... power was given him over all kindreds, and tongues, and nation. [8] And all that dwell upon the earth shall worship him, whose names are not written in the book of life of the Lamb slain from the foundation of the world. Rev 13:7-8 KJV

Now many men have had large empires like the Babylonians, the Romans, and the Spanish. The British of recent centuries ruled a significant portion of the globe. But none to date have had authority over "... <u>all</u> kindreds, and tongues, and nations. [8] And <u>all</u> that dwell upon the earth ... " Rev 13:7-8 KJV (*emphasis added*). Rev 13:7 says that he is "to make war with the saints and to overcome them ..." KJV. Thus he conquers the saints, the church, something no Roman Emperor ever did. In fact, in a real sense, the church conquered the Romans and their empire, not vice versa, Dan 2:44.

Ultimately, Satanism is about great and very harsh discipline. When the beast finally makes his appearance, many will wish for the mildness of a medieval Inquisition! He only rules for a very short period of time: three and one half years. (It can only be remarked, what a pitifully short period of absolute rule *for over two thousand years of work!*) This three and a half years is expressed in various ways in the Bible. It is called "time, and times, and half a time" Rev 12:14, "forty and two months" Rev 13:5 KJV, and as 1260 days Rev 11:3 (that is to say, 42 months of 30 days each). This very short period of time **is put to an end by Jesus personal coming**. *It will be very severe times for the church and the world,* and indeed, Jesus says "... However, when the Son of Man comes, will He find faith on the earth?" Luke 18:8 NASB. During this extreme stress, the church will be forced into "the wilderness" Rev 12:14, where she will be taken care of "for a time, and times, and half a time, from the face of the serpent," KJV. A special warning is given that all who worship the Beast will lose their souls, Rev 14:9-10.

This monster will be destroyed by the Second Coming of Jesus the Christ. Paul says that he writes 2 Thessalonians 2 so they know that this rebellion and this man has to come *just before the end,* 2 Thes 2:13. And the "man of lawlessness" will be destroyed by the brightness of Jesus' second coming, 2 Thes 2:8. The beast and the false prophet are thrown **alive** into hell, Rev 19:20, once again a clear indication that ***they are alive at the Second Coming of Christ!*** This is speaking of no ordinary opponent of God during the beginning or middle of the Christian age, but a special opponent who comes by the very power of Satan himself, very near the end, a short while before the *last trumpet,* when we rise *to meet Jesus in the air* to be with him forever, 1 Cor 15:52, 1 Thes 4:17.

Jesus is coming soon, Rev 22:20. We will not know the day nor the hour, but like Noah in Mtt 24:37-38, you will be able to see the day approaching, Heb 10:25. **Watching has a special moral quality.** Even though often unable to change events, it can produce a preparedness and resolution that makes us able to deal with events we cannot change. There are many things we cannot know, but we will be able to "see the day approaching," Heb 10:25 NASB. When you see these things come to pass you will know the Second Coming is near, right at the door. So be alert! For you do not know the time. "... And what I say unto you I say unto all, Watch." Mark 13:29, 33, 37. KJV

Then come the questions about the origins of the beast, and that also can be viewed from more than one point of view.

The "grave" is an important topic here. Some translations talk about "the grave" in Psa 16:10. What is it? It is what we call death, and what some call "the grave." When Jacob and his sons talk about Jacob dying, they speak of it as going to Sheol, Gen 42:38. The Greeks called it Hades or the underworld. Jesus calls it Hades in Lk 16:23. It is not just a "state of being," as some liberals say, but a place or places under the earth where the spirits of the dead stay before judgment. And it is "under," for Rom 10:6-7 asks who will go **down** to bring Jesus **up** from the dead.

It is a pit, an abyss, below the earth. God says "I make the nations quake ... when I make it go down to Sheol," Ezk 31:16 NASB. It is a pit. When God saves a man, "He keeps back his soul from the pit, and his life from passing over into Sheol," Job 33:18 NASB. It is a very deep place. "They are high as the heavens, what can you do? Deeper than Sheol, what can you know?" Job 11:8 NASB. Also there are lower places in the pit because the Palmist says, "... my life has drawn near to Sheol ... to the pit ... You have put me in the lowest pit," Psalm 88:3-4, 6 NASB. There are recesses in the pit, worse places without hope of rescue, because the King of Babylon "will be thrust down to Sheol, to the recesses of the pit," according to Isa 14:15 NASB.

Korah and the rebels with him went down alive into Sheol, Num 16:30, 33; and no doubt this wording is intended in part to be symbolic. The wicked do not return from this death, this Sheol. "When a cloud vanishes, it is gone, So he who goes down to Sheol does not come up," Job 7:9 NASB. They do not come back. But God keeps the righteous back from it, Job 33:18. Jesus was there for three days and three nights.

Of Korah and the rebels against God's authority it says, "So they and all that belonged to them went down alive to Sheol; and the earth closed over them, and they perished from the midst of the assembly." Num 16:33. A type no doubt of the rebells at the last day as will be led by the beast.

"For as Jonah was three days and three nights in the belly of the great fish, so will the Son of Man be three days and three nights **in the heart of the earth.**" Mtt 12:40 NKJV (*bold emphasis added*).

His body was in the grave, but his soul was "in the heart of the earth." But He was not abandoned there.

27 BECAUSE YOU WILL NOT ABANDON MY SOUL TO HADES, NOR ALLOW YOUR HOLY ONE TO UNDERGO DECAY.

31 he looked ahead and spoke of the resurrection of the Christ, that HE WAS NEITHER ABANDONED TO HADES, NOR DID His flesh SUFFER DECAY. Acts 2:27, 31 NASB.

In Romans it is called the Abyss where Jesus went for three days.

6 But the righteousness based on faith speaks as follows: "DO NOT SAY IN YOUR HEART, 'WHO WILL ASCEND INTO HEAVEN?' (that is, to bring Christ down), 7 or 'WHO WILL DESCEND INTO THE ABYSS?' (that is, to bring Christ up from the dead)." Rom 10:6-7 NASB

When Jesus died he went into the "abyss," which must be descended to enter. The word abyss itself, *abussos* ἄβυσσος, comes from *buthos* βυθός, a word for a great depth or a bottom, and the prefix "a" *sound* is a negative. So it is easily seen how the word abyss might be paraphrased as "the bottomless pit," as in the KJV in Rev 9:1-2. The pit consumes sinners, as "Drought and heat consume the snow waters, *so does* Sheol *those who* have sinned," Job 24:19. Still, in places it seems to be spoken of as the dead's waiting place till God's wrath comes.

"Oh that You would hide me in Sheol,
That You would conceal me until Your wrath returns *to You*,
That You would set a limit for me and remember me! Job 14:13 NASB

I find it interesting in discussing the last book of the Bible, that I would quote so much from what may be the first written book of the Bible, the book of Job. Some, especially those in the occult or the New Age, try to make agreements with death, but it won't work,

> [15] Because you have said, "We have made a covenant with death,
> And with Sheol we are in agreement.
> When the overflowing scourge passes through,
> It will not come to us,
> For we have made lies our refuge,
> And under falsehood we have hidden ourselves." ...

> [18] Your covenant with death will be annulled,
> And your agreement with Sheol will not stand;
> When the overflowing scourge passes through,
> Then you will be trampled down by it. Isa 28:15,18 NKJV

It is the place of the dead before judgment day. It is associated with destruction, and is called Abaddon, or Apollyon. "Sheol and Abaddon are never satisfied," Prov 27:20 NASB. There is no activity or planning there, Eccl 9:10. "Death cannot praise You," God says in Isaiah 38:18 NKJV. However, there is recognition there. In Isaiah men recognize the king of Babylon entering Sheol.

> [9] "Sheol from beneath is excited over you to meet you when you come;
> It arouses for you the spirits of the dead, all the leaders of the earth;
> It raises all the kings of the nations from their thrones.
> [10] They will all respond and say to you,
> 'Even you have been made weak as we,
> You have become like us.
> [11] 'Your pomp *and* the music of your harps
> Have been brought down to Sheol;
> Maggots are spread out *as your* bed beneath you
> And worms are your covering.'" Isa 14:9-11 NASB

Obviously, this applies to the ancient king of Babylon, but also he is a type, of the beast, the man of lawlessness-who briefly rules all the world. Yet when men see him enter Sheol, they will say words to the effect, "You have become as weak as we are, you are just a man, just like us, and maggots are your bed, and worms are your blankets." *The man of lawlessness is defeated almost before he starts.* The rich man in torment knows he is seeing Abraham, and he recognizes Lazarus far off living in comfort,

> And being in torments in Hades, he lifted up his eyes and saw
> Abraham afar off, Lk 16:23 NKJV

Also the rich man does not want his relatives to join him, and asks that Lazarus be sent to warn his brothers.

> [27] "Then he said, 'I beg you therefore, father, that you would send him to my father's house, [28] for I have five brothers, that he may testify to them, lest they also come to this place of torment.'" Lk 16:27-28 NKJV

Still there is more to tell here. There are two parts of Sheol. Notice the contrast between the beginning and the end of Isaiah chapter 57. It is rest for the righteous. "He shall enter into peace: they shall rest in their beds," Isa 57:1-2 KJV. But it is turmoil and torment for the wicked. "*There is* no peace, saith my God, to the wicked," Isa 57:20-21. If you go to the place of the wicked in Sheol, you will be in torment forever. But for the righteous dead it is called sleep,

> [13] But I would not have you to be ignorant, brethren, concerning them which are asleep, that ye sorrow not, even as others which have no hope. ... [16] For the Lord himself shall descend from heaven with a shout, with the voice of the archangel, and with the trump of God: and the dead in Christ shall rise first: 1 Thes 4:13, 16 KJV

It is evidently a different part of the world of the dead, called "Abraham's bosom" in Luke 16 where Lazarus rests.

Still, this pit, which is often called Sheol in the Old Testament, is a prison for the wicked awaiting trial. The wicked spirits are to finally go there, but they do not want to.

> [29] For He had commanded the unclean spirit to come out of the man. ... [30] Jesus asked him, saying, "What is your name?" And he said, "Legion," because many demons had entered him. [31] And they begged Him that He would not command them to go out into the **abyss**. Lk 8:29-31 NKJV (*bold emphasis added*)

The demonic spirits will end up there, but they dread the prospect. Where demons fear to go, Jesus went to pay the price for my sins and yours, if we will have it!

Then comes the next part of the story. **The beast of Revelation**, called "the man of lawlessness" in 2 Thessalonians 2, **is evidently in the abyss** prior **to his coming!**

> When they have finished their testimony, the beast that comes up out of the abyss will make war with them, and overcome them and kill them. Rev 11:7 NASB

This vile man "comes up" from there. Satan is restrained there for a long period in our age.

> [1] Then I saw an angel coming down from heaven, holding the key of the **abyss** and a great chain in his hand. [2] And he laid hold of the dragon, the serpent of old, who is the devil and Satan, and bound him

for a thousand years; [3] and he threw him into the **abyss**, and shut it and sealed it over him, so that he would not deceive the nations any longer, until the thousand years were completed; after these things he must be released for a short time. Rev 20:1-3 NASB (*bold emphasis added*)

So Satan and his choice men and spirits are restrained for most of the Christian age—imprisoned, limited, held captive in Sheol, the abyss—especially for an extensive period of time call symbolically "a thousand years." (But we should not make all of our views of Scripture dance to a single verse, and I trust that you can see that has not been the case.) Then the many evil spirits in the pit will be briefly released from the pit, the abyss, near the end of time, as can be seen from Rev 20:3, and also from Revelation chapter 9. In Revelation 9 the demons are pictured as locusts who harm all of those who do not belong to God, Rev 9:1-6. And who is the king of these spirits?

Topeth in the Valley of Hinnom seems to be used in Scripture as symbolic of the place of punishment. Cf. Jer 7:31, Isa 30:33, etc.

They have as king over them, the angel of the abyss; his name in Hebrew is Abaddon, and in the Greek he has the name Apollyon. Rev 9:11 NASB

And along with all these, Satan himself is released to do all that he is capable, just before the end.

[7] And when the thousand years are expired, Satan shall be loosed out of his prison, [8] And shall go out to deceive the nations which are in the four quarters of the earth, Gog and Magog, to gather them together to battle: the number of whom is as the sand of the sea.. Rev 20:7-8 KJV

It will be a time of war against everything which is holy and good and implied is that the beast is also released during this time when Satan and the demons are released in mass from the abyss. And of the beast it says,

"The beast that you saw **was, and is not, and is about to come up** out of the abyss and go to destruction. And those who dwell on the earth, whose name has not been written in the book of life from the foundation of the world, will wonder when they see the beast, that he **was and is not and will come**. Rev 17:8 NASB (*bold emphasis added*)

Notice what it implies here for the beast. He "**was and is not.**" It seems to imply that he has been on earth before, almost as if he is someone who is "known." At any rate, it seems he *used to be alive*, he "was"; but now (when the book of Revelation was written) he no longer exists, he "is not," he does not "exist" as a living being because he is now in Sheol. Then when the devil and his angels are released toward the end of time, then the beast comes "up out of the abyss and" goes "to destruction." "... he was and is not and will come." You cannot help but wonder as you think about these passages, what it will be like when this great champion of Satan presents himself before men. In the book of Daniel he is pictured as a man who wins through cunning and intrigue. If Antiochus Epiphanes is taken as a type of him, it is an astonishing picture we have.

> ²³ "And in the latter time of their kingdom,
>> When the transgressors have reached their fullness,
>> A king shall arise,
>> Having fierce features,
>> Who understands sinister schemes..
> ²⁴ His power shall be mighty, but not by his own power;
>> He shall destroy fearfully,
>> And shall prosper and thrive;
>> **He shall destroy** the mighty, and *also* **the holy people**.
> ²⁵ "Through his cunning
>> He shall cause deceit to prosper under his rule;
>> And he shall exalt *himself* in his heart.
>> He shall destroy many in *their* prosperity.
>> He shall even rise against the Prince of princes;
>> **But he shall be broken without *human* means**."
> Dan 8:23-25 NKJV (bold emphasis added)

Some will no doubt wonder, "Where in hell did this guy come from?" And that will be a better question than they ever imagined! Literally, that will be a subject. One can only imagine and speculate how he will reveal himself? Will he reveal things of his former life which only that person could have known? Will he in part by these means seek to prove his power over death and his "deity"? Intrigue? His success will be incredible. The devastation which he causes can scarcely be imaged. In the types of the beast, you can see types of the destruction that is described in the book of Revelation, but the fullness of these things await the genuine article. But no, he doesn't really have power over death, and he goes from the pinnacle of his "success" to his final destruction.

Still beyond all of this, the Hebrew word "Sheol" *sheol* שְׁאוֹל also seems to be used for hell, the place of eternal punishment. An evil woman's ways lead to Sheol, Prov 5:5. It is talking about hell because we all die physically. I think these are places in Scripture where the KJV is more correct in its translation, where it reads, "Her feet go down to death; her steps take hold on hell." And again, "Her house is the way to hell, going down to the chambers of death."

Prov 7:27 KJV. This is a case of using what some might call "functional equivalence," and is faithful to the original. Most modern translations do not use the word hell in the Old Testament, and many argue that it really is not there. That is technically true, but also it is plain from the context of many passages that Sheol is also used to describe what the New Testament calls hell. Remember that in the fewer words of ancient Hebrew, more words do double duty. It is the same thing in Prov 23:14, "You shall strike him with the rod And rescue his soul from Sheol," NASB. We all die. It is speaking of hell. And it has to be talking about the pit of hell in Psalm 30:3, where it says "You have brought my soul from Sheol, you have kept me alive that I would not go to the pit," NASB.

> "... For their worm does not die,
>> And their fire is not quenched.
>> They shall be an abhorrence to all flesh." Isa 66:24 NKJV

Capernaum will go to Hades because they have rejected the Christ, Lk 10:15. Again,this use of "Hades" seems to overlap the concept of hell. It is not just speaking of physical death.

Death is not permanent ... for some. At the end *all* the dead are raised, Rev 20:13; some to life and some to everlasting disgrace and shame, Dan 12:1-3. God says "Shall I ransom them from the power of Sheol?" Hosea 13:14 NASB. So we see the idea of being ransomed, redeemed, from the power of Sheol. This is quoted in 1 Cor 15:54-56, where it says "... *Death is swallowed up in victory.*" "*O Death, where is your sting? O Hades, where is your victory?*" NKJV. But we will not all sleep, 1 Cor 15:50-51. The righteous are not abandoned to Sheol, Psa 16:10. Now that was originally spoken of Christ but includes all those in Christ.

But "The wicked shall return to Sheol, all the nations that forget God," Psa 9:17 ESV. Even so, to return to something you must have first been there. So where is it that the wicked really go at the end? To where do those in torment return? It is what is called hell as in Mtt 23:33, "Ye serpents, ye generation of vipers, how can ye escape the damnation of hell?" KJV. This is permanent Sheol, the second death. "And death and hell were cast into the lake of fire. This is the second death," Rev 20:14 KJV.

"The fear of the Lord *leads* to life, so that one may sleep satisfied, untouched by evil," Prov 19:23 NASB. Things change "when morning comes."

> [14] As sheep they are appointed for Sheol;
> Death shall be their shepherd;
> And the upright shall rule over them in the morning,
> And their form shall be for Sheol to consume
> So that they have no habitation.
> [15] But God will redeem my soul from the power of Sheol,
> For He will receive me.   Selah. Psa 49:14-15 NASB

But when is the morning? It is when "... the God of peace will crush Satan under your feet shortly," Rom 16:20 NKJV. It is when Jesus rescues his people,

Psa 46:5. "The night is far spent, the day is at hand." Rom 13:12, NKJV. "The gates of Hades" will not prevail against the church Jesus builds, Mtt 16:18. The second death has no power over those who have the first resurrection, Rev 20:6. But what is "the first resurrection"? It is our death to sin, and our rising to walk in newness of life. It is in the new birth in baptism. It is in dying to this world and rising from the waters of baptism to live for Jesus, Rom 6:3-4. Jesus has the keys to death and Hades, Rev 1:18. The dead in Christ will rise to life. "Your dead will live. Their corpses will rise. You who lie in the dust, awake and shout for joy," Isa 26:19-21 NASB.

But of course, all of this starts with what Scripture calls a great uproar.

A Revolt, an Uproar, Psalm 2, Psalm 83

Then comes a popular theme in the prophets, and a good piece of the aspirations of the occult. This is about the ultimate *Strum und Drang*—The Storm and Stress which will encompass *ALL* the nations, and which will be without parallel. It is constantly spoken of by the prophets, but many have never even noticed the theme: an uproar of the nations. It is not an isolated theme. Like the story of the Messiah Himself, like the story of the great blessing and healing which he gives, like the story of the perfect reign and the heavenly bliss which will come, it is a story which runs all through the Scriptures, all the way to near the end of the book of Revelation.

One of the first places this uproar appears is in the second psalm. The psalm seems to start out with an incredible circumstance. The whole world seems to be in turmoil. The nations are in an uproar according to Psalm 2. The word is *ragash* רָגַשׁ, a commotion, a tumult, even it could be translated as a rage, although "uproar," almost like that of a wild mob, is a common translation into English. It is indeed related to *regesh* רֶגֶשׁ, a word for a group, a crowd, indeed even a mob! The King James Version says, "Why do the heathen rage?" It is concerning something wild and foolish that is coming about. The nations, the peoples, are trying something that is useless. Leading the nations in this futile enterprise are the kings of the earth. The rulers are working together against God, against "the LORD and against his" Christ, His Messiah, His Anointed. So here is pictured a raging commotion in all the world against God and His Christ, wishing for the ultimate "Independence Day" (is there a link here to some popular culture?) from the Mighty One Who sit in the heavens. They want to end all their obligations to Him, cut off their dependence on Him, cut the ties which go to Him, and end the bondage which their rebellion to Him has brought. They say,

"Let us tear their fetters apart

And cast away their cords from us!" Psa 2:3 NASB

The NIV is worth noting on verse one.

> Why do the nations conspire
> and the peoples plot in vain?

This is not about idle anger and hatred. "The nations conspire." "The peoples plot." This is active resolve and coordinated work. It is true that men are bound to God, that God rules and masters us all. The relationship starts with our creation by Him, receiving life by His grace.

> [1] Make a joyful noise unto the LORD, all ye lands. [2] Serve the LORD with gladness: come before his presence with singing. [3] Know ye that the LORD he *is* God; *it is* he *that* hath made us, and not we ourselves; we are his people, and the sheep of his pasture. Psa 100:1-3 KJV

God is the One who rules over us and does as He pleases. As Nebuchadnezzar so pointedly put it,

> [34] ... For His dominion is an everlasting dominion,
> And His kingdom is from generation to generation.
> [35] All the inhabitants of the earth are reputed as nothing;
> He does according to His will in the army of heaven
> And among the inhabitants of the earth.
> No one can restrain His hand
> Or say to Him, "What have You done?" Dan 4:34-35 NKJV

The fact of His rule is everywhere. As the old saying goes, "Man proposes, God disposes." Or again in the phrase, "Duty is ours, outcomes are God's." It is seen in the agencies He puts in charge, from the husband in the family, to the rulers in their places. In fact Paul says there is no power which the Lord has not put in place.

> ... For there is no authority except from God, and the authorities that exist are appointed by God. Rom 13:1 NKJV

It has already been covered, how God rules in the affairs of men. Proverbs chapter 16 gives a good summary of our limits, fore and aft.

> The lot is cast into the lap,
> But its every decision is from the LORD. Prov 16:33 NKJV

Still it is not that we cannot "want" something on our own.

> The preparations of the heart belong to man,
> But the answer of the tongue is from the LORD. Prov 16:1 NKJV

It is rather that God can and does over-rule men. He allows us within limits to reject Him, to even oppose Him; but at the end of the day we are not able to do just anything we want. He can make us succeed if that is His will ... or obstruct our path ... or leave us to our own very meager means.

Commit your works to the LORD
And your plans will be established. Prov 16:3 NASB

Can we then plot to do evil, to oppose God, to wrong another, and not be held to account? Hardly!

⁴ The LORD has made all for Himself,
    Yes, even the wicked for the day of doom. ...
⁷ When a man's ways please the LORD,
    He makes even his enemies to be at peace with him.
Prov 16:4, 7 NKJV

Again it says,

A man's heart plans his way,
But the LORD directs his steps. Prov 16:9 NKJV

This is hardly the "clock of the world" of the deists. We may delude ourselves, but we are indeed bound to the Lord of Hosts. His Son upholds us with the Word of His power, Heb 1:3. But if we are determined to live as fools who must be brought to account, and if we must at the end state all of this grace and bounty in the negative, then yes, we are so to speak on a short leash. So the wicked of the earth, who at some future point must include most of mankind, want to, "tear their fetters apart and cast away their cords from us!" But if we must engage in so asinine a quest, we see by the bounds which have been established, that it is all foolishness. There is no way that it can bring success.

³⁰ There is no wisdom and no understanding
And no counsel against the LORD.
³¹ The horse is prepared for the day of battle,
But victory belongs to the LORD. Prov 21:30-31 NASB

Empty, vain, useless, a vapor, stupid, hardly does justice to something so lacking in sense. This is something so dumb, it makes stupid look smart. This is indeed a picture of a world seeking to kick the slats from underneath itself, an appliance seeking to unplug itself, an empty clock face seeking to get it independence from any springs or battery or regulator. Such are the pictures that are to be seen in these verses.

This uproar I think is pictured also in the book of Revelation. It is interspersed with pictures of the work of Babylon coming to fruition and the beast coming to its head. The saints are assaulted and overcome, and the victory *seems* complete. Even the death of the beast is overcome in at least some measure, so much so that people think that there is no way to fight and overcome one who cannot even be killed. So they follow the beast in wonder and worship him and his image, Rev 13:4. But all is not well in this demonic utopia of oppressive discipline. The two prophets of Revelation 11 act as an Elijah and Elisha to this community of nations. Like these prophets of old, they are able on request to shut the sky so it will not rain, turn the waters to blood, and rain plagues on men who have rejected God and have consciously and voluntarily followed Satan. Desolations follow especially in those days, but the earth is so deceived—under mind control to this prince of darkness—that they will not repent, even when they know the source and know they are in the wrong.

> [20] And the rest of the men which were not killed by these plagues yet repented not of the works of their hands, that they should not worship devils, and idols ... which neither can see, nor hear, nor walk: [21] Neither repented they of their murders, nor of their sorceries, nor of their fornication, nor of their thefts. Rev 9:20-21 KJV

The climax of the great revolt seems to come after the suppression of the saints and all of Christianity, and after the persecution of all who even "**desire to live godly in Christ Jesus,**" 2 Tim 3:12 NASB (emphasis added). They do not have to be successful in the Christian life to warrant death at the hands of an ungodly world. They just have to "desire to live godly in Christ Jesus." But now the world has touched the apple of God's eye, and His retribution follows.

There are seven **last** plagues which come on men, beginning in Revelation 15. In turn, horrible sores afflict all who worship the beast. Then waters of the earth are turned to blood, and the sun of our solar system flares in heat which scorches men with fire. The men that are seen in the book of Revelation know what the source is of these plagues, but they are not repentant. They are angry with God who pays them back for their sin.

> And men were scorched with great heat, and blasphemed the name of God, which hath power over these plagues: and they repented not to give him glory. Rev 16:9 KJV

They are ready to fight. They are ready to fight God Himself. They are in an uproar, and the demonic powers gather them to war **against God Himself!**

> For they are spirits of demons, performing signs, which go out to the kings of the earth and of the whole world, to gather them to the battle of that great day of God Almighty. Rev 16:14 NKJV

God has acted. Men know it is God who has afflicted them. Men are ready to fight. They are in an uproar. Of course, God can only laugh at all of this.

> He who sits in the heavens laughs,
> The Lord scoffs at them. Psa 2:4 NASB

Then the Lord will repeat His decisions to them in His anger. He has long ago decided to send Jesus His Son to redeem men from their sins, to give them life and joy and great gifts forever and ever, and to seal it with a perfect reign of peace and prosperity, under the perfect ruler, Jesus the Christ. He will reign from the heavenly Zion, Psa 2:6; for God's true temple, His throne, is in heaven, Psa 11:4. What then is God's decree? It is that Jesus, His very own Son, has been begotten by God, Psa 2:7. What has He given Jesus to rule? The entire kosmos. And He is to rule with a rod of iron.

> [8] " 'Ask of Me, and I will give You
>> The nations for Your inheritance,
>> And the ends of the earth for Your possession
> [9] You shall break them with a rod of iron;
>> You shall dash them to pieces like a potter's vessel.' "
> Psa 2:8-9 NKJV

This rule by the Christ does not *begin* at the *end* of time. Rather, very clearly, He rules within time! He rules in middle of all of His enemies.

> [1] The LORD said unto my Lord, Sit thou at my right hand, until I make thine enemies thy footstool. [2] The LORD shall send the rod of thy strength out of Zion: rule thou in the midst of thine enemies.
> Psa 110:1-2 KJV

Notice several things here. This rule by the Christ is from heaven. He sits at God's right hand to rule, and God's true temple and His throne is in heaven. It is as referenced in many passages including Psa 11:4.

> The LORD *is* in His holy temple; the LORD throne *is* in heaven ... KJV

This is the heavenly Zion where Jesus the Messiah takes His seat beside His Father on His throne, stretches His scepter out over the nations, **and rules in the middle of them**, Psa 110:2! So this is speaking of a rule from heaven during history, not at the end of history. So you can see that there is more than one aspect to trying to cast off God and His Christ, because the psalm that is being studied is quoted in the New Testament. First let's notice that it is quoted as being a reference to Jesus the Christ.

> "God has fulfilled this for us their children, in that He has raised up
> Jesus. As it is also written in the second Psalm:
>> *"You are My Son,*
>> *Today I have begotten You.' "* Acts 13:33 NKJV

Again there are the references in Hebrews chapters one and five.

> For to which of the angels did He ever say:
>> "You are My Son,
>> Today I have begotten You"? And again:
>> "I will be to Him a Father,
>> And He shall be to Me a Son"? Heb 1:5 NKJV

Also look at Heb 5:5. These are clear references to Psalm 2 and to 2 Samuel 7 which was looked at in detail in the section on "Type and Anti-Type." It was noted in that section that *often* there are both a type and an anti-type in prophecy, and that in the case of 2 Samuel 7 Solomon is a type of the Christ, and that Solomon fulfills this according to 1 Kgs 8:17-20; and Jesus fulfills it (I would say ultimately) according to Heb 1:5. **What it amounts to is that God often chooses to instruct us on the big things which will happen, by a se-**

ries of models down through history. The Bible calls these models "types" or "copies" or "shadows," or "patterns." Then comes the third reference to Psalm 2 in the New Testament, the nature of the reference, and the mandates of the text. Peter also refers to this psalm in his sermon in Acts 4. He says that it was a prophecy of the opposition, trial and death of Jesus. He says that God

> 25 who by the mouth of Your servant David have said:
> *"Why did the nations rage,*
> *And the people plot vain things?*
> 26 *The kings of the earth took their stand,*
> *And the rulers were gathered together*
> *Against the* LORD *and against His Christ.'* Acts 4:25-26 NKJV

Then Peter refers to what had recently happened, about what he calls Gentiles who raged against the Christ, and about kings (plural) who worked against the Christ; that is both Herod and Pilate, who worked with the people of Israel, who worked together for Jesus' death.

> 27 "For truly against Your holy Servant Jesus, whom You anointed, both Herod and Pontius Pilate, with the Gentiles and the people of Israel, were gathered together 28 to do whatever Your hand and Your purpose determined before to be done. Acts 4:27-28 NKJV

All of this is true but then comes the next part of the study. This is that Psalm 2 seems to speak of something both deeper and more extensive than what is seen in the gospels, jarring though that story is alone. Here is the key point: *Psalm 2 seems to picture an understanding, a perception of revolution, a recognition of God and His rule over them, and an understanding and resolution to oppose that rule and overthrow those bonds,* which was completely absent in that early "cabal" (shall we say?) which worked for the crucifixion of Jesus Christ. Peter said the same thing in his earlier sermon which is recorded in Acts 3.

> "Yet now, brethren, I know that you did *it* in ignorance, as *did* also your rulers." Acts 3:17 NKJV

Peter seems to be speaking of both the Jewish leaders and the leaders of the nations as acting in ignorance. Clearly, Pilate and Herod did not realize the implications of what they were doing. Pilate, the one who imposed the final condemnation of Jesus to crucifixion, does seem to have been specifically warned by the Lord of the importance of what he was doing. His wife was warned in a dream and sent a message to him in court, that he should have nothing to do with that righteous man, Mtt 27:19. Such things might be of little consequence to many moderns, but dreams were taken much more seriously in ancient times, both among Jews and among the nations. Of the Jewish leaders also it is clearly said,

> "For those who dwell in Jerusalem, and their rulers, because they did not know Him, nor even the voices of the Prophets which are read every

Sabbath, have fulfilled them in condemning Him." Acts 13:27 NKJV

So how did the Jews act? In ignorance, they neither recognized Him nor the prophecies which they were fulfilling. But as has been shown, ***there is recognition in Psalm 2.*** There is *perception* and *rejection* and deliberate *revolution* against the LORD and His Anointed! If you must take it as referring to the trial of Jesus, just as a parallel to Isaiah 53, then one would have to say that it overstates the case, that it implies recognition and conscious revolt which is not there. But remember, *exaggerated language is one of the first signs of a type!* **There is recognition and deliberate revolt also spoken of in other places**—for instance in the parable of the tenant farmers in Matthew 21.

> [35] "And the vinedressers took his servants, beat one, killed one, and stoned another. [36] Again he sent other servants, more than the first, and they did likewise to them. [37] Then last of all he sent his son to them, saying, 'They will respect my son.' [38] But when the vinedressers saw the son, they said among themselves, 'This is the heir. Come, let us kill him and seize his inheritance.'" Mtt 21:35-38 NKJV

Here, in opposition to the events of the first century, as commented on by prophets being led by the Holy Spirit, there is recognition of the Christ, recognition that He is the heir of the land, and conscious decision to try to kill Him in order to take control of the land, the earth. **Remember:** *Scripture* **cannot** *be broken,* Jn 10:35. So there is recognition somewhere, and it comes to have telling results. If you look at the rest of the prophecies of the uproar of the nations, it is much broader than that which is seen in the first century.

So what is God's advice to these kings and rulers who conspire to revolt in Psalm 2?

> [10] Now therefore, be wise, O kings;
> Be instructed, you judges of the earth.
> [11] Serve the LORD with fear,
> And rejoice with trembling.
> [12] Kiss the Son, lest He be angry,
> And you perish *in* the way,
> When His wrath is kindled but a little.
> Blessed *are* all those who put their trust in Him.
> Psalm 2:10-12 NKJV

Kings, Presidents, Judges, show a little sense and do a couple of things. Worship the LORD, literally *Yehovah* יְהוָֹה, which is the name of God, and it is translated as LORD in most of our translations. Also worship the Son, Jesus. "Do homage" to Him it says in the New American Standard. The Hebrew is to kiss Him, *nashaq* נָשַׁק, as it is in many translations. But why kiss the Son, the One of whom the LORD says, 'You are My Son, Today I have begotten You.' The reason is that the Son rules over you. If He becomes angry with you, you may perish in the middle of your tracks, and His anger is easily kindled! But you see, Jesus was not made king until He went back to heaven *after* the resurrection. In the words of the parable in Luke 19, Jesus compares Himself to a certain nobleman, and says,

> ... A certain nobleman went into a far country to receive for himself a kingdom, and to return. Lk 19:12 KJV

The far country where He went to receive a kingdom is not just Rome as Herod so went, but to heaven. He is going to heaven in the end of Luke and the first chapter of Acts. He is pictured as entering heaven with captives in His procession, in Eph 4:8-9. It is from heaven that He rules and overrules, and from which He may decide to destroy a king or a president or a judge in moment if they displease Him! The psalm seems to say to these rulers, "**Fools, listen up!**" And this rule continues to the end of time.

> [25] For he must reign, till he hath put all enemies under his feet. [26] The last enemy *that* shall be destroyed *is* death. 1 Cor 15:25-26 KJV

So, yes, this psalm applies to the crucifixion, but also (and it would seem primarily) to the end of the age conflict, of which the first conflict was just a type. This is why Peter himself pictures this as an ongoing conflict.

> [29] And now, Lord, behold their threatenings: and grant unto thy servants, that with all boldness they may speak thy word, [30] By stretching forth thine hand to heal; and that signs and wonders may be done by the name of thy holy child Jesus Acts 4:29-30 KJV

These first century conflicts are things which over the centuries morphs into the great rebellion. You can see the continuation of this conflict and the things it involves. The psalmist Asaph says in effect, don't be silent Lord, speak up Lord, Psa 83:1. Your enemies, God's enemies, are making an uproar, Psa 83:2. But who are these enemies who are making an uproar, a commotion, a tumult? Are they conscious enemies? Yes. These are the ones who hate you it says, and they are the ones who hated Jesus.

> If the world hate you, ye know that it hated me before it hated you. Jn 15:18 KJV

This is talking about an irrational rejection, an emotional response, a visceral antagonism; one that has no foundation in fact, but only in feeling; among both the Jews of the first century, and finally among all the peoples of the world and their leaders. So they are making an uproar. In Hosea 10 it speaks of a tumult that will arise among your people, the people of Israel. In this tumult/uproar it says that ancient Israel will be destroyed.

> Therefore a tumult will arise among your people,
> And all your fortresses will be destroyed,
> As Shalman destroyed Beth-arbel on the day of battle,

When mothers were dashed in pieces with their children.
Hosea 10:14 NASB

Still there are other associations here, for four verses later Hos 10:8 says,

Then they will say to the mountains,
"Cover us!" And to the hills, "Fall on us!" NASB

In other words it is speaking of the kind of behavior that is consistently associated with the end of time in Scripture. Also this final tumult, this uproar, is associated with a revolt: a revolt of the civil powers against God's only Son, as was pictured in Psalm 2:1-3. Of course, God is just laughing at them in Psalm 2. The references are nearly universal in Scripture.

The heathen **raged**, the kingdoms were moved: he uttered his voice, the earth melted. Psa 46:6 KJV

So if you take it literally, the uproar is associated with the earth, on some final day, actually melting with heat. In Psalm 64 David speaks of it again as sort of a conspiracy, an action prompted by a "secret counsel" of wicked men.

Hide me from the secret counsel of evildoers,
From the **tumult** of those who do iniquity, Psa 64:2 NASB

In Psa 2:1 the word used is *ragash* רָגַשׁ for tumult or uproar, and in Psa 64:2 it is *rigshah* רִגְשָׁה for tumult or uproar, a word derived from *ragash*. There is this huge uproar which will come (the KJV translates it here as an "insurrection"), a historic event of incredible significance. No one here at the time will miss it, but God will subdue it, just as He subdues the waves of the sea when He wishes.

Which stilleth the noise of the seas, the noise of their waves, and the **tumult** of the people. Psalm 65:7 KJV

The nations are guided by the "secret counsel." David asks to be kept from their uproar, Psa 64:2. Asaph pleads to God,

Forget not the voice of thine enemies: the **tumult** of those that rise up against thee increaseth **continually**. Psa 74:23 KJV (*bold emphasis added*)

So here is almost a secondary sense. It is as if this revolt is going on "continually" through much of history, a conscious rejection of what God is and has and will do. It is implied to be a conscious rejection of God as was shown from Psalm 2, and Asaph says to not forget this Lord. It is clear that it is an uproar of the nationS, plural; and it causes God to gather His army for war.

A sound of **tumult** on the mountains,
Like that of many people!
A sound of the **uproar** of kingdoms,
Of nations gathered together!
The LORD of hosts is mustering the army for battle.
Isa 13:4 NASB (*bold emphasis added*)

So not only is there an uproar leading to war, but the Lord is gathering an army for battle. More is told in this early part of Isaiah 13, more about the Lord's intervention than about the uproar. So what is the uproar about? It is in Psalm 2 as a revolt against the authority of the Lord and His Son, but they are in an uproar to destroy the heavenly Jerusalem, the city of the Living God, according to Zechariah.

> For I will gather all nations against Jerusalem to battle; and the city shall be taken, and the houses rifled, and the women ravished; and half of the city shall go forth into captivity, and the residue of the people shall not be cut off from the city. Zech 14:2 KJV

At that time the Lord will fight, His armies will come.

> Then shall the LORD go forth, and fight against those nations, as when he fought in the day of battle. Zech 14:3 KJV

Jesus says of those days,

> [9] "Then they will deliver you up to tribulation and kill you, and you will be hated by all nations for My name's sake. [10] And then many will be offended, will betray one another, and will hate one another. [11] Then many false prophets will rise up and deceive many. [12] And because lawlessness will abound, the love of many will grow cold. [13] But he who endures to the end shall be saved. [14] And this gospel of the kingdom will be preached in all the world as a witness to all the nations, and then the end will come." Mtt 24:9-14 NKJV

Remember? It has been pointed out that the description of the siege of Jerusalem in Matthew 24 is also a type of the end of the world. Hated by many has happened, does happen. Hated by *all* nations, has not happened yet, but it will. Asaph, in addition, says they conspire against God's church.

> They make shrewd plans against Your people,
> And conspire together against Your treasured ones. Psa 83:3 NASB

"Shrewd plans" they are, "crafty counsel" in the KJV, and it is "with cunning they conspire" in the NIV. It is literally conspiracy, and that word is used of it many times in various translations of these eschatological conflicts. Paul says this secret power was already at work in the first century, 2 Thes 2:7, and according to 2 Thessalonians 2 this mystery will continue to work until the man of lawlessness is revealed, and Jesus will destroy this one by the brightness of His coming. They say, let us wipe out God's church, His holy people; and they work together toward this aim.

> [4] They have said, "Come, and let us wipe them out as a nation,
> That the name of Israel be remembered no more."
> [5] For they have conspired together with one mind;
> Against You they make a covenant: Psa 83:4-5 NASB

The real object is God, and His rule. All the nations are pictured as participating in these things, and it names specifically many of the nations of that time, the historic enemies of ancient Israel.

> [6] The tents of Edom and the Ishmaelites,
> Moab and the Hagrites;
> [7] Gebal and Ammon and Amalek,
> Philistia with the inhabitants of Tyre;
> [8] Assyria also has joined with them;
> They have become a help to the children of Lot. Selah. Psa 83:6-8 NASB

Deal with them as you dealt with Midian, it says in Psa 83:9. The daughters of Moab and Midian had seduced Israel in the matter of Peor, as is recorded in Num 25:1-4, 9. Phineas had stayed the anger of God in those things, Psa 106:28-30. So Israel made war on Midian and Moab and destroyed every male, Num 31:7-8. Again Israel is making war on Midian and crushing her in Judges 4 and Judges 7. The end for the nations that oppose God is compared to that. They will just be fuel for the fire in the words of Isa 9:4-6. For a child has been born who is "called Wonderful Counselor, Mighty God, Eternal Father, Prince of Peace," all spoken of the Son, *for the Father Himself is not just a "Prince."* See the built in contradiction if you reject Jesus.

Make our enemies like those people Asaph pleads, Psa 83:10-12. They have tried to destroy God's holy church, so make them like the dust, Psa 83:13. Make them like the dry timber in a forest fire, Psa 83:14. Jesus will come with fire and Isaiah describes it in Isa 13:9.

> Behold, the day of the LORD is coming,
> Cruel, with fury and burning anger,
> To make the land a desolation;
> And He will exterminate its sinners from it. NASB

Here is the classic picture of God intervening in anger to deliver His people in the day of trouble. It is a picture seen over and over again in Scripture and is also seen in Jewish secular apocalypses. It is described in 2 Thes 1:7-10 where it speaks of Jesus as intervening in flaming fire. Pursue them with your storm of vengeance, Psa 83:15. Fill their faces with shame and dishonor, Psa 83:16. There are two sides to the coin of God's intervention that is seen in Psalm 83. There are multiple types within history of God's final intervention. Finally, there is also a time which will be without appeal. So Psalm 83 talks about both things, as true and going to happen! So it says,

> Fill their faces with shame; that they may seek thy name, O LORD.
> Psa 83:16 KJV

Thus the psalmist first speaks of shaming the uproar of the nations so that they might seek God. This would apply to Psalm 2 as it speaks of the first councils which put Jesus death. It will also apply to when God delivers the unbelieving Jews in their time of stress so that they might believe and follow Him. But it also applies to a time of intervention from which there will be no remedy, no opportunity to repent, when all grace will have been frittered away. So the very next verse says,

> Let them be confounded and troubled for ever; yea, let them be put to shame, and perish: Psa 83:17 KJV

Both are clearly spoken of in the same psalm. There will be a final day of shame and dismay from which there will be no remedy, in which the humiliation will last "forever." May we not let some clever fool talk us out of the clear significance of "forever," and thus fatally postpone our personal opportunity for a Day of Salvation. Everyone will be resurrected in that day.

> [28] Marvel not at this: for the hour is coming, in the which all that are in the graves shall hear his voice, [29] And shall come forth; they that have done good, unto the resurrection of life; and they that have done evil, unto the resurrection of damnation. Jn 5:28-29 KJV

It is easy to observe that the Old Testament pictures and the New Testament pictures agree. Some will arise to everlasting life, and some to everlasting shame and contempt, Dan 12:1-3. Do it so they can know that the LORD alone is God, is the answer given in Psa 83:18. Everyone will have to know this in the end. Indeed, restore us Lord!

Tribulation and Rapture

Are there such things? There is such a thing as "tribulation."

There is tribulation in this life. The word tribulation itself means distress or suffering. The Greek word is *thlipsis* θλῖψις. We speak in modern America of being under "pressure," stress, strain, anxiety, or hassle; and this is the Greek word for being under pressure, under stress. Probably the most common word used to translate *thlipsis* in many translations is the word "tribulation." It literally means to press or to be pressing something or to be pressed. The word is sometimes translated "affliction," "trouble," or associated with being "pressed," as in passages like 2 Cor 1:8. It is also sometimes translated "distress" or "anguish," and a couple of times it is translated "persecution." In one passage the King James Version translates it as "burdened." It is used in the book of Acts when it is talking about the troubles that Joseph went through, and the famine that occurred in Egypt, Acts 7:9-11, and in verses 10 and 11 the word used is *thlipsis*, tribulation. You might call it being "under pressure."

Life includes much "tribulation." There are troubles (tribulations) in marriage, 1 Cor 7:27-28. There are troubles in being single. There are troubles in life. Such is the nature of life in a sinful world. Many fall away because of "troubles," "tribulations," cares, so it says in Mtt 13:21-22. Jesus Himself had troubles in this life, and in Jn 13:21 it speaks of when Jesus was troubled because of His betrayal and coming death. Still Jesus said not to let worldly things trouble us. "Let not your heart be troubled: ye believe in God, believe also in me," Jn 14:1 KJV. And there are special troubles for the Christian.

> Confirming the souls of the disciples, *and* exhorting them to continue in the faith, and that we must through much tribulation enter into the kingdom of God. Acts 14:22 KJV

In fact, in our troubles for Christ, we are filling up the afflictions of Christ.

> I now rejoice in my sufferings for you, and fill up in my flesh what is lacking in the afflictions of Christ, for the sake of His body, which is the church, Col 1:24 NKJV

Also there is a special time of trouble right toward the end of time, a time when Christians will be hated by all nations—the uproar.

> [9] Then shall they deliver you up to be afflicted, and shall kill you: and ye shall be hated of all nations for my name's sake. [10] and then shall many be offended, and shall betray one another, and shall hate one another. Matt 24:9 KJV

Jesus assures us that even though we have tribulation in the world, He has overcome the world, John 16:33. Everything will come out all right for those belonging to Jesus.

Tribulations began for Christians a long time ago, even in the first century. These early Christian troubles are spoken of in passages like Heb 10:32, where it says "you endured a great struggle with sufferings," NKJV. John the apostle was a partaker in tribulation, Rev 1:9. Paul tells Christians not to lose heart at his tribulations, Eph 3:13. The Thessalonian church had tribulation, 1 Thes 1:6. The first century church in Smyrna was to have tribulation, Rev 2:9-10, and evil doers in the church were to have tribulation, Rev 2:22. In a general sense there will be multiple difficult periods of time, "perilous times" KJV, "in the last days," 2 Tim 3:1, not just singular, but "times" plural, of tribulation or trouble. Much of our trouble is long term for our good. Scripture says we should endure troubles as discipline from the Father, Heb 12:7. So hardship, trouble, pressure, stress, tribulation, has purposes—that of training and testing us. So we both can and should glory in our tribulations, Rom 5:3. We should be like an athlete who rejoices in the trials of the training that leads to victory, or the soldier who rejoices in the struggles by which his army overcomes the enemy. The testing of our faith produces patience, Jas 1:24. So we should be glad. It is to train us and teach us, turn us from evil, and prepare us for life everlasting.

Still, beyond all of these things, there is also a Great Tribulation, Rev 7:14. The Greek text of Rev 7:14 literally calls it "the tribulation, the great," *tās thlipseōs tās megalās* (τῆς θλίψεως τῆς μεγάλης). Now when it is describing the greatest tribulation in the book of Revelation, it seems to involve someone called "the beast" making war on the saints and overcoming them.

> And it was given unto him to make war with the saints, and to overcome them: and power was given him over all kindreds, and tongues, and nations. Rev 13:7 KJV

The word "overcome" is also translated to "conquer," and indeed the Greek word used here (*nikaō* νικάω) means to conquer, have the victory over someone. The noun form of the word is translated "victory" in 1 Jn 5:4. From this we get our word "nike" as in Nike shoes or the old Nike missiles of the U. S. Army.

Now my friend, no anti-christ to date has overcome the church on a world wide basis. As you know, the Roman empire made war on the church, but the Roman empire did not conquer the church. Instead, the church of our Lord, the kingdom of righteousness and truth, conquered the Roman empire! This was prophesied in Daniel chapter two, which pictures the Babylonian empire, the Persian empire, the Greek empire, and the Roman empire, and it says that God's kingdom, the church, will conquer these empires, Dan 2:44. And that is exactly what happened. THE ROMAN EMPIRE NEVER CONQUERED THE CHURCH! In the end, even the mighty Roman Empire had to acknowledge Jesus as Master and Lord.

But the beast in the book of Revelation, indeed conquers, overcomes, has the victory over, the church, the saints of the Lord. On a world-wide basis, for he rules "over every tribe and people and tongue and nation," Rev 13:7. Now the Old Testament patterns clearly imply this will come about because of sin in the church. This point will not be discussed in detail, but it is easy to see from the text. Also you can see that the saints are not taken away before the beast makes war; rather the saints are overcome by the beast, and then the beast is personally destroyed by Jesus coming.

> And the beast was taken, and with him the false prophet that wrought miracles before him, with which he deceived them that had received the mark of the beast, and them that worshipped his image. These both were cast alive into a lake of fire burning with brimstone.
> Rev 19:20 KJV

This is a world-wide system which the beast heads in the book of Revelation. All who dwell on earth will worship this beast, Rev 13:8. "All" who dwell on earth worshipping anyone is something that no anti-christ to date has achieved.

Many Christians have heard so many false theories about the book of Revelation that they no longer believe the book, or maybe even, no longer believe prophecy. However, God still says that all will have to receive "the mark of beast" or they will not be able to sell or buy things, Rev 13:15-17. The world has seen many anti-christs (1 Jn 2:18) but **nothing of this magnitude** or that "overcomes" the church worldwide, or that suspends all ability to buy or sell without the worship of **one man**, has **ever** happened! So there is, literally, a great tribulation that is coming. This is a discussion of things which neither happened in the destruction of the temple in 70 AD, nor in the Roman persecutions of Christians in the following centuries. Such a period would be without parallel in the world, and that is what Jesus says it will be.

> "For in those days there will be tribulation, such as has not been since the beginning of the creation which God created until this time, nor ever shall be." Mark 13:19 NKJV

It seems that awful time in the future was foreshadowed by Jerusalem's destruction in 70 AD. But the 70 AD destruction it would seem is just a type of the terrible things yet to happen. Then after this special tribulation, there shall be signs in the heavens.

> [24] "But in those days, **after** that tribulation, the sun shall be darkened, and the moon shall not give her light, [25] And the stars of heaven shall fall, and the powers that are in heaven shall be shaken.
> Mk 13:24-25 KJV (*bold emphasis added*)

> [25] And **there shall be signs** in the sun, and in the moon, and in the stars; and upon the earth distress of nations, with perplexity; the sea and the waves roaring; [26] Men's hearts failing them for fear, and for looking after those things which are coming on the earth: for the powers of heaven shall be shaken. [27] And **then** shall they see the Son of man coming in a cloud with power and great glory.
> Lk 21:25-27 KJV (*bold emphasis added*)

But God will protect His faithful ones. Who or what can separate us from the love of Christ? Nothing according to Rom 8:35-37. Jesus will come to rescue His people.

But there is no "pre-tribulation" "rapture." The true saints of God will be here, to be tested and to be conquered, Rev 13:7. It is literally "the saints" who will be conquered, **not** the unbelievers. The unbeliever in contrast will just fold to the demands of this so-called "god." Jesus tells us to pray that we "may be accounted worthy to escape all these things that shall come to pass," Lk 21:36 KJV.

The concept of God's faithful being "caught up" to heaven is Scriptural, even though the word "rapture" is not really Biblical. It is a word associated with cultic theories of a failure of the kingdom God to come in the first century, and a "secret," "hidden," coming of Jesus before the end of time. But there is no secret, hidden, coming or "rapture." It will be a public event, and it will come soon—immediately after-this special time of trouble.

> [29] **Immediately after the tribulation** of those days shall the sun be darkened, and the moon shall not give her light, and the stars shall fall

from heaven, and the powers of the heavens shall be shaken: [30] And **then** shall appear the sign of the Son of man in heaven: and then shall all the tribes of the earth mourn, and they shall see the Son of man coming in the clouds of heaven with power and great glory.
Matt 24:29-30 KJV (*bold emphasis added*)

Then Jesus will gather His own, Mtt 24:31. You will not know the day or hour, but you will be able to see the day approaching, Heb 10:25. Jesus will come at the last trumpet according to 1 Cor 15:51-52, and 1 Thes 4:15-17. **Every** eye will see Him, Rev 1:7. There will be no secret or hidden coming. There is no second and then a third coming; but only a second coming, and it will not be secret or hidden. *Everyone* will see us rise to meet Jesus in the air! It is Jesus who rescues His people. Also it is not before tribulation ... it is after! Then a final time of trouble will come. Permanent trouble, or permanent glory and honor, Rom 2:7-11, in either heaven or hell. We are to be rejoicing in hope, patient in tribulation, continuing in prayer, Romans 12:12.

And many of them that sleep in the dust of the earth shall awake, some to everlasting life, and some to shame *and* everlasting contempt"
Dan 12:2 KJV

The only time to be saved is now. The only way to be saved is through Jesus. There is no mention of a second chance.

And what I say unto you I say unto all, Watch. Mk 13:37 KJV

It is foolish to believe in a special "rapture" that will never come, or not to watch and prepare for a tribulation that *must* happen *before* Jesus comes! Still Christians are just sheep for the slaughter. Much of the world takes Christianity to task for not being realistic about the world, but I am afraid to say that it is realistic in the extreme. It tells the Christians and the nations truthfully, that they are considered by the world system to be nothing more than sheep, something to be fleeced or slaughtered.

You see the sheep (and, yes, that often includes you and me) driving down the road, thinking and distracted, and maybe talking on the phone. Steven's wife has not announced it, but she has just cut him off. She thinks he deserves it. Steven would like to have someone but seemingly does not have access to his own. He has not talked to Connie, but he knows (or thinks he knows) that she would be willing, and it tugs at him. But what about ... the risk, our marriage, the kids ... me? Jesus? Mabel is telling Clois about Samantha loosing her job, and Cliff has just today tested positive for prostate cancer. Howard has just had another overdose and is in the hospital. Heather's talking to her friend. Her husband has just been caught ... again. The creep! The electric bill was really high this month, ... oh, that was my turn! They used to just wander around thinking about these things. Now they are driving around, talking on their cell phones, and the air waves are full of their problems.

All of this, of course, is much like the people of any country, any age, any century. For instance, this is just like the Jews of the first century, the ordinary Jews of the gospels. Again,

> Seeing the people, He felt compassion for them, because they were distressed and dispirited like sheep without a shepherd. Mtt 9:36 NASB

They need a Savior to deliver them. God decided to give them a Savior, even at the cost of the life of His Only Son. He came to save them, both from their own cares and their own stupidity, but even more than that ... from their very wrongs against Him! That is Love! Thank you LORD! Those who exploit and oppress them are in for big trouble ... forever! But the sheep still look very ... uh ... delectable ... uh ... vulnerable. What easy picking!

> As it is written, For thy sake we are killed all the day long; we are accounted as sheep for the slaughter. Rom 8:36 KJV

How were they treated in ancient times?

> They were stoned, they were sawn asunder, were tempted, were slain with the sword: they wandered about in sheepskins and goatskins; being destitute, afflicted, tormented; Heb 11:37 KJV

So in perspective, *all through history, the elect of God have been considered to be of NO value or worth, of no account ... expendable.* It says in the book of Revelation that the Great Prostitute is "drunk with the blood of the saints," Rev 17:6; as if she has literally been drinking the blood of Christians. Psalm 44, a song of instruction by the sons of Korah, first talks about God delivering His people. He gave them their land, pushing back their adversaries, and putting to shame those who hate God's followers. Then it speaks of God turning His hand against His people, and in this psalm it is not talking of the unfaithful. So the psalmist, like Jesus on the cross asks, why God has forsaken him? God causes them to run before their enemies, and then the psalmist says,

> You give us as sheep to be eaten
> And have scattered us among the nations. Psa 44:11 NASB

Sheep to be eaten, a flock to be scattered. The great whore drinks their blood and gets drunk with it! God, the psalmist says, has sold them out for almost nothing. Everyone makes fun of them. (Look, you can see it even in the movies, not just at the very last day, but also right now!)

> ¹² You sell Your people cheaply,
> And have not profited by their sale.
> ¹³ You make us a reproach to our neighbors,
> A scoffing and a derision to those around us.
> ¹⁴ You make us a byword among the nations,
> A laughingstock among the peoples.
> ¹⁵ All day long my dishonor is before me

And my humiliation has overwhelmed me, Psa 44:12-15 NASB

The innocent among God's people protest their faithfulness in the next part. They have not departed from the truth, though if you speak of ancient Israel here, it is plain that many did, and it was because of this that they were scattered. So it is also of future times of which the prophet Paul speaks. There will be plenty of apostasy and it will bring plenty of trouble on mankind. But also, in Rom 8:36 and Psalm 44, and other place, there is the cry of the faithful (few though they be, admittedly) in the midst of these troubles. Surely God will know if they were truly faithful.

> ¹⁹ Yet You have crushed us in a place of jackals
> And covered us with the shadow of death.
> ²⁰ If we had forgotten the name of our God
> Or extended our hands to a strange god,
> ²¹ Would not God find this out?
> For He knows the secrets of the heart. Psa 44:19-21 NASB

Instead, they have been faithful, yet in the words of Psa 44:22 they are considered only worth shooting.

> But for Your sake we are killed all day long;
> We are considered as sheep to be slaughtered. NASB

Even so, there is plenty of blame among us. Who can really say he is pure? Yes, even you of Jacob, too. We also have been much led astray. Those responsible for our welfare, the shepherds of government and the shepherds of the church, have led us astray.

> Woe to the shepherds who destroy and scatter the sheep of My pasture!" says the LORD. Jer. 23:1 NKJV

> My people hath been lost sheep: their shepherds have caused them to go astray, they have turned them away *on* the mountains: they have gone from mountain to hill, they have forgotten their restingplace. Jer. 50:6 KJV

Zechariah says the idols speak only of sin, and the fortune tellers of the people see false dreams and give the people empty comfort, so the people wander like sheep, Zech 10:2. They are consumed as in a slaughter house.

> You eat the fat and clothe yourselves with the wool; you slaughter the fatlings, *but* you do not feed the flock. Ezek 34:3 NKJV

When Zechariah himself speaks of the great false shepherd, the monster who pretends to shepherd the flock, he says that this beast will not care about the dying, or heal or help anyone, but instead he consumes everything, even tearing the hooves off sheep, Zech 13:7. Jesus warns us to beware.

> Beware of false prophets, which come to you in sheep's clothing, but inwardly they are ravening wolves Mtt 7:15 KJV

Thus it comes that we are deceived, and go astray.

> All we like sheep have gone astray; we have turned every one to his own way; and the LORD hath laid on him the iniquity of us all.
> Isa 53:6 KJV

And this One upon whom the LORD has laid the sin of us all, **He too is slaughtered like a sheep,** just as we have been and will be. He is our leader. He went before us, and showed us the way. Having a choice, but calmly submitting to the LORD'S will, He too suffers ... yes, even just like a sheep, like us.

> He was oppressed, and he was afflicted, yet he opened not his mouth: he is brought as a lamb to the slaughter, and as a sheep before her shearers is dumb, so he openeth not his mouth. Isa 53:7 KJV

This is, of course, Jesus. He is the Shepherd who gives His life for the sheep, Jn 10:11. He is the One who gave His life for us, by whose stripes we are healed. Peter follows up in some detail in chapters two through four in his first letter.

> Therefore, since Christ suffered for us in the flesh, arm yourselves also with the same mind, ... 1 Pe 4:1 NKJV

> But the end of all things is at hand; therefore be serious and watchful in your prayers. 1 Pe 4:7 NKJV

> [12] Beloved, do not think it strange concerning the fiery trial which is to try you, as though some strange thing happened to you; [13] but rejoice to the extent that you partake of Christ's sufferings, that when His glory is revealed, you may also be glad with exceeding joy.
> 1 Pe 4:12-13 NKJV

> For you were like sheep going astray, but have now returned to the Shepherd and Overseer of your souls. 1 Pet. 2:25 NKJV

In the end though, it will be the wicked who will truly and permanently perish be like sheep.

> [13] This is the way of those who are foolish,
> And of those after them who approve their words.   Selah.
> [14] **As sheep they are appointed for Sheol;**
> Death shall be their shepherd;
> And **the upright shall rule over them in the morning,**
> And their form shall be for Sheol to consume
> So that they have no habitation.
> [15] **But God will redeem my soul from the power of Sheol,**
> For He will receive me. Selah. Psa 49:13-15 NASB (*emphasis added*)

Once again this is what the Liberals detest and do not want to acknowledge: the Hebrew word Sheol is used of what is clearly Hell, unless you are blind.

What then can the righteous do? What is the proper reaction to these plots against the faithful? This is pictured in many different Scriptures from varying points of view. In many ways this is an overwhelming picture of what God will bring on sinful man, and what God will have His righteous ones endure for His glory and their glory. So how does one cope with this picture? If we are among those who have bowed their knee to God's One and Only Son, how do we have the courage to deal with such catastrophic events as will come upon mankind? The answer also is given in more than one place, including in some of the psalms of the Old Testament.

A good place to start is the perspective in Psalm 11. David felt the angst of these turmoils which surround us and sometimes overcome us and defeat us and cause us to defect. He gives the real answer, the answer to all Christians and all of history in this simple and profound psalm. In English it is an elegant 128 or 129 words in a mere seven verses. In Hebrew it is even more elegant: less than half that many words, yet giving the real answer to dealing with these things in its fullness.

In Psalm 11 disaster has already stricken the devout children of God. The foundations have already been destroyed according to verse 3. What does that mean? What are the foundations? They are the holy institutions which the Lord has founded for order in a sinful world. They might be listed in their order of creation. First comes the family as a bastion capable of producing righteous-ness.Then comes civil government (remember us talking about the covenant with Noah and his descendants?) as instruments to punish and suppress wickedness when it has gone too far. Finally there is the holy assembly of God's people, the church, to teach the ways of God to men, and to reconcile them to their Maker, and to be the pillar and the ground of truth.

In David's day, as in our day, they are often destroyed. The family is ruined, disrespect for its head is sometimes even encouraged, and its functions are usurped by a State which is ignoring its lawful functions. When the family "functions" it often concentrates on the things of men, not the things of God. And the State? The civil government? It is often subverted to private purposes, and it too has its lawful functions subverted. It is often turned to unlawful pur-poses along with its valid tasks. Such subversions of true function are often the very fabric of world history. In David's day it was personified in the kingship of Saul, who had stepped across his valid functions to take those of the priests of God and became politically afraid of decorated and celebrated war hero David ben Jesse. In David's time then the holy sword of God had been subverted to send armies in search of this war hero who scrupulously kept himself from real-ly being an enemy of the state. And what of the holy church of our Lord, which in that day was physical Israel and the temple services? There had been perva-sive neglect of true devotion to God, and the people of God willingly served in the pay of sin. The foundations were indeed in great part destroyed. Now the wicked were truly in power and aimed their arrows at the righteous.

> For look! The wicked bend their bow,
>> They make ready their arrow on the string,
>> That they may shoot secretly at the upright in heart.
> Psa 11:2 NKJV

If it is this way, then truly, "What can the righteous do?" Psa 11:3. David's adversaries are saying, "You'd better run boy! The wicked are in control, and aiming to kill you, and they have the armies of Israel at their disposal." Really? What can you do? David starts off with saying,

> In the LORD I put my trust;
>> How can you say to my soul,
>> "Flee as a bird to your mountain"? Psa. 11:1 NKJV

David is placing His trust in the Lord, depending on Him for protection. What more can you want? Are you also one of the unbelieving? If the Lord is the One protecting me, how can you say to me that I had better fly away like a bird to the mountains? Then he goes on to say that God is indeed in control, not David, not Saul, not the wicked among God's people. God is taking all of this in from heaven.

> [4] The LORD *is* in His holy temple; the LORD'S throne is in heaven;
> His eyes behold,
>> His eyelids test the sons of men.
> [5] The LORD tests the righteous,
>> But the wicked and the one who loves violence His soul hates.
> Psa 11:4-5 NKJV

What is there to fear? God is taking all of this into account. He is testing both the wicked and the righteous, and He hates violent men, the very kind of men idolized in many of our thrilling action movies. In the end God will make all things right. There is no need to fear. The Lord will redeem us. Final judgment and punishment will come. Yes, hell and fire and brimstone are even in Psalm 11.

> [6] Upon the wicked He will rain coals;
>> Fire and brimstone and a burning wind
>> Shall be the portion of their cup.
> [7] For the LORD *is* righteous, He loves righteousness;
>> His countenance beholds the upright. Psa 11:6-7 NKJV

Do not worry David says. God is in control, and fire and brimstone and a burning wind are the destiny of the wicked. But what if it is not just one nation, not just one people? What about when you have fled to the wilderness like David and all the nations have arisen against you. For these circumstances, God says that the He frustrates the nations, plural, according to Psalm 33.

Sing to the Lord it says in Psa 33:1, for praise is appropriate for the redeemed of God. Actually everything that man has and does should praise the

Lord, so it says to praise Him even with the lyre, with the harp, with the violin, with the trumpet, Psa 33:2. Of course, we should glorify Him with musical instruments. As Scripture says,

> For of him, and through him, and to him, *are* all things: to whom *be* glory for ever. Amen. Rom 11:36 KJV

All things are from Him and through Him and to Him; all things should praise Him. So of course, your chain saw and your bulldozer, are like your piano and bugle, and all of them should be used to glorify God also, but **not in the assembly** ... unless God so commands. All of our lives—even out of church, out of the assembly—all of our behavior and activities should glorify God, but not *all* of it is for our worship assemblies. It depends, of course, on what the LORD *commands* for our formal worship. Thus as it is written, we should sing to Him even a new song, and praise Him with all of our music, Psa 33:2-3. Why? Because He loves righteousness, and the earth is full of His kindness. For God *made* the world, Psa 33:6; all by the breath of His mouth, by His Word. Such means that we should fear Him, Psa 33:7-8. He has done awesome things and can even stack up water when it suits His purpose. It is not just a matter of work and making. God just speaks and it happens, Psa 33:9.

Then notice carefully, for God "nullifies the counsel of the nations," Psa 33:10 NASB. Now the nations have plans, many plans, which often go well beyond what God has commanded. But God frustrates those plans. A plan without God is a plan which only advances as far as God allows. Alexander the Great wanted to conquer all of the world. By God's grace he conquered much of it. But who stopped him? The Romans wanted to conquer all of the world. By God's grace they conquered much of the then occupied world. But who stopped them? Hitler wished to conquer much of the world. By God's grace he conquered much in the plan he had to preemptively employ. But who stopped him? The British tried to dominate the world, and many there thought of themselves as a new and better Rome, ruling by God's grace. They did come to rule about 25% of the earth, more than any other nation or king in history. They could truthfully say that the sun never set on the British Empire. Still, who set their limits, and who said to them, that they should go no further? The Russians more recently had their imperial ambitions and wanted to be the new Rome of the world. By God's grace they conquered much. But who stopped them? It does not do any good for evil men to plan against the true people of God.

> [9] "Be shattered, O you peoples, and be broken in pieces!
>> Give ear, all you from far countries.
>> Gird yourselves, but be broken in pieces;
>> Gird yourselves, but be broken in pieces.
> [10] Take counsel together, but it will come to nothing;
>> Speak the word, but it will not stand,
>> For God is with us." Isa 8:9-10 NKJV

The nations form their councils and assemble their men of understanding and insight, but it makes no difference. Most of their plans die with them, and the grave swallows their insight. God makes fools out of wise men and planners, turns their profound understanding into oatmeal mush, and yet confirms the words of His servants, Isa 44:25-26. But God's counsel stands forever, Psa 33:11; and His plans endure from generation to generation while men come and go like the flowers. Nations sink into their own pits, both our nation and other nations.

> [15] The heathen are sunk down in the pit that they made: in the net which they hid is their own foot taken. [16] The LORD is known by the judgment which he executeth: the wicked is snared in the work of his own hands. Higgaion Selah. Psa 9:15-16 KJV

How then can a nation be blessed? The blessing is on the nation that has the LORD as God, Psa 33:12. But that is not just *any* people who claim "the LORD is our God." Rather, it is the nation which God chooses, and that is the key: God does the choosing, not us. For us to be a part, we must please Him, satisfy Him, so that He would want to choose us. He looks from His dwelling place in heaven to see who will follow Him, Psa 33:13-14. What is this dwelling place in heaven? It is called Zion, Mount Zion, in other places, like Psa 48:1-2, and also in Psalm 11 as was pointed out. Physical Zion, even in the Old Testament, is only a type of the heavenly throne of God. The mount of assembly is in the far north, in heaven, according to Isa 14:13. At one time God looked from heaven and decided to destroy the earth with water according to Genesis 6. But now they are reserved for fire at a future date, 2 Pe 3:7-9. So how should we live but in holiness, 2 Pe 3:11-12.

Who saves a king? Who spares a nation? Not an army, and not strength and power. A horse or a tank or stealth fighter will not deliver, Psa 33:16-17. As David said when he met Goliath,

> [45] ... "You come to me with a sword, with a spear, and with a javelin. But I come to you in the name of the LORD of hosts, the God of the armies of Israel, whom you have defied. ... [47] Then all this assembly shall know that the LORD does not save with sword and spear; for the battle is the LORD'S, and He will give you into our hands."
> 1 Sam 17:45, 47 NKJV

The eye of the Lord is on those who fear Him, to keep them from death, Psa 33:18-19. Living in the fear of the Lord has an important place in Scripture. It is the beginning of wisdom, Prov 1:5-7. We need to just be patient and wait on Him, Psa 33:19-20. We hope in you, the psalmist says.

> Let thy mercy O LORD, be upon us, according as we hope in thee.
> Psa 33:22 KJV

We should not fear the uproar of the nations. God will care for us. We are looking for another world, a new heavens and a new earth, 2 Pe 3:13.

Victory Over Christianity: Gog, Magog

As has been repeatedly pointed out, just before the end of time, Satan will be released from his "prison" for a "short time," Rev 20:3. Also it has been noted, there will be a tremendous demonic release at this time, which is most vividly described in Revelation 9. Affliction will they bring, oh my goodness yes, but especially to the unsaved! Still they will work to a purpose. So what is this grand purpose? That the kings of the earth would work together to fight against God in "the great day of God."

> [13] And I saw three unclean spirits like frogs *come* out of the mouth of the dragon, and out of the mouth of the beast, and out of the mouth of the false prophet. [14] For they are the spirits of devils, working miracles, *which* go forth unto the kings of the earth and of the whole world, to gather them to the battle of that great day of God Almighty.
> Rev 16:13-14 KJV

These signs they perform are the fabric of the strong delusions and lies that will deceive the world according to 2 Thessalonians chapter two, and they prepare men to actually fight God in His coming. In Revelation 20 it describes it in similar form. In Rev 20:7 and 8 it says that Satan is released from his prison to deceive the nations of the world, and, just as in Revelation 16, to gather them for war. The armies gathered are, to all intents and purposes, numberless. They are like the sands of the seashore. And what is their purpose? They "surrounded the camp of the saints and the beloved city," Rev 20:9 NKJV. I really think it is talking about a dual subject. It should be remembered that these things will occur very close to the end, long after the mass conversion of the Jews to Jesus the Christ. So Gog and Magog are attempting to destroy "the beloved city," which if taken literally is physical Jerusalem ("the holy city," Mtt 27:53) and if taken metaphorically would be the church (" the city of the living God, the heavenly Jerusalem, ... the general assembly and church of the firstborn ..." Heb 12:22-23 NKJV). Also they are trying to surround "the camp of saints." This would clearly include those vile goyim converts to Jesus in Corinth, to whom Paul is writing as,

> Unto the church of God which is at Corinth, to them that are sanctified in Christ Jesus, called to be saints, ... 1 Cor 1:2 KJV

You may or may not take Rev 20:9 as *also* applying to literal Jerusalem (I am inclined to do so, but will not be dogmatic), and you may or may not be able to substantiate your position with other Scriptures (more about this later), but that part of the objective of Gog and Magog is to wipe out the church of our Lord should be without contest. This is not just a Jewish thing which is being discussed, *although the Jews at this time* ***will be*** *the leading lights in Christianity*. Rather this a Christian thing, a Jesus of Nazareth thing. As with all types, any types yet to come of these days, will fall short of the final description.

Then a couple of national names are given: Gog and Magog. Magog is an early historical figure in the book of Genesis. The sons of Noah were Shem, Ham and Japheth. The descendants of Shem are the Semites, and although this term is mainly used in the linguistic sense, they include the Hebrews, the Arabs, the Syrians, etc., (but not the Persians/Iranians who are Japhethites like most of us in the world). Ham is generally associated with the black peoples, but it includes Cush, and Mizraim (Egypt, and in fact this is what modern Israelis calls Egypt) and Put and Canaan, Gen 10:6. Most of the Caucasian people (as one might call them) come from the descendants of Japheth. It says of these peoples,

> From these the coastlands of the nations were separated into their lands, every one according to his language, according to their families, into their nations. Gen 10:5 NASB

So who are the first sons of Japheth that are mentioned? "Gomer and Magog ..." Gen 10:2. These are the people who settled the coastlands of the nations. Who were they? Where did they settle, of what peoples does the prophet speak? The old German commentary of Keil and Delitzsch gives an idea of the range of thinking on these things:

> Gomer is most probably the tribe of the Cimmerians, who dwelt, according to **Herodotus**, on the Maeotis, in the Taurian Chersonesus, and from whom are descended the Cumri or Cymry in **Wales** and **Brittany**, whose relation to the **Germanic** Cimbri is still in obscurity. Keil and Delitzsch (K & D in the notes which follow), *Commentary on the Old Testament, Vol. 1*, pg 162-163, Erdmans, Grand Rapids, 1986 (*emphasis added*)

Most scholars associate Magog with the origins of the Scythian peoples who inhabited the Caucasus region, and one of the ancestral lines of the modern Russian people. Keil and Delitzsch say,

> Magog is connected by Josephus with the Scythians on the Sea of Asof and in the Caucasus; but Kiepert associates the name with Macija or Maka, and applies it to Scythian nomad tribes which forced themselves in between the Arian or Arianized Medes, Kurds, and Armenians. (*Ibid*, pg 163)

It should be emphasized that the revolution against God, to actively fight against Him, involves *all* the nations of the world (including by inference even the unfaithful among God's own people), but that Gog and Magog are prominently mentioned as if they are the leaders of the nations in these things. Meshech and Tubal are also prominently mentioned in Ezekiel concerning these things, and K & D say,

> Tubal and Meshech are undoubtedly the Tibareni and Moschi, the former of whom are placed by **Herodotus** upon the east of the Ther-

modon, the latter between the sources of the Phasis and Cyrus. Tiras: according to **Josephus**, the **Thracians**, whom **Herodotus** calls the most numerous tribe next to the **Indian**. As they are here placed by the side of Meshech, so we also find **on the old Egyptian monuments** Mashuash and Tuirash, and upon the Assyrian Tubal and Misek (Rawlinson). (*Ibid*, pg 163) (*emphasis added*)

Once again notice what a broad range of modern peoples are thought to have come from these roots. Obviously, some ancient people knew more of these things than we do, but also obviously, archaeological research can be expected to give more update to our current information. K & D is adequate for the purposes here, and should be easy enough for the reader to find. References such as are seen here in Scripture are also included in the genealogies of the Bible books of Chronicles.

Then comes to the majestic picture of the conflict as given by the prophet Ezekiel. God tells Ezekiel in Ezek 38:1 to set his face against "Gog" of the land of "Magog." It calls "Gog" a leader of Rosh, Meshech and Tubal, and God instructs Ezekiel to prophesy against them. Compare Meshech and Tubal, already mentioned. K & D also make mention of Rosh,

> The Byzantine and Arabic writers frequently mention a people called Ῥῶς, Arab. Rûs, dwelling in the country of the Taurus, and reckoned among the Scythian tribes. K &D, *Vol 9*, pg 159

There is more to say from K & D but this will do. Then God says that Gog is the prince, the leader. God says He will put a hook in his jaws as you might hook a great fish, and God says He will turn him around with all his fine army. Notice another indicator of the breadth of the coalition against God. It includes Persia, Ethiopia, Put, and Gomer, Ezek 38:5-6. The indications from every side are that this is a very broad coalition.

God Himself then gives some advice to Gog and Magog: prepare yourselves and all your troops, and be on the alert; and after a long time, in the latter days, you will be called out to invade the "land" that is restored from war, Ezek 38:7-8. "Land"? What land? As has been discussed, *erets* אֶרֶץ, can refer either to a land or nation, or even all the earth as such. It does speak of Israel in many verses of this passage. I must acknowledge that it may be speaking of "Israel" metaphorically, as in Gal 6:16, Rom 2:28-29, etc., but indeed that is not the way it seems. Still there are other indications. It does seemingly speak of what someone might call a "camp," a "land of unwalled villages," Ezek 38:11. That might fit the pilgrims of the LORD regardless of nationality all over the world. And of the nations in Christ, the Word of God is emphatic that,

> [19] Now, therefore, you are no longer strangers and foreigners, but fellow citizens with the saints and members of the household of God, [20] having been built on the foundation of the apostles and prophets, Jesus Christ Himself being the chief corner*stone*, Eph 2:19-20 NKJV

So the nations in Christ are full "fellow citizens" with physical Israel. Now obviously in Ezekiel chapters 38 and 39, a "land of unwalled villages," does not apply to Israel of ancient times, in which often even most small villages were fortified at least to some extent. It could not even be stretched to include Jewish Palestine of the first century AD, but it might be said to fit a modern spiritual Israel of Christians as a "camp of the saints." Then notice Ezek 38:13.

> ' " 'Sheba, Dedan, the merchants of Tarshish, and all their young lions will say to you, "Have you come to take plunder? Have you gathered your army to take booty, to carry away silver and gold, to take away livestock and goods, to take great plunder?' " ' NKJV

So these armies which are invading the earth/land, from the north according to verse 15, arrive at Sheba, Dedan (which seems to refer to Persian Gulf communities), and Tarshish (Spain); and when they arrive there, the people are asking them, what are you here for? Plunder? Robbery? So at the very least this does indeed seem to be a world-wide phenomenon of armies coming against what God calls "My people," in verse 16. These armies seem to come to the complete surprise of God's people who are living at peace, and they will cover the "land" "like a cloud." It appears to be talking about strategic surprise of the highest order; not against worldly armies, but, seemingly, against peoples, against a religion, against the holy religion of the Most High God, "in the last days," Ezek 38:16.

I would say that this is clearly a part of the "uproar of the nations," discussed in the last section. *Is Gog another symbolic name for the beast?* Much of the text would fit this identification. God says,

> ... "Are *you* he of whom I have spoken in former days by My servants the prophets of Israel, who prophesied for years in those days that I would bring you against them?" Ezek 38:17 NKJV

In other words, God says He has spoken elsewhere through His prophets of this particular man. That alone would put Gog on a very short list. *If* he is to be identified with **the beast**, then the description in Revelation 13:7 fits: "it was given unto him to make war with the saints, and to overcome them ..." KJV. That could be easily implied from Ezekiel 38 and 39. Only God's intervention delivers Israel in Ezekiel chapters 38 and 39.

Of the enemies who attempt to wipe out God's people, God says He will shake the face of the earth because of them; and if the armies are all over the earth pursuing God's people, it would seem to imply a shaking of all the earth.

> " 'so that **the fish of the sea**, the birds of the heavens, the beasts of the field, all creeping things that creep on the earth, and all men who are on the face of the earth shall shake at My presence. **The mountains shall be thrown down**, the steep places shall fall, and <u>every</u> **wall shall fall to the ground**.' " Ezek 38:20 NKJV (*emphasis added*)

God goes on to say that He will call a sword against the earth, and that all of His enemies (seeing Him coming, it seems to imply), start fighting each other rather than follow foolish leaders who try to fight against God.

In general terms, the preambles of Ezekiel 39 are the same as in chapter 38. God is going to send Gog against the mountains of Israel. And what is the reason? It has already been discussed some of what may be the factors. Gog and his armies, it says, will "fall on the mountains of Israel." Of the leader personally God says He will knock Gog's bow out of his left hand and his arrows out of his right hand. Does this imply personal leadership and involvement of Gog in the fighting? Perhaps. Perhaps this also is talking about when the beast receives his "fatal" wound. At any rate, the armies will fall and will provide a great supper for the birds of the air, a fact attested to in more than one account of this great battle.

> [17] Then I saw an angel standing in the sun, and he cried out with a loud voice, saying to all the birds which fly in midheaven, "Come, assemble for the great supper of God, [18] so that you may eat the flesh of kings and the flesh of commanders and the flesh of mighty men and the flesh of horses and of those who sit on them and the flesh of all men, both free men and slaves, and small and great." Rev 19:17-18

Ezekiel says about the same thing.

> [17] ... "Speak to every sort of bird and to every beast of the field:
> 'Assemble yourselves and come;
> Gather together from all sides to My sacrificial meal
> Which I am sacrificing for you,
> A great sacrificial meal on the mountains of Israel,
> That you may eat flesh and drink blood.
> [18]   You shall eat the flesh of the mighty,
> Drink the blood of the princes of the earth,
> Of rams and lambs,
> Of goats and bulls,
> All of them fatlings of Bashan.
> [19]   You shall eat fat till you are full,
> And drink blood till you are drunk,
> At My sacrificial meal
> Which I am sacrificing for you.
> [20] You shall be filled at My table
> With horses and riders,
> With mighty men
> And with all the men of war," says the LORD GOD.
> Ezek 39:17-20 NKJV

The parallels are so striking as not to be coincidental. Then, it says the nations will know for sure that the LORD is God. First, let us notice that these two chapters of prophecy in Ezekiel, of the enemies of God working all over the earth to destroy all of God's people, attacking what is implied to be a peaceful people in unwalled villages, **has not happened in ANY way!** No such invasion has happened in ancient or modern history that really fits these chapters.

And there is a curious thing in Ezekiel 39. It seems almost to be a contradiction. On one hand, it speaks as if the birds and animals consume the dead, and it coincides with the final battle against God pictured in the last chapters of the book of Revelation. On the other hand, it seems to speak as if the dead are given a burial (though it takes a long time) and that this great battle happens **within** history, not at the end of history. For sure there are many battles, even some huge ones, within history. For sure there is a super battle against God at the end of history when the beast and the false prophet are thrown alive into hell, Rev 19:17-21. So where does Ezekiel fit? And there are other indicators.

> 22 ' "So the house of Israel shall know that I *am* the LORD their God their God from that day forward. 23 The Gentiles shall know that the house of Israel went into captivity for their iniquity; because they were unfaithful to Me, therefore I hid My face from them. I gave them into the hand of their enemies, and they all fell by the sword." '
> Ezek 39:22-23 NKJV

Does this, starting actually with verse 25, apply to only the first grand punishment of Israel that is portrayed in the Old Testament, that Ezekiel himself was a part of, or does it apply to the prophecy that Ezekiel has just finished in chapters 38 and 39, **or does it apply to both?** And if this part applies to 38 and 39, is it talking of some invasion **within history but which has not happened yet?** Or is it at the end of history, **or both?** *(In other words, is a type which hasn't happened yet involved, which will bear a resemblance to the day of battle at the last day?)* If there is a type yet to come it may well be the conversion of the Jews to Jesus of Nazareth which will come in their great time of stress (Deut 4:30, Romans 11, and all the other verses), and which will then be another type of the end of the world.

Notice that *the prophecy almost seems to point in both directions!* Surely "every wall" falling, all men being affected, and the mountains falling, would only seem to apply to the end of the world as we know it, as in,

> And the heaven departed as a scroll when it is rolled together; and every mountain and island were moved out of their places. Rev 6:14 KJV

Also Gog and Magog in Revelation 20 point all of this to the end, and it is followed in Revelation 20 with the final judgment of God.

My conclusion is that Ezekiel 38 and 39 applies literally to final battle against God, and the final suppression of Christianity, which occurs just before God intervenes at the end of history; and it applies symbolically to the great period of stress in which the Jews repent and turn to Jesus the Christ, which also is yet to happen.

Do all "end things,"
really just start
at the end?

Lab Work

What does all of this
mean to me?

False Christs and a Time to Flee

There will be false Christs who will appear, according to Mtt 24:23-24. It clearly indicates *multiple* false Christs. I can only laugh at some commentators. They speak as if, when there have been many failed attempts, then that means that there is no such thing as a real "false christ." Many of these false christs will be so effective as to even deceive God's chosen, if that were possible. Notice that you cannot fool those whom God has chosen. That is impossible. If anyone tells you, he is in here, or out there, or in the next room, Mtt 24:26, do not believe it.

The kingdom already exists, as has been shown, Col 1:13-14. It was established during the first century as prophesied by God's holy prophets. Christ will not come to earth to rule here. He rules from heaven even now, and does not need an earthly throne to do *whatever* He wants with *whoever* He wants, *remember?* We will rise to meet him *in the air,* 1 Thes 4:17-18. There will be no Christ here on earth at the end to start a new order *here.* There will be no earthly kingdom established at the end. The kingdom will be handed over to God, 1 Cor 15:21-24. *Did you remember?*

If you look you can see that this all seems to be in the context of false christs, and that Christ tells us that He will come like a flash of light, Mtt 24:27.

There is no "secret" Second Coming of Jesus Christ. If someone says "he is here" or "he is there" or "he is inside," it is a lie, Mtt 24:26.

> ¹⁴ Then the LORD will be seen over them,
> And His arrow will go forth like lightning.
> The Lord GOD will blow the trumpet,
> And go with whirlwinds from the south.
> ¹⁵ The LORD of hosts will defend them;
> They shall devour and subdue with slingstones.
> They shall drink and roar as if with wine;
> They shall be filled with blood like basins,
> Like the corners of the altar. Zech 9:14-15 NKJV

What have been the popular theories about the Man of Lawlessness?

He has been thought to be:	Popular With
1. A Roman Emperor (Nero, Caligula, Domitian, or some other Emperor.) A <u>past</u> event !	Many, perhaps most, modern scholars
2. The Pope	Most early Protestants
3. Some other man in history (Mohammed, Napoleon, Hitler, etc.)	Various
4. A Hebrew Pseudo-Messiah	Various
5. Some man (unidentified) who appears at the end of time.	Most Christians up to the Middle Ages

But "Wherever the corpse is, there the vultures will gather," Mtt 24:28 ESV. The corpse, the body, seems to refer to the resurrected body of the beast. Jesus will come publicly, in the heavens, but multiple false christs will come, and it seems to compare the false christs and the abomination to a dead body, a carcass. Remember, that a dead body, a carcass, is an abomination. You should read once again Revelation 13 in this regard, because *maybe, just **maybe**,* the abomination will be a dead body, the dead body of the future 'king of the North'. Once again, Scripture seems to speak of the beast after he is killed during his coming, and as if he both really *is* resurrected and as if he really *is not.*

If the beast is "like" Antiochus Epiphanes, then (not necessarily in order):

1   He will make war on 'the king of the South' (Egypt?)
2   He will make war on God's people, and many will fall with no help at hand, Dan 11:33-34.
3.   He will be successful against God's people, in part because of 'rebellion'/'transgression'. What could be called traitors among God's people help him, Dan 8:12, 13, Dan 11:32, 34.
4.   He will personally enter the "holy place" of God, and rob God's "temple". He will desecrate the "temple" of God, *ruin it,* and make it unfit for worship. It implies that he will set up an "idol" or "image" that desecrates in the Holy Place, Dan 11:31, Mtt 24:15, 2 Thes 2:4.

This image being put in place seems to be a signal for the start of a time of great stress, Mtt 24:15-22.

If the beast is like the unfulfilled prophecies of Antiochus Epiphanes, then:

1.   He will be successful at everything he does, Dan 11:36.
2.   He will conquer the "king of the South" (Egypt?), Dan 11:40, 42
3.   He will make war on God's people, and 'destroy' them Dan 8:24, break their power, Dan 12:7. Compare Rev 13:7.
    Clearly implied is that *most* of God's people will abandon the faith.
4.   He will exalt *himself* against everything that is called God or that is worshipped, Dan 11:36.
    (Compare the "man of lawlessness" in 2 Thes 2:4.)
5.   Implied is that he dies by no human hand Dan 8:25, near Jerusalem, Dan 11:45

If you want to put many of the popular interpretations of the Man of Lawlessness of 2 Thessalonians 2 into a chart, see the previous page.

Notice that 3 through 5 could be combined. Also note that without some big changes, number 2 is not plausible, although it looked very credible at one time, and I admit I have really done no analysis of the Popes in this book.

A good place to start on these things might be to list some of the characteristics of the man of lawlessness, and then see how various candidates stack up. See the chart at the top of the next page.

My friends, we need to be careful or we can be caught up in these things **at**

A Partial Check List on the Man of Lawlessness, 2 Thessalonians 2			
2 Thessalonians 2	**A Roman Emperor**	**A Pope**	**Others?**
Preceded and accompanied by rebellion, vs. 3	**NO**	YES	?
Sets himself up in God's temple as God, vs. 4	NO, though Caligula wanted to	(Yes? Or No? Qualifiedly so, depending on how you are quoting and interpreting many things)	?
Demands Exclusive worship as God, vs. 4	NO, absolutely not!	NO, absolutely not!	?
Accompanied by counterfeit signs and wonders, vs. 9	YES	YES	?
Deceives <u>all</u> except the few faithful, vs. 11-12	**NO!**	**NO!**	No one to date
Personally destroyed by Jesus' Second Coming, vs. 8	NO, absolutely not!	NO	?

almost any point in history. It clearly indicates that sin and rebellion by many of God's people seems to precede this, and this is what other prophecies indicate, for instance 2 Tim 4:3. It will literally be terrible times, 2 Tim 3:1ff.

It is proper for to observe a couple of things. First that there have been waves of messianic expectations (and anti-christ expectations) throughout New Testament times, even to our own day. If you really take a balanced view and study in detail past times and the forces at work, it can truly be said that these have really been continuous, with many men looking like bits and pieces of these prophecies (but not the whole), from the times of the Caesars to our own day. All along men have tended to look at the collapse of their own country/order-/civilization, or at other men who bore many marks of the lawless one, and have wondered whether this was the start of that great period of lawlessness predicted for just before the end. I would say that many of these were looking at mere "trumpets" of warning as in the vision in Revelation chapters eight and nine, NOT one of the "last plagues."

> And I saw another sign in heaven, great and marvellous, seven angels having the seven last plagues; for in them is filled up the wrath of God. Rev 15:1 KJV

Also clearly there have been certain periods of time when expectations were very high (perhaps rightfully so). One such period was toward the end of the first century; another was at the collapse of the Roman Empire (or "collapses" perhaps should be said, for Gibbon's *Decline and Fall of the Roman Empire* goes all the way to the 1500's AD)! No, Rome did not fall in a day as Babylon the Great will, but it was still something to watch closely. Another period was around 1,000 AD when many thought the Lord would come imminently. Expectations where high in the centuries leading up to the Renaissance. The occult has always thought of the triumph of Christianity as "the dark ages," and thought they were in some sort of "Middle Ages" which would lead to a New Age, a new occult age here on earth. The later Middle Ages were full of plagues and catastrophes that seemed indeed like the trumpets of judgment and war spoken of in the book of Revelation; and many were looking for the next shoe to drop, the next event to possibly confirm the nearness of the end. Many of the events of those days did indeed match much of prophecy, but there were loose ends here and there, no true world-wide rule, no anti-christ or beast that was quite big enough to fit the picture in the book of Revelation. And again, expectations were high from the mid-twentieth century. Many things seemed close, but nothing panned out.

So make sure you notice that the Biblical picture of the man lawlessness, the beast, is not an everyday portrait of an everyday politician or ruler, not even of a particularly bad or mean one. You can read of continual identifications through history, and new identifications are proposed all along, but this evil man himself is not an everyday person, but is in fact very extraordinary. It might should be asked,

Will the Real Christ, or Real Beast, Please Stand Up?

There are many who would like to be savior of the people, savior of the world, and their motives range from the well-meaning to the diabolical. There are even trails of types down through history, of both good men and bad, many of them never commented on in Scripture. Take the case of Joseph son of Jacob. It would be hard to find a more perfect type of the Messiah than Joseph. First of all Joseph was, like Jesus, the favored son of his father. All of the brothers knew this, and hated Joseph for it, and could not even talk to this "fair-haired boy" (to use modern slang) in civil terms, Gen 37:4. Both Jesus and Joseph were so hated by the brothers they were sent to save, that their brothers sought to kill them ... but in both cases failed.

So this favored son Joseph was committed to the pit to die forever and to end this intolerable favoritism. Joseph was placed in a literal pit in Canaan before the brothers changed their minds and sold him as a slave to rid themselves of him. So also Jesus was committed to the pit of the abyss, Rom 10:6-7; but neither could remain there. Joseph was "rescued" to a far land to in effect receive a kingdom, the position of second in command in Egypt. Similarly Jesus went to the far off land of heaven to receive a kingdom (Lk 19:12), and to be in effect the second in command to His Father.

Then the Son of their Father whom they had rejected became their ruler, and delivered them from famine and death. Jesus as has been shown, will yet deliver them from sin. As the sons of Israel face Joseph in Egypt, Joseph leads Judah to repentance and some very basic changes. You can read of these things in Genesis 43 and 44.

Joseph then at last had a revealing of Himself to his brothers, as also Jesus finally will have a revealing, as was shown. And at the last Joseph nurtured his brothers into a mighty nation in the Egypt of this world, before they entered the promised land. Similarly, Jesus (as has been shown from prophecy) will nurture His holy people into a mighty nation before they enter the ultimate promised land: Heaven.

But for all these parallels (and there are more than what have been recounted here), almost strangely, Joseph is never commented on in Scripture as a "type" or "shadow" of the Christ. I think perhaps God was trying to point out to us, through so obvious an example, that there are more things to learn from Scripture than all of what has been pointed out and commented on. So there are many types, many shall we say "prototypes" of the "ultimates," before the "ultimates" come. Even of the real beast!

Sometimes it is bewildering to have so many that fit parts of prophecy! And when you add in the pre-millennial idea of Jesus' coming back to this present earth to physically rule from physical Jerusalem for a thousand years (literally), then you have plenty of room for confusion. Nero, Domitian, Hitler, Stalin, Mussolini, Saddam Hussein, all have been seriously proposed as "the beast" of Revelation. Mussolini consciously tried to revive the ancient Roman Empire, and Saddam Hussein consciously tried to revive ancient Babylon. The occult has continuously put forward new candidates since ancient times. The Seed of the woman and the seed of Satan have had and will have an age long enmity, Gen 3:15, as has pointed out from the first. Additionally, the mystery of lawlessness has already been at work since at least the first century, 2 Thes 2:7, and quite likely centuries before the gospel first came.

The "beast" in Scripture is also about claiming the throne rightfully belonging to Christ.

It is a big claim to say that you have the throne of Jesus Christ. He was to be born as a child, to rule over the house of David and his kingdom. "... his name shall be called Wonderful, Counsellor, **The mighty God, The everlasting Father**, The Prince of Peace. Of the increase of his government and peace there shall be no end," Isa 9:6-7 KJV (*emphasis added*). There is to be "no end" to His reign! It is amazing how many of the prophets reflected Christ, but of course they were all moved by one Spirit, 2 Pe 1:21.

When Isaiah speaks of John the Baptist preparing the way for Jesus, he says they are preparing the way for "the LORD," Isa 40:3-5, and when He comes they say, "Behold your God," Isa 40:9. Psalm 72:8 says He will "have dominion also from sea to sea, and from the river unto the **ends of the earth**," KJV (*emphasis added*), but Rev 3:21 indicates Jesus is **now** sitting on His Father's throne **in heaven**! So to claim the throne of Christ is to claim the throne of everything, rule of the entire universe.

> *There have been and are and will be many false christs,*
> *and many "would be" "gods"*
> *who would claim divinity or something near it.*

Jesus said that **many** will come in His name, Mtt 24:5. He goes on to say that "if any man shall say unto you, Lo, here *is* Christ, or there; believe *it* not," Mtt 24:23 KJV, but take note, *this assumes Jesus will never again be on earth!* John tells us that anyone denying Jesus is the Christ is <u>*an*</u> anti-christ and also speaks of <u>*the*</u> anti-christ (singular) that is coming, 1 Jn 4:3.

We are clearly told that when Christ comes every eye will see Him, even those who pierced Him, Rev 1:7; and that far from establishing an earthly kingdom, at the end He delivers up the kingdom to the Father, 1 Cor 15:24. We will rise to meet Jesus <u>in the air,</u> "and so shall we ever be with the Lord," 1 Thes 4:17 KJV.

> *This struggle goes back to early Gnostic Heresies.*

Before the first century was over, the occult (what many today would call "the New Age") was infiltrating the church, trying to deny Jesus and His claims, and putting themselves up as prophets and "gods." Especially the gospel of John, the letters of John, and Paul's letters of Colossians, Ephesians, and first and second Timothy were written to refute their claims. These are the books to go to for refuting the key doctrines of witchcraft and magic. The occult hates these books and tries to destroy confidence in these books and their authors.

> *Then the "grail lore" came along somewhere*
> *in these false claims.*

The grail is supposedly the cup out of which Jesus drank at the Lord's supper. It is supposed to have caught His blood while He was on the cross, and the occultist claim it has extraordinary magic powers. Despite the clear testimonies of the eye witnesses in the gospels, they claim Jesus did not die at the cross. They claim He escaped to France, married Mary Magdalene, and had a family.

A bronze of Charlemagne from his time. Pehaps an authentic image.

The old French king Charlemagne, for

instance, and many of his descendants (the Carolingian line) have been quietly claiming to be descendants of Jesus Christ for well over a thousand years, as did the Merovingian kings; and most of European royalty are descendants of these lines of kings. The King Arthur myths are about this, as is the book *Holy Blood, Holy Grail*, and *The Da Vinci Code*, and many novels and movies. The Templars and the Crusades are in part about this. The occult Thule Society which helped spawn Adolph Hitler was into grail lore. Those who promote "grail lore," are both extensive and influential. (See for instance the articles in the *Dictionary of Gnosis and Western Esotericism*, published by Brill, "under the auspices of the Chair of Hermetic Philosophy ... University of Amsterdam.") C. S. Lewis' religious propaganda group "The Inklings" was involved in grail lore, and Lewis ties his trio of religious novels called "The Space Trilogy," into Druidism and grail lore. The Catholic church has rightly said these claims are opposed to Christianity, but some in the Catholic church (like for instance, Bernard of Clairvaux), were apparently involved. The grail lore implicitly treats Jesus as one god among many, as a god who can be accompanied or even surpassed by other "gods." It is nothing like New Testament Christianity. It is really part of the occult rejection of Jesus Christ and His claims as the "one and only" Son of God, Jn 3:16 NIV. It is a bizarre mixture of occult fantasy, occult forgeries, and just plain buffoonery. As Napoleon once said, "It is amazing what people will believe as long as it is not in the Bible." King Arthur of old, and the Roundtable and the grail lore are everywhere in our society.

Charlemagnes's crown, Vienna.

First let me say clearly that I do not think I have any particular Biblical reason for concentrating on the Carolingian line or those of other kings who have made at times some outrageous claims. Nor do I have any reason for supposing that all who are of these lines have made such claims. These families, like most families, have had their share of rascals, and I am sure they have had their share of good men of courage and ability and true faith in Jesus Christ. Still, such claims as are being discussed here have been present at times, and some of these people make a good public laboratory for testing ideas about prophecy and how many of these claims stack up to prophecy. They make a good place to practice what has been learned. They can make another good Prophecy Laboratory.

Shades of these claims and the behind the scenes struggles can be seen many places in history. Most of these attempts are unknown to the public, and many of them are even unknown to *history*, with the principals ignominiously perishing. *All* of these attempts have to date failed at complete success, and *most* have been very dismal failures. Many of the most foolish attempts are openly satirized *even by the occult*, but the most dangerous of these attempts are often from sources most would consider "respectable."

For instance, there is an extensive story behind the Holy Roman Emperor Frederick II (1194-1250), a member of one of those families claiming descent from Jesus Christ by Mary Magdalene. His dad was the Emperor Frederick I Barbarossa. Although he is not well-known in America, he was in many respects larger than life. Many picture him as "the first modern man" to rule, the pioneer of the modern state, and an enlightened despot before such was fashionable in Europe, and a rationalist, and a forerunner of the Renaissance. He was one of the first European kings to openly defy the Catholic church and excommunication. Historian Will Durant in his book *The Age of Faith*, says "this Frederick was his own Voltaire," pg 719. (But it must asked, what faith is this? For sure it is not that of Jesus of Nazareth!) He was such a controversial ruler that few will agree with all of these assessments, and there is still much to debate about him. Even so he was clearly a brilliant ruler. He was expert on falconry, and wrote a text on the subject. He had an array of language skills which were impressive by any standard, with varying levels of skill in Arabic, Greek, Latin, French, Sicilian and some German. He was a skeptic before skepticism was popular but publicly maintained an attitude of orthodoxy. He was an urbane sophisticate who could communicate and negotiate beyond the religious barriers of his time. Far after the Caesars and far ahead of his time, he tried to free government from rule by the Catholic church and to make himself the first of a long line of god-kings. Further, except for the opposition of the Catholic church he might have succeeded, and have been the start of a "millennium," and a "thousand year Reich" in 1228 AD!

Also these were times of great expectations. The Apocalypse and the time of the end was in the air in those days as much as in the mid 20th century. In Frederick II many expectations of the end and of the Christ and of the antichrist all seemed to come together. Peter of Eboli said of the babe Frederick, "this child in every way will be blessed," and reinterpreted parts of Virgil's "prophecy" as referring to Frederick. Many of the histories of this period are "quaint" by many modern standards. A bastard gets the polite term of "natural son," and many of the real issues between the church and Frederick are scarcely mentioned, or are dealt with only if they cannot be avoided. Sometimes you can see the historians writing as if "gosh, we don't know what this is all about," when obviously they do but at times do not want to lay out the issues plainly.

Frederick came to the throne in turbulent times, and continued the battle between the secular powers and the papacy. He both benefited and suffered from the papacy's "balance of powers" strategies for political survival in Medieval Italy. The papacy would often back the under-dog in the political struggles of the times but would later oppose them if they became a dominant power, always fearing the papacy would be eclipsed if any secular power became dominant in Italy. Pope Innocent III was his guardian as a boy, and Pope Honorius III crowned him Holy Roman Emperor.

Being raised in part in Sicily, he was subject to influences from Christianity, Judaism, and Mohammedism. Durant makes a point of saying that he gained "some of the lore of the Jews" (*The Age of Faith*, pg 715). He had among other things, also studied the occult, and Durant says he was led "To the replacement of the Bible with the classics, of faith with reason, of God with Nature, of Providence with Necessity ..." pg 724.

A man by the name of Michael Scot was an advisor to Freddy. Scot was an alchemist, a magician, a necromancer (one who speaks to the dead), and an astrologer at times to Frederick and Popes Honorius III, and Gregory IX. (Check out Deut 18:10-11 on these things.) According to Abulafia's biography of Frederick II, Frederick was "under the intellectual spell of the Scot." pg 263. Frederick was in his own times believed by many to be the anti-christ. Frederick had many things going for him from the occult perspective. He possessed "the holy lance." This was what later some have called the spear of destiny, the spear that supposedly pierced side of Christ on the cross. This spear became a symbol of legitimacy, especially in the West. Scientific testing estimates the spear's origin as early as the seventh century AD. There are some indications that the spear's origins are truly pagan, that is that it was originally supposed to be a spear of the Norse "god" Odin. According to various occult folklore, possession of this spear is necessary for mastery of the world. Hitler later also had possession of this once he possessed Austria. Figure out that one! (And a barrage of occult propaganda not withstanding, it does not seem plain to me that Hitler ever really took the spear that seriously. At least he did not seem to believe that he needed to personally take possession of the spear.)

Pope Gregory had first pushed Frederick to fulfill his vow to join a crusade to the Holy Land, and later excommunicated him when he failed to carry out his commitments. This was heavy stuff in those days. Many, if not most, kings believed in Jesus Christ and regarded excommunication with all seriousness. The Fourth Lateran Council of 1215 declared that if a ruler is under excommunication for a year, a ruler's subjects are released from all allegiance to him.

David Abulafia's *Frederick II, A Medieval Emperor,* (Oxford University Press,

The so-called "spear of destiny," or "The Spear o Longinus," which is supposed to have pierced the side of Christ on the cross. Possession of this spear is supposed to need to rule the world.

NY, 1988) is a current favorite standard biography in English, and is billed as "the first revisionist biography" of Frederick; and as dispelling the "distorted reputation" he has gained. Even so, in this instance he will do. Beyond that though, the Encyclopedia Britannica entry says that Kantorowicz, *Kaiser Friedrich der Zweite*, 2 vol. (1927–31), is still the most basic work."

In order to gain the throne of Jerusalem, Frederick in his mid-thirties married the 13 year old Isabella-Yolande, queen of Jerusalem. The parallels are striking in many ways. The beast in the book of Daniel is "Insolent and skilled in intrigue" "a stern king, a master of intrigue," Dan 8:23 NIV, and gains much by negotiation. Frederick saw himself as the "prince of peace," and it was in this role that he is primarily seen in the Crusades. Once in the Mid-East, Frederick gained much more by negotiation (intrigue?) with the Sultan al-Kamil of Egypt, than by battle, gaining among other things Jerusalem itself, Bethlehem, and Nazareth. Still many considered that these were gains made by treachery considering his chummy relationship with the Sultan.

In March 1229, still under excommunication, with no priest or bishop or pope to bless him and consecrate him to his new found duties, Frederick went to the church of the Holy Sepulcher in Jerusalem and **literally crowned** *himself* **King of Jerusalem!** This would in part fit the phrase in Daniel "on whom the honor of kingship has not been conferred, but he will come in a time of tranquility and seize the kingdom by intrigue," Dan 11:21. The crowd sang "David was thou in Jerusalem." Freddy then wrote, "It fills us with joy that our Savior Jesus of Nazareth also sprang from David's royal stock." H-m-m-m-m-m! Things were said at the time calling Frederick "a token of similarity to the Only-Begotten Son, as second Cherub, not a Seraph ..." (Right up there with the angels, right?) He now has himself referred to as like a son of God and as having "near divinity." When he returns to Sicily, his new code of laws referred to him as "Caesar" and "Augustus." Like Pope Innocent III, Frederick billed himself as "less than God, but more than man," Krantorowicz, *Frederick*, page 199. So there was more than a little pretense going around in those days.

What a picture of the "master of intrigue! He was now, as Abulafia says, "God's deputy," pg 199, and as with the later James I of England, he considered treason to also be heresy. Krantorowicz in *Frederick the Second, 1194-1250*, says,

The seal of Frederick II as King of Jerusalem

There is nothing sensationally new in this. All the Emperors since Charlemagne had held themselves to be the heirs and successors of King David, the chosen of God, and this was the claim of the imperial immediacy. The coronation formula has this in mind, "David thy son thou hast exalted to the summit of kingship." pg 201

In other words, such claims to divinity, and direct descent from the ancient King David of Israel had been going on all along among the Carolingian kings, in double talk such as is being recounted here. The claims were just more emphatic with Frederick. *Britannica* says,

Eschatological prophecies concerning his rule were now made, and the Emperor considered himself to be a messiah, a new David. His entry into Jerusalem was compared with that of Christ on Palm Sunday, and, indeed, in a manifesto the Emperor, too, compared himself to Christ. ... on the papal side the Emperor was branded as the precursor of the anti-Christ; on the imperial side he was hailed as a messiah. ("Frederick II." *Britannica Standard Edition.* Chicago, 2010.)

He claimed to be the "wonder of the world." In Abulafia's words, "Frederick was the new David ... the Christ King, higher than the common man, chosen to rule over all the earth from end to end," pg 188. He was ushering in a New Age, what many called a "Golden Age."

The 1909 *Catholic Encyclopedia* calls him "the reckless tyrant of Italy," and says, "His most prominent characteristic was his self-conceit. In Germany this megalomania was kept in check, but not so in Sicily." In his law code, the Constitutions of Melfi, Frederick speaks of himself as "Augustus" and talks of his "divine predecessors." He produced his "Augustalis coins in 1232, listing himself as "AVGVSTVS IMPERATOR" (see picture on the previous page). On the religious and the political side this was too much for a papacy which was itself claiming universal sovereignty! To all of this was Frederick's often open disdain for Christianity. Frederick supposedly joked about Moses, Christ and Mohammed as "three impostors," and he began to insist on taxing the clergy.

The "prophet" Joachim of Flore (1145-1202), had previously been proclaiming a new "Age of the Spirit" which would come and a "new order," to arrive in the year 1260 following a brief reign of the anti-christ. (Frederick lived from 1194 to 1250!) Note the dates of Joachim, whom many viewed as a prophet. This was well before Frederick's reaching his height. Many both then and now have debated whether Joachim was a fraud or a prophet, but part of the practical effect was that on one hand Frederick was seen as the messiah and on the other as the anti-christ. Still, this crowning in Jerusalem proved to be the turning point in his career. From here on it was an ongoing downhill battle. The excommunication was lifted after his return from the Sixth Crusade then reinstituted a second time by Pope Gregory IX in 1239.

Gregory just did not trust Frederick, either religiously or politically, and it seems with good reason. After these things Gregory again excommunicated the "self-confessed heretic," said he was "forerunner of the Antichrist," accused him of sodomy, and of being the "blasphemous beast of the Apocalypse." In turn, Frederick accused Gregory of being the anti-christ. Gregory died before Frederick did, but long term Frederick lost these battles, and his family, the Hohenstaufen, were defeated by the papacy by using diplomacy and war.

Like many would-be christs, after he died it was rumored that he would return and unite the world around himself. But don't hold your breath! Still, remember (as the occult clearly does), that the beast of Revelation is to have some sort of rising from the dead, and comes to this world from the abyss!

There is still another way that Frederick was like the anti-christ. Nothing of his doing was permanent. Except for the history specialist, he is virtually unknown to our modern world. Virtually none of his accomplishments survived his death.

> "... only He who now restrains *will do so* until
> He is taken out of the way." 2 Thes 2:7 NKJV

But from a Biblical perspective, how should he have been looked at if we had lived during his times? At the very least with great suspicion and careful watching. He made about all the claims he could get by with, as the christ, the messiah, and obviously a false one. He definitely had the will to be a world-wide false messiah and rule the entire world, and to oppress any opposition. Was his motivation strictly secular?

However, many things were missing. He did many incredible things but it cannot be said that he did "as he pleases, and no one will be able to withstand him," Dan 11:16 NASB, and there are hundreds of other small bits and pieces missing. Even so, though practically unknown today, it looks like he made a serious and credible attempt to be a world-christ in his day. Babylon does not want to call attention to these failures

There have been such attempts all through history, even though most did not even get as far as Frederick. If we are to be faithful to Jesus Christ, we would not want to worship or serve such a fraud. Nor would we want to be among those who *claim* to know Christ *but by their works* "**deny Him**" (Titus 1:16), *thus making our own selves into anti-christs who deny Jesus is really the Christ (1 Jn 4:3)*! And who among us has not at times denied Jesus by our actions! Jesus warns He will *not* physically be among men on earth again:

> 23 Then if any man shall say unto you, Lo, here *is* Christ, or there; believe *it* not. ...
> 26 Wherefore if they shall say unto you, Behold, he is in the desert; go not forth: behold, *he is* in the secret chambers; believe it not
> Mtt 24:23, 26 KJV

So the book of Revelation, and the warnings of prophecy have relevance to Christians all through history and will be especially relevant as we come closer

to the end. When serious replacement christs come to power, it is serious business, whether it is "the end" or not. If it is damnable to worship the true beast
who will be able to manage some sort of rising from the dead, have his priest to
cause all the world to worship him, and who is able to cause great signs and
wonders; **then how much more foolish** and damnable to worship some poor fool
who is never able to even dominate all of his own countrymen before he peris-
hes before all men. So Jesus says,

"And what I say unto you I say unto all, Watch." Mk 13:37 KJV

Some of the Stuart (or Stewart) line of kings also made some incredible
claims as if they were descendants of Jesus Christ. They called themselves "Jacobites." The best known Stuart to most Americans is James I, who was the first
Stuart king of England; but the Stuarts later lost England. Curiously, no one
seems to point out the significance of the language these kings and their followers used. To call one a Jacobite might mean they are of James the First, and of
course, James in Hebrew is Jacob or *Yaaqob* יַעֲקֹב, or the Greek is *Iakōbos*
Ἰάκωβος (Jas 1:1), or Jacob (or also "James" in English). But of course the ultimate Jacob is Jacob son of Isaac in the book of Genesis, and of course Jacob
became "Israel" and the Israelites. So the Israelites (the Jews if you will, although
that is technically inaccurate), could be called "Jacobites." You will find such
pieces of double talk up and down the line when you look at either the occult,
or those making pretensions to the throne of Christ.

James I gives us the imprints of many of these same issues. He was a well
known and blatant homosexual, so much so that in time everyone who needed
favors from the king planted their good-looking homosexual young men in his
court. Some of his love letters to his male lovers are still around. But there was
at least one good looking straight there at one time, whom the king came up to
and kissed on the mouth before a crowd. The man drew back, spit on the floor
in disgust, and wiped his mouth; and the king promptly banned him from his
court forever. Melville, leading preacher of the church of Scotland, called James
I, "God's silly vassal."

James I believed he was God's representative on earth. He said that "Kings
are called gods" from "Trew Law". James called it "Atheism" to dispute the
king. He thought himself above all law. When he first appeared before Parlia-
ment at the start of his reign, on March 19, 1604, he told a stunned and silent
crowd that, "I am the husband and all the isle is my lawful wife. I am the head
and it is my body. I am the shepherd and it is my flock." All of which is very reminiscent of Ephesians chapter five, and many other passages, describing our
Lord's relationship with His church. There is much more to be said up and
down the line on both sides, but I am just trying to give enough information so
that you can have a feel for how the issues lie, so to speak. At other times James
hedged or denied these claims, saying on one occasion, "I, James, am neither a
god nor an angel, but a man ..."

Like Frederick II, he called himself "the Prince of Peace." As part of this role, he overall kept England out of war, especially out of the wars for the survival of Protestantism in Europe. At a time when much of Protestant England was eager to enter the Thirty Years War on behalf of the Protestant Dutch and Germans, he remained overall aloof, though a few troops were sent. All of this had a part in the rape of Germany that cost the lives of about two-thirds of her population (talk about genocide!). Except for the intervention of Gustavus II Adolphus of Sweden, Germany would have been completely overcome by the Catholic armies. James' wife Queen Anne was, as many suspected, a covert Catholic. English historians seldom seem to comment on this, but it is clear from many events that the Stuarts often acted as if they thought they merited the aid and support of the Catholic church (and especially, why not, if you are the current "living" "Christ"?). It would appear they were repeatedly surprised and even a little offended that the Catholic hierarchy did not recognize their political efforts to help Catholicism and to move toward Catholicism. In the end though, the Gun Powder Plot moved James away from Catholicism. When Charles I in desperation tried to get Catholic help to maintain his throne and escape execution, he got nowhere. Will Durant commented on the English attitudes toward the Stuarts in the late 1700's. They could not forget

> ... the flirtations of the Stuart kings-Charles I and II, James III—with Catholic powers, mistresses, and ideas.
> Durant, *The Age of Napoleon*, MJF Books, NY, 1975, pg 360

It can only be described as ironic that James I, because of his association with the King James Version translation, became a symbol in America of fidelity to the older forms and language of Christianity. It is amazing the various idolatries that Mystery Babylon would have us embrace. On one hand they would have us worship some earthly king as "god." On the other hand, especially if the first doesn't really work, then they would have us worship some other silly thing. So James and Frederick would have had us take their word as the voice of God, and when revolutionaries started making their moves to replace these kings, their banners read, "Vox pouli, vox Dei." Or "The voice of the people is the voice of God." All I can say is, a pox on both their hou-

Some of the Stuart (or Stewart) kings. King James I is at the upper left. Charles I is at the right, who was desposed and beheaded by the revolution. "Bonnie Prince Charles is at the lower left.

ses! What does Christianity have to do with such nonsense on either side? Both the kings and the people are just men, and the LORD, He is God. Phillip II of Spain put it right: "Religion is being used as a cloak for anarchy and revolution." This was true of many of the forces working in the Reformation, and many good men were taken in by it. John Knox biographer Jasper Ridley in *John Knox*, makes the case well, describing Knox as "a shrewd political realist and a skillful diplomat, as well as a determined revolutionary," pg 320. He goes on to say Knox was "closer to the Russian Bolsheviks than to" the sincere non-conformist, pg 128-129; and that he was "one of the most ruthless and successful revolutionary leaders in history," pg 527. Great effects yes, and like all such things, part good and part bad, but often using teachings and means plainly contrary to the gospel.

Today a man by the name of Laurence Gardner claims to act as a representative for some "Stewarts." He claims to be "the appointed Jacobite Historiographer," and the "Presidential Attaché to the European Council of Princes." His book ***The Illustrated Bloodline of the Holy Grail, The Hidden Lineage of Jesus Revealed***, is about the "Holy Grail" stories, and it purports to give a detailed lineage of the "blood" of the Holy Grail. At one point it was published as a slick and lavishly illustrated picture book to sell for a mere $12.98. Gardner points to "HRH" (His Royal Highness), "Prince Michael Stewart of Albany" (Michel Roger Lafosse of Watermael-Boitsfort, Brussels, Belgium), as "the present head of the House" of Stewart (pg 219 of the full color edition of the book, 2004, ISBN 0-7607-6259-7). "Prince Michael" was also seen in an old early 2000's "House of Stuart" website, promoting his claims to Scotland's Crown, which seems to have been his objective. He basically claims descent from Jesus and Mary Magdalene through King James I of England. Gardner also recommends "Prince Michael's own compelling book," *The Forgotten Monarchy of Scotland*. As part of the "Messianic Grail Code" (and yes, "Messianic" is Gardner's term) he indicates that descendants of the "Holy Blood" should be the people's "Guardian," without the limitation of any parliament or church, "to act solely on the people's behalf," page 106 (all of which sounds incredibly like the earlier Stuarts). *So someone is taking all of this "grail lore" very seriously and is able to get their message promoted internationally!*

According to "Stuart, House of." *Encyclopedia Britannica. Standard Edition.* Chicago, 2011.

> The last **male** Stuarts of the British royal line were James II's son James Edward (d. 1766), the Old Pretender, and his sons Charles Edward (d. 1788), the Young Pretender (known as Bonnie Prince Charlie), who died without legitimate issue, and Henry (d. 1807), Cardinal Duke of York. (*emphasis added*)

They are saying that the house of Stuart no longer has any **legal** claimants to the British crown. "Prince Michael" in contrast is trying to prove his legitimacy. Nothing I have written here is the final chapter on "Prince Michael." These claims became prominent about the period of *The Da Vinci Code* book and movie, and stirred up quite a controversy on the Internet and in the British press. It is worth mentioning that there are several good refutations of *The Da Vinci Code* nonsense, including Garlow and Jones *Cracking Da Vinci's Code, The Hidden Agenda Unveiled*, Victor, 2004.

Will someone claiming descent from Jesus and Mary Magdalene end up fulfilling some key parts of Bible prophecy? *I honestly have no idea, but I am **not** inclined to think so*, despite the Establishment media push of the Da Vinci Code foolishness. The point is that there are claimants to the sovereignty of Christ from multiple angles: secular, political, "Christian," occult, and maybe others too. No doubt many of European Royalty, who have sincerely believed their "Holy Blood, Holy Grail" heritage, were merely accepting family myths they had been taught since childhood. So you can have "intent" in the legal sense that ranges all the way from those unwittingly misguided to the diabolical, and probably a little bit of everything in between. "Prince Michael" truly presents a side of the "divine rights of kings" controversy which most Americans haven't considered.

There have been continual claims concerning such things throughout history.

It all started in Gen 3:15, but is by no means over. There are actually many warring messianic strains **in the occult and out.** Many, like British occultist Aleister Crowley, would gladly claim to be the great beast of Revelation. They want to replace Jesus of Nazareth as king. And there is "one" who plots, who is not from Bethlehem but from Nineveh, Nahum 1:1, 11 (a type?). This "one" is a contemptible person who has not been given royal majesty, Dan 11:21. The "god of this world" (2 Cor 4:4), the "dragon" (Rev 13:2) is his authority.

An incredible man will come one day, with the full power and authority of Satan.

There have been continuous assaults to guard against throughout the Christian age. Many of the pseudo-christs and the "beasts" of history have a certain unity. They reflect the spirit of this world who is behind them. When God permits (2 Thes 2:7), a special lawless one will come by the activity of Satan (2 Thes 2:9, Rev 13:2); as the exclusive "god" (2 Thes 2:4). This one will be accompanied by awesome signs and wonders, 2 Thes 2:9-12 and Satan himself will give this one "his power and his throne and great authority," Rev 13:2. He will receive a fatal wound, but his fatal wound will be healed, and "**all** that dwell upon the earth shall worship him," Rev 13:8 KJV. To be actually "worshipped" by "all" is something which has never happened to date.

When this ultimate man of lawlessness is revealed, the veil will be lifted on very many of the "greatest" men of history, as having been all along, conscious and dedicated servants of Satan himself. The names and the details will be truly stunning. And the whole world will be stunned into worshipping the beast. Then they will have their victory, so to speak, for "one hour," Rev 17:12.

Who will this man be?

This author does not profess to know, but there are no shortages of men who would desire a messianic throne. As has been demonstrated, there have been quite a number outside of mainline Christianity who are taking all of this very seriously. *There have been many who have been willing to claim the throne of Christ if they thought they could, whether they were religious men or not!* There are many men who would like to rule the world, many of whom are not necessarily religiously motivated, but who would willingly do *anything* to get to that place, regardless of the risk. There is somewhere a true seed (singular) of Satan. (And there is a better than good chance that this work has not discussed any of those who are of the true Satanic line. Remember? He "was, and is not; and shall ascend out of the bottomless pit,," Rev 17:8 KJV.) Whoever are of this line (and I think 2 Thessalonians chapter 2 indicates they have been around for many centuries) they are without question **religiously motivated! Motivated by Satan!** Many down through history have been willing to be the great "beast" of Satan, all the way from Satanists like Aleister Crowley, to a wide variety of political leaders. But one thing for sure: if Jesus' kingdom was of this world, His servants would have fought at His first coming, to keep Him from being crucified, Jn 18:36.

Jesus Himself will be revealed from heaven, with a shout of command and the trumpet of God, 1 Thes 4:16. He will take vengeance on all those who know not God and obey not the gospel, 2 Thes 1:7-9. And the man of lawlessness will be destroyed by the brightness of Jesus' coming, 2 Thes 2:8; and he will be thrown alive into hell, Rev 19:20.

The Real Christ Will Stand Up!

[11] "So that He sets on high those who are lowly,
And those who mourn are lifted to safety.
[12] "He frustrates the plotting of the shrewd,
So that their hands cannot attain success."
Job 5:11-12 NASB

We Rest— Deliverance

It all seems hopeless,

at least in human terms

until the very end.

There will be Signs, Mtt 24:29-35

The special time of distress has already been discussed. It will be worse than anything in the world ever, Mtt 24:21-22. There is a "great tribulation" Rev 7:14, there is a special time of distress, and *that is not just pre-millennial doctrine!*

The signal for this distress is the abomination of desolation which is mentioned in Mtt 24:15 and Dan 11:31, and this seems to be the signal for the start of this special time of trouble.

Then somewhere in the midst of these things, trouble settles down. The beast, it seems, has won. The Lord of glory it would seem has cursed his throne with darkness and plagues, yet he and his kingdom have seemed to survive it all. The length of time involved in total is short, only three and one half years or forty-two months,or 1260 days, but there is no way (that I know of) to know precisely when to start the calculations, or when the end of 1335 days will come, Dan 12:12. All that not withstanding, blessed is the man who keeps waiting for it. Still for some period of time it *seems* that all righteousness has been lost. It appears that it will **seem so *even* to the elect!** This is why Jesus says that "Nonetheless, when the Son of Man cometh, shall He find faith on the earth?" Lk 18:8 KJV. Still it is known that a measure of normalcy will come before the very end.

> [37] "But as the days of Noah were, so also will the coming of the Son of Man be. [38] For as in the days before the flood, they were eating and drinking, marrying and giving in marriage, until the day that Noah entered the ark," Mtt 24:37-38 NKJV

Also it is known that when the Lord comes they will be saying that at last it will be "Peace and safety!" 1 Thes 5:3. At that time, the LORD of Heaven and Earth, Yahweh is His name, will call His own and all men to final account. The language of Rev 6:12-17 similarly seems to speak of these same ultimate cataclysms.

> [12] And I beheld when he had opened the sixth seal, and, lo, there was a great earthquake; and the sun became black as sackcloth of hair, and the moon became as blood; [13] And the stars of heaven fell unto the earth, even as a fig tree casteth her untimely figs, when she is shaken of a mighty wind. [14] And the heaven departed as a scroll when it is rolled together; and every mountain and island were moved out of their places. Rev 6:12-14 KJV

Now it seems from the evidence of the book of Revelation, this was written well after the fall of Jerusalem, and it mentions the same sun and moon signs! But even if you were inclined to quibble about the date of Revelation, the language sounds far broader than the fall of Jerusalem. Surely "the stars of heaven fell unto the earth," could be thought to speak of meteorites falling to earth. But then you get to sky splitting apart as a scroll, and then it sounds very reminiscent of more than one other passage in Scripture. Then it speaks of "every" mountain and island being moved out of their place, and it is then well beyond any description of 70 AD and the effects of the fall of Jerusalem at that time. It sounds like the end of the world, doesn't it? Of course, it is, and it goes on to say everyone is scared out of their wits and running for cover, including "every bondman, and every free man," Rev 6:15 KJV. Every slave and free man is running to get away from the presence of the Lord "For the great day of his wrath is come; and who shall be able to stand?" Rev 6:17 KJV. So the same extensions of language beyond anything historical are in both the book of Revelation and in the Old Testament prophets.

Scripture says that these astronomical signs will happen "**immediately** after the tribulation of those days," Mtt 24:29 KJV, and that is *after* what it calls the great tribulation, and of that "great tribulation," the fall of Jerusalem can be no more than a type, symbolic of the events of the end of the age. So there are signs in the heavens before Jesus Second Coming. It will be an unexpected experience, and an overwhelming experience, but there will be signs.

> 25 And there shall be signs in the sun, and in the moon, and in the stars; and upon the earth distress of nations, with perplexity; the sea and the waves roaring; 26 Men's hearts failing them for fear, and for looking after those things which are coming on the earth: for the powers of heaven shall be shaken. 27 And then shall they see the Son of man coming in a cloud with power and great glory." Lk 21:25-27 KJV

One would have to twist the *Scriptures **a great deal***, and *history **a great deal***, to make "distress of nations, with perplexity; the sea and the waves roaring; ... for looking after those things which are coming on the earth," fit a local event like the fall of Jerusalem, far away from the sea. Jesus tells the Jews: you should have known about the first coming. Mtt 16:1-3. Do you remember that Daniel 9 tells when Jesus would come, when he would be crucified, and when the new covenant would come? It was *because* they did *not* recognize these things, that the destruction of 70 AD came upon them, Lk 19:41-44. They should have been able to tell when these things were *near*, and some did, but most did not. Similarly, if we are awake we will be able to tell when the end is near, and we should not abandon the public services of the church *even then*.

> Not forsaking the assembling of ourselves together, as the manner of some *is*; but exhorting *one another*: and so much the more, **as ye see the day approaching**. Heb 10:25 KJV (*bold emphasis added*)

It is at that time, "then," that the sign of Jesus Christ's coming on the clouds with great glory will be seen, Mtt 24:30. Mk 13:26-27 is very explicit: "**then** shall they see the Son of man coming in the clouds with great power and glory," KJV (*bold emphasis added*), with great power and spectacular brightness. He will come from "the ends of the heavens," in a perceptive translation of Isa 13:4-5 in the NIV. As they saw him leave in a cloud, so He will return, Acts 1:11.

He will come from heaven, very clearly in 1 Thes 4:16. He will gather all his people at some point in time. Isa 11:12, and in the broadest sense Mtt 24:31, fits that.

> And he shall send his angels with a great sound of a trumpet, and they shall gather together his elect from the four winds, from one end of heaven to the other. KJV

Similarly Isaiah speaks of a very inclusive gathering.

> ⁶ "I will say to the north, "Give them up!'
>> And to the south, 'Do not keep them back!'
>> Bring My sons from afar,
>> And My daughters from the ends of the earth—
> ⁷ **Everyone** who is called by My name,
>> Whom I have created for My glory;
>> I have formed him, yes, I have made him." "
>
> Isa 43:6-7 NKJV (*emphasis added*)

If there is a temptation to take Isaiah in the most restricted sense of the physical Jews, note the gathering pictured in Isaiah 43 is of " **Everyone** who is called by My name ... Whom I have created for My glory," "Everyone" can only fit the gathering of the elect at the end of time. It is at a trumpet call, Mtt 24:31. At that time, He will gather out of his kingdom everything that is offensive and causes stumbling, Mtt 13:40-43, ... perhaps even you and me!

Now some say that there are no signs of Jesus coming. It is true that we will not know the day or the hour. But notice that: *Matthew 24 was written to tell us what are the signs are of his coming, Mtt 24:3.* He could have said, "Well there are no signs." End of story, but he gave us Matthew 24 to give us signs of the three events dealt with. Notice that *2 Thessalonians chapter 2, was written to discuss **signs** of the end!*

> ² not to be quickly shaken in mind or alarmed, either by a spirit or a spoken word, **or a letter seeming to be from us, to the effect that the day of the Lord has come.** ³ Let no one deceive you in any way. For the day <u>will not come</u> **unless the rebellion comes first**, and the **man of lawlessness is revealed**, the son of destruction.
>
> 2 Thes 2: 2-3 ESV (*underline and bold emphasis added*)

That is a clear and accurate translation of 2 Thes 2:2-3. So Jesus says,

> And when these things begin to come to pass, then look up, and lift up your heads; for your redemption draweth nigh. Lk 21:28 KJV

Now learn this lesson, Jesus says in Mtt 24:32-33. When fig trees of Palestine become green and the leaves sprout out, then you know summer is near, and so when you begin to see these astronomical signs, and the quaking of men, you will know that He is very near, even though you will not know the day or hour, still you will know that He is just at the door. So this is just like knowing when summer is near, or winter is near. It's just like knowing when flowers will bloom. You will never know the exact day or hour, but you will be able to see when it is near. You will not know the day and the hour when freezing weather will happen, but there will be signs that it is coming. *Pay attention! Not knowing the day or the hour does NOT preclude signs of nearness, and this is true both in nature and in Scripture.*

Then notice what is to many the great stumbling block.

> [34] Verily I say unto you, This generation shall not pass, till all these things be fulfilled. [35] Heaven and earth shall pass away, but my words shall not pass away. Mtt 24:34-35 KJV

First, it needs to clearly seen that Matthew 24 *obviously* speaks of the destruction of Jerusalem in 70 AD, and *obviously* speaks of the Second Coming of Christ at the end of time. No one seriously denies this, who believes the Scriptures at all. The problem is sorting out the destruction of first century Jerusalem, from the description of the second coming and of "the end of the age" (which are *all* in Mtt 24:3). Some demand a single line of demarcation. Marcellus Kik in his *Matthew 24* probably made as good of an attempt at this as I have seen, but, as has been repeatedly shown, all such attempts fall to the ground. As repeatedly shown, they will not even stand up to the internal evidence in Matthew 24; and *that is **not** the **normal** way that prophecy works when it has a type!* Review again the chapter on "Type and Anti-type," and the examples given there.

Now the word generation, or the Greek is *genea* (γενεά), is often translated "generation," and this is the sense we often use the word, meaning 20 or 30 or 40 years: a generation, however you might figure it. Still the *primary meaning* of the Greek word is of all of the people of a certain race, tribe, or ethnic group, with their ancestors and descendants. To use *genea* as a "generation" as we use the word is only a secondary application of the Greek word, and so it is with all of the standard Greek lexicons. But note Mtt 23:33-36 which has the same word used in a different context.

> [33] Ye serpents, ye generation of vipers, how can ye escape the damnation of hell?
>
> [34] Wherefore, behold, I send unto you prophets, and wise men, and scribes: and *some* of them ye shall kill and crucify; and *some* of them shall ye scourge in your synagogues, and persecute *them* from city to city: [35] That upon you may come all the righteous blood shed upon the earth, from the blood of righteous Abel unto the blood of Zacharias son of Barachias, whom ye slew between the temple and the altar. [36] Verily I say unto you, All these things shall come upon this generation. Mtt 23:33-36 KJV

First of all, the word "generation" in Mtt 23:33 is a cognate word, *gennāma* (γέννημα), and in context it is speaking of the entire "race" of Jews (in the broad-

est sense), or the entire tribe of Jews since early Old Testament times as being a
"brood," a "tribe," of snakes and that "upon you may come all the righteous
blood shed upon the earth," that is to say, on the Jews! Wow! It is surely not talking of all this guilt falling on just the Jews from say 30 AD to 70 AD, but it is
talking about all of this falling on the Jewish people, without limitation to just a
few in one century, for the crimes of many centuries. Therefore, this "generation"
will be held responsible for the blood of all the prophets ... since the beginning
of the world. But God's word is explicit that the son will not suffer for the
father's sins, nor the father for the son's, Ezek 18:20. No, it is clearly speaking
of the guilt of the tribe, the family, as a whole. This as much as any passage is
an indication of the sort of "nation guilt" that the Jews are so fond of ascribing
to others (like for instance the Germans of World War II). So this text would
NOT fit, *if it were applied* to just *those Jews* who lived in the first century. But if
you use the primary meaning of the word, that of an entire race or tribe of the
same physical descent, then it makes more sense, as if to say: "Upon the Jews as
a whole, will fall all of the blood of the prophets ..."

Also the phrase "all these things will come upon this generation," is in Mtt
23:36 literally **"All these things shall come upon this generation"** *panta epi
tān genean tautān* (πάντα ἐπὶ τὴν γενεὰν ταύτην.), and in Mtt 24:34 the
phrase is literally upon **"all this generation"** *panta tauta genātai* (πάντα ταῦτα
γένηται).

I would like to suggest that the phrase as used in Mtt 24:35 is **a deliberate
double meaning**, both to make you think and to instruct and to clearly indicate
the nature of the "type" that is used here. The point is that the destruction of
Jerusalem in 70 AD is a type of the end of the world; and that destruction of
physical Jerusalem would occur before 30-40 years are over (which it did); and
that the Jews as an ethic group will not pass away, before the Second Coming
and the end of the world arrives! **It is a type and an anti-type all clearly put
in one single passage, just as for instance in 2 Samuel 7!** Similarly it is for
Mtt 23:35-36 which was discussed above. Heaven and earth will pass away, but
not Jesus' words, Mtt 24:35. "Scripture cannot be broken," Jn 10:35

Let us hear the conclusion on these "signs" of various events in Matthew
24. We are not going to be able to understand Matthew 24 or New Testament
prophecy, without understanding Old Testament prophecy. So when it is read
about seeing the abomination standing "in the holy place" in Mtt 24:15; there
need to watch and read and understand something about the parallel passages
in for instance Daniel 12. They (along with other passages) are intended to be
used together. Nothing could be more fatal to understanding than using the so-
called "scholarly" standard of refusing to use these books together (which is
falsely called "Biblical scholarship").

> ... O fools, and slow of heart to believe all that the prophets have spo-
> ken: Lk 24:25 KJV

Many of the answers, it is true, are "sealed" until the end, Dan 12:9. Not everyone is going to understand, for "none of the wicked shall understand; but the wise shall understand," Dan 12:10 KJV. Hear O Israel what the prophet Amos says:

> Surely the Lord GOD will do nothing, but he revealeth his secret unto his servants the prophets. Amos 3:7 KJV

God has *revealed* (not hidden) His plan to His chosen ones.

> "No longer do I call you slaves, for the slave does not know what his master is doing; but I have called you friends, for all things that I have heard from My Father I have made known to you." Jn 15:15 NASB

God's friends will know. It will be like the days of Noah when most men did not realize the truth of these matters until the flood came and swept them all away, Mtt 24:39. Noah knew. He had been warned, Gen 6:13. He had been told to get ready, Gen 6:14. Noah had been *told* to get in the ark, Gen 7:1. Noah *knew. And we will know!* Not the day and the hour! But we will know!

> [26] "And just as it happened in the days of Noah, so it will be also in the days of the Son of Man: [27] they were eating, they were drinking, they were marrying, they were being given in marriage, until the day that Noah entered the ark, and the flood came and destroyed them all."
> Lk 17:26-27

So it will be like in the days of Noah. *And we will know!* Not the day and the hour! But we will know! The world was evil. The world was violent, and full of evil desires, Gen 6:5-7. There had been some very good men around, like Enoch, who it says walked with God. But the people overall did not love God, and Enoch's righteousness was rare beyond all normal measure. It will be like that when Jesus comes again.

Similarly, it will be the same as in the days of Lot, Lk 17:28-30. The men and women of Sodom had become very wicked, Gen 18:20-21. It had become so evil, that the pleading and prayers of the righteous Abraham were insufficient to save it. Still there was a righteous man there, Lot. God knew how to protect him, while getting ready to destroy Sodom. Lot knew, or was told, that the destruction was coming, that it was very near. Lot tried to warn the men his daughters were engaged to marry, but they would not listen. It will be the same way when Jesus comes. There will be some righteous men and women around. God will protect them, although many will be near to perishing in the catastrophe as Lot himself came near to perishing. Like Lot, if they are spiritually awake, they will know when it is about to happen. They will not know the exact time, but they will know when it is near. They will try to warn others ... but many of their attempts will fail. The trumpet sound will come, 1 Thes 4:16. We are warned; do not look back my friends, do not look back, Lk 17:31-33. Some will be taken and some will be left, Mtt 24:40-41.

And here is the last sign: THE Tribulation will come to an **end** *before* the Second Coming of Christ, Mk 13:24! It will be "But in those days, **after** that tribulation ..." (*emphasis added*). All of this tags on to the discussion of the blissful lack of awareness of those who were by then doomed in their sins in the days of Noah and in the days of Sodom.

> But ye, brethren, are not in darkness, that that day should overtake you as a thief. 1 Thes 5:4 KJV

This is as plain a statement as you will get. If you will not believe this from Paul the Apostle, then surely you will not believe me. The faithful Christian is not in darkness for this to take him like a thief. This is clearly telling us the same thing: we will not know the day or the hour, but there will be signs. *Now notice carefully:* **if that day takes you like a *thief*, then you are in _darkness_, NOT in the light!** We will not know the day or the hour, but it will not catch us by surprise, because we are NOT in the darkness, but are sons of light and sons of day! 1 Thes 5:5, so we won't be surprised. But those in darkness will stumble because they do not have any light!

> [11] And for this cause God shall send them strong delusion, that they should believe a lie: [12] That they all might be damned who believed not the truth, but had pleasure in unrighteousness. 2 Thes 2:11-12 KJV

It will not be secret: every eye will see him, even those who crucified Him, Rev 1:7. That includes, Julius Caesar, Genghis Khan, the crew of Christopher Columbus' ship, your maternal grandmother in France or England, or in Antioch in the 12th century. It means Adam and Eve and their sons and daughters.

It will not be secret: He is coming on the clouds of heaven, in much the same way that He left. In Acts 1:9-11 Jesus is talking to His disciples as He is lifted up into a cloud. They are standing there staring at the sign, dumfounded, and then two "men" dressed in white appeared beside them and asked why they staring up into the heavens. Jesus will come back in the same way that He went to heaven! His sign will appear in the sky according to Mtt 24:30, and everyone will start crying as they realize that all those things they had heard were indeed true. He was seen *personally* as he left, and he will be seen *personally* as he comes. Every eye will see Him.

It will not be secret: It will come about with loud noises! A loud command will be uttered. He will come with a shout and the voice of an archangel, that is to say, the voice of one of the ruling angels, 1 Thes 4:16. It will be loud. A loud trumpet call, "the trumpet of God" in 1 Thessalonians 4, and it is called a "great trumpet" in Mtt 24:31; such a trumpet, of such pitch and frequency, that it will actually wake the dead in Christ and they will be gathered from one end of the universe to the other.

It will not be secret: It will be with a roar! The universe will pass away with a roar as men perish in the chaos, and the elements themselves melt with incredible heat, 2 Pe 3:10. Everything that is made of perishable matter is to be shaken to pieces so that only the unshakable will remain, Heb 12:26-27. If you are not frightened by such a prospect, **you will be!** *You will see it with your own eyes as you rejoice at His coming, or cry bitterly about your sins!* The universe will disappear like smoke, Isa 51:6-8.

It will not be secret: This universe, with the earth, will be destroyed! The stars will fall and the powers of the heavens themselves will be shaken, Mtt 24:29. Then the old universe will be folded up and put away, like old clothes, Psa 102:25-27 (Heb 1:10-12). Every person will see this. Even if you die today.

My friend, we are not going to just wake up one morning, and talk to our friends, and realize that the true Christians are missing. We will know when it happens, you and I will see Jesus coming to get his own, we will see it, whether we *are good or bad!* Your Christian friends may disappear some night because they oppose the Prince of Darkness of this World, and a goon squad from unrighteous armies seizes them, but not because of the Second Coming of Jesus. My friends, we have been taught lies, so that we will accept a kingdom of this world, ruled by the Prince of this World. But God's kingdom has never been of this universe. If it was of this world, His disciples would have fought to keep Him from being seized at His first coming, Jn 18:36! No the kingdom did not come with careful observation of the rise of battlements and the digging of trenches, for the kingdom of God is within men of faith for this present age, Lk 17:20-21.

Is Jesus coming in November? Will you know when He will come? Will you have a body of life in the future life?

God uses prophecy to tell us of these things?

Then Comes The End, 1 Cor 15:23-34

It never was intended that man should live, only to die forever. However, the promise of the tree of the knowledge of good and evil in the garden was that, if you eat of it, you will die, Gen 2:16.

But each in his own order dies or comes to life eternally, 1 Cor 15:23. The Greek word is *tagma* (τάγμα), which is the word for a military order or array, a file or line of men or the sequence in which the ranks of men may pass a line or road. It was a word in classical Greek for a cohort, which is more or less the equivalent of our battalion or regiment. There is an order to creation. There is an order to nature, and there is order to men's rising from the dead. There will be order in the world to come, and some will sit on twelve thrones judging all Israel, Matt 19:28. But Christ is the first fruits from the dead, the primary one, the firstborn from among the dead, Col 1:18. He will take first place in *everything!* Then the end will come when Jesus hands back His rule to the Father, 1 Cor

15:24. But some things have to happen *before* the end.

> Then shall they deliver you up **to be afflicted,** and shall **kill you**: and ye shall **be hated of all nations** for my name's sake.
> Mtt 24:9 KJV *(emphasis added)*

> And many false prophets shall rise, and shall deceive many.
> Mtt 24:11 KJV

> "For false christs and false prophets will rise and show great signs and wonders to deceive, if possible, even the elect." Mtt 24:24 NKJV

> But he that shall endure unto the end, the same shall be saved
> Mtt 24:13 KJV

But the kingdom itself will not end. It will enter new phases, yes, be enjoyed in new ways, but pass away? No, it will have no end, Lk 1:33. It will not pass away, and the Lord's dominion will never cease there, and it will never be destroyed, Dan 7:13-14. But the present world system will end. Sin and death will pass away. Rot and rust will pass away. Grinding and wearing out will be no more for those worthy to enter the life to come. The corrupt systems of Satan and of evil men will pass away.

The last enemy is death, 1 Cor 15:26. Death will be terminated. It is the Devil who holds the power of death, whom Jesus will destroy, Heb 2:14. Death and decay will end. He will swallow up death forever. Isa 25:8. Death and Hades will be thrown into the lake of fire, Rev 20:13-15.

Christians are to rule the world to come, the new heavens and new earth, Heb 2:5. We have a foretaste of the world to come, Heb 6:4-5, and that is for us, for you and me. Jesus will sit upon His throne, Mtt 25:31-33. All of the nations of this world will be gathered to appear before Him, and He will separate men as a shepherd separates the goats from the sheep. Men will receive the rule of cities and the rule of angels, Lk 19:12, 16-19, and 1 Cor 6:2-3. The apostles will rule with the Lord himself, Mtt 19:28-30, and we will sit with Jesus on His throne, Rev 3:21. He will wipe away every tear, Rev 21:4. The entire universe will rejoice on that day. The rivers will clap their hands and the mountains will sing together for joy, Psa 98:1-9. It will be a day of refreshing and wealth such as you have never seen, Isa 66:10-14.

Do not be deceived. Come to your senses, Paul says. There is no point in being baptized into Christ's death if there is not a resurrection. Why would we suffer for Christ, if there is no resurrection, 1 Cor 15:30-32? If God does not really judge ... if God will not really raise His blessed ones and punish the wicked, then why not just whoop it up now, as they also said in the Old Testament. "Let us eat and drink; for to morrow we shall die," Isa 22:13 KJV. We see it again in Isa 56:12.

It comes on you as a trap if your heart is weighed down with dissipation and drunkenness. Jesus has appeared once for all to deliver us from sin, Heb

9:26-28. But this is just the beginning.

All things have been committed to Me, Jesus says in Mtt 11:27. There is only one eternal thing that you can really "earn," and that is death. For the **wages** of sin is death, but the **gift** of God is eternal life in Christ Jesus. But life, true life, is a **gift**. We just have to commit ourselves to God.

Those in Christ carry around in their bodies the death of Jesus, 2 Cor 4:10-12; so that the life of Jesus will also be made manifest to the lost. In the end, if they *refuse* to turn, if they will not *accept* the terms of pardon, God's fire will consume them.

> 8 Your hand will find all Your enemies;
>   Your right hand will find those who hate You.
> 9 You shall make them as a fiery oven in the time of Your anger;
> The LORD shall swallow them up in His wrath,
>   And the fire shall devour them.
> 10 Their offspring You shall destroy from the earth,
>   And their descendants from among the sons of men.
> Psa 21:8-10 NKJV

The nations were angry, they were in an uproar, and the time for judgment came.

> 18 And the nations were angry, and thy wrath is come, and the time of the dead, that they should be judged, and that thou shouldest give reward unto thy servants the prophets, and to the saints, and them that fear thy name, small and great; and shouldest destroy them which destroy the earth. Rev 11:18 KJV

Times of Refreshing: Heaven is a Universe

"The night is almost gone, and the day is near." Rom 13:12 NASB

Peter in his second letter tells us in chapter three of things that will be: of the Lord coming like a thief, and the earth and the stars passing away with a roar, being destroyed, with intense heat, and the heavens themselves burning, and even the elements melting with incredible heat. Then the best of good things will come it says, a new heavens and a new Earth, 2 Pe 3:13. This is what is usually called heaven. We wonder, what will this be like? But you know something? We are told what it will be like, **and** we are *told that* we are *told*. Scripture emphasizes over and over, since the world through its wisdom did not come to know God.

> 20 Where *is* the wise? where *is* the scribe? where *is* the disputer of this world? hath not God made foolish the wisdom of this world? 21 For

after that in the wisdom of God the world by wisdom knew not God, it pleased God by the foolishness of preaching to save them that believe. 1 Cor 1:20-21 KJV

We know *nothing* as we should know,

> And if anyone thinks that he knows anything, he knows nothing yet as he ought to know. 1 Cor 8:2 NKJV

But we "speak the wisdom of God in a mystery," 1 Cor 2:7, 9 KJV, and it is hidden wisdom that was decided before the ages of this earth ever began. God does reveal these things to His chosen ones. That which eye has not seen and ear has not heard, to us, His chosen ones, *God has revealed those things* through the Spirit,
1 Cor 2:9-10. *We are told about* those very things which eye has not seen, nor ear has heard! But what is weak and shameful will be destroyed first.

> Behold, the LORD makes the earth empty and makes it waste,
>> Distorts its surface
>> And scatters abroad its inhabitants. Isa 24:1 NKJV

> [18] And it shall be
>> *That* he who flees from the noise of the fear
>> Shall fall into the pit,
>> And he who comes up from the midst of the pit
>> Shall be caught in the snare;
>> For the windows from on high are open,
>> And the foundations of the earth are shaken.
> [19] The earth is violently broken,
>> The earth is split open,
>> The earth is shaken exceedingly.
> [20] The earth shall reel to and fro like a drunkard,
>> And shall totter like a hut;
>> Its transgression shall be heavy upon it,
>> And it will fall, and not rise again.
> [21] It shall come to pass in that day
>> That the LORD will punish on high the host of exalted ones,
>> And on the earth the kings of the earth. Isa 24:18-21 NKJV

But at the present time the creation is subject to decay, corruption, running down, vanity, futility. In physics this is called entropy or the Second Law of thermodynamics. Things run down. ***But the world to come will not be subject to entropy.*** *The second law of thermodynamics will not be an operating law,* for the creation itself also will be set free from its slavery to sin and death into the freedom of the glory of the children of God, Rom 8:20-21. Look carefully, the creation *itself* will share *freedom* of the *glory of the children of God.* It will be glorious when God's children are revealed. The creation will sing at Jesus' coming, rejoicing at their liberation from decay and death. Psa 96:10-13 says, "... all the trees of the forest will sing for joy before the LORD, for He is coming, For He is coming to judge the earth," NASB. You will laugh and jump for joy, "and skip about like calves from the stall," Mal 4:2-3 NASB. They will come with a shout to Mount Zion, Jer 31:12-13.

> And he that sat upon the throne said, Behold, I make all things new. And he said unto me, Write: for these words are true and faithful.
> Rev 21:5 KJV

All things will be made new! "... your bones will flourish like the new grass," Isa 66:14 NASB. Paul speaking of these days tells the Thessalonians that he prays that "your whole spirit and soul and body be preserved," 1 Thes 5:23 KJV.

> 22 For we know that the whole creation groans and labors with birth pangs together until now. 23 Not only *that*, but we also ... even we ourselves groan within ourselves, eagerly waiting for the adoption, the redemption of our body. Rom 8:22-23 NKJV

It is talking about waiting for the heavenly Jerusalem (Revelation chapters 21 and 22), "Jerusalem above," to be revealed. It is so alien to our world of sin and death. How do you describe a world with no death, no decay? How do you describe woods with no fallen trees, no rotting plants, no wilting flowers, no stumps, no dead limbs, no fallen birds, no perishing rabbits, no hungry foxes, no mold or decomposition, no moss that lives on death, no maggots because there is no death. Can you imagine a grocery store without a cash register because there is no dishonesty? A town with no policemen because there is no crime, with no doctors because there is no sickness. A town with no hospitals because there is no surgery. A place without morticians because there is no death. A place without locks because there's no stealing. How do you describe air without smog, an earth without an end, a world without a sea, highways without a horse or a cart or a donkey or a car? A home without a mortgage? We can taste it! It will be *nothing but open doors* because none but the righteous dwell there. We long for it! And all who wish to do wrong will not be allowed.

> For without *are* dogs, and sorcerers, and whoremongers, and murderers, and idolaters, and whosoever loveth and maketh a lie.
> Rev 22:15 KJV

With what words can you express it? The prophets do it this way: as a place where, "weeping shall be no more heard in her, nor the voice of crying," says the LORD, Isa 65:18-19, 21-24, 25 KJV. "For, behold, I create new heavens and a new earth: and the former shall not be remembered, nor come into mind," Isa 65:17 KJV. This is about a **universe** that has not been ruined by the revolt of its creatures. A **new** universe, without sin and death. This is what Peter is referring to when he says that "we, according to his promise, look for new heavens and a new earth, wherein dwelleth righteousness," 2 Pe 3:13 KJV. Where is this promise he speaks of? You can read of this as the period of the restoration of all things, in all the prophets since Samuel, Acts 3:21, 24. There will be peace among God's creatures.

> [4] But with righteousness shall he judge the poor, and reprove with equity for the meek of the earth: and he shall smite the earth with the rod of his mouth, and with the breath of his lips shall he slay the wicked. [5] And righteousness shall be the girdle of his loins, and faithfulness the girdle of his reins. [6] The wolf also shall dwell with the lamb, and the leopard shall lie down with the kid; and the calf and the young lion and the fatling together; and a little child shall lead them. [7] And the cow and the bear shall feed; their young ones shall lie down together: and the lion shall eat straw like the ox. [8] And the sucking child shall play on the hole of the asp, and the weaned child shall put his hand on the cockatrice' den. [9] They shall not hurt nor destroy in all my holy mountain: for the earth shall be full of the knowledge of the LORD, as the waters cover the sea. Isa 11:4-9 KJV

Let us think about these verses a little. The wolf and the lamb and the leopard and the goat and the calf and the young lion and the "fatling" will all be led by a little boy. The Hebrew is *naar qaton* (נַעַר קָטֹן) *literally "a boy little." So there are little boys there,* and they can play with and lead the most dangerous of animals, along with the meekest of animals. **But there are little boys there!** A nursing child will play by the hole of cobra, and the weaned child will put his hand on the vipers den. The Hebrew uses the word for those nursing against the word for those weaned, **so there will be nursing children there, and weaned children there.** However, we will not be married there, as we are on earth, Mtt 22:30. The Lord will be our husband, 2 Cor 11:2. Remember?

But there will be children there!

> [21] Thy people also *shall be* all righteous: they shall inherit the land for ever, the branch of my planting, the work of my hands, that I may be glorified. [22] **A little one shall become a thousand, and a small one a strong nation**: I, the LORD, will hasten it in his time.
> Isa 60:21-22 KJV (*bold emphasis added*)

A little one in heaven (this could not apply to this present earth) will become a clan, and a small one will become a mighty nation, Isa 60.22. The land will be called Beulah, that is "married." Compare both the New American Standard and the King James Version on Isa 62:4. There will be children there. We will have offspring, and we will plant and grow things. To go back to Isaiah 11, it says in verse 9 that they will not hurt or destroy in all My holy mountain. But this is not a mountain of this world that can be touched (compare Heb 12:18). Not even the most bizarre greenies envision man in this present world, as ever being so much at one with his environment. Scripture indicates that through the end of the age there will be vicious wolves in the flock of God, many only to be dealt with and punished at the end of the age, and while this age lasts "evil men and seducers shall wax worse and worse, deceiving, and being deceived" 2 Tim 3:13 KJV. No the prophecies being dealt with here only apply to the age to come, spoken of in Heb 2:5 and many other places. We will build houses and inhabit them, plant gardens and eat of their fruit. **There will be building, planting, doing, eating!**

A ceaseless rule of peace and prosperity will come. How do you spot the verses about heaven? It is the "forever" verses, it is the "never again" verses, it is the "no longer" verses. "Forever" and "never again" is *only* in the world to come.

> [4] And they shall see his face; and his name *shall be* in their foreheads. [5] And there shall be no night there; and they need no candle, neither light of the sun; for the Lord God giveth them light: and they shall reign for ever and ever. Rev 22:4 KJV

Of the Messiah it says, "The sceptre shall not depart from Judah, nor a lawgiver from between his feet, until Shiloh come; and unto him *shall* the gathering of the people *be*," Gen 49:10 KJV. That is Jesus. He is so prosperous that "He ties *his* foal to the vine, and his donkey's colt to the choice vine; He washes his garments in wine," Gen 49:11-12 NASB. Tie your donkey to your choice vine? Wash your clothes in wine? Try pricing that at your local supermarket! That is prosperous in the terms of any age! The prophet Amos says that the plowman will overtake the reaper.

> "Behold, the days are coming," says LORD,
> "When the plowman shall overtake the reaper,
> And the treader of grapes him who sows seed;
> The mountains shall drip with sweet wine,
> And all the hills shall flow *with it*." Amos 9:13 NKJV

In other words, the new earth will be so fruitful that it will be time to plow again, before there is sufficient time to harvest all that has grown last season! They will still be treading the grapes of last years bountiful harvest when it is time again to plant seed in the fields. But it is not just about what you can plant and then harvest, but it speaks as if the mountains themselves can without intervention, produce "sweet wine"; this is to say, new wine, and the mountains themselves are pictured as dripping with sweet wine flowing from the hills. If one takes the NASB or the KJV in one sense, it is talking about a time after the hills melt, that is to say, clearly after the melting of 2 Pe 3:10-12. One might question that, and look for an idea more to the immediate context as the NIV and the NKJV do, but this is clearly speaking of fruitfulness which is beyond that of this earth. It is the heavenly Jerusalem, and every tear will be wiped away, Rev 21:1-5. Man will have access to the tree of life once again, and there will not be any curse, Rev 22:1-3.

"You fool! That which you sow does not come to life unless it dies;" Paul says in 1 Cor 15:36 NASB. You and I must die, and this universe must die, for the eternal to come to fruition. Still, *even in this life* one can have a foretaste of powers of the age to come, Heb 6:4-5. And what should be done? Can we live forever in this flesh?

> Now I say this, brethren, that flesh and blood cannot inherit the kingdom of God; nor does the perishable inherit the imperishable.
> 1 Cor 15:50 NASB

So why not change? Change for the better, for a better life and a better world, not marred by sin! Why not give your very *life* to Christ? Why not die to life here to gain life forever? Do not live for now; live forever! Why not gain the treasure in the field, the pearl of great price Mtt 13:44-46? Why not give up your sins for the fruit of righteousness? Why not, just like Paul, "Get up and be baptized, and wash away your sins, calling on His name," Acts 22:16 NASB, and follow forever, here and there, the ways of righteousness.

²⁹ He gives strength to the weary,
And to <i>him who</i> lacks might He increases power.
³⁰ Though youths grow weary and tired,
And vigorous young men stumble badly,
³¹ Yet those who wait for the LORD
Will gain new strength;
They will mount up <i>with</i> wings like eagles,
They will run and not get tired,
They will walk and not become weary.
Isa 40:29-31 NASB

Biographical Information

Neal Fain was born in Georgia and converted to Christ in Dallas, Texas in 1962. He attended Harding University from 1965 to 1967, preaching as a student, graduating with a degree in Bible and Biblical Languages. He lived in Alaska for over 30 years, both preaching and teaching, and much of that time self-supporting. He retired from a major oil company in 1999, followed by preaching in North Carolina. He is now retired to Tennessee, preaching, teaching, researching and writing.

From listening to popular views, he early took a rationalistic view of prophecy, and only slowly realized its importance to the entire Christian age, not as an "accidental" extra, but as something needed for both conduct and preparedness, "a lamp shining in a dark place."

****

My interest in prophecy came in a round about way. I came to realize that all Scripture was inspired and was profitable for doctrine, 2 Tim 3:16-17, and thus that if we were neglecting the Old Testament (or any of the Bible really), then we had no assurance of being "adequate ... for every good work"! Also I discovered that many had no idea of what to do with much of the Old Testament, and had no answers when asked specifics about many passages in the prophets. I accepted the proofs of the church as the beginning of the kingdom of God, but could not accept the neglect of the Old Testament, although I knew we would use it differently from the way we use the New Testament. For a long time I just pondered these things.

Then in the middle 1970's I was doing some lessons on Christian evidences, and decided to do a lesson on the crucifixion of Christ as foretold in Psalm 22. I figured, rightly, that these were irrefutable evidences for Jesus of Nazareth as the Christ of God. I proceeded to analyze the psalm line by line, and imagine my astonishment when I discovered prophecies in Psalm 22 which irrefutably had NOT been fulfilled, and which were indeed repeated in the New Testament as not yet fulfilled! That was my wake up call, and the rest was just following the insights and trails of evidence which proceeded from there, and trying to figure out by what mistakes we had come to such a serious neglect of so much that was intended to be a "lamp" of our age, 2 Pe 1:19.

That original study material from Psalm 22 is included in the section in this volume on "Time and Image in Prophecy."

Neal Fain

www.ingramcontent.com/pod-product-compliance
Lightning Source LLC
Chambersburg PA
CBHW060246100426
42742CB00011B/1654